"We Will Stand by You"

"We Will Stand by You"

Serving in the Pawnee, *1942–1945*

by Theodore C. Mason

University of South Carolina Press

Copyright © University of South Carolina 1990

Published in Columbia, South Carolina, by the
University of South Carolina Press

Manufactured in the United States of America

Library of Congress Cataloging-in-Publication Data

Mason, Theodore C.
   "We will stand by you" : serving in the Pawnee, 1942–1945 / by
Theodore C. Mason.
      p.   cm.
    ISBN 0-87249-709-7
   1. Mason, Theodore. 2. Pawnee (Ship) 3. World War, 1939–1945—
Personal narratives, American. 4. World War, 1939–1945—Naval
operations, American. 5. World War, 1939–1945—Campaigns—Pacific
Area. 6. Tugboats—Pacific Area—History—20th century. 7. United
States. Navy—Biography. 8. Seamen—United States—Biography.
I. Title.
D774.P36M37   1990
940.54'5973—dc20   90–35438
                                             CIP

CONTENTS

For my *Pawnee* shipmates
William J. Miller
and the late
Donald J. Aposhian,
Dale H. Gerber,
and Harley A. Schleppi:

Friends of diverse qualities who shared an uncommon valor.

PREFACE AND ACKNOWLEDGMENTS

When I first proposed writing an account of my wartime service in the U.S.S. *Pawnee*, I was met with skepticism and lukewarm interest. Many professional navymen and not a few civilians who have served in the Navy harbor the conviction that the only ships worth writing about are combatants: battleships, carriers, cruisers, destroyers. But a fleet tug? Why would anyone want to read about a stubby, unglamorous vessel whose functions are towing, salvage, and firefighting? My *Battleship Sailor* memoir has been successful, I was told, because I had recalled my service in a dreadnought, and because I had been provided with a fiery denouement in the attack on Pearl Harbor. How could I hope to duplicate that kind of drama in recalling the ho-hum, pull-and-push duties of a mere auxiliary ship of the Service Force?

I did not agree with these assessments. I could not engage the *Pawnee* in another Pearl Harbor debacle, fortunately; but she had performed with honor and, at last, honors in the Solomon Islands and Western Pacific, where she had had her own defeats and victories, her tragedies and triumphs. My small contributions to the defeat of Japan had been of more consequence in the *Pawnee* than they had in the radio gangs of two battleships. Furthermore, the story of a fleet tug had never been told. I had an opportunity to tell it in depth and in detail as an involved participant, focusing on the ship's commissioning and 25-month war cruise to the Pacific.

Reading the descriptions of the Pacific War by the professional historians and the high-ranking officers or their biographers, I found myself longing for more objective and irreverent treatments. Almost always they were written from an elitist viewpoint in which the failures of the powerful were excused or glossed over, while the enlisted men who made their successes possible were treated as faceless and voiceless pawns of war. Relying heavily on library research, the journalists and "pop" historians all too often perpetuated and extended the perspectives and occasional factual errors of their sources.

Samuel Eliot Morison was commissioned by the Navy to write its official history of World War II naval operations. On those occasions when he mentioned enlisted "bluejackets" and Marines (whom he once described, quoting an American historian of an earlier time, as "rude humanity, trained only for fighting and destruction"), he seldom dignified them with full names. Usually they were patronizingly identified as Yeoman Doe, Radioman R. Roe (R. M. Roe for an act of exceptional valor). As admirable as such histories are in their reconstructions of battles, campaigns and grand strategies, they generally lack understanding of, and identification with, the young Americans who did the fighting and dying. That kind of empathy must come from within the ranks of Morison's "rude humanity."

"I want to bring out the idea that wars are fought by men, and not just by their tools," the noted artist-illustrator McClelland Barclay said shortly before volunteering for invasion duty in the Solomon Islands on board *LST-342*. A tool of war employed by the Japanese killed him and most of his shipmates in July 1943. The remark of this 53-year-old lieutenant commander of the Naval Reserve embodies my most compelling reason for writing "*We Will Stand by You.*" Wars are fought by men who are mostly young, generally naive, and largely kept in ignorance by their leaders. Here in the *Pawnee* crew of 85 enlisted men and 9 officers was a microcosm of men at war: their reactions to the savagery around them, their interactions with each other, their doubts and fears, their performance of duty where failure could result in the loss of men and ships. I knew, or at least was acquainted with, every man and officer of the *Pawnee*—and there were many more than the 94 because of the Navy's personnel policy, admirably defined as "chronic turbulence," whereby men were continually being transferred onto and off the ship. If I have failed to make my account of the *Pawnee's* men at Nomobitigue Reef, Rendova, Bougainville, Peleliu and in the Philippine Sea gripping and instructive, I cannot plead the ship's noncombatant, "stretcher-bearer" status. The fault is mine.

Some readers, including a few shipmates, may not agree with certain of my comments, criticisms and conclusions. This is a personal account; the opinions expressed are my own, unless otherwise specified, and must not be charged to any shipmates or others who helped with my researches. I did make painful efforts to be accurate as to fact, with one exception and that a matter of good taste. In reconstructing dialogue, I have removed that most popular noun, gerund, adjective and verb in a sailor's vocabulary. Those who desire the scatological verity so popular today, often as a substitute for content, can insert the expletive at will.

Developing my memoir of Pawnee service from idea to outlines, from rough drafts to print, has been more difficult and time-consuming than I had foreseen. It could not have been accomplished at all without the generous help of old shipmates, friends, and other research sources.

Heading the list is William J. Miller, Pawnee quartermaster who retired from the Navy in 1961 as a master chief journalist for a career as a Navy Department civilian. When he retired again in 1981, he was deputy director of the Sea Power Presentation Program. Bill's access to Navy personnel, offices and sources from his home base in Arlington, Virginia, was simply without price, as were his extensive correspondence and critical readings of chapters in progress.

I. J. H. (John) Day, who retired as a chief warrant boatswain, is another Pawnee shipmate who provided detailed recollections and essential technical descriptions and drawings relating to seamanship and salvage operations.

The late Le Roy E. Zahn, Pawnee yeoman, shared a wealth of primary source documents, along with many photos. Especially valuable was a war diary he kept. Since the ship's deck logs for 1943 were written under some wartime censorship stricture, Le Roy's diary was essential in accurately retracing the ship's movements for that critical year in the South Pacific. I could even name the films we saw.

Rodney Wolcott is another Pawnee shipmate who provided helpful recollections and technical sketches. The late Calvin Rempfer, ship's communication officer, passed along radio message decodes which made an important contribution to my account of the rescue of the cruiser Houston.

Dr. Dean C. Allard, director of the Naval Historical Center in Washington, D.C., promptly supplied ships' histories, action reports and other materials. He also gave encouragement and support when they were most needed. My thank-you to him is particularly heartfelt.

Deck logs for the Pawnee and Pennsylvania, as well as a number of photos, were supplied through the good offices of Dr. Timothy K. Nenninger of the Navy and Old Army Branch of the National Archives. A full book of plans for the U.S.S. *Sioux*, a sister of the *Pawnee*, came from the Navy Sea Systems Command. Charts of South Pacific areas were provided by the Defense Mapping Service.

The *Dictionary of American Naval Fighting Ships* provided useful ship biographies. (I must append a minor criticism, however, of the *DANFS* entry for the *Pawnee*. Four short paragraphs seem entirely inadequate for a ship that earned seven battle stars and a Philippine Republic Presidential Unit Citation while I was on board.) And I must thank the friendly staff of the Driftwood Library in Lincoln City, Oregon, for many helpful services.

John A. Hutchinson, a flag radioman in the attack transport *McCawley*, rates a "well done" for articulate eyewitness testimony. His written reminiscences helped me correct the accounts which have been published about the sinking of the "Wacky Mac" and the near loss of *Pawnee* and her crew.

Others who shared their memories and memorabilia of the South and Central Pacific include:

Robert H. ("Rebel") Boulton. "Long Glass Signalman," his candid, unpublished memoir of Navy service in the *California*, *Camanga* and *Oakland* before and during World War II was a useful source. My friend and "prune barge" shipmate also gave me a 1/2400 scale-model diorama of *Pawnee* towing *Houston* from Formosa (Taiwan), which occupies a place of honor on my desk.

K. E. ("Tommy") Thompson provided recollections, drawings, and technical data about the *Lipan*, a sister of the *Pawnee*, in which he served as a quartermaster from 1947 to 1949.

Roy T. Cavanagh typed and sent many memories of his service as a Marine artilleryman on Guadalcanal and other islands in 1942–43.

Donald G. Collver, a retired boatswain's mate, abandoned the sinking cruiser *Astoria* at Savo Island in August 1942, and was assigned to the Lunga Point boat pool. His memories contributed to my descriptions of Navy actions and bases in the lower Solomons.

Clair E. Boggs, a retired chief warrant officer, furnished lively memories of his service in the cruiser *Honolulu* at Pearl Harbor and in the Solomons during the desperate early days following the landing on Guadalcanal.

Ted Blahnik put me in touch with a number of destroyer sailors, survivors of the campaign for the Solomons, through his office as national president of the Guadalcanal Campaign Veterans.

Mario T. Sivilli headed a radio team that set up a harbor entrance control post at Peleliu. His memories and snapshots were helpful in my account of the invasion of that blood-stained island. (My friend would not forgive me if I did not add that he also served in the battleship *North Carolina.*)

The late Theodore C. Wilbar, a junior officer in the cruiser *Houston,* kept a daily journal as his ship was torpedoed and torpedoed again while under tow by *Pawnee.* His permission to quote from his narrative enabled me to include facts previously unreported about his ship and crew.

Walter J. Raczynski of Worcester, Massachusetts, who served in the cruiser *Canberra,* offered background and comments on my chapter 14 account of the days of "CripDiv 1." (Walter has written and self-published his own book about that celebrated event, *The Battered Remnants of the Blue Fleet: History of the Heavy Cruiser USS Canberra.*)

John L. Whitmeyer, another *Canberra* survivor, made an equal contribution to the accuracy of my "CripDiv 1" chapter.

Earl E. Smith, a longtime close friend, will not see this book; he died in September 1989. But he did read it in manuscript, offering his usual vigorous and well-founded criticisms based upon his own 22-year naval career and his wide experience as writer, editor and screenwriter. He is sorely missed.

It has been a pleasure to work with the scholars and gentlemen of the University of South Carolina Press. I am especially indebted to Kenneth J. Scott, director of the Press; to Earle W. Jackson, managing editor, who gave my manuscript a generous and insightful copy editing; and to Dr. William N. Still, Jr., director of the Studies in Maritime History series.

Finally, a *merci! merci!* to my lovely wife Rita Jeannette, who indulged me, at substantial sacrifice, in this long and costly labor of love. She remains *ma belle femme sans pareil.*

Theodore C. Mason

"We Will Stand by You"

Chapter One

PLANK OWNER

Life can only be understood backwards, but it must be lived forward.

Søren Kierkegaard

"South Pacific here we come," said Radioman John See in a tone of resigned bravado.

A few minutes before, we had backed clear of Pier 54 in the *Pawnee* and passed under the San Francisco–Oakland Bay Bridge. Now Alcatraz was on our starboard beam, Fort Mason to port, and the Golden Gate Bridge was dead ahead. Overhead, several hungry gulls flapped escort against a stiff breeze.

"Not quite yet," I said. "We have to pick up our diving and towing gear at San Diego, I'm told. Then we're off for Pearl and the SoPac."

When I had stood out of San Francisco Bay in the battleships *California* and *Pennsylvania*, civilians waved encouragement and American flags from the pedestrian lanes of the bridge. No one seemed to notice the *Pawnee*, a new fleet salvage ship we had put in commission three weeks before. From 220 feet up she must have looked small and unmartial, a mere coastal patrol vessel of some kind, on this sunny late morning of 30 November 1942.

My own feelings were as ambivalent as See's. For many a young serviceman this outbound passage already had proved a voyage of no return. In mid-November a series of sanguinary night surface actions off Guadalcanal in the Solomon Archipelago had thwarted a major Japanese effort to

1

retake that malarial island. While our full losses had not yet been announced, I knew that hundreds of cruiser and destroyer sailors who had
participated would not be coming back. In the future there would be many
more whose last sight of their country was this bridge and this fair city on
its hilly peninsula. The South Pacific was where the *Pawnee*'s rescue services were needed, and that was where we had to go. I hoped we would not
be found wanting.

We passed between Point Bonita and Mile Rocks, and the Pacific
Ocean baptized the *Pawnee* with spume-blown whitecaps. She buried her
stubby bow clear to the bulwarks. Spray hurtled back over the 3-inch gun
platform where See and I were standing and misted the closed ports of the
pilothouse some thirty feet above the water line. The *Pawnee* came up
smartly, rolling easily with the impact, and attacked the next turbulent sea
with a fine, controlled abandon. I had been told that the Indian-class ships
pitched and rolled rather heavily but had excellent seakeeping characteris-
tics. Now I believed it.

"This is the *Pawnee*'s real shakedown cruise," I shouted. "By God, she
loves it!"

"She may but I don't," See groaned, staggering away in a doubled-up
position. "Shit, I'm going to be sick!"

He had plenty of company in his misery, for two-thirds of this wartime
crew had never been to sea before. Numbers of young seamen began heading for the side. They were joined by firemen and motor machinist's mates
lurching up with ashen hue from the engineering spaces. Some took to
their bunks and others lined up at sick bay for relief. They got little sym-
pathy from "Doc" Ortalano, a pharmacist's mate of the old school.

"Ain't no pill or cure for seasickness," he growled. "You candy-ass
boots get back to your stations."

At 14 knots and zigzagging, *Pawnee* skirted the California coast. We
passed Santa Cruz and Monterey, the misty headlands of Big Sur and the
Gibraltar-shaped dome of Morro Bay Rock. Off Santa Barbara, I thought
about the Japanese submarine which had surfaced nine months before and
tossed twenty-five shells at a nearby oil refinery. If I were an enemy sub
skipper, I probably wouldn't waste torpedoes on a ship like the *Pawnee*,
which was 205 feet, 3 inches in over-all length by 38 feet, 6-3/4 inches in
extreme breadth, and displaced 1,450 tons. I would save them for fat oilers
and slow freighters. But I well might chance a surface engagement with
my 5.5-inch (14-cm.) deck gun, feeling I would have this auxiliary ship
outgunned.

The enemy C.O. would have been right. We had a 3-inch 50-caliber
dual-purpose gun just forward of the captain's cabin, on an extension of the

boat deck. If this antique weapon, which had been original equipment in the *California* at her 1921 commissioning, had ever sunk a sub or brought down a plane, I hadn't heard about it.

For close-in anti-aircraft defense, *Pawnee* was provided with four 20-mm. Oerlikon air-cooled machine guns in "tubs" on the bridge wings and the after ends of the boat deck. Our defenses against submerged submarines consisted of sonar listening and echo-ranging gear in the pilothouse and a pair of Y-gun depth-charge projectors on either side of the after-deck, or fantail.

Even if skillfully employed, these weapons were grossly inadequate against any determined attack. We had three gunner's mates in the ship's complement, I had noted. But the men who would actually aim and fire the guns were novices, and our gunnery officer, Thor Eckert, was a Reserve ensign fresh from midshipmen's school.

I had taken little comfort from these facts until I met Cy Hamblen at a 20-mm. mount while *Pawnee* was still making daytime training cruises around San Francisco Bay. A powerfully built, balding man in his thirties, Hamblen was a former Marine who had seen service at the International Settlement in Shanghai and later worked for lumber camps in the Vancouver and Longview areas of Washington.

"When this little fracas came along," he said with a crooked grin, a cigarette dangling from one corner of his mouth, "I couldn't stay out. Being D.I. for a bunch of boot gyrenes wasn't for me—too much horseshit—so I got me a motor-mac rating."

I was glad to have such a man as a shipmate, especially when he told me he would be instructing our seamen in the 20-mm. guns, as well as the .30- and .50-caliber machine guns which would be broken out and installed along the boat-deck rails and on the flying bridge at general quarters.

"Don't worry, Sparks," he promised. "I'll soon whip these hayseeds and range riders into shape."

As we continued south, I remembered something else Hamblen had told me. Although our rated speed was only 16.5 knots, we could coax another knot or two from our power plant in an emergency. That was probably enough to outdistance an enemy I-boat in a stern chase. "He who fights and runs away . . . " was a sound if inglorious precept for a salvage ship like the *Pawnee*.

I had never expected to serve in such a vessel, for I had been a battleship sailor. When my first duty ship, the *California*, was sunk at Pearl Harbor, I had been transferred to the *Pennsylvania*, flagship of the seven seaworthy capital ships. During the epic Coral Sea and Midway engagements, the old battlewagons of Task Force 1 had served as a distant covering force should the Japanese sink our carriers and threaten Hawaii and the West Coast. On direction-finder watch in early June, I had picked up the weak radio signals of a *Mississippi* scout seaplane down in a heavy fog. The plane and its crew of pilot and radioman-gunner had been saved.

"Ted, that was well done," said Lt. Proctor A. Sugg, my radio officer in both battleships. He had been impressed, he added, with my abilities and devotion to duty. "Have you ever thought of trying for Annapolis?"

I said I had requested an appointment from my congressmen after high school, but hadn't even been given the chance to take the entrance examination. Sugg reminded me that there were one hundred appointments a year from the enlisted ranks of the Navy and Marine Corps.

"If you'd like to bone up for the qualifying exams, I'll give you all the help I can. Think about it."

I told him I doubted that my math was adequate for the engineering-oriented curriculum at the Naval Academy, but I appreciated his offer and would certainly consider it.

I gave Annapolis a great deal of thought while Task Force 1 milled around off the California coast on a variety of training exercises and gradually steamed south, entering San Pedro Bay on 19 June in a long column of division guides. Quite apart from my deficiencies in mathematics, which study could remedy, I was concerned about the Spartan atmosphere at the Academy. The discipline was so remorseless, I had heard, that it made the Battleship Navy seem like a cruise of Sea Scouts. Under the hazing I would encounter, especially severe on former enlisted men, I feared I might lose my temper and deck some starchy upperclassman with a name like Thomas Starr King III (chosen for the *Pennsylvania*'s "sundowner" captain, Thomas Starr King II). If I couldn't abide the indoctrination considered necessary to produce career naval officers, I would be shipped back to the fleet in disgrace.

After Pearl Harbor I began to look at my officers in the brutal light cast by a devastating defeat. I had always disapproved of the Navy's Brahmin caste system, which erected unyielding barriers between officers and enlisted men, "gentlemen" and "gobs." But I had thought the former were at least competent, aware of their responsibilities to the second-class shipboard citizens whose lives they held in their hands. Their utter failure at Pearl Harbor made me wonder just what kind of officers the Annapolis system produced. With a few notable exceptions, most of the ones I had met seemed arrogant snobs who led by coercion rather than by example, who bullied their inferiors and toadied to their superiors. The Naval Academy definition of an officer and gentleman seemed different from mine.

A balancing factor was the quite egoistic one of personal safety. If I made it to Annapolis, I would be far from combat for three or four years. The war might well be over by the time I was commissioned. A prudent man would think well on that. A man less prudent would think about his conscience. Would it accuse him, down the years, of showing the white feather? I was, I finally decided, one of the less prudent ones. As much as I wanted to go to college, I had better do it as a civilian.

When we got under way for San Francisco, I found Sugg on the flag bridge, saluted and gave him my decision.

"I'm very sorry to hear that, Ted," he said. "Can you give me your reasons?"

I could give him a secondary one. "Sir, I keep thinking about the senior officers in the *California*. If Annapolis produces leaders like them, I'm afraid it's not the place for me."

"I'm sorry you see it that way," Sugg replied, his tone a shade less cordial. "Whatever you do in the future, you'll find incompetent men at all levels of authority. But it's your decision."

Sugg had been an executive with NBC Radio in San Francisco before he reported to the *California* as radio officer in April 1941. In his high-tension, high-stakes corporate world, one simply did not turn down an opportunity for advancement. I had, I supposed, failed to live up to his conception of me. I was probably being a damn fool, as well. Before the shattering defeat at Pearl Harbor, when I still placed unquestioning faith in my officers, I would have subordinated myself to the Navy's autocratic system, and it would have rewarded me. That is what makes conformity so attractive. Now, as a rebel prideful and disillusioned, I faced the prospect of Japanese bombs and torpedoes somewhere in the Pacific. No wonder Lieutenant Sugg was disappointed in me.

On 3 July 1942 I received my orders. I had been transferred to the receiving station at Yerba Buena (Goat) Island for assignment to new construction by Service Force Pacific.

At Goat Island's moldering receiving barracks, built during the Spanish-American War as a naval training station and little changed since, I spent days milling around with hundreds of other sailors on the main-deck "bull pen." At last I found my name on a transfer list a bored yeoman had just posted on one of the bulletin boards. The Service Force had detailed me to a ship named the *Pawnee*, under construction at the United Engineering yard in nearby Alameda.

All I knew about the Pawnees was that they were a nation of Plains warriors, now confined to a reservation in Oklahoma. I found a first-class quartermaster with several red hashmarks on the left sleeve of his undress blues.

"Wheels, I've just been assigned to the *Pawnee*. Hull AT-74. Can you tell me what type of ship she is?"

"Indian-class ship," he said. "Let's see. Yeah, she's one of the new ocean-going tugs."

I looked at him in dismay. The word "tug" evoked images of the small, squatty harbor workboats, their bulwarks lined with auto tires, which assisted battleships in and out of their berths.

"My God," I said. "An ocean-going tug! Do they really go to sea?"

The quartermaster grinned. "Damn right. They're over 200 feet and around 1,400 tons. Crew of ninety or so. We use 'em for salvage, firefighting and deep-sea towing."

"What kind of duty are they?"

"Damn good if you draw an old Mustang skipper—and you probably will, cause he's got to be a salvage expert." He grinned again. "Yeah, they're good duty if you don't mind towing some cripple along at five knots for weeks on end, where you're a sitting duck for any Nip sub that happens along. Good luck, Sparks."

From a mighty battlewagon, a force flagship, to a lowly fleet tug! Sugg must really have been sore at me for refusing the Annapolis exam. Why not shore duty at Dutch Harbor, Unalaska, or maybe a nice new ammo ship? Then the delicious dark humor of my plight dawned on me, and I laughed. Why not view this assignment as a promotion? The dreadnought's fifty years of glory had ended in a chaos of fiery destruction at Pearl Harbor seven months before. Better the insignificant *Pawnee* than duty in the new queen of battles, the ungainly and unmajestic flattop.

After several glorious months of liberty, leave and Shore Patrol duty in San Francisco's Chinatown, I was transferred to Treasure Island—site of the Golden Gate International Exposition of 1939–40, now a strategic naval base—where the *Pawnee* crew were assembling at Barracks E.

I looked around curiously at the sailors writing letters, lounging on their bunks, gathered in small groups for bull sessions or preparing to go on liberty. A working party of seamen in dungarees was scrubbing the woodwork and oiling the plank deck. A second-class machinist's mate in undress blues was strumming softly on a mandolin.

These were the men I would go to sea with. Together we would share travel, strange ports of call, hard work, danger and, perhaps, tragedy. None of us, after sharing these things, would ever be quite the same. They seemed a fairly typical cross-section of America: tall and short, lean and thickset, pale and olive-skinned, blond, brunet and red-haired. Most were very young. In the segregated Navy of 1942, all were white.

From service in two battleships I knew that a few among this ship's company were destined to become true comrades. Some would be friends of lesser degree. Others would be no more than acquaintances, no matter how long we served together. A few I would learn to actively or passively dislike, and they would dislike me in turn. Regardless of that, we were all bound together now by silken, invisible ties. "Shipmate" is a word of infinite meanings.

Were there heroes among us? Although they were always in short supply, it was very likely in a group of this size. Were there cowards? Again, most likely. One could not tell by studying faces. Only grave events separated the men of valor from those who valued personal safety above honor. Among us also would be the inevitable eightballs and incompetents. As with the faint-hearted, I hoped they would be quickly discovered and weeded out before they could endanger the ship and all our lives. But I was certain of one thing. Most of these men were patriots who sincerely wanted to serve their country.

"Hey, Mason," a voice shouted. "What the hell'd you do to rate this glorified wye tee?"

It was my *California* shipmate Jim (Papoose) Evans. I hadn't seen him since we lost our ship at Pearl Harbor. He had been a striker then but now was sporting the rating badge of a third-class signalman.

"Turned down a shot at Annapolis," I said, very glad to find a familiar face. "How about you? They catch you doing your Indian war dance on the flag bridge?"*

"Shore duty in the Islands," the lanky Texan explained. "You know Pearl. I got sick of it and put in for new construction. By God, I think I'm on the Great Spirit's shit list."

After we had caught up on the whereabouts of mutual friends from the "Prune Barge," I asked him what he thought of the *Pawnee* crew.

"Bunch of boots and V-6s around here," Papoose said with the fine scorn of a Regular Navyman. "Lot of fireman ones and motor-mac twos who can't tell a ship from a boat. We got a few seagoin' POs like Wilson there"—indicating a tall, sandy-haired, hard-faced coxswain—"and Miller over yonder"—a muscular blond quartermaster third. "And some real salty chiefs and firsts from the *Yorktown*. They're mostly at Alameda on precommissioning detail."

"When do we do it?"

"Around six, seven November, I hear. Hey, you got any wampum? Let's go ashore."

---

* In the summer of 1941, Evans's "war dance" had triggered a full-scale brawl between two deck divisions and the radiomen and signalmen at Nanakuli Beach, Oahu. See my *Battleship Sailor* memoir (Annapolis, Md.: Naval Institute Press, 1982), pp. 175–80.

The next day a first-class radioman strode briskly into the barracks. "I'm looking for my new radioman second," he announced.

"Yo," I said.

"Bob Proctor," he replied, holding out his hand. "And you must be Mason. I imagine you prefer Ted to Theodore." He had a tanned, pockmarked face and prematurely white hair. I guessed he was in his early forties.

"Ted, am I glad to see you," he continued. "I've been at United Engineering for weeks making sure those monkeys get our radio gear installed shipshape and Bristol fashion. Let's have some java and get acquainted."

Ship's service was near the pedestal where the statue of Pacifica had once stood. Raised as a symbol of peace and civilized dealings among the nations bordering the Pacific Ocean (including Japan), she would have been out of place in the new Treasure Island anyway, I thought. The snarl of radial engines from the Navy airstrip at the north end of the island, where thousands of fair-goers had once parked their cars, was a constant reminder of the true state of the world.

Over coffee and rolls, I learned that Proctor had been recalled from the Fleet Reserve, making him a "retread." He had had to leave a cushy job as a radio announcer in Jacksonville, Florida. That, I thought, explained the breezy manner and pear-shaped vowels.

The *Pawnee*'s radio equipment consisted of two late-model receivers, the RBA for low-frequency reception and the companion RBB for high frequencies, a short-wave radio piped to the crew's spaces and the wardroom, and a TBL all-purpose transmitter. We had neither a search radar nor a TBS (talk-between-ships) transceiver rig. They would be installed later, as the equipment became available. We also lacked a direction finder.

I asked about personnel.

"Well, there's Ray Figlewicz. Third class about to make second. Regular Navy but you'll be my leading petty officer, naturally. I couldn't have asked for anything better than a battleship radioman! Then we have a third class named John See and a striker, Howard Murphy. Both V-6s but they can copy the Fox. Oh yeah, we also have a radio technician named Bell. He's not a CW man, though."

Proctor noted my pained look. "I know. That means four on and twelve off around the clock." It was obvious he didn't intend to stand any watches. "But we'll secure the shack anytime we're alongside a tender. And we're going to find a bright seaman and train him ourselves. That's a promise!"

"What's our skipper like?"

He made a circle with his thumb and index finger. "Four-oh! Name's Frank Dilworth. A Mustang jay-gee who'll make lieutenant shortly. He was one of the Navy's top chief bosuns—served in the *Lexington* and the new battlewagon *Massachusetts*, you'll be glad to know. And as fine a gentleman as you'd ever want to meet. You're going to like him."

That, I commented dryly, would be a welcome change.

On 6 November liberty was canceled: we would leave for Alameda at 0800 the next morning. The high excitement of the recruits was evident when we boarded the buses in front of Barracks E. I, too, felt the drama of this morning, when we would commission a shiny new ship and become plank owners—charter members of the crew.

As my bus approached pierside at United Engineering's yard on the Oakland Estuary, I got my first look at the *Pawnee*. She seemed solid and stolid in wartime gray, a compact and not altogether lovely lady. Her forecastle was high and narrow, terminating in a slightly flared bow, her two-level superstructure was set well forward of amidships, and her fantail was long and low in the water. Accustomed to the graceful, greyhound lines of Navy combatants, I found my new ship chunky, thick-chested and more than a little hump-shouldered. She had, after all, been designed not for fighting but for the hard, unsung work of towing, salvage, rescue and fire-fighting. Her utilitarian purposes were revealed not only by her lines but also by a tripod mainmast at the after end of the boat deck which supported a tall, 10-ton derrick boom.

The *Pawnee* was, I remarked with more ingenuity than insight, a sort of Eskimo dog of the seas. Maybe even a bulldog, since she was supposed to hang on tenaciously to her tows.

These opinions drew a lecture on marine architecture from Quartermaster William J. ("Bill") Miller, who was well-read in the subject. He had joined the Naval Reserve in his home town of Rochester, New York, in 1938, was ordered to active duty to commission the cargo ship *Castor* in early 1941 and soon transferred to the Regular Navy.

"This is one fine-looking ship, Mason," he said in a sharp, upstate New York accent. "Take a look at her extreme sheer. She makes one continuous curve up from fantail to bow. The sheer is accented by those two half-round pipe bumpers that parallel the deck line along her freeboard. Now check her top hamper. It's in harmonious balance with the rest of her hull. Hey, a short and stocky girl can have good lines, too. How about Mae West?"

Boarding the *Pawnee* across the brow, I automatically paused and faced aft to salute the flag. No flag was flying from the staff. Grinning at my momentary confusion, Miller explained that until a ship was formally commissioned, she was not yet in the Navy and didn't rate a national ensign.

A ladder down from the fantail led to two crew's compartments which were even more austere than I had expected. A single coat of gray paint had been daubed on the bulkheads; the overheads were a maze of piping, cables and conduits. In place of the peacetime linoleum, the decks had been sprayed with a gritty gray Gunite. Except for narrow access lanes, every foot of space was taken up with three-high bunks in double tiers and banks of lockers. Living here, the *Pawnee* crew would have all the privacy of animals at the zoo and a good deal less room. Simple coexistence would require endless tact and forbearance.

The right-arm rates and seamen took the larger forward compartment; the engineering force, electrician's mates and radiomen claimed places in the after one. Seamen and firemen were assigned top bunks and bottom lockers. As a second-class petty officer, I rated the middle facilities. Soon all ninety of us, along with half a dozen warrant officers and ensigns, were assembled on the fantail at dress parade for the commissioning ceremony. A Marine honor guard and Navy band were drawn up on the pier.

"Attention!" someone shouted.

Out of the corner of one eye I saw a captain, a commander and a lieutenant junior-grade approach a table set up abaft a huge towing winch which was tucked away under the break of the boat deck.

"Carry on."

At parade rest, I examined the three officers. The four-striper obviously was the representative of the commandant of the 12th Naval District. The three-striper wore the corps devices of a chaplain, and the one-and-a-half striper was Frank Dilworth, my commanding officer. He was a man of middle height and build with a full face upon which a hint of a smile played. He was, I guessed, a man who smiled easily and often. He was wearing rimless glasses and looked more like my high-school English teacher, Robert Ramsey, than a battleship chief boatswain who recently had been commissioned.

While I was still marveling at this, the chaplain gave the invocation and the captain read his orders for the delivery of the ship.

"Commission the U.S.S. *Pawnee*," he commanded.

Dilworth relayed the order to an older officer wearing the single stripe of an ensign. He was, I soon learned, our executive officer and navigator, another former enlisted man named W. P. Hoag, Jr. "Attention" was sounded on the bugle and the band broke into "The Star-Spangled Banner."

With chills chasing up and down my spine, I watched the national ensign being slowly raised to the top of the flag staff. At the same time the thin ribbon of the commission pennant was hoisted to its staff at the very top of the mainmast. Out of sight at the bow, the 48-starred Union Jack was being two-blocked. Now the *Pawnee* was ours. Would we take her to glory—as had the crew of the first *Pawnee*, a Federal gunboat that harassed the South all through the Civil War—or to grief?

"Last man off the ship from this crew gets the commission pennant," Miller said. "I wonder who it will be?"

"Let's hope it's not Davy Jones," I said.

Our new commanding officer read his orders in a pleasant and, it seemed to me, rather studious voice. What must he be thinking in this moment of personal triumph? It was a long, arduous climb from "deck ape" to a commission and command of his own ship. I did not know him yet but I wished him well.

"I assume command of the U.S.S. *Pawnee*," he said. Then he turned to his exec.

"Set the watch!"

That was my cue to join the port watch in a race to our stations. We would miss the remarks of the transferring officer and Dilworth's address but that hardly seemed important. Proctor had given me the honor of setting the first radio watch.

The radio shack was a snug compartment which shared the first superstructure deck with the captain's cabin, just forward, and the exec's stateroom to starboard. With Proctor to guide me, I switched on one of the two motor-generators which powered our receivers and tuned the RBA to 26.1 kc. The Fox schedule transmission from NPM Pearl Harbor came in loud and clear—strength five, readability five—on my headset. I inserted a log sheet in the Underwood mill and typed across the top:

"First radio watch in USS PAWNEE set at 1100 hours on 7 November 1942 at Alameda, California. Operator: T. C. Mason, RM2c, USNR."

Proctor already had encoded the *Pawnee*'s international call sign, NUMA, for that day and scotch-taped it to the receiver at eye level. On the rolled-up log, I began typing the headings of all the numbered messages transmitted by NPM to the Pacific Fleet. If a dispatch came in for AT-74, I would insert a message blank over the log sheet and copy the text for decoding by our communication officer. We didn't expect any messages until our shakedown cruises were completed but *semper paratus* (always ready), the motto of the Coast Guard, applied to Navy radioman as well.

Within half an hour the word was passed to man the special sea detail. The diesel engines started up with a deep belch of exhaust gases—a Titan suffering from indigestion, I thought—and a furious clatter of steel against steel which soon subsided to a high-pitched roar. The *Pawnee* would be a noisy ship under way, very unlike the whisper-quiet *California*, which had a turbo-electric drive, or the pleasant low throb of the *Pennsylvania's* geared turbines. The deck beneath my feet vibrated as power was applied to the screw through the reduction gear. The *Pawnee* eased away from the dock and stood down the Oakland Estuary at one-third ahead.

Proctor had gone to the bridge, establishing a precedent which would cause a good deal of griping and barbed humor among the radiomen in the future. When he returned, he was smiling.

"Smooth as silk," he enthused. "Captain Frank took her away from the dock like he'd been handling one of these Able Tares for years."

"I'll bet it was a little tense up there."

"Only among the Reserve ensigns," he chuckled. "The skipper has a chief quartermaster named Earl Clark who really knows his stuff. Came to us from the subs."

"How did our green seamen do?"

"Just like you'd expect. Some of these kids have never even been in a rowboat before. But our bosun's mate first is an old sea dog name of Paul Campbell. He bailed out of the *Yorktown* when she went down at Midway. He'll shape 'em up—or he'll get 'em shipped out."

By noon we were moored at the Naval Supply Center on the Oakland side of the estuary and the work of provisioning the ship began. It was an all-hands evolution that went on far into the night and would continue for the next three days.

The radio gang assembled in the shack, anxious to avoid the working parties. Proctor let them stay, since we had plenty of work of our own. While we were updating the communication manual, encoding call signs and familiarizing ourselves with the tuning of the transmitter and receivers, I had a good chance to evaluate the men I would be working with on the closest of terms.

Ray Figlewicz was a slender blond Pole from Chicago. He seemed quiet and introspective, given to long silences. I thought I detected an undertone of envy, as if he believed he should be Proctor's second in charge. That attitude of Regulars toward Reserves was all too familiar to me from service in the *California.* But I had the rating and that was the Navy way, whether he liked it or not.

B. H. Bell, our technician, was not a sailor and never would be. He seemed out of place aboard a ship; a radio lab or workshop was his proper milieu. A little older than the rest, he had a bland, rather cold face and manner. I read him as intelligent and ambitious. He lost no time in complaining that there was nothing for him to do until our radar arrived.

"How would you like to learn the code?" I asked. "I see we have a practice oscillator and key. I'll be glad to teach you."

"So you can have another watchstander on the Fox schedule?" he retorted. "No thanks."

John See was a curly-haired, rosy-cheeked Midwesterner with a square-hewn face that was pleasant rather than comely. His friendly, open manner reminded me of many another small-town boy I had met. I found him cheerful and cooperative and knew he would do his duty and cause no problems.

Howard Murphy, our striker, was a short, sturdy, baby-faced Texan with an infectious Irish smile and wit. Proctor already had told me he was a radio-school graduate who could copy more than 20 words a minute. Since the Fox sked was running at 18 wpm and repeating headings and five-letter code groups, we could put him on watch immediately. He had enlisted fresh from high school, where I gathered he had got by on charm and native intelligence rather than hard work. Perhaps he had been somewhat spoiled by his parents; perhaps he was a bit of a rebel. But I thought I understood rebels.

The division petty officers soon began coming straight to Dilworth for answers to their questions about the stowage of gear, the daily routine in port and personnel assignments. He seemed remarkably informal and approachable for a commanding officer.

In late evening our lean, olive-skinned first-class cook found him outside the radio room.

"Captain, we gotta issue night rations to the men. How many sandwiches should I make?"

Dilworth considered the question for a moment. "What do the Regulations call for?"

"Two per man, sir."

"Well, make two each, then. And make up some extras for anyone who wants them."

The cook's mouth fell open. Like Campbell, he had served in the *Yorktown*, where everything was done "by the book." "Aye, sir," he finally managed.

Proctor winked at me. "What did I tell you, Ted?"

The rest of the month was spent largely on daylight cruises around San Francisco Bay. Once a plane buzzed us and some of the topside seamen looked alarmed. But it was only a Navy trainer having a little fun while taking the official photos of the *Pawnee* for the archives. In late afternoons we moored at the South Pier in the Port of Tradewinds and half the crew was given liberty.

On my duty nights I listened to the water lapping at the *Pawnee*'s hull and enjoyed the curious and comfortable isolation that is never felt so strongly as in a Navy ship. We were at Treasure Island but no longer a part of it. On the Bay Bridge the amber sodium-vapor lights glowed feebly behind their metal shields; the traffic was only a distant hum. San Francisco retreated into a dim, shimmering mirage to the west. I knew that Berkeley sprawled across its hills on the *contra costa* side but couldn't see the city of my birth. The air had the bracing smell of canvas and tarred hemp and salt water, and I could hear the distant moan of foghorns.

I thought of the thousands of sailors in their hammocks at Yerba Buena and their iron bunks at T.I. and was glad the waiting was over and I was in my own ship again. This one was small, compact and informal. Only two decks and a hundred feet or so separated my living spaces, mess hall and duty station. Best of all, there were no "brass hats" around demanding their perquisites and enforcing minute regulations. Here the spit and polish would be minimal and the personal freedom far greater than was possible in a larger ship.

One of those freedoms was the ability to explore the *Pawnee*, from the anchor windlass machinery to the after steering-gear room, and from the ammunition magazines at the double bottom to the flying bridge and the searchlight platforms.

The ship's diesel-electric drive employed four General Motors V-12 engines, each rated at 750 horsepower, which were close-coupled to their DC generators. The electric power developed—500 volts at 1100 amperes—passed through a propulsion-control panel to four powerful electric motors which drove the reduction gear. A 67-foot-long shaft 12 inches in diameter coupled to the reduction gear rotated the 12-foot bronze screw. The screw was especially pitched at 12.5 degrees for towing operations and, as a quartermaster remarked, "for pulling other skippers' mistakes off the beach."

Two of the four main engines could be taken off the line and used to power the high-voltage salvage and firefighting pumps, as well as the towing winch and derrick boom.

Two 100-kilowatt auxiliary generators driven by 3-cylinder diesel engines supplied the other power requirements of the ship at sea. In port, a 60-kw generator powered by a 6-cylinder Cummins diesel provided lighting and other electrical services. Freshwater was supplied by a distilling unit of 500-gallon capacity located on the upper level of the engine room. Cy Hamblen, who ran the "evaporator," would have been considered one of the most important crewmen even if he had never seen a gun. When his gear broke down, we took saltwater showers. Nearby, a boiler provided steam for the galley and ship's heating.

On the lower level, the engine room also accommodated the two motor-generators that converted DC to AC current for our radio receivers and a third, larger motor-generator that powered the TBL transmitter. Later, I would curse the genius who had located this vital radio equipment in the hottest part of the ship. In the tropics, despite my best efforts and the help of an electrician's mate, I could never get more than 100 volts of the specified 110 at the receivers.

But that concern was in the future as *Pawnee* passed San Pedro Bay, marked by the long, bisected shape of Santa Catalina Island to starboard and the cliffs of the Palos Verdes Peninsula to port. I remembered that Los Angeles had justified its reputation as a suburb of Hollywood by staging a phantom air raid just two days after the I-boat attack at Santa Barbara. Unfortunately, the casualties were real. Some two thousand rounds of A.A. ammunition were fired into the clear night skies; the falling shrapnel injured dozens of residents who refused to take cover. When the all-clear was sounded, five people were dead from traffic accidents and heart attacks. Lt. Gen. John L. DeWitt's Western Defense Command maintained against all evidence that enemy planes had penetrated our air space. It was, I thought, a performance worthy of an Oscar.

On the morning of 2 December I spotted the old lighthouse on the heights of Point Loma and knew that San Diego was just beyond. The *Pawnee* changed course in a wide lazy turn, passed two sea buoys and a lowered submarine net and entered the crescent-shaped channel. On another sun-drenched day in October 1940 I had departed this channel in the oiler *Neosho*, bound for Pearl Harbor and service in the *California*. Now the *Neosho* was at the bottom of the Southwest Pacific, torpedoed and scuttled during the Battle of the Coral Sea the previous May, and the battered *California* was at Puget Sound Navy Yard for refitting and modernization. So far, I had been luckier than my ships.

Off the port beam now were the red tile roofs and wide green lawns of the Naval Training Station, where I had taken boot camp and radio school. On the Grinder the marching recruit companies made geometric splashes of white against the tan asphalt. I, too, had drilled with a Springfield service rifle on that Grinder. It was an experience I would not want to repeat but I was glad I had had it.

Still changing course to conform to the channel, we passed the Marine Corps Recruit Depot, where the moving rectilinear shapes were brown on brown. I freely admitted to a sailor's prejudice against those Marines who served as seagoing cops. In the *California* and *Pennsylvania* they had regularly brutalized and beaten up the prisoners confined to the brig, obviously with the tacit approval of the ships' officers.

As we neared the Broadway Pier, a yard tug chuffed up on our starboard side. After a shouted dialog with Dilworth, the tug maneuvered the *Pawnee* to her berth.

Proctor came into the radio shack, still laughing. "The old retread chief on the YT had orders to put us alongside the dock. The skipper could have done it himself no sweat, but he just smiled. 'Let's keep everybody happy,' he said."

Dilworth shortly made another contribution to the general welfare by granting overnight liberty to two of the three sections of the crew on a daily basis. By 1700, only thirty men were still on board.

Before I went ashore I had an unpleasant duty to perform, something I had been debating all the way down the California coast. I made up my mind to break my informal engagement to Helen Hazelton.

Helen was a hazel-eyed brunette of twenty-two, as pretty, gracious and charming as "the girl next door" of popular lore. Working in Hawaii as a civilian employee of the Army when the Japanese attacked, she was repatriated to her native Bay Area in the *Lurline*. When my aunt introduced us over cracked crab at Fishermen's Wharf, she was a secretary in a San Francisco firm. In a sense, we had shared the century's most dramatic and stunning event. That alone made her special.

By imperceptible degrees during my months at Yerba Buena, our relationship moved into that elevated perception, a product of propinquity and desire, which countless bad novels and worse films have portrayed as "love." Just as naturally, we drifted into an engagement.

But now I was going back to war, and that would demand 100 percent of my energy and dedication. I could no longer afford the soft feminine bonds which had made my precommissioning time so memorable. They would keep my thoughts focused on the States and might turn me weak and pusillanimous, unable to serve either myself or my country.

As I drafted the letter breaking our engagement, I remembered that Helen's boss disapproved of me. He told her I was "too hard." He had met me twice, once when I had Shore Patrol duty in Chinatown and again over drinks at the Garden Court of the Palace Hotel.

"Do you think I'm too hard?" I had asked Helen.

She squeezed my hand. "Of course not, Ted. You are the sweetest lad I have ever known."

I laughed and laughed. "I don't think anyone in Chinatown would agree with you. They are probably right, I'm sorry to say. But this goddam civilian doesn't understand the problem. How could he? He wasn't at Pearl."

I understood the problem. War was a mindless brutality, the ultimate dehumanizing experience. Facing it again, I didn't think I was hard enough. That a fine sensitive young woman had to pay part of the price of that was lamentable, but later the price might be higher still. I justified my unchivalrous action by quoting Hamlet's words: "I must be cruel, only to be kind." I would be gone a long time. She was free to find another more deserving than I.

I took the letter to J. R. Moodie, the ship's censor who also was my communication officer. He was a small, mild-mannered ensign who looked of college age—an English major, perhaps. I was sure he was having his own problems mastering the electric cipher machine, supervising the radio-men and signalmen and qualifying as an officer of the deck. That made him just the sort of comm officer Proctor and I wanted.

"You write well," he said rather diffidently. "Not many enlisted men know Shakespeare, I'm sure. Not many officers do, either, I have discovered. But was it necessary to be so, er, harsh?"

"I thought so, sir."

"Miss Hazelton must be a very fine young lady."

"She is, sir. She is the kind who would wait for me, no matter how long I am away. That is not fair. Now she can find someone else."

Moodie shook his head. "You may be making a great mistake. This kind of young lady is not easily replaced."

I wondered if he was facing a similar decision. "It wouldn't be my first mistake, sir."

He sighed. "Very well, Mason. I hope she's still around when we return."

"So do I, sir."

I put on my tailor-made dress blues and laid aft to the fantail. Near the gangway I was approached by a seaman second class.

"Mason, my name is Jimmie Sewell," he said in the accents of the Deep South. "Mind if I sorta tag along? I hate to go ashore by myself."

So did I. This fellow still wore a boot-camp sun tan, but he was in his early twenties and had the confident air of a city dweller who had been around.

"It might get a little wet out there. I just lost a fiancée."

"Maybe you'd like to talk about it. I'm game if you are."

"Okay, Jimmie, let's go."

We got acquainted over drinks at a serviceman's bar. Sewell proved a good deal more worldly than the average recruit and he could hold his liquor. We decided to go roller skating at a rink off lower Broadway and picked up two pints of bourbon on the way.

The thunder of hundreds of metal rollers made an atonal obbligato to the music from a tinny amplifier. The orbiting skaters were a colorful medley of costumes and uniforms, male and female, the young and the younger.

Sewell and I hadn't been skating for a long time and our frequent pit stops for whiskey and Coke did nothing to improve our coordination. As usual, a few habitués were displaying their skills, weaving and whirling past the clumsy with insolent grace. I had to grab for the rail to keep from falling when one tall civilian in black pants and a white satin shirt, skating backward with a brunette partner, brushed against me at high speed.

"You see that soda jerk?" I asked Sewell. "This is the only skill he's ever mastered and he thinks he's king of the mountain. He'd better give us a wide berth."

But the fellow ignored our threatening looks. He made a game of passing as closely as possible without making contact. His girl friend pirouetted in a flash of brown legs under her short skirt. Her scornful laughter floated back to us.

Perhaps she looked a little like Helen, though obviously she was no lady. Perhaps she didn't and I simply was spoiling for trouble.

"Hey, you soda jerk," I shouted. "Try that one more time."

On their next lap the pair slowed down and skated in circles around us. "Were you talking to me?" the man asked in a mean voice.

"You're the only jerk here," I said. "You'd better belay the near-misses."

"Yeah? Or else what?"

"Or else I'm gonna drag you out of here and teach you some goddam manners."

"I haven't decked a sailor for at least a week," he said with a sneer. "Let's go."

We changed into street shoes and went to the vacant lot which adjoined the rink on the Broadway side. The word had spread like wildfire and half the skaters followed us outside.

It would be a bare-fisted fight to the finish, the kind that was a court of last resort for disputes where I had grown up. As usual, I had picked someone bigger than I was.

Bigger and possibly better. The civilian very soon proved he had other skills than roller skating. He connected with a solid overhand right and I found myself on the ground. My head felt as if it were full of rocks grating against each other.

Back on my feet, I brought both arms straight up in front to protect face and body, dropped into a crouch and waded in. He hit me with a wide-angle hook and I went down again. I got up, ducked a right-hand lead and connected with a whistling left hook to the body. The civilian doubled up in pain and gave ground. I decided he was lacking in fortitude and charged. He nailed me on the way in, and I was down for the third time.

I was taking fearsome punishment. Punches I should have blocked or slipped were making contact. The alcohol had slowed my reflexes. But it also dulled the pain. The crowd receded to a blurred white ring around us. The face in front of me was my enemy, all my enemies combined, and it was not sneering now.

We stood at close range and exchanged blow for blow without a semblance of boxing or defense. My nose and mouth were bleeding but so were my opponent's: his fancy white shirt was smeared with gore. The mob loved it and howled for more, as mobs always do.

Now it was a question of endurance and desire. I thought I saw a shadow of fear in the tall man's eyes. He should have won the fight long before now and walked away a hero to his girl friend of the scornful laugh. Instead, this sailor kept getting up and coming back for more.

I drove a right fist to his face and he spat blood. He tried to clinch but I got the left hand free and hooked it repeatedly to his midsection. Now he was weakening and I knew I would win. I brought up my right from ground level in a sweeping bolo punch, a blow I had learned from watching the Filipino fighters at the Honolulu Civic Auditorium. He fell to his hands and knees, gasping for breath.

He might have risen: I shall never know. For the Shore Patrol had arrived en masse and were trying to force their way through hundreds of spectators who refused to give ground before their shouts of, "Gangway! Shore Patrol!"

Half a dozen seamen formed a cordon around me.

"We-uns gonna carry you-all outta here," said one. "The bluecoats has done arrived."

The crowd parted obligingly as the sailors spirited me from the lot and down a dark street. One of them ran to find a cab.

"Ah ain't seen a fight like that in a coon's age," another said admiringly.

"Sho nuff," a third added. "You-all got real grit!"

Sewell and a second group of seamen soon arrived with my opponent. "He wants to shake your hand," my shipmate explained.

"Why not?" I replied, wiping blood from my face. That was the way it was done in Placerville.

We shook hands.

"You're one tough sailor," he said with a twisted grin.

"You're one tough civilian," I said with a grin equally twisted.

"Not for long," he said. "I'm going in the Navy next month."

"By God, we'll be glad to have you."

My six rescuers insisted on accompanying me to the Broadway Pier and paying the cab fare. These young Southerners were still in boot camp, but they already knew what being a shipmate meant.

So did the petty officer from the *Yorktown* who had the gangway watch the next evening. This time the Shore Patrol had succeeded in apprehending *Pawnee* sailors. They arrived at the brow escorting two wayward right-arm ratings.

"Permission to come aboard," snapped the SP spokesman.

"Permission denied."

"These men have been arrested on serious charges. You are to make them prisoners-at-large pending a captain's mast."

"Oh yeah? What charges?"

"Drunk and disorderly and fighting with civilians."

"Is that all? Advance with my men and show your papers."

The SP handed over the report forms. Without reading them, our petty officer tore them into ribbons, balled up the strips and threw them over the side.

"That's what I think of your goddam arrest chits."

"You can't do that," the SP protested. "It's a violation of Navy Regs. These men are on report."

"Tough shit." He put his hand on his forty-five. "Now get your ass off my ship."

The Shore Patrol had no alternative but to obey. They knew an enlisted gangway watch had the same authority as an officer of the deck. When the captain was notified of this incident, he earned the plaudits of the crew by doing nothing.

Meanwhile, our chief petty officers were demonstrating their own brand of shipboard savoir-faire, one honed by long Navy service. The *Pawnee* was lacking a few articles they considered necessary for her efficient operation. They sortied for a "midnight requisition" at the San Diego Destroyer Base. By some arcane means, they appropriated two ladders, miscellaneous tools and a bicycle—the latter for transportation to the CPO club at any Navy base we might visit. Again, Captain Dilworth may have chuckled but he did nothing.*

On the morning of 9 December we departed the continental limits of the United States and set our course west-southwest for grim, gray Pearl

---

* Shipmate Bill Miller adds a postscript. "In May 1945, back at San Diego, I ran into some of the destroyer base CPOs. They still remembered the *Pawnee* chiefs and their 'heist.' The dexterity with which it was accomplished was appreciated."

Harbor, a place of defeat and death I had no reason to love. Behind us on 200 fathoms of HGPS (high-grade plow steel) wire rope 2 inches in diameter was the great hollow hulk of *ARD-1*, the first of a family of floating dry docks designed to provide major repairs for wounded ships in the forward areas.

The *ARD-1* was 485 feet long and had a lifting capacity of 3,500 tons, ample to accommodate destroyers, submarines, and all manner of small merchant ships and Navy auxiliaries. Essentially, it was a floating graving dock fitted with a tanker-type prow to facilitate deep-sea towing. The small crew were housed in a rudimentary superstructure at the forward end. They could communicate with the *Pawnee* by flashing light or flag hoist to the yards of a stick mast.

I stood on the fantail, well clear of the taut tow wire, and watched the skyline of San Diego diminish and at last disappear. Our new mascot, a nondescript gray wharf kitten we had named "V-6," was cavorting at my feet but I scarcely noticed. I was leaving my country for many months, even years, and possibly longer than that. I thought of Alan Seeger's lines, "I have a rendezvous with Death / At some disputed barricade . . . "

Pawnee and I had our own rendezvous to keep. Death was notoriously fickle and might pass us by. Whichever way our appointment went, I had prepared myself. I had burned my emotional bridges, even the ones to my family: a sacrifice made easier by the divorce and subsequent adoption which had darkened my childhood years. I would continue to write the Masons regularly and my father occasionally, but from a distance beyond miles. I had hopes, but no false ones, and declined the baggage of regrets. Henceforth, so far as I could discipline myself, I would live in the very hour of every day. It was the only sane way for a man at war to live.

Chapter Two

TO THE
SOUTH PACIFIC

It is required of a man that he should share the passion and action of his time at peril of being judged not to have lived.

Oliver Wendell Holmes

" 'Water, water, everywhere, / And not a drop to drink'," Electrician's Mate Donald J. Aposhian said, waving an arm toward the horizon.

"Ah, 'The Rime of the Ancient Mariner'."

"Well, we're not going to let our V-6s shoot any albatrosses, are we?" Aposhian quipped. A tall, ruggedly handsome Armenian from Salt Lake City, he had a wry sense of humor and a philosophic turn of mind that I appreciated. We had quickly become good friends.

"It's funny," I said. "I thought of that poem the first time I ever went to sea, in the *Neosho*. Especially the lines, 'As idle as a painted ship / Upon a painted ocean'."

"Looks that way, doesn't it? Hell, our beards may be as long as the Mariner's before we make a landfall."

Pawnee was crawling across a vast expanse of the Pacific due south of the Hawaiian Islands. The cobalt ocean was as flat as a mill pond, so unruffled it might indeed have been a painted seascape. The cloudless sky above was painted, too, an intense cerulean blue. The scene gave an impression of infinite space against which our puny progress could scarcely be measured.

In fact, we had all four engines on the line, turning the shaft at 120 revolutions per minute, and our speed of advance was 9 knots. Astern on 1,240 feet of tow wire was the fat black shape of *ARD-5*, a younger sister of the floating dry dock we had towed to Pearl Harbor. She was heavily laden with unassembled Quonset huts, flatcars piled high with cargo, a steam locomotive and a yard tug. Our sole escort, a mere speck in the van, was a steel-hulled sub chaser.

Our destination was an island in the South Pacific most of us had never heard of: Espiritu Santo in the New Hebrides chain. Our dogleg course would take us well to the east and south of the Japanese-held Marshall and Gilbert Islands.

We had just spent three weeks at Pearl Harbor and were not sorry to leave. Arriving on 20 December, we had released our tow and moored alongside the *Medusa* at the Repair Basin for work on our already temperamental engines and steering gear.

I looked across the main channel to Ford Island and battleship row. A year after the air raid, two ships were still there, but the concrete interrupted quay at the head of the line was empty. That was where the *California*, flagship of Vice Admiral William S. Pye's battle force, had moored, where I had witnessed the entire attack from my maintop battle station, where I had lost ninety-eight shipmates. Between Berth F-3 and Ford Island was the now placid lagoon through which I had swum to the sanctuary of a bomb crater. In my imagination, the stench of blood still hung over Pearl Harbor.

At the next quay astern was the *Oklahoma*, in the same upside-down position she had assumed before my unbelieving eyes that Sunday morning. Only her keel, part of her flat bottom and the starboard screw were above water. More than 400 bodies were entombed with her.

At the rear of the line the twisted and broken *Arizona*, blown apart by bombs on 7 December, brooded over the harbor. She was a reminder to every ship standing out that this enemy was the most formidable the Navy had ever faced—and that warfare by gentlemen's rules was as dead as the 1,100 men of Battleship Thirty-nine.

I found her a reminder, also, of the Navy's sometimes cavalier attitude toward casualties. I vividly remembered the day in late March 1942 when I departed Pearl Harbor in the heavy cruiser *Louisville*, bound for San Francisco and duty in the *Pennsylvania*. Admiral Pye had retained command of his battle force, reduced now to seven capital ships and a squadron of destroyers, and I had been selected for his flag radio complement.

The admiral and his retinue of staff officers, all in spotless whites, came on board a few minutes before the *Louisville* cast off. They were greeted on the quarterdeck with full honors by the captain and his department heads. Admiral Pye, a very short, rotund man, was beaming and smiling as he exchanged pleasantries with the cruiser officers, who had assumed the slightly subservient postures and expressions typical of such naval ceremonies.

"You'd think the admiral was running for office," I told my buddy, Radioman J. K. ("Jawbones") Madden. "All he needs is a baby to kiss."

"How the hell you think he made admiral?" the irrepressible Madden replied, puckering up his mouth and making smacking sounds.

I looked toward Ford Island. "This great smiler lost most of his battle line, including our ship, right over there. He lost 2,000 sailors. When he was Acting Commander-in-Chief, after Kimmel was fired and before Nimitz arrived, he lost Wake Island. What the hell is he laughing about?"

"That's easy," Madden jested. "He's happy because he didn't get what he deserved—a general court-martial."

I couldn't decide. His performance might have been deliberately staged for the benefit of the jittery enlisted men and junior officers. Perhaps he was concerned about morale and wanted to project an air of calm confidence, like a football coach rallying his squad after a 0 to 20 first quarter. On the other hand, it might be that his forty years as a naval officer had made him grossly insensitive to the human cost of the most humiliating defeat ever suffered by the U.S. Navy. Regardless of his reasons, I would have much preferred him scowling on deck, sulking in his quarters and scheming revenge, a nautical Napoleon on his own retreat from Moscow. Then I would have known he cared.

Radioman J. F. ("Red") Goff, a buddy in Battleships 44 and 38, had once described Honolulu as the absolute armpit of the world. Under martial law and a curfew, I warned the *Pawnee* seamen and motor macs, the city had descended to another part of the anatomy. They went ashore anyway and soon returned laden with grass skirts, bad liquor and souvenir photos of themselves dandling dusky island lasses on their knees. (The folks back home didn't have to know they had paid these "models"—and that a pose is all they got for their money.) There were lines everywhere, they reported. The longest ones extended down the stairways and along the sidewalks from the second-story bordellos of Hotel, River and North Beretania streets. We prewar petty officers laughed in a pardonably superior way and went to Bloch Recreation Center, inside the navy yard gates, where we could play pool, drink ten-cent beer, listen to a Navy band and watch a free movie.

As we headed south our shipboard routine of four hours on duty and eight off was varied only by periodic gunnery, first-aid and fire drills, the occasional sighting of a C-47 transport headed for Christmas Island and, once, a floating object which was quickly identified as an uprooted palm tree. By day we saw flying fish, grinning dolphins that played tag across our bow until they tired of such a slow and clumsy opponent, a whale blowing to port. By night we watched the luminous phosphorescence in our wake and talked of the States and our home towns and the women we had known.

Day and night the engines pounded noisily but rhythmically. *Pawnee* rolled easily in a moderate swell, her stem parting the waters with a muffled plashing sound. As I had learned on our passage to Pearl, when my ship had a large tow against which she could spend the thrust of 3,000 horses, she snugged down with her fantail low in the water and rocked as gently as a cradle. Behind us, *ARD-5*, tried to steer her own course, tending first toward one quarter and then the other. She was restrained in her wanderings by our automatic towing winch, which payed out on the tow wire under conditions of overload or sudden strain and shortened it to the preset length when the load returned to normal.

From our bridge came the sharp, echoing ping of the sonar gear. Our tranquility was an illusion which could be shattered at any moment by a submarine broaching to engage or the deadly track of the torpedo. Even here death was lurking in the midst of life, as I now knew it always did. War only sharpened one's perception of its immediacy.

With time on my hands, I continued my explorations of the ship. I was especially concerned with the location and arrangement of the three radio antennas, which might have to be repaired under battle conditions. The one for the transmitter was strung between the tops of the foremast and tripod mainmast, a distance of about 55 feet, and was forestayed to the ship's single raked funnel. The two receiver antennas paralleled the foremast between a flying bridge atop the pilothouse and the signal yards. Lacking radar, *Pawnee* already was myopic of vision. Without these slender conductors of electromagnetic waves, she would be deaf and dumb as well.

I made my most pleasing discovery in the athwartships passage on the main deck which gave access to the radio shack and bridge. The passageway served also as a line of demarcation between officers' country, just forward, and the crew's spaces. There in a 4 by 6 foot metal cabinet secured to the after bulkhead, I found the ship's library.

The selection of books had been made by someone of catholic taste and leftist views—probably a Roosevelt New Dealer operating sub rosa in the Navy Department, I told Aposhian. For along with the usual popular novels there were the works of John Steinbeck, Ernest Hemingway, John Dos Passos, Upton Sinclair, and Jack London. London was represented by *The Sea-Wolf, Martin Eden* and *The Iron Heel,* all three recommended to me by an erudite stevedore on the San Francisco waterfront. Since the latter novel prophesied the seizure of power in America by a fascist-type organization, I had never expected to find a copy in a Navy ship's library. The nonfiction section included the five-volume *Outline of History* by H. G. Wells and *The Rise of American Civilization* by the Beards, Charles and Mary. I even found anthologies of English and American poetry.

I set out to read, or reread, all these books, beginning with H. G. Wells. That this could be considered preparation for college in the future did not conflict with my intention to live for the hour. Since the age of nine or ten, reading had been one of my great pleasures.

I thought about the *Pennsylvania,* whose oppressive routine was designed to keep men too busy to think. The *Pawnee* lacked a "squawk box" for passing the word, and our bosun's mates could find few occasions to use their shrill "bird whistles." I thought about Annapolis, whose midshipmen were too occupied with drilling and cramming for engineering exams to read Wells or London. The two Socialist authors were probably on the proscribed list, anyway. Here I could indulge myself in my reading habit, even at the cost of some lost sleep.

Approaching the equator, it became obvious that the score of "trusty shellbacks" in the crew were planning special and no doubt severe initiation ceremonies for us seventy "pollywogs." With some apprehension we noted low-voiced conversations with the skipper, found some compartments like bosun's stores and the paint locker off-limits, heard loud guffaws from CPO quarters which were not a happy augury for the rest of us.

It hadn't taken long to discover that all the *Pawnee's* chiefs and senior firsts were Navy career men. In making the rounds of the ship I had met most of them and decided we were in capable hands. On the bridge were Chief Earl Clark, F. H. Jobson, quartermaster first, and Irvin John Henry Day, signalman first. (The latter already was convinced that Dilworth was a rare breed of skipper. Day had been at Pearl Harbor in the *Argonne* when the Japanese attacked and didn't return to the States until 6 November, the day before our commissioning. Dilworth granted him five days' emergency leave so he could put his affairs in order before reporting to the ship.) Maintenance of the seven diesel engines was the province of W. B. Arnold, chief motor machinist's mate. Chief Electrician's Mate F. J. Heinrich was responsible for the propulsion-control and power-distribution panels and associated motors. The deck force rated a chief boatswain's mate, R. F. Coffey, as well as the more visible Campbell.

These were the men who really ran the *Pawnee*, regardless of what the ship's organization table said. If the Reserve ensigns and the warrants who filled officers' billets were smart, they would leave them alone to do their jobs. I had a feeling that Dilworth—who already was being called "Captain Frank" by the careerists—understood this fact of small-ship life thoroughly.

Any doubts about our enlisted elite had been removed when first-class POs Proctor, Jobson, Day, Campbell and S. S. ("Doc") Ortalano (who ran sick bay as the ship's sole medical attendant) were moved into chief's quarters, amidships on the second deck. Henceforth, they had very little contact with the crew except on duty: they were destined for quick promotion to chief or warrant. Meanwhile, they slept on inner-spring mattresses, ate in the CPO mess, which was always supplemented by "midnight rations," and used the chief's head. They also enjoyed a very special privilege which I only discovered years later. On occasion Ortalano broke out a pint bottle of 180-proof pharmaceutical alcohol (used for sterilizing instruments, scrubup and formulating medicines like elixir of terpin hydrate). Mixed with canned grapefruit juice, the "white lightning" made a potent nerve tonic.

The second-class petty officers of the Regular Navy—supplemented by a few thirds like Quartermaster Miller and Coxswain C. B. Wilson who would soon make second—occupied the next echelon of authority. Although a Reserve, I belonged to this group by virtue of prewar service in the Battleship Navy. Our privileges were far fewer than our responsibilities. We bunked in the crew's compartments and had to share head and mess facilities with the seamen and firemen. The perceptive observation that "familiarity breeds contempt" applied with special force in the confined quarters of a Navy ship. Required to give orders to men who knew them too well, the seconds often had the hard choice of enforcing discipline through channels, with the report, or unofficially with their fists. They looked longingly toward the lordly privacy of the chiefs' spaces and spent extra hours at the training courses for advancement in rating.

Almost without exception, the rest of the petty officers were Reserves; many had never been to sea. They were relegated to the third echelon in the rigid Navy class and caste system. They might be competent diesel mechanics, storekeepers, soundmen, yeomen or bakers, but that did not make them sailors by any means. They would have to prove themselves, and their performance under stress would be the measure of their acceptance.

Most of the seamen and firemen who made up the fourth echelon had enlisted after the war began in the V-6 classification of Reserves. They would serve for the duration of the national emergency plus six months. Being green, untried and unnautical, they were segregated in one section of the forward crew's compartment. It would be the job of the Navy Regulars to turn them into sailors. Until that happened, if ever, they could expect few favors. I knew how they felt, for I had faced the same problem when I reported to the *California* in October 1940. They were fortunate, I thought, to be serving in the *Pawnee* under a benevolent C.O., not in a battleship under a martinet.

But even the seamen had a group they could feel superior to. At the very bottom of the ship's social order were the officers' servants— two cooks, one Filipino and one black, a black steward's mate and a Filipino mess attendant. (I shall have more to say in later chapters about these "untouchables.")

The *Pawnee* had the surprising number of nine officers. With the exception of the captain and his exec, they were a yeasty mix of pink-cheeked ensigns—"90-day wonders" to the crew—and older warrant officers of long enlisted service. Even in this small salvage vessel, the rigid hierarchical system which separated officers from enlisted men was maintained. The only modification was that the warrants did not have their own quarters and mess, but bunked and ate with the rest of the officers. Officers' country, forward on the main deck, was off-limits to enlisted men unless they were invited or had urgent business there.

That this medieval system was an anachronism in twentieth-century America occurred to few crewman. The Navy had been organized that way since its beginnings during the Revolutionary War, when the customs and traditions of the aristocratic British Royal Navy had been adopted nearly intact. Most Americans paid lip service to democracy, I reflected, but didn't really believe in it. They were perfectly willing to grant special privileges to an elite of the well-born, well-educated and well-to-do. When a grizzled mariner like Campbell saluted an upstart ensign with no sea duty and called him "Mister Hughes," there was not a trace of irony in his voice or manner—or if there were, I could not detect it.

I considered the class system of the *Pawnee* more than a little ridiculous, but it was nothing to laugh about. If a man got into trouble there would be no one to turn to. The ensigns knew too little about the ways of the Navy to go to the mat for an enlisted man, and the warrants knew too much. The latter had not moved up into what I called "the curious limbo of the broken stripe" by rocking any boats. The captain was the only officer in this ship with authority, and I was thankful that he appeared to be a man who remembered his origins and took his perogatives lightly. Under another kind of commander, *Pawnee* could easily become a hell ship.

On 16 January, the day before we reached the line at 160° 09′ west, Admiral Davy Jones suddenly appeared on the forecastle with a message for the captain and a sheaf of summonses directing the pollywogs to appear before His Majesty Neptunus Rex, ruler of the raging main, the next morning. Although he was wearing a cocked hat over a long rope-yarn wig and a flowing great coat, the admiral looked suspiciously like Boatswain's Mate Campbell. Since the war, most ships had greatly curtailed the boisterous crossing-the-line ceremony but *Pawnee* was not going to be one of them.

The next day I lined up with the other off-duty pollywogs along the port rail. We were shoeless and wore nothing but dungaree pants. One by one we were called before King Neptune and his Royal Court for sentencing and punishment.

The "throne" was set up on the forecastle just outside the curve of the wardroom mess. Neptunus Rex looked properly regal in golden crown and flowing beard, with a long cloak over his shoulders. He was holding the traditional trident in one hand and a proclamation in the other. Despite this disguise, I thought he greatly resembled Quartermaster Frank Jobson. On his left was Davy Jones; on his right was six-foot two-inch Queen Amphitrite, clad in a grass skirt and a well-stuffed bra. A tin-foil tiara was tied around her head over a stringy Navy swab. If I hadn't known better I would have thought the role was being played by Signalman Second Frank ("Irish") Driscoll.

When I came before the court, Neptunus Rex looked displeased. "Scribe, who is this miserable landlubber?" he inquired.

"Mason, T. C., Your Majesty," Davy Jones growled.

"Pollywog, prostrate yourself before the throne!" Neptune roared.

I did so.

"Now kiss the foot of Queen Amphitrite."

I obeyed. She winked at me.

"Read the offenses of this lowly pollywog," Neptune ordered.

"Your Majesty, he is charged with being a Reserve of the V-3 class, which is only one small step above the lowest form of animal life, the V-6. He is charged with pretending to read books to impress his superiors when he doesn't even know how to read. He is further charged with being a liberty hound and with committing assault and battery upon overage 4-Fs."

"How do you plead, landlubber?"

"Guilty as hell, Your Majesty."

"Execute the punishment."

I was seized by several attendants and doused repeatedly in a canvas water tank. When I emerged, dripping and breathless, other shellbacks applied electric shocks to my wet skin with padded "devil's forks." Shuddering involuntarily from the prods, I was steered to an 8-foot-long canvas tube.

"Into the tube, landlubber."

When I hesitated, I was hit with high-velocity streams of water from fire hoses manned by grinning shellbacks. As soon as I recovered my balance, I dived head-first into the mouth of the tube. The wet canvas closed around me and I had a feeling I was suffocating in its coarse embrace. I lost no time in kicking and squirming the rest of the way.

Back on my feet, I found the remaining shellbacks lined up along the starboard weather passage. They were armed with canvas-covered shillelaghs which they brandished impatiently.

"Run for you goddam life, pollywog!"

I sprinted the gauntlet to the fantail while each man in turn took lusty whacks at my posterior. Canvas stuffed with wet paper makes a most effective flail. At the end of the line Aposhian was waiting to grip my hand.

"Welcome to the Ancient Order of the Deep, buddy!"

From the wings of the bridge Captain Dilworth looked down upon the proceedings with a benign smile, obviously delighted that a centuries-old tradition of the sea was being observed despite the war. The initiation had not been gentle, either for the enlisted men or the Reserve officers, but it had been kept well within the bounds of a rough good humor. As much as the long, slow cruise, it had brought all hands together in that camaraderie which shipboard duty can engender. As we moved ever deeper into the Southern Hemisphere, the *Pawnee's* climate of controlled permissiveness made her a happy ship, the first one I had ever served in.

Gradually, the days got warmer and more humid. In the engine room the blowers were unable to dissipate the heat generated by the four big diesels and temperatures soared as high as 125 degrees Fahrenheit. With one exception, the black gang endured these conditions stoically. Engine rooms in the tropics were hot and nothing could be done about it.

After supper nearly everyone off duty assembled on forecastle or fantail to enjoy the mild breeze generated by our forward progress. Strange new constellations appeared in the sky, looking brighter and closer than the familiar ones of the Northern Hemisphere. John Day, who was learning celestial navigation from Chief Quartermaster Clark, pointed out glittering Orion, the brilliant dog star Sirius in Canis Major, brightest in the heavens, and the irregular geometry of Centaurus. The short rear legs of the Centaur nearly touch the four stars that form the Southern Cross. I stared long at it, remembering that Robert Louis Stevenson had come this way . . . and Somerset Maugham . . . and London in the *Snark.* The Cross seemed more a symbol of adventure and romance than of piety. Would I find any of these? Adventure depended upon one's definition. Romance seemed out of the question. A little godliness, given the purpose of my transit of the South Seas, might be in order.

On 21 January we changed course to 270° and headed due west for Espiritu Santo. As we passed north of Samoa, our sub-chaser escort was detached. Alone with *ARD-5,* we crossed the International Date Line near the Fiji Islands on Sunday the 24th and lost Monday. That was quickly forgotten when the ship's yeoman, Le Roy Zahn, handed out our shellback cards. We also received a second billfold card, the coveted Order of the Golden Dragon, awarded for crossing the 180th Meridian at Latitude 00°-00'-00". The captain's thoughtful gesture may have fallen outside of Navy Regulations—we had crossed the dateline far south of the equator— but it further endeared him to the crew.

After breakfast on the 29th I went to the bridge. Dilworth was in the pilothouse and I saluted.

"Good morning, captain."

"Good morning, Mason." He smiled as he touched his cap. "What do you think of the New Hebrides?"

Looking around, I saw islands of various sizes on both quarters, our port beam and ahead. Some had jagged volcanic mountains; all were covered with dark green rain forest. Against the shorelines, heavy surf was breaking upon coral reefs. The only sign of human habitation was an occasional smudge of gray smoke.

"They don't look too friendly, do they, sir?"

"Not very. They remind me a little of the coast of Panama. I am told some of the natives still practice cannibalism here."

"Sir, I've changed my mind about requesting special liberty."

I found Day at the pelorus on the port wing.

"Have these islands got names, or are they still uncharted?" I inquired.

"They've got names you won't believe," he said. "Back there are Pentecost and Ambrym. On our port hand is Malekula. Dead ahead are Ile Malo and Espiritu Santo."

"It sounds like we're steering a course between heaven and hell."

That drew a tight grin from the normally serious signalman. "It'll be hell if we hit that mine field at the entrance to Segond Channel. It sent the *President Coolidge,* an Army transport, to the bottom last October—and before that, the destroyer *Tucker.* We'll have a pilot, though."

We came into the mile-wide channel between Espiritu Santo and a small island named Aore with the pilot at the conn, the tow snubbed up close to our stern with a wire bridle and Condition Afirm set throughout the ship for maximum watertight integrity. We released ARD-5 at 1653 and moored alongside a yard oiler for refueling.

We had been under way for 19 days and had covered nearly 4,000 miles. The *Pawnee* had performed flawlessly. The crew had shaped up well, too, proving we could handle routine towing operations. But, in my opinion, we weren't yet ready for the Solomon Islands, 500 miles to the northwest. *Pawnee's* sister ship *Seminole* already had been lost there, sunk by concentrated fire from three Japanese destroyers off Lunga Point, Guadalcanal. Before we threw down any gauntlets, we needed time to finish making sailors of our seamen and junior ratings.

The Navy apparently agreed. We spent the next four weeks in the waters around Espiritu Santo on a variety of towing and salvage duties. We moved lighters around Segond Channel, stood by to assist the storied carrier *Enterprise* and other men-of-war into the channel, salvaged a plane that had crashed in shallow water and delivered the remains to Pallikulo Bay, near the Army-Navy airfield. We placed camels (wooden floats that served as caissons) along one flank of a torpedoed merchantman, *El Capitan*, and pulled a French interisland steamer off the beach at Pallikulo. At night we moored to the big new destroyer tender *Dixie*. The crew had a chance to draw small stores, get haircuts, buy gedunks (ice cream sundaes), attend church services on Sunday morning. Most importantly, our mail was waiting for us at the fleet post office ashore. The Navy base, code-named "Button," was being built up rapidly across a former coconut plantation by a battalion of Seabees. Occupying sloping terrain above Segond Channel, it faced the prevailing southeast trade winds.

Right now that was no particular advantage, for this was the summer monsoon season in the New Hebrides. By day the clouds hung heavily in a leaden sky. The temperature climbed into the 90s and the relative humidity was close behind. Balefully, the sun set behind Espiritu Santo in a promise of worse for tomorrow. Around midnight relief often came with heavy rain squalls that chased the topside sleepers belowdecks. But the sun rose just as angrily as it had descended, sopping up tons of moisture. The dense jungles and groves of coconut palms seemed to boil like giant cauldrons, and there was a fever in the air. Then we were glad we were not ashore, for this was one of the most notorious malarial regions in the world. At Base Button, we heard, the sailors and Seabees "ate atabrine tablets like candy" against the threat of the dreaded *Anopheles* mosquito and turned as yellow as mummies.

"There's an old Navy saw that 'the worst shore duty is better than the best sea duty'," Proctor said after one trip to the beach in a quest for spare parts. "The guy who came up with that pearl of wisdom never spent any time at Santo."

At 2000 hours on 1 February the general-alarm klaxon reverberated throughout the ship. The crew double-timed to general quarters under our first "Condition Red." Proctor left me in charge of the radio room and went to the bridge. The other radiomen laughed and skylarked, treating the air raid as a joke.

"Knock it off," I said sharply. "And put your helmets on. You guys haven't seen what one bomb can do. Believe me, it ain't funny."

Proctor soon reported that big Kawanishi flying boats from the Solomons were overhead for the fifth time in the past eleven days. Whether by coincidence or design, their first air raid on 21 January had caught Secretary of the Navy Frank Knox and the Pacific Fleet's ranking admirals, Chester Nimitz and William Halsey, conferring in the seaplane tender *Curtiss*. If one of the eight bombs dropped that night had scored a providential hit, the whole course of the Pacific War might have been changed. The Japanese had no better luck in welcoming *Pawnee* to the New Hebrides. All their bombs exploded harmlessly in the channel.

As February passed I spent most of my spare hours in the mess hall reading the histories of Wells and the Beards and trying to ignore the sticky heat. Often a crewman would join me in the hope of discovering our next port of call. I was accustomed to that, for radiomen—along with yeomen, quartermasters and signalmen—held a special status in every ship's company. They were the conduits through which nearly all outside information, whether by radio, mail or flashing light, reached the ship. Although such vital intelligence as sailing orders was usually coded or classified, to be deciphered or opened only by an officer, the crew always believed that the petty officers involved were "in the know." Naturally, the radiomen and other ratings did little to discourage this notion, since it occasionally prompted small "perqs" such as a piece of hot apple pie from the galley or an illicit can of grapefruit juice. While I sometimes did get a quick look at message decodes, in this instance Ensign Moodie had shown me nothing, and even Proctor agreed with the scuttlebutt that we would soon be in the Solomon Islands. The Japanese had just evacuated Guadalcanal, ending six months of jungle warfare, and fallen back on the New Georgia group in the Central Solomons. *Pawnee's* salvage services would doubtless be needed when we invaded those islands.

On 25 February Dilworth attended a sailing-orders conference in the *Dixie*. A war correspondent wearing a white brassard embossed with a green

"C" on his khaki uniform came aboard for transportation. He disappeared into the wardroom and wasn't seen again for three days. The crew expected nothing more from the correspondents, who were widely regarded as so many "trained seals" writing what the Navy told them to. The proof was in the stories they filed, which bore little resemblance to what actually happened and often turned defeats into victories. As further evidence, they consorted only with officers, ignoring the enlisted men. If a real writer like Hemingway ever came aboard, I told my shipmates, he would soon appear in the crew's quarters—with a bottle.

On 26 February we stood out of the channel in company with a small convoy. Lashed alongside was a rusty old coastal transport which had been holed amidships by a torpedo that passed clear through without detonating. As soon as we cleared the minefield, we strung the cripple on 200 fathoms of cable and set a course nearly due south. Our destination was not Guadalcanal but Noumea, New Caledonia.

Three days later we steadied astern of the convoy commander and shortened our towline to 66 fathoms. We were entering a strait which wound its tortuous way among dozens of small islands, each with its sentinel reef against which great combers rolling up from the southeast drove and broke into feathery white surf. The jade-green waters of placid lagoons glittered in the sunlight as if promising treasure to those who stayed awhile. It was an invitation we could not accept. To the northwest was a passage through the great barrier reef which almost completely girdled the 250-mile-long by 30-mile-wide island of New Caledonia. The approaches to Noumea, near its southern tip, looked like a graveyard for ships on the foul ground of shoals or coral banks. There should be plenty of work for *Pawnee* here.

I compared scuttlebutt with other off-duty crewmen assembled along the weather passageway outside the mess hall. Noumea had once been a French penal colony, a Devil's Island of the South Pacific. When the Americans arrived in the spring of 1942, New Caledonia was divided between loyalists of Vichy France, the puppet government of that Nazi-occupied country, and the followers of General Charles DeGaulle, the Free French. Many Vichyites would have preferred to see the flag of the rising sun, for they had prospered from a lucrative trade with Japan in the iron, nickel and chrome ores of New Caledonia. Even the Free French, now in nominal control of the colony, were hostile to the Americans and fleeced them unmercifully ashore. But we were there in force because of the island's strategic importance, and the French were simply a nuisance that must be tolerated until we had driven the enemy from the Solomon Islands.

Noumea was the headquarters of Admiral William F. ("Bull") Halsey, commander of all South Pacific forces. He lived in the former Japanese consulate on a hill overlooking the harbor, which must have amused him as much as it did the enlisted men, who all knew of his hatred for the enemy. His offices, the best he could commandeer from the peevish French, were an ugly, barrackslike building near the waterfront, which probably amused him and his staff not at all. The Bull himself could, on occasion, be seen strolling nearby in shorts and T-shirt which revealed a large fouled anchor tattooed on his arm, souvenir of a summer cruise when he was still a midshipman. I rubbed the bird tattoo on my left shoulder, acquired during a bibulous liberty in Honolulu in the summer of 1941, and thought more of Halsey for his violations of the priggish Annapolis code. We also chuckled over an eyewitness report, passed along from Halsey's chauffeur to the CPO club at Santo. The Bull had got roaring drunk one night at the officers' club and started swinging at his staff captains. We only hoped the Scotch hadn't spoiled his aim.

Nearly all this scuttlebutt was true. It was only the beginning of our reluctant education about Noumea and the *Calédoniens*—and about the South Pacific Theater. Under the Southern Cross, the truth often was more bizarre than the contrived tales of novelists.

At four knots it took nearly five hours to thread Bulari Passage, put the lighthouse abeam to port, skirt the tip of an offshore island and enter the Great Roads. Noumea spread across the hills to the east in a motley of nondescript buildings with red roofs. On a peninsula to the north, the tall chimneys of a nickel smelter were belching flames and foul smoke. We took in this uninspiring scene of colonial enterprise and decided it didn't really matter that only 5 percent of the crew would be granted liberty at one time—and that only for a few hours in the afternoon.

With a yard tug assisting, we put our tow alongside *ARD-2*, a Pearl Harbor veteran which was anchored near the offshore island that formed one protective arm of the Great Roads, and dropped our hook nearby. The island, I learned, was infamous Ile Nou, where the convicts from France had once been confined. We could see grim stone dungeons and, on a hill commanding the harbor, a French artillery post. We also saw newly constructed docks fronting rows of Quonset huts and steel warehouses, for the island had been taken over by the Navy and was being converted to a major repair base.

Near our berth, a listing Liberty ship seemed abandoned to rust and barnacles. Water lapped in and out of a hole at least twenty-five feet in diameter in her number four hold. She was the *Edgar Allan Poe*, torpedoed about the time of the *Pawnee*'s commissioning and already forgotten. The dissolute genius for whom she was named would, I thought, have appreciated the irony. Her forlorn silhouette reminded me also that the waters between the Solomon Islands and Australia were teeming with Japanese submarines that had sunk or heavily damaged a number of merchantmen in the past year.

We refueled from a yard oiler and spent most of the next two weeks moored portside to the *Argonne,* another veteran of the Pearl Harbor attack. Formerly a submarine tender, the 22-year-old vessel had a limited repair capability; her principal role had been that of flagship. Since 1941 the flags of three admirals had flown from her main: W. L. Calhoun, Commander Base (now Service) Force; Robert L. Ghormley, the first Commander South Pacific, and his bolder successor, Halsey. When the latter moved ashore in November 1942, she had become the station ship at Noumea. Now her diesel mechanics came aboard and tinkered with our cantankerous main engines. We checked them out by returning to Bulari Passage, passing our tow wire to the badly leaking destroyer *Shaw* and putting her in the floating dry dock at Ile Nou. The *Shaw* had gone aground at 25 knots while screening a task group and been pulled off the reef, despite a badly corrugated bottom and the loss of both propellers, by our sister ship *Menominee.**

Back alongside the *Argonne,* Aposhian and I arranged a liberty together. We had heard that Noumea occupied the same position in the anatomical scale as Honolulu but wanted to see this onetime penal colony for ourselves. Besides, it was a good chance to learn some French.

The whaleboat deposited us at the fleet landing on a rubble-filled embankment called, rather grandly, the Grand Quai. A left turn and a short walk, we had been told, would bring us to the most famous establishment in Noumea, the Pink House. The only enlisted man's brothel in the South Pacific, it was a joint venture among the Army, the Navy and the civilian authorities and a model of efficiency. The line extended along the waterfront for a block or more. Upon entering the drab premises, you surrendered your I.D. card, paid your five dollars and took potluck. That might be a Javanese, a Chinese, a half-caste Polynesian or, if the luck was running good, the single Frenchwoman. Before your I.D. was returned, you

---

* The *Shaw,* a *Mahan*-class destroyer commissioned in 1936, was in this same ARD-2 dry dock during the Pearl Harbor attack. Hit by three bombs, her magazines detonated and demolished the forward part of the ship clear back to the bridge. Fitted with a false bow, she made it to Mare Island Navy Yard under her own power for full repairs. She survived the war, winning 11 battle stars.

were required to take a full service prophylaxis. Aposhian and I shuddered at the thought and headed for the nearby business district.

We passed the Rue Général Gallieni, where Halsey ran the South Pacific from his spavined barracks, and soon came to the Place des Cocotiers, a four-block-long plaza in the center of town. No doubt it had been planned as a verdant oasis, but the grass was trampled and brown, the coconut palms which gave the place its name were shedding their fronds, and even the orange blossoms of the squatty poinciana trees looked faded by the summer sun.

We paused to look around. The rickety, unpainted buildings had roofs of corrugated tin plate whose eaves overhung the narrow, uneven sidewalks. All the shops were closed, some with iron shutters. We peered through dust-coated windows of the others at shelves which were bare except for a few American and Australian products. The fall of France had cut off all trade with the homeland, so we looked in vain for French perfume, lingerie, gowns or champagne.

Mixed in with the shops and offices were private residences hidden behind high walls with locked gates. The French, we had heard, had a passion for privacy. Some of the taller buildings were decorated with gingerbread balconies of rusting wrought iron giving this listless city what little atmosphere it possessed. Noumea, we decided, looked like a run-down, third-rate New Orleans.

Glancing neither left nor right, an elderly French gentleman in a white tropical suit approached at a brisk gait. He had a neatly trimmed mustache and goatee in the style of Napoleon III. When Aposhian greeted him, he responded with the barest nod of recognition and marched on down the Rue Anatole France. Aside from a few native Melanesians and Tonkinese imported from French Indochina, the only people we saw on the streets were wearing American uniforms. The Noumeans seemed to consider themselves under enemy occupation.

"You'd think we were the Nazis," I commented.

"If you want to make an enemy," Aposhian observed, "just save a man from himself."

At last we found a *mercerie,* French for a five-and-ten store, which was just opening for business. The small, brisk woman behind the counter spoke English. Everything had been closed because Noumeans took a three-hour lunch, from 11 to 2, she told us. We bought a guide booklet for Americans written by a local scholar and two English-French readers. She brightened at that and favored us with a smile.

We asked if there was any place we could buy a drink. All the cafes were closed in the daytime, she said regretfully (meaning, we assumed, they were reserved for the French). The Grand Hotel du Pacifique, Noumea's best, had been taken over by the Americans as an officers' club, she added with even more regret. But there was a small bistro on the other side of the Place des Cocotiers that should be open now.

It was our turn to smile. Behind open French windows, the brightly lighted room was jammed with sailors huddled around small tables. The only civilian in sight was the proprietor, a stout mustachioed fellow of middle age. He informed us he had genuine American whiskey for one dollar per glass. Despite the outrageous price, triple that of Stateside, he obviously wished to announce his solidarity with the American fighting men. On the left breast of his jacket he wore a single red ribbon, probably for service in World War I.

"Here's one local who loves American sailors," I told my buddy. "Just as long as their money holds out."

The bar at the far end had been closed off except for a service window. Behind the counter was a slender, olive-skinned barmaid who proved as flirtatious as French women were supposed to be. We received an ounce of whiskey in the bottom of a six-ounce glass, a coquettish smile and a few words of greeting in broken, heavily accented English.

Naturally, we got the same idea as every other American in the place. After savoring our first bourbon since San Diego, we went back for refills. My shipmate turned on his considerable charm and we exchanged names: hers was Yvette. We returned again and yet again, each time to a friendlier reception, a fluttering of long lashes over large brown eyes and even a moue or two. I could see why the owner had placed a barrier between her and her customers. French women, Aposhian and I agreed, were probably the most charming and sensual in the world. The only thing we couldn't understand is why these admirable qualities were wasted on Frenchmen.

On our last trip to the bar Yvette suddenly reached across the counter, took a firm grip on my hair and pulled.

"Hey, it's real," I protested. "I just haven't had a haircut recently."

"*Beaux cheveux*," she murmured, still running her fingers through my hair. "*Beau marin.*"

I wondered why she had selected me. There were a dozen other sailors in the place, Aposhian especially, who were better-looking and more personable than I. She could have any one she wanted.

She seized the collar of my undress whites and pulled me close. "Ted, you got Jeep?"

I passed from surprise to astonishment. Hastily, Aposhian thumbed through the dictionary section of his reader.

"No Jeep, Yvette," he said with a huge grin. "But he has boat, uh, *bateau. Petit bateau.* You go?"

She giggled and slapped me lightly across the face.

"Ah, *oui,*" she said. "You come back *vendredi,* is Friday. We go in *petit bateau!*"

On our way back to the ship Aposhian and I marveled at the glorious unpredictability of women. But how to take advantage of that fact? We would have to bribe or cajole the gangway watch into looking the other way while we "borrowed" the whaleboat. Then we would have to avoid the Shore Patrol at the fleet landing. If we eluded them, we would probably be challenged or even fired upon by the Harbor Patrol. Under wartime security in a foreign port we knew nothing about, a pleasure cruise seemed out of the question. We would almost certainly be apprehended and brought back to the ship under guard. Not even the benevolent Captain Frank could save us from a summary court-martial, or worse.

"Well, buddy, at least you know you haven't lost your touch," my shipmate said consolingly—a little too consolingly, I thought. "All the Constitution guarantees is the pursuit of happiness, not the attainment."

"General Sherman said it better," I grumbled. " 'War is hell.' "

Chapter Three

THE "DIRTY DELL"

On St. Patrick's Day we picked up French Pilot Vincent Gap, cleared the harbor and headed southeast from the lighthouse for Nomobitigue Reef on a crucial salvage job. The store ship *Delphinus* had gone aground there and the brass hats at Noumea wanted her off without delay. She was one of only three or four "beef boats" with refrigerated spaces making the run from Auckland, New Zealand, to the forward areas with chilled and frozen provisions.

We arrived in mid-afternoon to a scene no crew member ever forgot, for here is where we would spend the next three weeks. The *Delphinus* had driven up onto the reef for nearly half her 329-foot length. A heavy surf was breaking around her, rolling clear over the reef and roiling the waters of the adjacent lagoon. Across the lagoon, a few hundred yards away, a small atoll wore the familiar crown of coconut palms and casuarinas.

The rollers were a dirty foaming brown. They had painted the reef the same color. Apparently the *Delphinus* had ruptured some of her fuel tanks upon jutting coral heads. Bobbing up and down in the surf were hundreds of large metal globes which were soon identified as net buoys from the crippled ship's cargo. (A radio message from NCX Noumea warning us to be alert for numerous floating mines in the area gave our officers one of the few laughs they would enjoy at Nomobitigue Reef.)

The crew of the *Delphinus* soon had reason to regret that the Navy had changed their ship's name from *San Mateo* when she was acquired from the Munson Line the previous year. For Bill Miller, in an inspired moment, coined the sobriquet she would carry for the rest of her service career—the "Dirty Dell."

40

Adding insult to grievous injury, Miller hailed the crewmen with this question in his bullhorn voice:

"Hey, how you guys like shore duty?"

When that elicited no response beyond scowls and profanity, he tried again.

"What happened? Your navigator shoot the truck light for a star?"

More profanity and clenched-fist salutes.

"These Dirty Dell people are a surly lot," Miller complained. "No sense of humor!"

I knew little about marine salvage but this was my opportunity to ask questions and learn. Our skipper had been one of the top warrant boatswains in the Navy; he had mastered his profession in the oiler *Cuyama* and the carrier *Lexington* before putting the *Massachusetts* into commission. If he couldn't extricate the *Delphinus* from the embrace of the coral reef, I doubted that anyone else in the Navy could.

I watched closely as we anchored to seaward of the cripple in 35 fathoms of water with 60 fathoms of chain on the forecastle deck. By slowly paying out the chain, we maneuvered into position for passing our tow wire across. Once it was secured to the stern of the *Delphinus*, we heaved in on our anchor with the windlass while paying out the tow wire. Soon the taut wire and the anchor were both stopped off. The captain ordered one-third ahead on our engines to maintain a steady strain and adjusted our course to keep the *Pawnee's* head into the fresh southeast breeze.

It soon became apparent that a strong 5-knot tidal current was making up along the reef and exerting a mighty force against the *Pawnee's* beam. With the ship caught in the bight between the anchor cable and the towline, it was necessary to continually change headings and speeds to keep her headed up and away from danger. When I came on watch at 2345, a heavy rain squall was passing through, visibility was 450 yards, our heading was 144 degrees true—and the Dirty Dell had not moved an inch.

All the next morning we kept changing headings and propeller revolutions against the effects of wind and tide, but Nomobitigue refused to release the store ship from its gap-toothed grip. The wind increased to Force 6, driving heavy swells before it from the east. Two hundred yards off our port beam, giant breakers were combing against the reef. Our anchor was dragging and setting us down toward the fury of white water. At 1225, Dilworth ordered the tow wire cast loose. Until the weather moderated, further operations could only jeopardize his ship.

We spent most of March 19th trying to find a suitable holding ground for our anchor. The available charts, which dated from the turn of the century, showed the land masses and reefs far out of position and gave no information on the type of bottom, which could be determined only by examining the anchor each time it was pulled. Mostly it came up with wet sand and bits of coral wedged between the flukes and the shank. This type of bottom would not hold our anchor when we heaved around with the windlass to assist the main engines in taking a strain on the tow wire. The problem was compounded by continuing heavy swells and the shifting tidal current. Meanwhile, a yard tug arrived with a 500-ton lighter (an unpowered, flat-bottomed barge) and we transferred salvage pumps and gear to the *Delphinus*.

By 1800 hours our 2-inch tow wire was back aboard the recalcitrant store ship and we were ready to try again. We were going ahead two-thirds and heaving around on our anchor when a signal light began blinking urgently from the bridge wing of the *Delphinus*: CEASE PULLING!

The wire was cast off and we winched it in with many Anglo-Saxon expletives. Apparently the Dirty Dell had shifted and sprung new leaks in her perforated bottom. It would be necessary to patch the leaks and lighten ship before towing efforts could resume. We put the engines on standby, received the lighter from the YT, strung it astern and turned in.

But not for long. About 0230 the starboard quarter of the *Pawnee* shuddered under a booming metallic impact. Within a few seconds the anvil blow was repeated. It sounded as if dud 5-inch shells were striking the ship just above the crew's compartments.

We sprang from our bunks.

"What the hell's that?"

"We're under attack, goddam it. Let's go!"

With a single patrol craft guarding the seaward approaches, it would be easy for a Japanese sub to slip through. We poured topside in various states of undress, some with and some without helmets and life jackets. A fog had set in and visibility was 50 yards.

Out of the mist a large, flush-decked shape emerged, rose high above the fantail and crashed down upon the bulwarks with a rending and crumpling of metal. The 500-ton lighter was running amok in the heavy swells and battering the starboard side of the ship.

One of the main engines was started to power the towing winch. Efforts to snub in the lighter proved fruitless. It was like a wild thing determined to break free and escape Nomobitigue Reef.

Now it shifted its attack to our counter, rearing and plunging to smash at the heavy steel roller chock which supported the towing cable. Only when the swells subsided did the lighter consent to once again ride obediently astern. *Pawnee* had sustained numerous bruises and contusions.

Wide awake now, Aposhian and I had a cup of coffee in the mess hall. It was 0345.

"I tell you, Ted, this goddam coral reef is alive," he said somberly. "It's out to get us like it got the Dirty Dell, and who knows how many other ships? Have you seen those shark fins? They're just cruising around waiting for fresh meat!"

Over the next ten days I would remember Aposhian's words and come to believe them. On the bridge, Miller and Day told me, the captain was doing everything "by the book," just as the 1941 edition of Knight's *Modern Seamanship* said it should be done. But the late Austin M. Knight and the officers of the department of Seamanship and Navigation at the Naval Academy, who had revised and updated the admiral's text, had never contemplated the assistance of a stranded vessel under the conditions which prevailed off New Caledonia. The charts were inaccurate and incomplete, the holding ground was poor, the currents were strong, a heavy sea was running, and the masters of both ships had no knowledge of local conditions. It must have been with some dismay that our captain read the authors' final word on the subject on page 613: "If all other methods fail, resort must be had to regular salvage operations, the description of which is beyond the scope of this book."

If the Navy's seamanship bible could not tell the skipper of an ocean-going salvage vessel what to do when standard methods failed, who then could he consult? The Navy had no special salvage manual and in fact had always turned over its tough salvage jobs to civilian firms like Merritt, Chapman and Scott Corporation on a "no-cure, no-pay" basis, Day informed me. That left only God, he suggested ruefully.

Our morale was not improved by the arrival on board of five officers and thirty enlisted men, transferred from the *Delphinus* by motorized barge for further transfer to Noumea. They were dirty and unshaven, morose and dispirited by their misadventures on the reef. Aboard their ship, they reported, were tons of frozen beef destined for our fighting men in the Solomons. If the ship wasn't taken off the reef soon, it would have to be dumped overboard. We licked our chops and prayed that some of the beef would find a place in our larder before the officers' messes at Noumea claimed the choice cuts.

Time and again we shifted anchorages—using both anchors now—and took a maximum strain on the cripple with all four engines on the line. Inevitably, the anchors dragged, the *Pawnee* was set down toward the reef by wind and tide and we had to maneuver desperately to avoid going aground. From where I stood outside the radio shack, it seemed that only Dilworth's artful ship handling was keeping us from joining the Dirty Dell. Sooner or later, I feared with Aposhian, Nomobitigue would prevail.

On 29 March it almost did. All that day, gigantic swells rumbled in from the southeast, crested and fell upon the reef with murderous intent, a force of nature as uncontrollable as avalanches in the high Sierras. Without warning, both anchors began dragging. The *Pawnee*, caught "in irons" between tow wire and anchors, was helpless to maneuver. Quickly she passed the danger bearing as she was swept down toward the reef.

On our bridge, the captain gave an order and a signalman leaped to his blinker light: CAST OFF TOW WIRE ON THE DOUBLE!

As soon as the umbilical cord which bound us to the cripple was free, we were under way from this hazard. Only to encounter another. The tow wire had dragged and fouled in our propeller. When efforts to free the wire failed, we could do nothing but anchor at a safe distance from a ship that we now devoutly believed was a Jonah, cast up upon a reef which was, as Aposhian had said, vengefully alive.

Moodie soon arrived in the radio shack with an encoded message addressed to Commander Service Force, South Pacific, with an information copy to Commander South Pacific. I tuned up the TBL, raised NCX Noumea on the local ship-shore frequency and transmitted the message while the other radiomen looked on enviously. Under wartime conditions of radio silence, sending a message was a rare privilege.

As soon as I had a receipt from the NCX operator, I switched off the TBL, made the required log entries and shook my head sorrowfully.

"Tomorrow, men," I predicted, "the shit will hit the fantail."

It did. Shortly after noon a steel-hulled patrol craft flying signal flags denoting "Senior Officer on Board" stood in. She was followed by the *Antares*, a creaky 5,000-ton ex-cargo ship now classified as a "miscellaneous auxiliary," and a yard tug with a 500-ton lighter alongside. A party of officers debarked from the PCE and boarded the *Delphinus* for an inspection. They ignored the *Pawnee*, which had sent a diver down despite continuing heavy swells in another futile attempt to clear the tow wire from our propeller.

"Of all times for those SOBs from Noumea to arrive," a bosun's mate muttered, staring across at the Dirty Dell. "We look as foolish as a kid caught behind the barn with his pants down."

Early the next morning two officers came aboard and stormed toward the bridge. I saw them as they passed the radio room: a captain wearing a mean scowl followed by a lieutenant commander whose scowl was even meaner. They were, I soon learned, Roy T. Cowdrey, Halsey's ship repair officer, and Emile C. Genereaux, the renowned West Coast merchant sailor and salvage expert, now C.O. of the *Menominee.*

Cowdrey proceeded to "chew out the skipper," according to John Day, who had the bridge watch. He wanted an explanation of our failure to get the *Delphinus* off the reef. He had reports that we were sending swimming parties to the lagoon between high tides instead of making all preparations for the next pull. He was especially irate because Dilworth had proposed floating a barge alongside the cripple to recover some of the beef which was scheduled to be dumped overboard to lighten ship.

"I want that beef over the side immediately!" Cowdrey raged.

"You should have seen the way Captain Frank stood up to this four-striper," Day said admiringly. "He was thinking of the morale of the crew. I tell you, I was proud of him."

Silently, the crew lined the bulwarks as side after side, ton after ton of prime New Zealand beef was jettisoned from the Dirty Dell. I had heard that sharks could detect the presence of blood at great distances. Now I had proof. Swiftly moving dorsal fins announced the arrival within minutes of those great elemental feeding machines, first by dozens and then by hundreds.

In the shallow waters I could see their shimmering shapes, as fearsome as nightmares, closing the ship in random crisscrossing patterns. As each half of beef splashed it was struck repeatedly. Chunks of flesh as large as a man's head were ripped away. Within seconds, the sharks were attacking the next carcass. The water boiled white in the turbulence of thrashing bodies.

I had read descriptions of feeding frenzies and thought them exaggerated. They were not. Sharks leaped nearly clear of the water, their gaping underslung jaws snapping at nothing. Others, disoriented, banged into the side of the *Delphinus* at full speed. A sailor tossed a torn life jacket overboard: it was swallowed in one gulp.

The awesome ferocity of this primordial scene left me speechless. To these predators a sailor was just another slab of meat. A man overboard would live no longer than a heartbeat or two.

"Makes it a little hard to believe in an all-loving God, doesn't it?" Aposhian remarked.

John Day's reaction was more pragmatic.

"We're eating Aussie goat meat and these sharks are dining on T-bone steaks. They're getting the feast we should have enjoyed!"

After disposing of an entire ship's cargo of beef, the sharks were still ravenous. Like thieves quarreling over the take, they began turning on each other. A great white a dozen feet long veered suddenly and tore a chunk from a smaller one. In an instant, many others joined in. The victim disappeared before my eyes. The carnage soon became general and the water frothed red with blood.

"In this world the big ones eat the little ones," Aposhian said. "The Armenians found that out in Turkey in 1915."

Letting go a volley of curses, a gunner's mate ran to the bridge. He wanted to rig a machine gun and open fire. Every dead shark was a shark that wouldn't eat a sailor. Reluctantly, Dilworth denied permission. We all understood why.

Listening to Armed Forces Radio on the ship's short-wave set, it was obvious that the big ones were assaulting the big ones all over the world and the little ones were in mortal peril from both. In January, Red Army troops had broken through to Leningrad, ending the longest siege of the war and forcing the Germans into retreat toward the hapless Baltic States. In February, Field Marshal Friedrich Paulus surrendered the pitiful remnants of his Sixth Army—90,000 of the original 300,000 men—to the Russians at Stalingrad. Meanwhile, Field Marshal Erwin Rommel's Afrika Corps was trapped between British and American armies advancing from two directions in North Africa, despite a temporary U.S. setback at Kasserine Pass, Tunisia. In March, American planes destroyed all eight transports and four of the eight escorting destroyers of a Japanese troop convoy in the Bismarck Sea as it approached Lae, New Guinea. But in the Atlantic, German U-boats operating in wolf packs sank twenty-one Allied ships in the biggest convoy battle of the war. The nations of Western Europe continued to suffer under the brutal German occupation, heartened only by massive flights of Allied bombers passing overhead to attack German strategic targets. Some day, those who survived would be liberated.

With an armada of sharks patrolling Nomobitigue Reef, diving operations were impossible. We received a towline from the *Antares* and were taken into the lagoon through a break in the reef. While a seaman on the boat deck "rode shotgun," our divers soon cleared the tow wire, which had taken three turns around our propeller shaft. We got under way with only a slightly scored shaft and reanchored near the now indescribably filthy *Delphinus*.

Several seamen decided to go fishing. They attached a large hook to a length of stout manila line which was passed through one of the port davits on the fantail. Baiting the hook with a slab of salt pork, they dropped it over the side. Almost at once it was taken by a giant fish. Setting the hook, they shouted for reinforcements.

Eagerly, a dozen seamen brought in their catch hand over hand.

"My God," one shouted, "it weighs at least a ton!"

"It's a shark," another yelled as the head broke water. "The biggest goddam shark I've ever seen!"

The great white was at least fifteen feet long. As it dangled helplessly under the davit, one of the seamen unsheathed his hunting knife. Dashing in, he buried the knife to the hilt in the shark's belly and disemboweled it with one ripping downward motion. Blood spurted all over the fantail.

"Aaaaah!" shouted the assembled crewmen. Two or three ran in with their knives for the coup de grace.

We had found a suitable outlet for our hostility, which extended from Nomobitigue Reef to the Dirty Dell and from the callous officers of the South Pacific Force to the cannibalistic creatures of the sea. Soon the great white was stretched out on the fantail in a pool of blood and crewmen were gouging at the serrated rows of triangular teeth for souvenirs.

Cy Hamblen came up from the engine room, wiping his hands on a piece of cotton waste. He was grinning with satisfaction.

"That's more like it," he announced. "I think we're just about ready for the Solomons."

But first we had to get this jinx ship off the reef. Another small tug arrived with a 500-ton lighter laden with two Eells anchors, plate shackles and other gear. Cowdrey had returned to Noumea but Genereaux remained aboard to direct operations. The bridge became a very crowded place.

The commander was a brawny six-footer with piercing hard eyes. Because of the perpetual stubble of unshavable beard on his pugnacious jaw, he was soon nicknamed "Black Jack" by the crew. When he doubled one great ham fist and rasped his orders, there was no doubt how he had enforced discipline in the merchant service. I doubted there was a man in the ship—and that included our two light-heavyweight boxers, Seaman Ralph Taylor and Officers' Cook Dick Garrett—who could stand against him in a brawl, even though Genereaux was in his early forties. He might have stepped straight from the pages of a Jack London novel, a sea wolf in a Gallic mould.

We soon discovered that his knowledge of ship salvage was unequaled in the South Pacific. The new lighter was brought alongside to port. Fifteen fathoms of die-locked chain and several 100-fathom lengths of 1¼-inch wire rope were shackled to each Eells anchor. We took the lighter in tow and let go the anchors well offshore on the starboard and port quarters of the *Delphinus*. Since the stranded ship had no power, the cables were run through roller chocks on her stern and back to the *Pawnee*, where they were secured to the two auxiliary wing drums of our towing winch. We had just laid beach gear anchors which would exert an extra pulling force when we took a strain on our main tow wire.

Campbell, now a chief bosun's mate, shook his mastiff head in perplexity as he reached for a cigarette and a Zippo lighter.

"In all my years in the Navy," he rasped, "I never seen such a lashup before." Neither, apparently, had the authors of *Modern Seamanship*.

The next morning Genereaux pulled another rabbit from his salvage hat. Before we passed our 2-inch wire to the *Delphinus*, it was shackled to a "Liverpool bridle" which was rigged along our starboard quarter, the direction of the prevailing current set. The bridle was stopped off with 3-inch

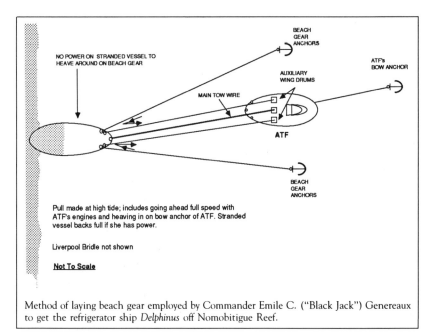

Method of laying beach gear employed by Commander Emile C. ("Black Jack") Genereaux to get the refrigerator ship *Delphinus* off Nomobitigue Reef.

manila "lazy jacks" to provide an ingenious spring-action on the anchors. Instead of being "in irons" between tow wire and anchors when the current set us down toward the reef, *Pawnee* was free to shift directions at will while still maintaining a pull on the cripple. The technique was a common one in the days of sail, Genereaux said. Apparently, it had been lost to the Navy through generations of steam propulsion.

At high tide on the early morning of 4 April we were ready for a supreme effort. We went full ahead on our main engines while hauling in on the Eells anchors and heaving around on our anchor windlasses. This time the anchors held fast in the coral and sand.

An hour later, at 0637, the *Delphinus* gave a convulsive lurch. Then she floated clear of malevolent Nomobitigue Reef with a port list. Crewmen gathered along the weather passages with their morning coffee responded with cheers, applause and rebel yells.

To the accompaniment of flashing signal lamps, the crew of the *Delphinus* cast off the beach gear wires and manhandled the tow wire to the bow. By 0800 we had increased our scope of wire to 250 fathoms and were under way for the Southern Passage to Noumea at 6.9 knots. The Dirty Dell had flooded her ballast tanks and now assumed a starboard list. A tug came alongside with extra dewatering pumps while *Pawnee* maneuvered to maintain a minimum pitch and roll on the precariously afloat "reefer."

Looking back at the wave-battered, oil-smeared hulk, now minus the forward gun and part of the superstructure, Aposhian and I decided we had no reason to congratulate ourselves on our first tough stranding job. It had taken nineteen days and the services of half a dozen other craft to get one 6,000-ton store ship off the reef. In the process we had ourselves nearly gone aground, saved only by Dilworth's seamanship. But he had, partly out of concern for his crew, incurred the wrath of "Slim" Cowdrey and been forced to practically relinquish control of his ship. "Black Jack" Genereaux's knowledge of beach gear and the Liverpool bridle had made the floating of the *Delphinus* look easy. He would get all the credit from the brass, and our fine, humanitarian skipper probably would become a scapegoat for the Navy's weakness in salvage. With this assessment, John Day agreed.

We were not pleased that our prophecy came true. After putting the Dirty Dell into dry dock, we returned to Nomobitigue Reef to recover the beach gear and salvage airplane parts that had been landed on the islet behind the reef when the *Delphinus* lightened ship. Within three days we were moored to the *Argonne* at the Great Roads.

On Tuesday, 13 April, a slender, youthful lieutenant commander named Flave J. George reported on board. The word passed to every compartment and work station nearly as rapidly as if we had had a P.A. system. George's orders came directly from Halsey's Comsopac headquarters. Lieutenant Frank Dilworth had been summarily relieved of his command.*

---

* He reported for duty in the *Argonne*. In 1944 he commissioned the attack cargo ship *Uvalde* as executive officer and participated in the landings at Lingayen Gulf, Luzon, in January 1945. Promoted to lieutenant commander, he became C.O. of the *Uvalde* in September

With long thoughts and impassive faces we assembled at quarters for the brief change-of-command ceremonies. Captain Frank stood straight and proud and read his detachment orders in a firm voice with only an occasional hint of a quaver. But there were tears in his eyes. My own eyes were moist, and I was not the only one. We knew that never again would we serve under a commanding officer who treated his men with such respect and consideration.

If George was aware of our resentment, he certainly didn't show it. He moved and spoke with a kind of debonair assurance which hinted at a privileged background. What that background had been no one knew, but he looked more like an English gentleman than a salvage expert. A high-bridged nose dominated a thin, intelligent face. His smile was rather perfunctory and his eyes seemed to survey the world with a cool skepticism. He was a man, I thought, who would trust his own judgment and confide in no one. I hoped he would prove half as competent as he gave the impression of being.

In the mess hall afterward, a number of us compared notes and agreed that the fine carefree days of no inspections, few regulations and muster on work stations rather than at quarters were over.

"In five months Captain Frank never held a single captain's mast," one senior petty officer pointed out. "He didn't have to—we took care of that."

"No one is ever gonna call this new guy 'Captain Flave'," another said.

"Who ever heard of a goddam Reserve commanding a Navy salvage ship?" a third asked, forgetting about Genereaux. "Well, we got one now."

Various theories were advanced for Dilworth's peremptory relief. A plane had snooped on a swimming party in the lagoon and reported it to Comsopac. The skipper's sharp exchanges with Cowdrey over the beef had put him on the shit list. Genereaux had done a hatchet job on our captain. The scuttlebutt reported that "Black Jack" was spending most of his time in Tulagi Harbor bringing up a Jap destroyer that the Bull wanted as a souvenir. The Dirty Dell incident was a good chance to consolidate his position as Halsey's fair-haired salvage boy. With the traditional loyalty of most Regulars toward their commanding officers, our failure to get the *Delphinus* off the reef was glossed over.

1945. In the immediate postwar period, he commanded and subsequently decommissioned the battle damage repair ship *Oceanus* and the special cargo ship *Castor*. He retired in 1949 after thirty years of service and lived in San Diego with Myrtle, his wife of more than fifty years, until his death in 1987.

Author, right, with *Pawnee* shipmate Jim Sewell and unidentified woman at Patrick's nightspot in downtown San Diego in early December, 1942. Mason's left eye is still discolored from skating rink fight with civilian. (Photo from the author's collection.)

Lieutenant Frank C. Dilworth, USN, commanding officer of the *Pawnee* at her commissioning on 7 November 1942, a man admired and respected by his crew. (Photo courtesy of Myrtle Dilworth.)

Boatswain's mate Winston ("Pappy") Schmidt, oldest man in the crew, sporting a Gay 90s mustache and described by author as having "the physique of an oak tree." (Photo courtesy of Le Roy E. Zahn.)

Author's close friend, Donald J. (Flash) Aposhian of Salt Lake City. (Photo from the author's collection.)

Pawnee radioman John See poses with one of the "dusky island lasses" of Hotel Street, Honolulu, against painted backdrop of Waikiki. (Photo from the author's collection.)

Radioman Clennon W. (Bill) Bowser, member of the *Pawnee*'s dedicated radio gang and a valiant shipmate. (Photo from the author's collection.)

Unhesitating execution of orders by two resolute *Pawnee* shipmates helped save ship from destruction off Rendova. At left, William J. Miller in undress whites after the ship returned to Pearl Harbor in December 1944.

At right is I. J. H. (John) Day at Noumea in early 1944, shortly after he was promoted to chief quartermaster. (Photos courtesy of William J. Miller and John Day.)

Harley Alexander Schleppi of Houston, Texas, a man fit for a bottle, a brawl or a seduction. (Photo from the author's collection.)

The able and dedicated Yeoman Le Roy E. Zahn was the "champion correspondent" of the crew. (Photo courtesy of Le Roy E. Zahn.)

Lieutenant Commander Flave J. George, the intrepid commanding officer of the USS *Pawnee* during the Solomon Islands Campaign. (Photo courtesy of Le Roy E. Zahn.)

Author with Yvonne (Pat) Leckie at Luna Park, Sydney, in early 1944. (Photo from the author's collection.)

The crew of the USS *Pawnee*, ATF-74, assemble on the fantail during a brief break in the action in the Central Solomons. Author is third from left in second seated row. (Photo courtesy of Le Roy E. Zahn.)

Lawrence Goodfox, Jr., president of the Pawnee Tribal Council, with ship's cap and photo. The ship, after 24 years in the Reserve Fleet, was broken up in 1971. The Pawnee people, although greatly reduced in numbers, endure on their reservation in Oklahoma. (Photo courtesy of Le Roy E. Zahn.)

Chief Pharmacist's Mate Salvadore S. Ortalano (third from left) considered lectures of crewmen a necessary part of his sick bay ministrations. Other *Pawnee* chiefs in photo are, from left: Robert Cunningham, chief carpenter's mate; Lorenzo D. Armstrong, chief motor machinist's mate, and Paul L. Campbell, chief boatswain's mate. (Photo courtesy of Le Roy E. Zahn.)

Author (left) and shipmate Dale Gerber on Hotel Street, Honolulu, in January, 1945. Mason has just tipped his white hat over one eye at the approach of the ubiquitous Shore Patrol. (Photo from the author's collection.)

"How the hell can they blame the skipper when no one in the Navy knew anything about frigging beach gear or Liverpool bridles?" was one defense.

"That's an aye," John Day said. "Captain Frank did everything by the book, just like Knight said it should be done. He kept us off the beach. His only mistake was wrapping that tow wire around our screw. That certainly doesn't warrant being relieved of his command."

"It boils down to one thing," was Aposhian's summary. "Captain Frank is just too nice a guy to be a skipper in this man's Navy in wartime."

A committee of officers and senior enlisted men drafted a letter of appreciation for Dilworth. A collection was taken for a farewell gift, which all hands eagerly subscribed to. No one cared that this was a violation of Navy Regulations.

The letter and gift were presented as he prepared to leave the *Pawnee* for the last time.

Reading the fulsome but heartfelt words of praise, his eyes teared again.

"I'm sorry I didn't have a chance to say goodby personally to every member of the crew," he said with a wan smile. "I will certainly remember you all."

One of the chiefs saluted him. "Captain, we will never forget you," he said in a choked voice.

I do not think any member of the crew ever did.

From: The Officers and Men of the U.S.S. PAWNEE.

To: Frank C. Dilworth, Lieutenant U.S.N.

As our own individual ships sail into the impenetrable haze of future years, your friends of the PAWNEE will look back upon the days that we worked and laughed and worked together. During that time the entire complement of your ship has developed admiration, appreciation and respect for you, not only as an officer, a gentleman, and a leader of men, but also as a friend. This letter, and this gift, are intended to be a small token of our esteem you so fully deserve.

And when our ships are reaching the horizon of the future, each of us will save for you a special place in our hearts. As you leave the PAWNEE, each of your officers and men bid you farewell and wish you Godspeed.

Chapter Four

KING SOLOMON'S ISLANDS

Kill Japs, kill Japs. Kill more Japs.

William F. Halsey

"Guadalcanal off the port bow!"

That word from the bridge watch emptied the mess hall of idlers. We lined up along the bulwarks for our first look at this famous island, already a symbol of the courage and tenacious fighting qualities of our Marines. Three days before, we had departed Espiritu Santo for Tulagi in a small convoy, a large fuel-oil barge in tow. En route we doubled our lookouts, held numerous drills (including abandon ship) and conducted A.A. firing practice daily. Three sonar contacts sent us racing to general quarters on false alarms. If we needed any further reminder that we were entering the combat zone, it was provided by an empty life raft afloat near San Cristobal, the southernmost island of the Solomon Archipelago.

Along the serrated coastline of kidney-shaped Guadalcanal, the tall coconut palms stood like closely spaced sentinels—or, as one imaginative crewman suggested, like a brown picket fence with a green trim on top. Behind the coastal plain, crumpled foothills rose in successive tiers into mountain peaks that were cloaked in drifting cumulus. The deep green mantle of the rain forest was broken here and there with patches of lighter-colored kunai grass. They gave the island a scabrous appearance, as if it had been stricken with leprosy. I knew I could never look at Guadalcanal objectively, for too much American blood had been expended to secure it. The name was burned into the national consciousness with red-hot streams of tracers, as Stalingrad was for the Russians.

A C-47 transport approached, losing altitude, and disappeared behind the sentinel groves. It must be making a landing at Henderson Field, I thought. Henderson Field! That insignificant ribbon of air strip a mile inland was what the whole fierce struggle for Guadalcanal had been about. For whoever controlled Henderson controlled our vital sea lanes to Australia and New Zealand; and controlled, too, the means of climbing or denying the ladder of the Solomons toward the great Japanese base at Rabaul, New Britain.

Bob Shirley, one of our motor macs, came up from the engine room, mopping with a towel at the perspiration coursing down his face. He looked with distaste toward Guadalcanal.

"If I had my druthers, Mason, I think I'd take Santa Catalina Island."

I remembered that the stocky, outgoing Shirley was a Southern Californian. "Did you ever go dancing at the Casino there?" I asked.

"Many times. What I wouldn't give to be on the 'great white steamer' right now, heading for Avalon! The music was good—Jan Garber, Dick Jurgens, Freddy Martin—the girls were bad, and the booze flowed like water. I've seen five thousand people in that big circular ballroom on a summer evening."

Papoose Evans looked down from the bridge wing. "Hey, Ted. Tulagi off the starboard bow. 'Ironbottom Sound' and Savo Island dead ahead. Another goddam Pearl Harbor!"

Lieutenant (junior-grade) James S. Lees, who had relieved Ensign Hoag as executive officer-navigator three weeks before, was standing on the wing. He lowered his binoculars and gave Evans a sharp, annoyed look. Papoose ignored it. I knew very well what he meant: we both had abandoned the burning battleship *California*, sinking at Berth F-3, on the morning of 7 December 1941.

Shirley and I went forward for a better look. Savo was the jagged, truncated cone of an extinct volcano. On the early morning of 9 August 1942 the bodies of hundreds of American sailors had drifted over its fringing reef and piled up on the coral sands, food for sharks as they washed in and out with the tides. They were the flotsam of the worst defeat ever suffered by the U.S. Navy at sea—the Battle of Savo Island.

I pointed to the waters in the lee of Savo. Down there were the heavy cruisers *Quincy*, *Vincennes* and *Astoria* and the Australian cruiser *Canberra*, I told Shirley. Our peacetime gold braids had been taken totally by surprise again, just like Pearl, and with less reason. Some of the dead had been my shipmates in the *California*. This time it was a Japanese surface force which got clean away.

Shirley looked thoughtful. "It's going to be rough up here, isn't it?"

"It has been, and it will be, especially for the tin-can and cruiser sailors," I replied. "Let's hope the Navy sends all the seaweed politicians back to shore duty and finds some combat commanders."

I realized I was violating my usual practice of being optimistic, even if I had to force it. Seeing Ironbottom Sound had brought back bitter memories of Pearl Harbor, the defeat which taught me the meaning of fear, shattered my naïve confidence in my officers, and left a legacy of anxiety that it might happen again. But my misgivings must be borne alone, during the dark watches of the night, not shared with shipmates.

"Well, let's look at it this way, Bob," I said with a shrug. "When those COs yell 'Corpsman!', we're going to be there to render first aid. That's what the *Pawnee* was designed to do."

"What do you think of our new skipper?"

"I've heard a lot of sea stories about how gung-ho he is. We're sure as hell in the right place to find out."

As I said this, I glanced toward the bridge. Now Lieutenant Lees was fixing me with a critical look. I cared as little about that as Papoose had. Lees, I was told, had come to us from duty in some old ocean tug called the *Cahokia*. Before the war, he had served in the seaplane tender *Tangier*. He hadn't been at Pearl Harbor and he hadn't been at Savo Island.

"Oh, how I wish I was in the stag line at the Casino!" Shirley said.

The *Pawnee* heeled over in a 45-degree turn to starboard and pointed her stubby prow at a large, densely forested island deeply notched with coves and inlets: Florida of the Nggela group, I learned. In a bight of the island was Tulagi Harbor, named for the narrow, 2-mile-long island that screened it from the sea on the Guadalcanal side.

Athwart the mouth of the harbor, as we approached at slow ahead, were two even smaller islands connected by a causeway: Gavutu and Tanambogo. I enjoyed letting the names roll off my tongue—they seemed to evoke all the mystery of the South Seas as London, Stevenson, and Herman Melville had depicted it—even as I puzzled over the evidence of civilization. (I discovered later that the causeway and the few impermanent-looking shore installations were the work of the ubiquitous Lever Brothers.)

There was further evidence of the white man's presence at the seaward end of Tulagi: a wharf, a few prewar buildings and a cluster of Quonset huts. But as we moved deeper into the harbor nothing could be seen but green water and darker green jungle, which grew right to the strand and cantilevered over it. The sun had disappeared behind Florida Island, and a rank smell of decaying vegetation drifted to me. The air was so heavy with water vapor that breathing was an effort. My blue dungarees were soaked through with perspiration. The moisture condensed on the hot steel bulkheads of the ship and ran in rivulets to the deck.

I felt a shiver of apprehension. The ambience of the place was purely malignant. One sensed that death had visited Tulagi Harbor often: it was almost a palpable presence. Several hundred Marines had lost their lives taking Tulagi, Gavutu and Tanambogo, and the Japanese casualties had been ten times that. A number of vessels rested on the bottom under these murky waters, sunk during the first American raid on Tulagi the previous May. The New Zealand corvette *Moa* was there, too, lost only a month before we arrived. Probably, there were others I didn't know about. Already, the place was called "Ironbottom Bay," a fitting companion to the sinister Ironbottom Sound.*

By 1730 we had released our tow and found our assigned anchorage near the small island of Makambo. Captain George called away the motor whaleboat and headed for the wharf at Tulagi base.

"He's lookin' for action," Papoose Evans said morosely, scanning the silent and nearly deserted harbor. Overhead, a lone scout plane made hasty flight toward Henderson Field. "He doesn't hafta worry, fer crissakes. The action's gonna come lookin' for us!"

Papoose, too, had heard the sea stories. George, we were solemnly assured, had commanded a sway-backed ex-sailing ship, a two-masted motorized brigantine, in Guadalcanal waters during the struggle for the island and had had more narrow escapes from the enemy than the fictional Horatio Hornblower. Lending credence to this tale was the fact that the vessel existed. I had seen her just before we left Espiritu Santo and marveled that any man would be so brash as to take her to sea, even in peacetime. Why the Navy would have commandeered such a moldering hulk and put a commissioned officer on board was never explained. Others assured us just as solemnly that George had been skipper of the cargo ship *Aludra* when she was sunk by a Japanese submarine in the Solomons the past November but had saved the entire crew.**

---

* Many veterans of the South Pacific insist that the proper nickname for the body of water between Guadalcanal, Savo and Florida Islands is "Ironbottom Bay." I have followed the usage of Samuel Eliot Morison and other naval historians.
** The brigantine, which was manned by a crew of enlisted men, had been pressed into service at Tulagi for emergency fuel-oil storage during the Guadalcanal Campaign. The *Aludra* was still afloat at the time of *Pawnee's* first passage to the Solomons, 13–16 May 1943. She was sunk five weeks later by the submarine *RO-103* just south of Guadalcanal. The casualties were 2 dead and 12 wounded.

Regardless of which story one believed, the consensus was that George was one of those exceptional men (foolhardy, thought some) who gloried in action and sought it out at every opportunity. When I later learned the facts—that he had commissioned the 500-ton net tender *Catalpa* as officer-in-charge in 1941 and taken her to the Fiji Islands and Funafuti, Ellice Islands, for routine duty during 1942—I kept them to myself. By that time most of the *Pawnee* crew fervently believed that our captain had a St. Christopher's Medal around his neck, a four-leaf clover in his pocket and such rapport with the higher powers that he would manage somehow to return them safely to port. I was a half-believer myself. Secretly, I wondered whether George found the outrageous tales of his exploits amusing, or whether he deliberately cultivated them for purposes of morale. Myths seem to spring up spontaneously around natural leaders like Flave J. George.

After supper Aposhian and I took coffee and cigarettes at the port bulwark outside the mess hall. Tulagi, we decided, was one of the most depressing places in the world. It made forlorn Espiritu Santo seem almost fit for human habitation.

My shipmate nudged me. "Take a look at that, Ted. A welcoming committee, by God!"

A dugout canoe paddled by a young Melanesian native was coming alongside. The youth waved a friendly greeting, white teeth gleaming in a chocolate face, as he stood up and grasped our sea ladder for balance. He was slender and of medium height, probably still in his teens. His kinky hair was a burnt-orange color. He was chewing betel nut; the red juice ran down one corner of his mouth to his chin, making it necessary to expectorate freely and often. Just like one of our big-league baseball players, I thought.

He began speaking in a high-pitched babble of Pidgin English, the *lingua franca* of the Solomons, I had heard. At first I could only make out an occasional word. My buddy, an excellent linguist who spoke fluent Turkish and Armenian, did better. "He wants cigarettes," he translated for the growing cluster of crewmen at the rail. Packages of Luckies, Camels and Chesterfields were soon produced and tossed down to our host, who plucked them nimbly from the air with his free hand, smiling broadly and bowing politely in thanks. Hershey bars were next and were received just as gratefully.

Following this exchange, our one-sided conversation took a new turn. "Good Lord," Flash said, "he's talking about religion. The *Christian* religion!" By listening carefully, I was able to pick up some of his ingenious patois, the marvelously flexible English language wrenched from its customary grammar and syntax for communication across races and cultures in the most basic of terms. The Melanesian was indeed talking about Jesus Christ, whom "big fella belong sky"—this accompanied by the rolling of eyes and the swinging of an arm upwards to encompass the heavens—had sent to these islands to save "alla same black fellas" from their sins. He spoke of the virgin birth, the disciples, the miracles and the resurrection, urged on by Aposhian's questions in his own improvised brand of pidgin. Obviously, British missionaries had preceded the Japanese and Americans to this eerie place.

With the onset of darkness, our visitor reluctantly departed. We watched him paddle toward the mouth of a river that emptied into Tulagi Harbor, turning often to wave to his new friends, and felt better. The life of the Solomon Islanders went on around Ironbottom Bay despite our murderous intrusions. One day we would be gone and the missionaries could return to continue their proselyting.

Did it do any good, I wondered aloud, to teach religious concepts so foreign to the tribal customs and traditions of these Stone Age islanders? Could our preachers and doctors and traders bring them into the twentieth century? Should we even try?

"Hell, yes!" shouted Dale Gerber, a motor mac who had come aboard just before the *Delphinus* salvage. Blond, slope-shouldered and well-muscled, he looked what he had been: a middleweight fighter in the Rocky Mountain region, as well as a cab driver, bartender, fry cook and general roustabout. He had been drawn to us because Aposhian was a fellow "Jack Mormon" and I liked to discuss boxing.

"That's right," I said. "You're saving money to send your little sister on a mission to convert the heathens, aren't you?"

"The gentiles," Aposhian corrected with a grin. "In the Church of Jesus Christ of Latter-day Saints, all non-Mormons except the Jews are gentiles."

"Even these black savages," Gerber added. "I figure they're better off spouting the Bible than tossing each other into their stewpots."

Aposhian was firmly dedicated to the "one-world" and "four-freedoms" idealism of Wendell Willkie, Republican presidential candidate in 1940, and Sumner Welles, former undersecretary of state. He agreed with Gerber, provided the natives were protected by government from exploitation. But I was not so sure. My readings in H. G. Wells, the Beards and London's *The Iron Heel* had made me somewhat skeptical about the altruistic tendencies of capitalism.

As if to fulfill Papoose's prediction, the large signal searchlight at Tulagi base soon flashed out "Condition Red." I wished we had emulated the example of the PT-boat tender *Niagara*, which was moored up-harbor at the river mouth where it was well disguised by the overhanging branches of the rain forest. Not for the last time, I wondered what criteria the port directors used in assigning anchorages. Safety seemed to be far down the list. But this night the Japanese planes were looking for bigger game at Henderson Field. We saw nothing and heard only the distant drone of their engines.

The next morning we recrossed Ironbottom Sound en route to Lunga Roads. Here, in the same waters that had closed over the four cruisers was fought the desperate Battle of Guadalcanal on the dark and bloody Friday of 13 November 1942. Rear Admiral Daniel J. Callaghan had led his task force of 13 ships (5 cruisers and 8 destroyers) down between 2 columns of enemy ships comprising 2 battleships, 1 light cruiser and 14 destroyers. In a terrifying melee that soon lost all semblance of order, the Japanese were turned back from their Guadalcanal bombardment mission with the loss of two destroyers and the battleship *Hiei*. The price was very high: antiaircraft cruisers *Atlanta* and *Juneau* (never designed for a night surface engagement) and destroyers *Barton*, *Cushing*, *Laffey* and *Monssen*. All these valiant ships except *Juneau*, which was torpedoed by submarine *I-26* while retiring toward Espiritu Santo the next morning and disintegrated instantly,* rested at the bottom of Ironbottom Sound. So did more than a thousand American sailors, including Rear Admiral Norman Scott in the *Atlanta*. Admiral Callaghan was killed on the flag bridge of the badly damaged heavy cruiser *San Francisco*. And Savo Island received another sacrificial offering of American blood.

As we put Savo on our starboard quarter, I remembered that my ex-fiancée had known the deeply religious, almost mystic, Callaghan when he was commanding officer of the ship in which he lost his life on Bloody Friday. She told me he was an exceptionally handsome man with a shock

---

* Capt. G. C. Hoover of the *Helena* was relieved of his command by Admiral Halsey for abandoning more than 100 *Juneau* survivors without leaving so much as a life raft in the water for them. He did ask a passing B-17 to relay a request for rescue to Comsopac headquarters. The message was never delivered; only 10 men survived. Among those lost were the 5 Sullivan brothers of Waterloo, Iowa. The Navy christened a new destroyer, *The Sullivans*, in their honor and changed its policy of allowing brothers to serve in the same ship. (Morison, Samuel Eliot, *History of the United States Naval Operations in World War II* [Boston: Little, Brown and Co., 1967], Vol. V, pp. 257–58.)

Two eyewitnesses strongly disagree with Morison's claim of more than 100 *Juneau* survivors. Both screenwriter Earl E. Smith, then a yeoman in the *Fletcher*, and Ted Blahnik, then a boatswain's mate in the *Helena* and now national president of the Guadalcanal Campaign Veterans, maintain that no one who saw the explosion believed anyone could have survived.

of thick gray hair and a kindly disposition, whom she and her girl friends of those prewar days in Honolulu called "Uncle Dan." Hearing some of the hellish details of the battle from survivors, it seemed to me that Callaghan's tactics certainly were flawed but none could deny his valor and the valor of his sailors. Desperate courage sometimes forces its own luck. I hoped that my fellow Americans would remember, and honor, their sacrifice.

The open roadstead fronting waterlogged Lunga Point was crowded with shipping, for this dismal place at the delta of the Lunga River was now the principal supply and service center for the lower Solomons. Rusty merchantmen at anchor were discharging cargo into tank lighters; an oiler was offloading aviation gasoline to quench the consuming thirst of hundreds of planes of Air Solomons. Other supplies were being ferried by 36-foot Higgins boats to Navy attack transports and cargo ships painted in various camouflage measures.

Closer inshore was the "spitkit" flotilla of small coastal transports and wooden patrol craft which provided passenger and freight service to Tulagi-Florida and the recently occupied Russell Islands. Tied up at the old Japanese dock and moored nearby were the prototypes of new tank and infantry landing ships and craft of strange designation (LST, LCT, LCI) and even stranger appearance. They looked, I said, like they had been fabricated in a vacant lot by a bunch of mad metalsmiths. Aposhian theorized they had been designed by Rube Goldberg, the famous cartoonist of bizarre inventions, while Gerber claimed that any bright 10-year-old with a good erector set could have done better. Before many weeks, we would get much better acquainted with these slow, clumsy, unseaworthy and invaluable beaching vessels. Too well acquainted, many crewmen thought.

From our anchorage on the outskirts of the roads, we watched the captain heading for the scattered shacks, Quonset huts and supply dumps of Lunga Naval Operations Base in the motor whaleboat. Typically, he was standing well forward, as if urging the coxswain and engineer to greater speed.

"I'll bet ya ten bucks right now that *Pawnee* is in the first wave when we hit the next beach," Bosun's Mate Wilson predicted to no one in particular. The bet was not covered. But the captain soon returned, looking noncommittal if not disappointed, and we spent the night at anchor.

On mid-afternoon of the following day, 18 May, we were suddenly ordered to return to Tulagi. The message went out over the mysterious grapevine that keeps a Navy ship's crew informed (or, more often, misinformed): "Something's up. A Jap air raid, maybe. Or a visit from the Tokyo Express."

At 2000 hours "Condition Red" sent us to general quarters, where we remained until midnight. Japanese planes in sizable numbers were approaching from the upper Solomons. If they followed their usual pattern, they would pass just north of Florida-Tulagi, make a westward loop over Indispensable Strait, the waters separating Guadalcanal and Malaita Islands, and commence their bombing runs on the Lunga Point area through Sealark Channel. Or, they could just as easily turn south over Florida Island and attack Tulagi Harbor.

Proctor, recently promoted to chief radioman, lost no time in taking the up-ladder to the bridge. Within thirty minutes he returned with a report I found hard to believe. We had just had our first battle casualty. That in itself was not surprising but the man's identity was. A survivor of a ship sinking early in the war, he was a Regular of three years' service whom I considered one of our stalwart petty officers.

On the darkened bridge, Proctor told me, it was very quiet as crewmen strained to pick up the first faint vibrations of the enemy's approach.

The vibrations became a whisper that slowly increased to a vibrant hum. A voice sounded off from one wing of the bridge:

"Here they come!"

Startled, the sailors looked toward the new sound. A shadowy figure was standing there transfixed, staring up into the night sky.

"Here they come!" The voice had a deep, hoarse quality overladen with a tremolo of terror.

The hum of engines swelled into a throb.

The voice, too, was louder. "Here they come!"

All hands looked to the captain. He summoned a messenger with a come-closer gesture of one hand and said a few inaudible words. The seaman tiptoed through the adjoining chartroom and double-timed down three ladders to the second deck.

Now the planes were just north of us. Would they turn south? The petty officer thought so.

"Here they come. O God, here they come!"

Pharmacist's mate Ortalano arrived, conferred briefly with George and approached the frozen figure on the bridge wing. With soothing words and a firm grip on the man's elbow, he steered him below to sick bay. The petty officer went as numbly as if he were sleepwalking, Proctor told me just before returning to the wheelhouse.

The sound of the bombers gradually receded as they moved toward Lunga Point and Henderson Field. Proctor reported parachute flares and searchlights probing the sky, "just like a big Hollywood movie premiere," the bright flashes of our A.A. guns against the horizon and the brighter explosions of bombs. A couple of enemy planes fell in flames, "the biggest, brightest shooting stars you ever saw."

Most of the shipping at Lunga Roads undoubtedly had made for the comparative safety of the open sea. No flares had yet illuminated Tulagi Harbor, so we were reasonably safe, too. Why would the Japanese concern themselves with one small auxiliary ship among so many bigger targets like the Tulagi shore facilities, anyway? Because, I told myself, the enemy did not always act in a rational manner. If a returning pilot were hit by the intermittent fire from our 40-mm. batteries on Florida and the heights above Tulagi, he might select any nearby ship for his funeral pyre.

But none was hit that night over the harbor. At Henderson Field, I later learned, 14 men were killed and 20 wounded. Translated to the brutal optimism of the official communiques, "casualties were light." The families of the dead and wounded might not have agreed.

I kept thinking about our own casualty. There was nothing I could do to help; nothing I could say to him now. I wanted him off the *Pawnee* before his fear infected everyone. It was a fear I understood better than most of the crew, for I too had lost a ship. To a true sailor, his ship-home seems as immortal as youth and her loss is a shattering blow which cannot be forgotten and never quite forgiven. She has proven mortal after all, a mere thing built by fallible men, and if she is mortal so is he. All the more important, then, to steel himself against the possible loss of the new mistress. Had the petty officer, once a man of valor, been trying to escape this painful knowledge in a dream of home, mother, sweetheart, even peace? If so, that had been a tragic mistake. Those images must be consciously suppressed, as I had done before leaving the States. There was no way that a thinking man—a man capable of creative imagination—could fight a war part-time.

I remembered that he often had paced the bridge from wing to wing through the wheelhouse complaining we had nothing to shoot back with. He didn't accept my argument that that very lack was our best defense, that the enemy seemed interested only in sinking combat ships or knocking off waddling freighters.

"If I have a choice between being a hunter or a ground hog," he had growled, "I'll take being a hunter every time."

Accepting this tough-talking combat veteran at face value, I had hoped he would get his avowed wish, transfer to a cruiser or destroyer. I should have known better. The brave words were a smokescreen for a fear he had been unable to admit even to himself.

In high school I had performed in a one-act play, *The Valiant*. As the protagonist, a man unjustly facing the death penalty, I had quoted the thematic lines from *Julius Caesar*:

> Cowards die many times before their deaths;
> The valiant never taste of death but once.

Now I understood the words I had mouthed as a callow sixteen-year-old. They were not very different from my own San Diego resolution to live henceforth in the very hour of every day. That is what my shipmate had failed to do.

The day after the air raid we hooked onto an empty oil barge and joined a convoy to Espiritu Santo, where we would stay for the next three weeks. Our war neurotic was transferred to a repair ship for duty and, I hoped, psychiatric treatment. My real hope was that he would one day have a chance to redeem himself. Failing one's shipmates under combat conditions is a terrible burden to carry for a lifetime.

After fueling ship and swinging at anchor for two days, we moored alongside the *Dixie* in Segond Channel. The crew had a chance to gorge themselves on gedunks and attend the nightly movies. The ice cream was made of powdered milk and eggs and strong vanilla extract and tasted even worse than the prewar gedunks served in the *California* at Pearl Harbor. The films tended toward the inspirational: *Flying Fortress*, *A Yank at Oxford*, *When Johnny Comes Marching Home*. For variety we whistled at Dorothy Lamour, that sailor's favorite, in *Pardon My Sarong*. The religious ones like Yeoman Le Roy Zahn and Doyle Saxon, a freckle-faced motor mac who had brought his mandolin along from Tennessee, attended church services. They were joined by other shipmates, perhaps not so pious, who had been sobered by the Henderson Field raid, the crack-up of our petty officer and the promise of much worse to come.

Personally, I was more sobered by the smiling face of Burton Bell, our radio technician. His continual "ear-banging" and "curtain-hanging" (from enlisted men who stood outside officers' staterooms and tugged on the curtains which served as doors in some ships) had finally resulted in his transfer to some undisclosed station. Since commissioning day he had done little but occupy the second chair in the radio shack and complain that he had nothing to do.

"That's really good news, Bell," I said. "It means we'll be getting our radar gear soon. Yeah, we'll have a new radar and no radio tech to keep it operating."

"Just read the instruction manuals," he said with a self-satisfied smirk. "They'll tell you what to do."

"Just like you learned the code, I suppose." Then I had to laugh at this superb example of the Navy way. I put out my hand.

"Oh, hell. Good luck to you."

A couple of days later Chief Proctor came bustling into the radio shack while I was double-checking our call-sign coding and announced that a materiel inspection was scheduled for the next morning.

"You know the drill—a general field day for the radio gang," he said, rubbing his hands together as if in anticipation of a glorious time. "You'll take care of it, won't you, Ted?"

"Whose idea was that?" In her six-month career, *Pawnee* had thus far escaped materiel and personnel inspections.

"Lieutenant Lees. He's Regular Navy, you know—a Mustang."

"Yeah," I said. "I know."

Since Lees occupied the stateroom next to the radio compartment, I had seen him often since he replaced Hoag as exec. He was about 5 feet 9 inches tall, no longer slender at thirty-five, and had the kind of face I associated with district attorneys and high-school principals. According to scuttlebutt, he had gone from quartermaster first class directly to warrant officer (an exceptional accomplishment in the peacetime Navy). Shortly after the war began he received a commission. Already he had been promoted from ensign to junior-grade lieutenant and was determined to go a great deal further than that, if I judged his ambition correctly. He treated all enlisted men, even the chiefs, with a frosty reserve that signaled to me his intention to widen the distance between himself and his antecedents. It was wise to be very prudent and correct in dealing with such a man.

Accordingly, I summoned the other radiomen.

"Some of you have asked me what duty in the battlewagons was like," I said with a smile I hoped was not too sardonic. "Now you're going to find out for yourselves. We're having a real honest-to-God Battleship Navy field day."

As usual, Figlewicz had been the last to arrive. He was now a second-class but still far junior to me. I had recently passed the written examinations and been elevated to radioman first class.

"What the hell for?" he asked petulantly.

"The exec will be around tomorrow for a materiel inspection. We're going to pass it with a four-oh mark. Why is that important? Because it will keep him off our backs for a while. So let's turn to."

Two hours with soap, cleaning rags, brightwork polish and swabs removed the accumulated grime and tarnish of Noumea, Nomobitigue Reef and Espiritu Santo.

"Be sure to clean the tops of the receivers and the TBL," I instructed Murphy. "Lees will be checking them. In the *California* the exec came around with white gloves. He always went for the radio gear and the overhead."

Lees appeared shortly after breakfast on Friday, trailed by Ensign Moodie, Chief Proctor and Yeoman Zahn with his notebook. After looking around the room, he peered into the narrow air space between the TBL transmitter and the after bulkhead. Then he ran his index finger across the top of the TBL and examined the result minutely.

"Very shipshape," he commented. The comm officer looked relieved. Proctor beamed his pleasure. Zahn scribbled in his notepad, poker-faced as always.

"Let's see, Mason," the exec continued in what for him was a friendly tone. "You served in the battleships, didn't you?"

"Yes, sir," I replied. "The *California* and the *Pennsylvania.*"

"Well, I hope you'll continue setting a good example for our newer men, who haven't had that privilege."

I wondered how much of a privilege it was to have 98 shipmates killed and 61 wounded in a shattering defeat for which I held the Pearl Harbor admirals and battleship captains responsible. I was framing a suitably ironic reply when Proctor saved me.

"I'm sure he will, Mr. Lees," he said in his best officers' voice, which managed to convey respect, bonhomie and subservience all at once. "Mason is an outstanding petty officer."

Lees gave me a hint of an enigmatic smile as he and his entourage departed. I had little trouble interpreting this to mean: "And you had better keep on being one, Mason."

The notes taken during Lees's thorough inspection of the ship were soon posted on the crew's bulletin board. He was not satisfied with the condition of the forecastle deck ("needs chipping and painting"), the anchor chains ("wire-brushing and painting") and the jack staff ("provide better stowage"). Furthermore, when the manila lines were not in use they should be "faked down neatly on deck." Moving below, the paint work in the forward and second-platform holds was dirty, the overhead in the refrigeration compartment needed painting and there was a "lot of work to be done in the general storeroom." The chiefs' quarters came in for special attention: the overhead needed cleaning, as did the head, and clothing was adrift. On the other hand, the motor room "looks good," the control room was "excellent" and the engine room was "very nicely kept up." In general, he concluded, "painting throughout the ship shows lack of proper instruction and supervision." The list of forty-three items contained no mention of the radio room.

"The chiefs better get squared away," one sailor chuckled as he read the two-page memo. "Most of this stuff is their responsibility."

Another agreed. "The exec jumped from first class to bosun, from what I hear, so he was never one of the boys in chiefs' quarters. I figure he's a little sensitive about that."

"He was never one of the boys, anyway," I observed. "Not even in boot camp."

"That's true," Aposhian said. "He swallowed the book of Navy Regs in the detention barracks. Guys like that are always with us. We have a couple more down in crew's quarters right now."

On the evening and mid watches, meanwhile, I was writing my own booklet of regulations in the form of a procedures manual for the radio gang. When we returned to the Solomons, the fate of the *Pawnee* and her crew might depend upon a radioman knowing exactly what to do in any emergency: a loss of signal, a damaged antenna, an enemy attack, a sinking ship. The completed manual ran to ten or twelve single-spaced pages, neatly bound between stiff brown covers.

I was proofreading the mimeographed copies late one evening when Lees stepped into the radio shack.

"What have you got there, Mason?" he asked without preamble.

I sat up straight in my chair, glad that the room was still shipshape and I was wearing clean dungarees and a *Dixie* haircut of regulation length. I explained the purposes of my manual.

"Where did you get that idea?"

"My idea, sir. I always wondered why it wasn't done in battleship radio gangs."

"Let me see." He leafed back and forth through the pages. "Mind if I borrow this for a couple of days?"

"Of course not, sir."

He returned the copy without comment. Some weeks later, in the Russell Islands, Lees again made an abrupt entrance to the radio room. He was shaking out his right hand.

"Writer's cramp," he explained with a wry smile.

"Official correspondence, sir?"

"Oh, no. I'm drafting an organization book for the *Pawnee*. It's something that's long overdue for ships of this class."

"That seems like a fine idea, sir."

"It's also a lot of work. Well, goodnight, Mason."

In September the "U.S.S. PAWNEE Ship's Organization Book" was distributed to all officers, CPOs and leading petty officers. The forty-four pages of detailed regulations covered everything from daily routines in port and at sea to messing, berthing and emergency bills, and from the duties of the chief master-at-arms to mail censorship and the compensation of the ship's-service storekeeper, barber and laundryman.

The organization book suffered the fate of all such documents (including mine). It was greeted with dismay, roundly reviled ("A catalog of thou-shalt-nots," Aposhian gibed) and largely ignored. But I had little doubt a copy found its way to Commander Service Squadron South Pacific, whose staff officers appreciated such dedication. If so, it had achieved at least one of its purposes.

A series of emergency drills and gunnery exercises on 9 June confirmed reports that our next port of call would be somewhere in the Solomons. On the 14th we pulled an errant Liberty ship off the beach. The next day a curly-haired seaman second from Los Angeles named Costa J. Aronis, soon to prove an invaluable addition to the crew, reported on board.

C. J., whom I nicknamed Ronnie, had a prominent Grecian nose dominating a serious face that looked drawn and older than its nineteen years. He had contracted that scourge of the New Hebrides, malaria, while on Higgins boat duty and had volunteered to go to sea.

"I would have done anything to get off that stinking island," he said with fervor. "Christ, Ted, I was either shaking like a leaf with the chills or burning up with fever. I must have lost twenty pounds and I sure can't afford it."

He was happy to be in the *Pawnee* even though we were going north. "Better the Solomons than being shipped home in a pine box. Besides, I didn't enlist to sit on my tokus in the rear areas. I'm going to be a gunner's mate."

On the 16th, the day before our departure, a number of urgent radio messages in plain language informed us that a large troop convoy approaching Guadalcanal had been attacked twice by torpedo-carrying Bettys. Another urgent message the next morning, as we were getting under way with a yard oiler in tow, announced an attack on the shipping at Lunga Roads by 24 Val dive bombers and 70 Zero fighters.* The enemy had been driven only from Guadalcanal, the Nggela group and the Russells. He still owned the rest of King Solomon's Islands, from New Georgia to Bougainville, more than 300 miles to the northwest.

---

* The attacks on the transports were beaten off by fighter interceptors from Guadalcanal and by excellent ship maneuvering. Of the 94 planes in the Lunga attack, 93 were shot down at a cost of 6 U.S. fighters. Freighter *Celeno* was bombed but was beached and saved with the help of two of *Pawnee*'s sisters. *LST-340* was also bombed, beached and saved.

During the tense four-day passage through the waters of "torpedo junc-tion," our A.A. gunners took target practice, using the bursts from the 3-inch gun as an aiming point. Again, we rehearsed our emergency drills. I spent many hours in the radio room, sending Morse code at slow speeds to our new striker, Clennon W. (Bill) Bowser. Certain that no radio-school graduates would come our way, Proctor had kept his promise to let me train a bright seaman.

I selected Bowser, a tough, square-faced kid from a blue-collar section of Denver. He had two of the qualities I sought: attitude and desire. He was as highly motivated to escape the deck gang as Aronis had been to flee Espiritu Santo. Only time would reveal whether he had the third attribute, aptitude. I wasn't even sure what criteria the Navy used in selecting its radio-school applicants beyond the extent of formal schooling and a high score in intelligence tests. Based upon my observations of superlative radio-men I had known, I thought a certain mental agility, a self- rather than group-oriented nature and good eye-hand coordination more important than I.Q. scores or grades completed. (Whether I was right or simply lucky, Bill Bowser learned the code with remarkable ease and was standing watches long before I thought he could qualify.)

Once again I watched in fascination as we passed the now historic place-names: Guadalcanal, Savo Island, Ironbottom Sound, Gavutu-Tanambogo, Tulagi. We cast off the tow wire, moored the oiler alongside to port and picked up an officer-pilot for the brief transit to Purvis Bay, a wide estuary in the Florida Island coast ten miles east. Recently it had been chosen as the anchorage for the cruisers and destroyers of the Third Fleet. Tulagi was short of suitable berths, Miller explained: the water was too deep in most places.

Purvis was even wilder and more desolate than Tulagi. Again the jun-gle ran riot, halted reluctantly only by water. In all that endless mosaic of green, rain forest and bay, the only contrast was the occasional brief irri-descence of a parrot or parakeet flitting from tree to tree. Then a band of cockatoos took noisy flight above the canopy. Their wings flashed a daz-zling white in the sun, purer than the satin of a bridal gown.

I remarked to Gerber that the Solomons really belonged to the birds. Only they could fly free above the corruption of the jungle and the shark-infested waters.

Gerber was not impressed by the angelic white of the cockatoos. "You've got that a little wrong, buddy," he cried in his customary louder-than-life voice. "The goddam Solomons are *for* the birds!"

We anchored the yard oiler far up the estuary, cast off and got un-der way for Tulagi. As if to validate Gerber's opinion, the *Pawnee* gave a sudden spasmodic lurch and stopped dead in the water. We had gone hard aground on a coral outcropping.

To the consternation of the bridge watch, all efforts to dislodge the ship failed. Captain George could not be held accountable, since the pilot had the conn, but he was not pleased at our inauspicious departure from the new fleet anchorage. Some crewmen, loyal still to the memory of Captain Frank, thought our dilemma amusing. They found the interloper George remote and standoffish, delegating entirely too much authority to his exec. The embarrassing explanations he would have to offer his superiors might give him a little proper humility.

"That's all well and good," Bill Miller interjected, "but what if the Japs come over tonight? We'll make a damn fine target, immobilized here in a cabbage patch of coral heads."

We thought about that when the klaxon sent us to general quarters at 2100 and decided Miller's point was well taken. Obligingly, however, the enemy ignored us in favor of a nuisance raid on Guadalcanal.

With no lighters or yard tugs available, the only solution was to lighten ship by pumping thousands of barrels of diesel oil into Purvis Bay. We finally floated free at high tide thirty-six hours after grounding and proceeded to Government Wharf, Tulagi, to take on 72,000 gallons of fuel. The officer-pilot's faulty navigation had not proved tragic, only embarrassing and wasteful. (Later we heard rumors that he had committed suicide. I thought about Nomobitigue Reef, where our problems were compounded by obsolete charts just as his were, and hoped he had not paid such a price for forgivable human error.)

Up close, there was more to Tulagi base than had met the eye from our anchorage near Makambo Island. Until the Japanese invaded in early 1942, Tulagi had been the capital of the British Solomon Islands Protectorate. The Government House was of substantial timber construction, painted white, and had a roof of red corrugated iron. It was now the headquarters of the base commander, Captain O. O. ("Scrappy") Kessing. He was celebrated in Third Fleet wardrooms, Ensign Willson told me, for the liquid hospitality he dispensed. (For the enlisted men, of course, not so much as a stray can of beer was available.)

Tulagi once had such typical British amenities as a cricket pitch and a small golf course, I was told. The cricket pitch had been converted to a baseball field; the golf course provided a suitable cleared area for nondescript wooden service and supply buildings. The shops and shacks of the old Chinese quarter had been bulldozed for a village of green Quonset huts.

On a hillside commanding the harbor stood Admiral Halsey's already famous billboard, which admirably if crudely expressed the leitmotif of our presence in the Solomon Islands:

KILL JAPS, KILL JAPS.
KILL MORE JAPS.
You will help to kill the yellow
bastards if you do your job well.

A couple of thousand yards west of Tulagi, at Sesape, was the gim-crack base for the motor torpedo boat squadrons. Late every afternoon the PTs roared out of the harbor, rocking the *Pawnee* with their tumultuous wakes. We cursed them as they went by, disbelieving the Stateside propaganda which had made the public think they were so many Jack-the-giant-killers. From what we had heard, the PTs were skippered by glory-hunting ensigns and jay-gees from the Ivy League colleges whose basic qualifications were wealthy parents and summer experience handling sailboats off Cape Cod. We considered them disorganized, trigger-happy and at least as great a menace to us as to the Japanese.

Toward the end of June Halsey gave us a more pressing concern than the dashing mosquito boats. Once again he had ordered "Attack Repeat Attack" and a full-scale invasion was imminent. The targets, as reported by scuttlebutt and confirmed by decoded radio traffic, were the islands of the New Georgia group in the Central Solomons.

On 29 June 1943, we recrossed Ironbottom Sound and joined an armada of attack transports, destroyer-transports, tank landing ships (the new LSTs) and their destroyer screen at Lunga Roads. The *Pawnee* would "help to kill the yellow bastards" by providing lifeguard service.

Chapter Five

TIN FISH AT RENDOVA

Life, to be sure, is nothing much to lose;
But young men think it is, and we were young.

A. E. Housman

Before taking the evening watch, I stepped onto the boat deck for a breath of air and a look around. The date, which would live in the memory of every *Pawnee* crewman, was 30 June 1943. The ship was making 15 knots and rolling easily in a slight swell as she proceeded on a northwesterly course up Blanche Channel. There was no moon; the rain clouds hung low and threatening. The enemy-held islands of New Georgia on the starboard hand and Tetipari and Rendova to port were visible only as vague masses of deep purple against the horizon.

That morning U.S. Marines and soldiers had established beachheads on New Georgia, Rendova, and the neighboring island of Vangunu. Three hours ago, a message of "urgent" priority was put on the Fox schedule. The *Pawnee* was ordered to a position between the northern tip of Rendova and Mbalumbalu Island to take over the towing of the attack transport *McCawley* from the cargo ship *Libra*. The "Wacky Mac," once the Grace liner *Santa Barbara* and now the flagship of Rear Admiral Richmond K. ("Terrible") Turner, Commander Amphibious Force, South Pacific, had been torpedoed and was in danger of foundering.

Out of the menacing darkness ahead, a dim blinker light flashed out a challenge. Slowing, *Pawnee* answered and began a wide turn to reverse course. Now I could just make out the high, bulky outline of *Libra*, moving slowly southeast with the 9600-ton transport in tow. The *McCawley* was listing to port and riding deep at the stern.

We eased alongside the *Libra*'s port quarter. Her seamen, working mostly by feel, secured a ⅝-inch wire messenger to the tow line and prepared to pass it across to our fantail. There was a minimum of low conversation between the crewmen of the two ships; even the curses were muffled. Everyone was well aware that we were deep within Japanese-controlled waters, and submarines or surface combatants might make an appearance at any moment.

It was now 1945 hours, time to relieve the watch. The last glimmer of light was gone, swallowed up in a blackness of suffocating depth. Knowing the radio shack would be hot and airless, I stopped by the galley for a cup of strong coffee. Being alert was especially important on this tense, threatening night, when radio was our sole means of receiving new instructions or warnings of danger.

For a couple of hours, little happened. I copied every message heading, checking the coded call signs against the list I posted daily on one receiver. When any listed sign was broadcast over NPM Fox, we copied the entire dispatch for the communication officer to decode. Fixed to the other receiver with Scotch tape was my typed reminder to the radiomen: "IF IN DOUBT, COPY THE GOD DAMN THING!"

Periodically, Murphy gave me a progress report on our tow. After we received the messenger, the *Libra* cut the tow wire loose from her bitts. Ignoring the darken-ship precaution, she briefly used an acetylene torch, pulled clear and departed the area at top speed.

"We were lit up like a goddam Christmas tree," Murphy complained. "If the Japs didn't know we were here, they sure as hell do now!"

To their further consternation, our deckhands heaved in on a severed messenger. It, too, had been burned through in the hasty torching of the *Libra*'s tow wire. With *McCawley* now adrift, we proceeded to reverse our heading. We would lay our bow alongside the *McCawley*'s port bow and send three crewmen aboard to heave up and secure our own tow wire to the cripple. Her flag personnel and crew had been taken off by the escorting destroyers *Farenholt*, *Ralph Talbot* and *McCalla* hours before.

Just as Murphy was leaving, the full-throated roar of our four diesel engines filled the radio room. The *Pawnee* trembled violently. The loose gear on our work table fell off onto the deck; my shipmate was pitched against the door. We were backing away under full power, obviously from imminent danger.

The shattering blasts of two almost simultaneous explosions rode over the racket of the diesels. They were followed by a third so loud I thought we must have been hit by gunfire from an enemy destroyer or cruiser.

Pawnee reversed power and slued around on hard left rudder. TORPE-DOES! I braced myself for a monstrous impact. There was none. The rudder was brought back amidships as we gathered momentum under maximum shaft revolutions. The ship had easily made her rated speed of 16.5 knots on our shakedown cruises. I felt sure she was exceeding that now. Even the metal grilles on the TBL transmitter were vibrating noisily.

The door was thrown open and Chief Radioman Proctor bolted into the radio shack. His tanned face was drained of color; his nearly white hair seemed to be standing straight up on his head.

"My God!" he exclaimed in a loud voice. "We just had eight or ten torpedoes fired at us! The goddam *McCawley* went down in 30 seconds! We're hauling ass for Tulagi at 21 knots!"

The shack was soon full of radiomen and other kibitzers, some with action reports from topside, others but recently rousted from their bunks and anxious to learn what happened.

What did happen constituted the most frightening, and fortuitous, 4 minutes in the history of the *Pawnee*. Even today, at reunions of her sailors, the events of that night of 30 June 1943, "when the tin fish flew at Rendova," are endlessly rehashed.

As the *Pawnee* made her approach to the *McCawley*'s bow, Coxswain Norman Hazzard stood on the shoulders of Bosun's Mate Winston ("Pappy") Schmidt and Motor Mac Rodney Wolcott and groped for a hand-hold on the transport's deck fittings. But our ship veered out slightly in the near-zero visibility, and Captain George backed away for another pass.

By 2024, we had again closed to less than 100 feet from the Wacky Mac. "I hear American voices out there!" Schmidt shouted.

Almost at the same moment, several topside sailors spotted underwater objects running toward us fast and true. Their sinister tracks left an eerie afterglow in the phosphorescent waters.

"Torpedoes off the starboard bow!"

On the flying bridge, Captain George took one look and gave an order. Chief Quartermaster Earl Clark relayed it down the voice tube to the pilothouse:

"*Emergency back full!*"

One of the torpedoes coursed past our stem with a scant 3 or 4 feet to spare.

A few seconds later, a pair of torpedoes hit the *McCawley* with a fatal one-two, the first at her port quarter and the second just forward of her bridge. The latter apparently set off a powder magazine. A flash of light that must have been visible for many miles momentarily turned night into day.

As *Pawnee* continued backing away, another torpedo skimmed by our bow.

"Torpedo off the starboard quarter!"

"*All ahead full!*" came the orders from the flying bridge. "*Full left rudder!*"

This maneuver checked our sternway just in time. The torpedo passed by our counter—some said under our counter—in another razor's-edge escape from death.

The bow of the *McCawley* rose straight up in the air as high as our foremast and balanced there precariously, like a dolphin swimming on its tail. The gun platform which had been welded to the forecastle fell off into the sea. Then the bow disappeared as the transport sank to the bottom of Blanche Channel, 340 fathoms down. The time was 2028—just 4 minutes after the sighting of the first torpedo tracks.

The screening destroyer *McCalla* had been patrolling some 1,500 yards off the troopship's starboard side during the attack. Now she swiftly circled around the *Pawnee* and headed in the direction from which the attack had come. As she raced past with turbines whining, her signal light blinked:

PROCEED TO SEA AT MAXIMUM SPEED

Pawnee was already complying, careening down Blanche Channel with all four diesels clattering and her shaft turning at 150 rpm. Crewmen not on watch gathered in small groups to marvel at our escape from the McCawley's fate and to praise the coolness under fire of our skipper. He won the admiration and fealty of the crew that night off Rendova; through all the weeks and months of our torturous advance up the Solomons to Bougainville, he never lost our loyalty.

Dale Gerber pushed into the still-crowded radio shack, coffee mug in hand. He had been on watch in the engine room. He swore that he had heard two torpedoes thunk against the shell plating of the ship. Somehow, they had failed to detonate.

His report was received with skepticism until Arsenio Albano, the Filipino officers' cook, provided verification. On duty in the wardroom pantry, Albano had distinctly heard the sound of a torpedo scraping against the bottom of the ship.

In the light of these accounts, some crewmen gave thanks that the Japanese long-lance torpedo had proved less deadly than its reputation.

Others, accepting "Pappy" Schmidt's warning about American voices, thought we had come under "friendly" surface attack from a U.S. submarine: the poor performance of our torpedoes was common knowledge in the South Pacific. Bill Miller argued, more credibly, that the torpedoes had been fired from such close range that they porpoised deep before reaching their normal running depth. Consequently, they had only "kissed the keel" with a glancing impact insufficient for detonation.*

During the attack, John Day had stood beside Helmsman Bill Miller at the controller, or annunciator. Unlike the standard engine-room telegraph, it permitted direct control of the main engines from the pilothouse. The two men had unhesitatingly executed the orders passed down from the flying bridge in a split-second response that was decisive.

"That's the closest I've come to cashing in my chips since Pearl Harbor," Day said with profound relief. "You know, I'm a backsliding Catholic and haven't been to mass for years. But when we passed into the open sea, I crossed myself with the Father, Son, Holy Ghost sign and said two Hail Mary's!"

Whether we attributed our escape to Divine Providence, chance or skillful ship handling, the men of the Pawnee were certain of one thing. After the night of 30 June 1943, we were living on borrowed time.

Our speed in departing northwest Rendova gave rise to the belief that the Pawnee was the fastest ocean-going tug ever built. Not long after, a sailor from the McCalla met Quartermaster Miller at Government Wharf, Tulagi.

"Say, Wheels, what's the Pawnee's rated speed?" he asked.

Miller told him, with slight exaggeration, that it was 18 knots.

"You're a lot faster than that," the other replied, shaking his head in amazement. "When we were bailing out of Rendova, you passed us by—and we can do 34 knots!"

The other legend to emerge from this action was that the Pawnee had been touched by destiny and would henceforth lead a charmed life. Destroyer sailors of the various task groups felt cheered when we were operating in the forward areas, ready to rush in with first-aid and ambulance

---

* Captain George apparently gave little credence to Schmidt's report, although it was clearly heard by Miller in the pilothouse. In his action report of 1 July 1943, "U.S.S. McCawley APA4, sinking of by enemy submarine action and events pertaining thereto," George wrote: "It is believed the conning tower of the submarine was seen to break water at a distance estimated to have been about 700 yards."

services, if needed. Some of the fabulous luck of the *Pawnee*, they reasoned, might rub off on them.

Sometimes it did. But not often enough.

A surprise almost as great as the torpedo attack was the discovery that the "enemy" was neither a Japanese nor an American submarine. It was our own motor torpedo boats.

Unknown to us, six mosquito boats of PT Squadron 9, led by Lieutenant Commander Robert B. Kelly in *PT-153*, were prowling the waters around Mbalumbalu Island that evening. Kelly had orders to intercept enemy forces which might try to reinforce the Viru Harbor area of New Georgia. The commander of the Attack Group, Amphibious Force, had informed Kelly that all friendly shipping was clear of Blanche Channel.*

When Kelly's radar picked up surface bogies at 7,000 yards, he closed the range to a point-blank 600 yards. Identifying the targets as "what appeared to be a large destroyer, a 7,000–10,000 ton transport and a small destroyer or transport," he ordered his first section of three boats to attack.

PT-153 fired all four of her torpedoes and claimed four hits on the transport, followed by "a large internal explosion."

From the starboard quarter of Kelly's boat, *PT-118* (Lieutenant junior-grade D. Kennedy) fired two torpedoes at the "small transport or destroyer and observed two direct hits. As the *PT-118* retired following *PT-153*, her target appeared to be sinking by the stern."

PT-158 (Ensign W. C. Sells), the rear boat in the right echelon formation, unleashed two torpedoes at a "large destroyer. The target maneuvered radically and no hits were observed although one torpedo appeared to have passed under her. The other was a near miss." Ordered by Kelly to "press home the attack," Sells fired his last two torpedoes in a stern shot at a "retiring destroyer" from 1,000 yards, but straddled the target.

Fortunately for *Pawnee*, the three boats of the second section trailed behind Kelly in a column of echelons and could not attain a firing position. The section leader's voice radio had failed shortly after departing the newly established base at Rendova Harbor, and he missed Kelly's order to join the initial attack from a beam position. But Ensign O. H. P. Cabot of *PT-160* moved forward, apparently on his own initiative, and fired one torpedo at a "small transport." He missed. He then gave chase to "a destroyer

---

* The following account of the PT-boat attack is based upon the action report of R. B. Kelly, Commander Motor Torpedo Boat Squadron 9, dated 1 July 1943.

retiring to the South at high speed" but was unable to close. When the destroyer reversed course after about 30 minutes, Cabot thought he "recognized the silhouette of a friendly ship, and so retired to the East."

The two remaining PTs also retired to the east, toward New Georgia, and lay to. A "destroyer" approached from dead ahead and made a high-speed turn to port (east). *PT-159* (Lieutenant O. W. Hayes, the section leader) fired two torpedoes in an overtaking shot. Both missed. In *PT-162*, Ensign J. R. Lowrey exercised what the sailors in the *Pawnee* and *McCalla* would have considered rare good judgment. Not certain of the target's identity, he withheld his fire.*

"Due to the strange behavior of the vessels attacked as reported by the various boat captains the next day, this command has reason to believe that the attack must have been delivered against our own forces," Kelly wrote in his action report. "[There were] no communications between the forces ashore and the boats. It is considered imperative that satisfactory communications be established immediately."

Kelly's claim that he had no contact with his superiors is given a different interpretation by John A. Hutchinson, then a radioman second class in Admiral Turner's flag complement. After the *McCawley* was torpedoed in the late afternoon of 30 June, Turner shifted his command to the destroyer *Farenholt*, where Hutchinson and his fellow radiomen set up flag communications "in a radio shack so small you had to go outside just to turn around."

"My first priority was to establish contact with our PT Boat Squadron 9," Hutchinson writes.** "The original orders for Operation Toenails called for the PTs to sink any vessels in Blanche Channel . . . after sunset. It was mandatory to inform them that the Wacky Mac, along with her

---

* The "small transport or destroyer" which took two reported direct hits from *PT-118* and appeared to be sinking by the stern obviously was the *Pawnee*. The "large destroyer" which maneuvered radically to avoid the torpedoes of *PT-158* must, again, have been the *Pawnee*. During the attack the destroyer *McCalla* was on the far side of the *McCawley*, according to the *Pawnee*'s action report of 1 July 1943. The "small transport" taken under fire by *PT-160* must also have been the *Pawnee*. She thus avoided at least five, and possibly seven, torpedoes. The one fired by *PT-158* which seemed to pass under her may have been a dud, or it may have porpoised because of the close range and "kissed the keel."

Had the larger, deeper-draft *McCalla*, a new *Bristol*-class destroyer, been on the action side, she almost certainly would have been sunk. Her luck held, as did *Pawnee*'s, in the pell-mell withdrawal down Blanche Channel. The overtaking shots fired by *PT-158* and *PT-159* all missed.

** Letters to author of 8 June, 1 and 11 August, 12 November 1984. Written recollections of "The Wacky Mac," 8 June 1984.

towing tug, the *Pawnee,* and two destroyers, the *McCalla* and the *Ralph Talbot,* would still be in the critical area.

"Despite every effort and utilizing all of our appropriate frequencies, as set up in the Comm Op Plan for the invasion, I could not raise Kelly by radio. As the time grew short, I began broadcasting a 'blind' plain-language message addressed to the PTs, warning them of the presence of our ships. No acknowledgment was ever returned by Kelly or any of his boats. . . .

"When the Mac went down, the *McCalla* and *Pawnee* assumed the torpedoes came from Japanese submarines, and the first reports I received went on to the admiral with that assumption. We still lacked all communication with the PT squadron.

"By the time the *Farenholt* got the flag contingent back to Guadalcanal, I had gone some 80 hours with barely any sleep. Jeeps took us over to the admiral's camp at Koli Point.

"Then a message came in from Robert Bolling Kelly, reporting that he and his PTs had sunk a Japanese transport trying to reinforce their troops on Rendova, and that he had taken on enemy destroyers as well. Admiral Turner read the report and burst into gales of laughter.

"I asked about a reply.

" 'Just four words,' he said. 'That was the Mac!' "*

Even without possessing all these facts, the crewmen of the *Pawnee* seethed with righteous indignation over the shoot-'em-up tactics of PT Squadron 9. The PTs should be confined to the rear areas, where their depredations would be limited to knocking over privies with their backwash. Better yet, Gerber shouted, send 'em all to Dugout Doug's command in Australia. Aposhian had a more subtle idea. Their insignia, he said with one of his infectious slow grins, should be changed from the mosquito to the black widow spider, which attacked and devoured its own mate.

For the next couple of weeks, *Pawnee* was under way nearly every day among Tulagi Harbor, Purvis Bay and Lunga Roads on a miscellany of salvage and towing duties.

"The bastards think this is a yard tug," griped Bosun's Mate C. B. Wilson, the tall Texan with the sandy hair in slow retreat from his temples

---

* The sinking of the *McCawley* had one fortunate consequence. Operational control of the PTs in the South Pacific was switched from naval base commanders to Admiral Turner and his successor as Commander III Amphibious Force, Admiral T. S. Wilkinson. A PT liaison officer was assigned to the III 'Phib staff. Thereafter, the attack boats were usually kept well clear of Third Fleet operating areas.

whom I had first met at Treasure Island. "Dammit, the *Pawnee* is a deep-sea rescue ship."

Dale Gerber had a different reason for questioning this deployment of our ship. "When a fighter has been knocked out or badly hurt," he said, speaking from experience, "he should climb back in the ring as soon as possible. Otherwise, he'll get glove-shy and lose his nerve."

I concurred, remembering the time I had taken an elbow to the solar plexus during an intrasquad basketball scrimmage and been knocked cold. As soon as I had recovered my senses and my breath, Coach Brown sent me back in. "I don't want you afraid to mix it up under the basket, Mason," he had growled.

Something like that could easily happen to the crew. Already, some men were showing the effects of the shocking four minutes off Rendova. They were visiting sick bay with vague complaints which Chief Ortalano diagnosed as "nothin' but nerves," adding in his irascible and pedantic way: "You guys ain't been out here long enough to go Asiatic." They had become irritable and short-tempered; it had been necessary to break up a couple of fights in the crew's compartments. More ominously, a few had become uncommunicative, given to long brooding silences. The antidote was to return immediately to Rendova–New Georgia.

On the night of 5–6 July, a task group of 3 light cruisers and 4 destroyers under the command of Rear Admiral W. L. Ainsworth met 10 destroyers of the Tokyo Express in Kula Gulf, that inhospitable body of water lying between the northern end of New Georgia and Kolombangara. Despite the fact that the Japanese ships were encumbered with troops and supplies for the defense of the airstrip at Munda Point, New Georgia, we learned later, Ainsworth's superior force hardly distinguished itself: it sank one destroyer. (Another was lost when she ran aground near Vila Harbor, Kolombangara.) In return, long-lance torpedoes scored three deadly hits on the *Helena*, one of our proudest and most combat-tested light cruisers, which jackknifed and sank. *Helena* had been with me at Pearl Harbor, where she was torpedoed at Ten Ten Dock and nearly lost. She had been with Admiral Callaghan at Ironbottom Sound on Bloody Friday, 13 November 1942, emerging miraculously with only minor superstructure damage. Now her luck had run out: hundreds of her crewmen were adrift or clinging to her still-floating bow section.

Captain George, according to the scuttlebutt, made a call on the base commander at Tulagi to volunteer our services as a rescue ship, but was turned down. Two fast destroyer-transports, *Dent* and *Waters*, escorted by four destroyers, were selected for this hazardous—and successful—mission deep within the enemy-controlled zone of the Slot. *Pawnee* was dispatched instead to Oloana Bay, Vangunu Island, to get *LCT-322*, a 126-ton tank landing craft, off the beach.

Since it is a good example of American ingenuity and ability to improvise—two qualities that helped us wrest the Solomons from the Japanese—this minor salvage operation is perhaps worthy of note.

Looking at a map of the Central Solomons, New Georgia Island resembles the head and thorax of a praying mantis about to devour Rendova, with Vangunu forming the abdomen and smaller Gatukai, just to the south, the ovipositor.

Between Vangunu and Gatukai is Wickham Anchorage, an extensive lagoon sprinkled liberally with reefs, shoals and nameless islets. Ten miles to the west is shallow Oloana Bay, a nipple-shaped depression in the rugged Vangunu coastline. In the predawn hours of 30 June, four companies of Marines had been disembarked there against heavy seas and high winds. The "Elsie Tare" we were seeking had been part of a support echelon that followed the next day in a driving rainstorm.

As we approached Oloana, moderate swells were breaking across the barrier reef which partially sheltered the bay and rolling up on a wide crystalline strand to the east. A fair current was running and a stiff breeze rattled the mast fixtures. When the fathometer indicated we would soon be in shoal waters, the captain sent Quartermaster Miller to the bow to take soundings with the hand lead.

While *Pawnee* maintained headway, Miller grasped the long, braided-cotton line by its wooden toggle and swung the 7-pound lead back and forth until it was describing a wide arc. Heaving it forward dextrously, he called out the depth in fathoms just as the ship was passing the now perpendicular line:

"By the Mark Seven!" he shouted to the bridge in his stentorian voice, indicating 42 feet of water.

Repeating the procedure, he called out the new depths: "By the Deep Six!" "By the Mark Five!"

At the latest reading, the captain anchored and sent Miller out in the whaleboat to make additional soundings of the surrounding area. Then he cautiously moved in close to shore. We reanchored with less than 10 feet of water under our keel.

Driven off course in the storm, the Reserve ensign conning *LCT-322* had missed the entrance to Oloana Bay by a couple of hundred yards and been swept onto the shelving beach. His ungainly, 112-foot-long craft broached in the surf. High seas had pushed the LCT well ashore; she rested, starboard side to, at least 35 feet from the water's edge.

The captain consulted with his exec, warrant boatswain and chief boatswain's mate. They decided to swing the LCT's stern around to starboard and haul her off stern first through a break in the jutting coral heads. A 1⅝-inch bridle was landed and rigged around the craft's small pilothouse.

Since the vessel had no power, running the 2-inch towing hawser across coral, surf and sand proved difficult. The first attempt, using our 30-foot motor launch to carry a hauling line attached to the hawser, failed when the line parted as the boat was maneuvering in the surf. Operations were secured for the evening, but someone remembered that the Seabees were already ashore and clearing the jungle with their power equipment. Why not employ a bulldozer to land the tow wire?

As always, the Seabees were cooperative. Early the next morning, the hawser was made up with a 50-fathom shot of 1⅝-inch wire. The wire was passed to a 20-ton bulldozer, which churned across the beach under full throttle, spewing sand. The wire was soon safely ashore and secured to the bridle on the LCT.

Now the *Pawnee* shifted to seaward and put one main engine on the towing winch. Two more bulldozers appeared out of the jungle. While the ship took a strain on the hawser, going full ahead, all three dozers pushed away at the LCT's port quarter. Slowly and reluctantly, the 126-ton craft swiveled around at right angles to the beach, stern end to.

At high tide the big pull began. I watched the LCT inching across the sand toward the surf, with the bulldozers pushing and rocking at her bow, and marveled at the resourcefulness of my countrymen. Never in the history of savage Vangunu Island had there been such a sight as this. Americans had designed and built the big yellow earthmovers to supplant backbreaking labor with pick and shovel in the peaceful pursuits of government and industry. When war came, they repainted them in service drab and shipped and transshipped them 8,000 miles, to a place so remote it did not even appear on their maps. They had brought them ashore against the fury of nature and the enemy. Now they were using them for a purpose their designers could hardly have visualized, against a setting of coral reef, rain forest and extinct volcano utterly foreign to the American experience.

My countrymen had not adapted to Stone-Age Vangunu, as the Japanese were trying to do. They had brought America with them: the America of limitless invention, of C-2 cargo ships and C-rations, of Cokes and chocolate bars, of prefabricated landing craft and Caterpillars. How could any foreign enemy defeat men like these?

Ten minutes after *Pawnee* went full ahead on the 2-inch towing hawser, *LCT-322* was off the beach and waterborne, showing only minor damage to her superstructure. Under her own power she chuffed into Oloana Bay and disappeared from our sight.

At 0600 on 13 July, *Pawnee* got under way for the Slot, that now-infamous strait that separated the two island chains of the Solomons, east and west. By late morning the temperature was in the nineties. The sun rose toward the zenith in a sky of pale, hammered blue. On either side of the Slot, the shimmering shapes of purple islands rose into fierce peaks.

I sat in the mess hall with Aposhian, Gerber and Murphy. Our long-sleeved chambray shirts and dungaree pants were soaked with sweat. Some crewmen removed their shirts, but I remembered the horrific burn cases at Pearl Harbor, where the uniform of the day had been white shorts and T-shirts, and gulped more salt tablets instead. Despite the weather, the four of us were drinking hot coffee, which we swore was better than any soda pop in the Solomons.

When one of the quartermasters passed through the mess hall, Murphy accosted him. "Hey, Miller, where the hell we going?"

But Miller, as usual, was close-mouthed. "North," he shot back, without breaking stride.

" 'North'," Murphy muttered. "What concerns me is just how damn far north we're going. If the old man told Miller to set a course for Tokyo Bay, that's what he'd do." He mimicked Miller's foghorn voice and upstate New York accent. " 'Aye aye, Captain! Shall we take the northern or the southern approach, sir?' "

Shortly after the noon meal, while we were still idling in the mess hall, I saw a *Fletcher*-class destroyer pass the open door. Having copied several urgent messages on the midwatch that morning, I knew that Admiral Ainsworth's Task Force 18 had been in action. I moved outside to the port bulwark, followed by the others.

Two light cruisers were approaching in column open order. Although the waters of the Slot were almost glassy smooth, the leading cruiser was throwing up a huge bow wave. What had been the forecastle deck had collapsed, obviously from massive torpedo damage, and was hanging down vertically into the water, anchor chains still dragging. The ship was literally scooping up the water and propelling it out in front of her. I thought about the bulldozers at Oloana Bay.

"Ted, isn't that the *Honolulu?*" Aposhian asked.

A check with the bridge confirmed that she was in fact CL-48. She had escaped Pearl Harbor with minor damage from a near miss and now was retiring from Kula Gulf with a survivable wound. The *Brooklyn*-class light cruisers had only five inches of belt armor, not nearly enough to withstand the impact of a long-lance torpedo in a vital area.

Behind her came a cruiser of nearly identical lines, which we identified as the *St. Louis*. At Pearl Harbor she had eluded two torpedoes fired by a midget submarine near the channel entrance. This time her adversary was more formidable. Her bow had been nearly severed by torpedo and was projecting out at a sharp angle to her hull. She was displacing even more water ahead and to one side than the *Honolulu.*

We exchanged messages with the lead cruiser by signal light. Our offer of assistance was apparently declined, for the two warships were soon far astern as they beat their ponderous way south. I thought about their battle-weary crews. Some men would be rejoicing, secretly or boisterously, that they would be out of action for many months and far from the Slot, the most dangerous waterway in the world. Some would be angry, speaking of retribution against "the slant-eyed bastards." Some would give thanks to their Protestant or Catholic or Hebrew God for deliverance from the fiery hell of night surface battle. And some would be sad, mourning the deaths of buddies and shipmates. The *Honolulu* and *St. Louis* had lucked out, but that did not mean that all of the crews had. As I knew from experience, any time a ship was hit there were certain to be casualties.

"We could have taken one of them babies in stern first, and the *Menominee* the other one," said Bosun's Mate "Stinky" Higgins. "That woulda saved a hell of a lot of wear and tear on their hulls and power plants. Shit, they're probably going full ahead to make 10 or 12 knots."

"Yeah," another rating agreed. "But them cruiser commanders don't think it's manly to accept a tow. They have to be heroes. They'd back all the way to Purvis if they had to."

We had just seen some of the results of the Battle of Kolombangara, where Admiral Ainsworth once again tried to chase Japanese destroyers with cruisers. In the resulting turn into torpedo waters, the destroyer *Gwin* exploded and was later scuttled, with heavy loss of life, and the rickety Australian cruiser *Leander* was so severely damaged by one torpedo that she was out of action for the rest of the war. The *Honolulu* and *St. Louis* did not rejoin the fleet until the following November, too late to participate in the campaign for the Northern Solomons. The only enemy loss, I learned later, was the storied cruiser *Jintsu.* Rear Admiral Shunji Izaki, who had defeated Ainsworth's force of 3 cruisers and 10 destroyers with 1 light cruiser and 5 destroyers, was lost with his flagship.

At the time, however, we believed that Task Force 16 had sunk five Japanese ships and, for neither the first time nor the last, celebrated an imaginary victory. Had we known the facts, we would have been even more critical of the cruiser captains and admirals than we already were. Meanwhile, our "jarheads" and "dogfaces" continued to tighten their grip on Rendova and New Georgia. Soon they would take the strategic airfield at Munda Point, making possible new offensive moves to the north.

It seemed as if the momentum of the Solomon Islands Campaign had shifted to the American side, although no one doubted that the Japanese resistance would be bitter and fanatical. Would they continue their futile strategy of feeding in ships, planes and men piecemeal, to be gobbled up by attrition, or would they concentrate their still-formidable forces for one all-out "decisive engagement"?

The answer to that question was a matter of some concern to the crew of the *Pawnee*. On 15 July we were ordered to the Russell Islands, now one of the most advanced of the advance naval bases. Lying about 60 miles west of Tulagi, the Russells flanked the two principal routes to the Central Solomons: Blanche Channel and the Slot. There we would have a head start of several hours when we operated to the north in support of our faster cruisers and destroyers, which continued to be based at Port Purvis.

As at Guadalcanal and Tulagi, Lever Brothers had preceded us to the Russells. The broad coastal plains on the two principal islands of Banika and Pavuvu—separated north and south by a narrow channel appropriately named "Sunlight"—had been extensively planted with coconut palms. Behind the copra plantations, the intimidating jungle seemed to occupy every square foot of the low, featureless hills. Here and there in the islands' irregular shorelines, slow-moving streams debouched muddy water in fan-shaped patterns, cocoa-brown against the prevailing aquamarine. Evidently the Russells received even more rainfall than Tulagi. We felt sorry for the soldiers, Marines and Seabees who had occupied the islands in late February, shortly after the Japanese evacuated their troops, and had been living in the mud ever since.

We stood into 3-mile-long Renard Sound, which half-bisected Banika from the east, and found the first signs of the Navy's presence: an unkempt-looking interisland transport and a couple of sub chasers. An airstrip for Marine Corsair fighters had been hacked out of a coconut grove by the Seabees and paved with crushed, rolled coral. The handsome, gull-winged F4Us were lined up in open revetments along the field. They compared with the stubby, carrier-based F4F Wildcats and F6F Hellcats as a hummingbird does to a bumblebee, I thought.

We soon received the unwelcome news that we were sharing the Russell Islands with a motor torpedo boat squadron. Our apprehension was somewhat allayed when we learned that the PT base was at Wernham Cove, which overlooked Sunlight Channel at Banika's southern tip. The greater the distance between the *Pawnee* and the "black widow spiders," the greater our peace of mind.

Once again, the port directors had followed their maxim of "safety last." Our anchorage was a couple of hundred yards off the end of the fighter strip.

"That gives the Japs two targets to aim at instead of one," I said with as much elan as possible. "With any luck they'll get confused and miss both of them."

Some of my shipmates were not so sanguine. They observed that there was nothing between us and the enemy now except some fighter planes and two PT-boat squadrons, one here and the other at Rendova Harbor.

"If we have to make a break for the open sea," one cynic said, "these Ivy League bastards'll make another torpedo run on us. They can't tell a Navy ship from a maru!"

On our second day in the Russells, I had the 1600–2000 dog watch. At 1730 NPM broke into its routine Fox sked transmissions with an urgent-priority message addressed to all ships and bases, South Pacific Forward Areas:

CONDITION RED SOLOMONS X 98 PLANES REPORTED EN ROUTE GUADALCANAL

I flipped open the cover to the bridge voice tube.

"Message pick-up. Condition Red!"

Within a minute, the message form had been delivered to the captain and the G.Q. klaxon was blaring. In five minutes, all our guns were manned and lookouts were sweeping the skies with their binoculars. Below-decks, the four diesel engines were being warmed up and put on standby, and electrician's mates were at the main control panel in the motor room, ready to supply power to the propeller shaft through the reduction-gear motors. On the forecastle, the bosun's mates and seamen of the special sea detail, wearing helmets and lifejackets, were clustered around the anchor windlass. Ashore, the Corsairs were scrambling from the airfield, climbing steeply to gain altitude.

Figlewicz arrived, grumbling about missing evening chow. Tersely, I instructed him to warm up our transmitter, which was already tuned to the emergency ship-shore frequency. There were few targets of opportunity in the Russells, but Pearl Harbor had taught me the bitter lesson of preparedness.

Far up and out of sight to the northwest, the F6Fs and F4Us of Air Solomons broke through the screen of Japanese Zeros and fell upon the fragile Betty bombers. Not a single enemy plane came over the Russells; only three or four, we heard later, penetrated to Henderson Field. An hour after general quarters had sounded, the crewmen were finishing their interrupted supper, filled with raucous high spirits that masked the relief we all felt.

The following evening we received a proper Japanese welcome to the Russells. Earlier, our whaleboat had made a run to the beach. Our commissary stores officer, Warrant W. O. Armstrong, had wheedled a variety of fresh provisions and two quarters of beef from the Marines. At supper, we enjoyed the first decent meal we had had in weeks. Then we assembled on the fantail to exchange scuttlebutt, memories of home and tales of conquest.

From the perspective of the Russell Islands, the American woman appeared to combine the best qualities of Pocahontas, Nefertiti, Madame Pompadour and Lillian Russell. In addition to her other attributes, she was invariably possessed of a voluptuous figure and a libido to match. Each of us listened with interest or resignation to these narratives, awaiting the first opportunity to break in with a topper. It soon was apparent that a young lady from Puyallup, Washington, who boasted both a 38-inch bust and a desire of insatiable dimensions, was the leader in the Miss Passion contest. But she had stiff competition from talented misses in Pocatello, Idaho, Chattanooga, Tennessee, Tuscaloosa, Alabama, and Big Spring, Texas. Others of no mean accomplishments could be found in Salina, Kansas, Shawnee, Oklahoma, and Rochester, New York. Not wishing my native state of California to suffer by comparison, I submitted a couple of entries of my own.

About 2200, Aposhian, Gerber and I tested the air in the after crew's compartment and decided it would poison a buzzard. Lying on damp mattress covers in their triple-tiered bunks, sleeping men stirred restlessly, mumbled incoherently, sighed loudly, gurgled and snored. A couple were wide awake, staring into infinite distance and thinking the long thoughts of men at war. The compartment smelled of sweat, hanging cigarette smoke, hot steel and body gasses. My buddies and I went back up the ladder and stretched out on the steel deck of the fantail, making ourselves as comfortable as possible across two or three lifejackets. Topside, at least, one could breathe the air and wait for the southeast trades to bring their cooling breezes from the Roaring Forties.

I was just dozing off when the klaxon was activated from the bridge: AH-OU-GAH . . . AH-OU-GAH . . . AH-OU-GAH! Gerber and I were up with the first sounds. Shaking Aposhian awake—he was a heavy sleeper—we raced for our battle stations. As soon as the radio shack was fully manned, I stepped out onto the weather passageway. I could see nothing but a few dim stars among the heavy clouds that were scudding across the sky. But I heard something: the faint sound of an airplane. The sound grew perceptibly louder, as it passed over the airstrip, and then faded. Instead of the smooth purr of a radial engine, it had a nervous, unsyncopated beat, as if one or two cylinders were not firing.

"Washing Machine Charlie" was paying us a nocturnal visit. He was already famous for his Henderson Field social calls, and now the Russells were included in his itinerary. The planes were Zero float types, I had heard. The pitch of the propellers had been deliberately set to produce the erratic chitter that had earned the pilots the sobriquets of Washing Machine or Bed Check Charlie.

The next time I stepped outside, Charlie was back. I thought I saw a ghostly shape flit between two clouds but couldn't be sure. When the hell will he drop his bombs? I asked myself. Waiting for this fiendish fellow to complete his mission was a trifle unnerving. I knew he had slight chance of hitting the *Pawnee* from his height, which I estimated at 5,000 or 6,000 feet. But it was not impossible: in war, nothing was. I could visualize Charlie in his cockpit, wearing a black leather helmet and thick goggles, giggling sadistically and shouting down at me: "Amelican, you die!" You've been watching too many Hollywood war movies, Mason, I thought, smiling to myself.

After more than an hour of this psychological warfare, I heard him approaching again. "Now, damn you," I said aloud. Within a few seconds, as if in obedience to my order, sheets of flame shot up from the coconut grove adjoining the airstrip. The dull *crump! crump!* of bombs echoed across Renard Sound. The rackety engine retreated into silence, and the all-clear was passed. But Charlie had kept thousands of men up until after midnight. And some of them, I knew, would not fall asleep again for many hours.

Over the next couple of months we were to get better acquainted with Charlie. Our familiarity brought a certain contempt, always a dangerous attitude in a war zone. For Charlie sneaked in under the surveillance of the radar station one moonlit night and aimed two bombs at us. They exploded with thunderous sound and huge cascades of salt water between the ship and the airstrip. *Pawnee*, caught in the shock waves, vibrated like a tuning fork. Dishes came clattering down in the scullery, and a few crewmen were pitched from their bunks. But I was in the satisfying position of being able to say:

"I told you Charlie couldn't handle two targets at one time. He missed us by fifty yards."

Aware apparently that Americans were inveterate moviegoers, Charlie occasionally varied his timetable to check out the latest Hollywood films. On 12 August we prepared to enjoy one of our rare nights away from Blanche Channel with movies on the fantail. The screen and projector were rigged, and stewards brought chairs from the wardroom for the officers. The enlisted men, following the hoary Navy custom, sat behind them on hard wooden mess benches.

"In the States the coloreds have to sit in 'Nigger Heaven' at the theaters," Flash Aposhian joked. "They're better off than us. They can see the screen."

Promptly at 1930 the captain arrived and signaled with a casual wave of his hand that the film could begin. It was *A Seven Day Leave,* starring Victor Mature and Lucille Ball. "The handsome hunk," as Victor was known, was just beginning to make progress in his campaign to inherit $100,000 by marrying Lucille when a Higgins boat appeared alongside.

"Hey, you on the *Pawnee,*" a voice bawled. "Condition Red. Douse that goddam screen!" Somehow, the bridge watch hadn't got the word that Charlie was overhead. We knocked over chairs and benches in our haste to man our battle stations.

This time the A.A. gunners ashore had a surprise for Charlie. Powerful searchlights began to probe the sky. Soon he was caught and held in brilliant white light, like a moth against a light bulb. Before he could escape into cloud cover, our 40-mm. and 90-mm. guns opened up. Charlie was hit almost immediately. The searchlight beams followed him down as he fell into the sea in devouring flames.

The projector operator appeared on the bridge. "Should I secure the movie gear, sir?" he asked the captain.

A fleeting smile crossed George's face. "I don't think Charlie will be back tonight," he said. "Let's see the rest of the film."

"Captain, we should get an assist on that plane," one of the quartermasters observed. "We lured Charlie down to ogle Lucille Ball."

"Quite so," George agreed. He seemed absolutely unruffled by the incident.

Aposhian, too, was in rare form that evening. "The Japs send whores to the forward area for the use of the sailors and soldiers. Whores and sake. What does the Navy send us? Flag-waving goddam war movies!"

On the late afternoon of 25 July, I copied an "OP" (operational priority) dispatch from Commander Task Group 31.3 to *Pawnee.* It ordered us back to Oloana Bay on a salvage job that would prove as unforgettable in its way as our narrow escape from PT Squadron 9. We got under way at 0300 the next morning and arrived at the entrance to Oloana Bay, where we had salvaged *LCT-322,* about 0745.

Aground in the inner bay was an LST, one of those "large slow targets" that had been employed offensively for the first time in the South Pacific during the landings on the New Georgia group. Or rather, what we saw was the buoyant, cargo-carrying forward section of *LST-342*. The ship had been torpedoed by a Japanese submarine in the early morning of 18 July. The 100-foot-long after section, which housed the superstructure, crew's quarters and diesel-powered machinery, had broken off and was somewhere on the bottom of the outer bay.

Since our ancient British Admiralty charts indicated foul ground, Captain George ordered our motor launch and whaleboat lowered so working parties could take soundings of the inner harbor and inspect the blackened hulk. Evidently, her cargo of gasoline, ammunition and other flammable materials had caught fire after the torpedoing. They reported waters barely deep enough to float *Pawnee* at low tide. The long, tunnel-like hold of the tank landing ship was lightly aground at the bow but rested heavily on the after port corner. Fortunately, the transverse bulkhead had held. The captain's solution was to haul the hulk off bow first after sluing it to starboard.

It was not until *Pawnee* shifted berths to the inner harbor and ran the 2-inch tow wire with the motor launch that the salvage party made the grisly discovery. The men came back pale and shaken.

"My God!" one said. "The top deck is covered with bodies and pieces of bodies. Some of 'em are still draped over the gun tubs. They're stinkin' in the sun. I tell you, it's a goddam charnel house. I never seen nothin' like it."*

With as little as one foot of water under our keel, four pulling attempts were required before the LST was clear of the reef and floating free with a 5-degree list to port. The date was 27 July 1943, my 22nd birthday.

We came alongside to prepare the hulk for sea. The stench was so overpowering that Chief Ortalano had to sprinkle a solution of formaldehyde over the remains. He selected a working party of reluctant seamen and junior petty officers. Armed with brooms and scoop shovels, they boarded *LST-342* for a gruesome field day.

"Everything over the port side and into the drink," Ortalano ordered, his nose wrinkled and his round face set in lines of distaste.

---

* The few survivors were rescued on the afternoon of 18 July. Among the dead was Lt. Cdr. McClelland Barclay, USNR, a well-known artist and magazine illustrator who in 1940 volunteered for active duty in the Navy's recruitment program. Barclay had finished a portrait of General Douglas MacArthur shortly before joining the crew of the ill-fated LST.

Just then A. Head, a Negro of dignified bearing who was our leading officers' steward, appeared at the bulwarks. He was carrying a prayer book. "What you doin' here?" the chief demanded. "If you wanta stick around, grab a shovel."

"Chief, I am an ordained minister of God," Head replied in a quiet but firm voice. "I am going to give these men a Christian burial service."

Ortalano removed his cap and scratched his crew-cut head. He was a Catholic, although he probably had not been to church for many years. He was also a Southerner from New Orleans. A voice from the bridge resolved his dilemma.

"Chief, let him go aboard," the captain said. "He is in fact a minister."

"I'll be God damned," Ortalano muttered even as he replaced his cap and tossed a salute toward the bridge. "Aye aye, sir."

I stood outside the radio shack, watching in fascinated horror. I knew I should leave, but I couldn't tear myself away. With shovels and brooms, followed by high-pressure hoses, the working party cleared the weather deck of arms and legs and other less-recognizable pieces of bodies. Some of the men held handkerchiefs to their faces with one hand while working with the other. A couple rushed to the lifelines, overcome with nausea. I saw one perfectly formed leg, slightly flexed at the knee. It had been severed near the hip as neatly as if a surgeon had performed an amputation.

All during the macabre cleanup, Officers' Steward Head read and re-read the committal from the Protestant burial service, his voice strong and vibrant with emotion:

"Unto Almighty God we commend the soul of our brother departed, and we commit his body to the deep; in sure and certain hope of the resurrection unto eternal life, through our Lord, Jesus Christ, Amen."

When Head came over the port bulwark, his book clutched to his breast, several men reached out a helping hand. I, too, had been moved by his performance. "Well done, Reverend," I said.

He looked up with a brief, pleased smile. "I am glad I could be of service in this sad hour." He returned to the wardroom and his duties as an officers' servant with as much dignity as if he were passing down a church aisle during the recessional.

We had the remains of *LST-342* in tow and were under way for Renard Sound well before noon. I passed through the chow line with my tray, but I couldn't eat. While the conversations ebbed and flowed around me, more subdued than usual, I sipped a cup of coffee and thought about "the nightmare 'T'," as Bill Miller had cogently dubbed it. That severed, disembodied leg kept returning to my mind with photographic clarity.

Once it had belonged to a young American lad. It had obediently done everything its owner commanded: walked, run, bicycled, swum, danced, marched; and had, I hoped, been intertwined with a woman's. At Oloana Bay in the Central Solomons it had become, in a second, a useless piece of decaying flesh to be ruthlessly shoveled over the side with expended shell casings and other debris of war. I did not think the young man's family would approve of our method of disposing of his remains. My countrymen could be remarkably crass and unfeeling, I reflected. Only a Negro officers' steward had brought a proper reverence to the occasion.

I thought, too, about the late owner of the Samurai sword. Not long before our mission to Vangunu Island, we had moored alongside this very LST at Tulagi Harbor. A seaman no more than 18 or 19, a friendly and outgoing Midwesterner, had paid us a visit. He wanted to show off his prize war souvenir, an authentic Japanese sword. In the mess hall, we examined the long, gracefully curved weapon, which was sharp enough to shave the hairs on a man's forearm.

While my shipmates were exclaiming over the intricate design of the hilt and the superb workmanship of the blade, I marveled at a society which carried feudal weapons into modern warfare. It seemed to me as foolish a fixation on the past as if our officers had carried dueling pistols. But Aposhian reminded me that our officers wore swords of their own at changes of command and other ceremonials. Furthermore, he pointed out, they were nearly useless as weapons, whereas a Samurai sword could easily take a man's head off. The Japanese officers, I had to agree, were little different from ours in their slavish adherence to tradition.

Meanwhile, several *Pawnee* sailors had decided that a genuine enemy sword was much superior to the souvenirs they had already collected: grass skirts from Noumea and necklaces or bracelets of cat's-eye gems from Espiritu Santo. The bidding reached as high as $200—more than two months' pay for a second-class petty officer—but the LST sailor refused to sell.

"When I go home," he said with a disarming smile, "this sword is goin' up on my living room wall. Any time I get the itch to travel, I'll look at that sword. And I'll think about the Solomons. I swear, that'll cure me of ever leavin' town!"

Now the Samurai sword was on the bottom of a bay with a name known to few men. The homesick sailor probably was there, too. The severed leg that was shoveled over the side might even have been his.

It all seemed a terrible waste.

Chapter Six

KENNEDY AND MOOSBRUGGER

Heroes are created by popular demand, sometimes out of the scantiest materials . . . such as the apple that William Tell never shot, the ride that Paul Revere never finished, the flag that Barbara Frietchie never waved.

Gerald White Johnson

After delivering *LST-342* to the repair base at Carter City, Florida Island, we returned to the Russells for a brief hiatus from Blanche Channel and the Slot. It was a break in the action made memorable not for the movies we saw (*Yankee Doodle Dandy*, with James Cagney, and a trifle called *Here We Go Again*, in which ventriloquist Edgar Bergen shared top billing with his wooden dummy, Charlie McCarthy), nor even for a softball game we won, but for an attempt on the life of our mascot, V-6.

In the minds of many of the crew, the *Pawnee's* narrow escapes from torpedoes off Rendova and bombs in Renard Sound had confirmed the San Diego wharf cat as a potent good-luck charm. Our latest reminder of sudden death in the Solomons had only added to her value as a talisman of almost mystic proportions. She was petted and pampered and given the best the crew's galley had to offer. In the universal manner of cats, she accepted all this attention as no more than her due. She did not seem to have any special favorites, dividing her time between the crew's and CPO's quarters. Sensing perhaps that she was an enlisted cat of uncertain lineage, she never ventured into officers' country.

91

On a typical late afternoon in the Russells, the sun was sinking into a cloud bank behind Pavuvu Island. The temperature had dropped into the 80s as long shadows inched across the fantail toward the roller chock at the ship's counter. A couple of seamen were working off their extra-duty hours by painting the depth-charge launchers and towing bitts. Half a dozen petty officers, Aposhian and myself included, were seated on the after hatch cover drinking coffee and discussing the course of the war.

Within the past month the Americans and British had invaded Sicily, stopped a German counterattack at the beachheads and moved inland to capture Syracuse and Palermo. In Italy, Dictator Benito Mussolini had been deposed and arrested and his successor, Marshal Badoglio, was attempting to negotiate an armistice. The RAF had hit Hamburg with four devastating raids, and U.S. bombers had penetrated Hitler's air defenses to cripple the Ploesti oil field and refineries in Romania. On the vast Russian front, the German offensive at the Kursk salient had been stopped and our Communist allies were counterattacking. In the Central Solomons, the Tokyo Express was running between Rabaul and Vila Plantation on Kolombangara, and we expected a surface engagement very soon in Kula or Vella Gulf.

Despite these encouraging developments, we still anticipated a long war. So far, we were only nibbling at the edges of the vast German and Japanese conquests. In the Solomons, it had taken a full year to advance from Guadalcanal to New Georgia, a distance of only a hundred miles. We agreed with Winston Churchill that this was not even the beginning of the end, only the end of the beginning. Our cynical motto was:

> The Golden Gate in forty-eight;
> The breadline in forty-nine.

While we talked V-6 had been rubbing against one sailor's legs, elevating her hindquarters when petted and meowing piteously.

"Poor little bitch," he said. "She's in heat and there ain't no tomcats within a thousand miles. She's as hard up as we are."

V-6 moved over near a member of the deck force whom I shall call Rampling. Since he was something of a loner we paid no attention to him until we saw him approaching the starboard bulwark. He was carrying V-6, holding her at arm's length as if she were contaminated. Before anyone could stop him, he had tossed our mascot into the water.

"You crazy bastard!" Aposhian shouted. "What have you done?" He started for him, closely followed by me and the others.

My Armenian buddy was normally slow-moving and of a reflective temperament, qualities which had earned him the ironic nickname of Flash. Now his handsome face was contorted with rage. He seized Rampling by the shirtfront and shook him as a terrier does a rat. He was pulling his right fist back to strike when Chief Campbell interposed himself.

Reluctantly, Flash dropped his hands. "If I ever catch you ashore, Rampling," he promised, "I'm going to beat you within an inch of your life!"

Meanwhile, two petty officers had scrambled for the sea ladder. One of them dived into the water, seized the terrified cat by the nape of the neck and passed her to his companion on the ladder. She broke free of his grip, launched herself into the air and hit the fantail running. Pausing only to shake herself vigorously, she scampered under the towing winch and could not be lured out until her coat had dried and she had made herself presentable again.

"Don't worry, Aposhian," Campbell rumbled. "We'll fix that Reserve. Just wait and see." A few weeks later Rampling was transferred off the ship.

Aposhian was delighted. "There are three kinds of men you should never trust, Ted," he counseled. "Never trust a man who doesn't drink. He doesn't know what it means to be a shipmate. Never trust a man who smokes a pipe. He's a miser and a cheapskate. And never never trust a man who doesn't like animals. The S.O.B. has his polarities reversed."

My friend's advice led to a discussion of the Navy's liquor policy. Navy ships had been bone-dry since 1914, not because the officers wished it that way but because Secretary of the Navy Josephus Daniels and his successors did. Abolished along with the traditional wardroom wine mess was the regulation which permitted crewmen to purchase beer from "bumboats" (limit three bottles per man). Deprived of even this minor comfort, the enlisted men devised many ingenious ways of smuggling liquor aboard, despite the severe penalties if caught. (The rum-running techniques ranged from simple bribery of boat coxswains or the ship's "Jimmy Legs" to switching the contents of shaving-lotion vials to taping bottles to shins or rib cage.)

In the Solomons, however, there was nothing to smuggle. The officers controlled the supply. It was well known that Admiral Halsey was a two-fisted drinking man who, like Aposhian, mistrusted teetotalers. No sooner had a forward naval base of shacks and Quonset huts been established than an officers' club opened for business. It was stocked with bourbon, Scotch, gin and brandy shipped in as essential war supplies from the States.

Where the enlisted men had access to bars and liquor stores, they didn't care. "Let 'em have their goddam officers' clubs," was the prevailing sentiment. "I wouldn't want to drink with 'em, anyway." But in the Solomons the booze-for-officers-only policy was blatantly discriminatory, and was deeply resented by many sailors.

Gradually, a few of the benefits of Halsey's tolerant attitude toward liquor trickled down to the enlisted men. Some ships began carrying beer in defiance of Daniels's famous Order 99 and issuing it to the crew on special occasions. The usual ration was two cans per man.

Pawnee, though, stocked no beer. I assumed the captain wished it that way and was inclined to agree with him. What good were a couple of cans of uncured beer? They only left one thirsty for more. In the forward area, abstinence was the best policy. For all hands.

George had another way of bolstering the crew's morale. He scheduled a softball game with one of the coastal transports based in the Russells. Our volunteer team took the 30-foot motor launch to Banika Island, where the Seabees had laid out a ball diamond in a clearing among the coconut groves. The infield had been bulldozed flat and smooth, but the outfield was left in its rough, pristine condition. The captain put himself in left field. I chose second base, my old position with the De Molay team in Placerville's summer softball league.

When the game began I had trouble concentrating. I kept thinking of the remarkable contrast between the American-made infield, laid out to the precise dimensions called for in the rulebook, and the wild and pagan surroundings in which it was set. It was almost as great a culture-shock as seeing those Navy bulldozers at Oloana beach. Then I became engrossed in the game, with all its nostalgic references to those warm summer nights in my home town.

A junior officer came to bat lefthanded. He was sandy-haired, stocky and cocky. I wondered why he was wearing an officer's cap, with its gold band across the visor, rather than the unobtrusive garrison type worn by Captain George. He reminded me of a junior officer of the watch in the California, recently graduated from the Naval Academy, who was puffed up with his own vainglory. "Bear a hand, sailor!" he would bawl at members of returning liberty parties for no other reason, so far as I could see, than to break them into double time.

"Come on, Mac," I shouted. "Hit it right down here." Despite the fact I hadn't played for several years, I had an unusual confidence in my reflexes and timing that afternoon.

The officer obliged with a sharply stroked grounder. I scooped it up and threw him out at first.

On his next at-bat I repeated the message. I received a glare and a high Texas Leaguer into short right field. Turning my back to the infield, I outraced the ball. Just as it settled into my hands, I stumbled over a rock and fell down. Remembering to relax and "fall easy," I rolled over and came up triumphantly clutching the ball, to the cheers of my shipmates.

Despite my exhortations to "try me again," my opponent singled to the opposite field on his third time up. Captain George fielded the ball neatly and threw it back to me. The next batter lofted a drive into center field. I planted myself at second, squarely in the base path. The officer came barreling toward me. I braced myself to give him a rolling football block. At the last second he did a fadeaway slide around me, losing his cap in the process.

He came up angrily. "That was interference, sailor. You were blocking second base. I should have taken you out of there."

"Why don't you try, Mac?"

We started for each other but several players from both teams got between us. Dale Gerber came running in from the outfield to stand beside me.

"You can't talk to him that way," one of the transport crewmen told me indignantly. "He's an officer!"

Like all too many of my shipmates, this sailor accepted his status as a member of a permanently inferior social class. I didn't.

"Not here he's not. He's just another softball player."

The redhead recovered his cap and put it on at a salty angle as he stood on second.

"What's your name and rate, sailor?" he asked in a conversational tone.

"Mason. Radioman first. What's yours?"

He smiled. "I sure wish I had you on my ship. Maybe I'll speak to Commander George about it."

I smiled. "I sure wish I had you ashore in civvies."

"That would be interesting. But never the twain shall meet, I'm afraid."

"Not until after the war."

To the crew's surprise, the captain made no move to intervene in this dispute. He stayed in left field, polishing his sun glasses, an amused smile on his face. The *Pawnee* won the game, 13 to 7. As we left the field, the coastal transport team was breaking out the beer.

In the launch, Gerber went into extensive and loving detail on the sanguinary outcome of a fight between the APc officer and me. He assumed, as good friends will, that most of the blood would be spilled by my adversary. While I demurred modestly, we did agree on one thing. If the Reserve officer had swung first, I would have been presented with a golden opportunity.

Our interlude of movies and softball ended abruptly on 6 August with orders to proceed to "Point X-ray" in Ferguson Passage, well to the northwest of Rendova. From a quick look at the message decode, I learned that six destroyers under the command of Frederick Moosbrugger would be making a sweep of Vella Gulf, hoping to intercept the Tokyo Express. The charts showed that narrow, reef-lined Ferguson Passage led from the Solomon Sea to Blackett Strait. Blackett Strait opened into Vella Gulf, which separated the enemy-held islands of Kolombangara and Vella Levalla. From Point X-ray, *Pawnee* would be only 10 or 12 miles south of Moosbrugger's Task Group 31.2.

The moonless night of our deepest penetration into the Central Solomons was sweaty with more than humidity. A thick cloud cover blacked out the stars and reduced visibility to a couple of miles. Occasionally, the clouds parted to reveal the vague shapes of land masses which, we knew, were New Georgia and Rendova. Twice before midnight we sighted ships moving swiftly down Blanche Channel on opposite courses. They were friends, not foes. We passed the northern tip of Rendova, marked by the 3400-foot conical mountain of the same name, and put Arundel and Wana Wana Islands on our starboard beam.

At 0150, general quarters was sounded. Anxiety showed on the faces of the radiomen. We were now in the Solomon Sea, with Japanese forces ahead of us and on both sides. Had we encountered an enemy destroyer or submarine—or were Commander Kelly's "friendly" PT-boats lining us up in their sights again?*

Proctor hurried up the ladder to the bridge. He soon reported that the call to battle stations was precautionary. The looms of three explosions had been sighted from the direction of Vella Gulf. Our destroyers must have joined battle with those of the Express. If our ships were burning and sinking, *Pawnee*'s services would be desperately needed: I told John See to stay alert for an urgent distress message. That possibility meant also that enemy ships might even now be breaking into Blackett Strait, just to the north. To elude them would require all of Captain George's skill and daring and *Pawnee*'s storied luck. But no messages came. We secured from G.Q. at 0300, reasonably confident that the Express had been derailed in Vella Gulf.

Two hours later we were rousted from our bunks for morning general quarters. When we secured, about 0630, I went to the bridge to shake the cobwebs of too little sleep and too much nervous tension.

---

* Rear Admiral Theodore S. Wilkinson, Commander III Amphibious Force, apparently had little more confidence in the PTs than we did. On this night, he ordered Kelly to operate in southern Kula Gulf, well removed from Moosbrugger's destroyers—and from *Pawnee*. (Morison, p. 213.)

At the port wing Papoose Evans was focusing his binoculars on an object off the bow, where small islands were strung out along their reef in a wide semicircle. While I looked, the cays became a necklace of emeralds set in platinum upon a field of electric blue.

"Long night, buddy," I said. "Where are we?"

Evans smiled a little grimly. "No-man's sea. Ferguson Passage. The old man wouldn't bail out till he was damn sure there weren't any cripples in the gulf."

He pointed. "There's something over there on the reef near that two-bit island. Looks like it's part of a small craft, Jap's or ours. Here, take a look."

The islet was about the size of my high-school athletic field. A cluster of coconut palms and casuarinas occupied the high ground, a few feet above a circlet of sand that flashed in the morning sun. It was, I thought, the prototype of all the South Sea islands the cartoonists drew for their stale shipwreck jokes.

The object on the fringing reef was a dirty, faded green. It didn't resemble any part of a vessel until I tilted my head and examined it from down under.

"Hey, Papoose. It looks like the forepart of a Higgins boat or PT—but it's upside down."

Evans took the glasses back. "By God, I think you're right. It's the bow end of a PT turned turtle. How the hell did it end up aground in Ferguson Passage, and where's the rest of it?"

"Are you going to report it to the skipper?"

He laughed. "A goddam PT-boat? Hell, no. Christ, there are slant-eyes all around us."

The reaction of my buddies to this unique sighting was the same as Papoose's. The laughter was mocking but not heartless. We assumed the crew had been rescued by the nightly PT patrol. What, we asked, had the goddam Harvard-Yale war heroes done now?

Gerber had an explanation.

"This ninety-day wonder prob'ly got in the way of one of our tin cans and was run down," he said to more laughter. "You know how the can skippers hate those PTs—and they ain't the only ones!"

No one took his words seriously, of course; they were interpreted as typical American humor by gross exaggeration. When the facts became known, they matched my friend's wild surmise so closely that we were left speechless (all but Gerber). Once again in the South Pacific, truth had proved more outrageous than fiction.

On the black night of 1–2 August, the PT base on Lumberi Island, Rendova Harbor, sent 15 boats to blockade the southern and western approaches to Blackett Strait. They encountered 4 destroyers of the Tokyo Express on a run through Vella Gulf to Vila. In a series of poorly executed, laissez-faire attacks, the PTs launched a total of 30 torpedoes without scoring a single hit. From our admittedly biased perspective, this was a typical performance of the "black widows" when they faced anything more formidable than a drifting cripple.

The failure of the blockade was obscured by the fate of one of the participating motor torpedo boats, *PT-109*. Her skipper, a 26-year-old Harvard graduate named John F. Kennedy, was leading two other PTs on a slow sweep down Blackett Strait when he encountered the *Amagiri*, retiring toward Rabaul at 30 knots from her successful reinforcement mission to Vila.

"Ship at two o'clock!" a lookout shouted.

For a few unredeemable heartbeats, Lieutenant (junior-grade) Kennedy thought the contact was another PT. By the time he spun the wheel to evade, it was too late. The *Amagiri* sliced his fragile craft in two like a knife going through butter.

Two crewmen were killed by the impact of the sharp steel prow against moulded plywood. The eleven survivors (an officer was along as a passenger) sought refuge on tiny Plum Pudding Island in the Gizo Reef, later swimming to Olasana, a larger island a couple of miles south. They were rescued in the early morning hours of 8 August, the day after the *Pawnee's* own mission to Ferguson Passage. The battered, topsy-turvy bow section had drifted southwest with tide and current until it rested, temporarily at least, on the reef where Papoose had spotted it.

The incident should have ended there: a minor misfortune of war, rating a line or two in the official histories. But this particular junior-grade lieutenant was the son of the immensely wealthy and powerful Joseph P. Kennedy, a former Chairman of the Securities and Exchange Commission, head of the U.S. Maritime Commission and Ambassador to Great Britain. He also was a business tycoon, a heavy contributor to the Democratic Party, and a man with presidential ambitions for one or more of his four sons. The young Kennedy's singular accomplishment in Blackett Strait—and his real exploits in towing a burned enlisted man to safety and helping effect the rescue of his men—were the subject of a John Hersey article, "Survival," in the *New Yorker* of 17 June 1944. Of such raw materials are legends manufactured and heroes made.

But in August 1943 we had no knowledge of Kennedy's connections in very high places. If anyone had predicted that a "goddam Harvard-Yale war hero" of the Solomons would one day be President, we would have laughed him off the ship. Officers from the PT squadron stationed in the Russells occasionally visited the *Pawnee*, where they took snapshots of each other "shooting the sun" from the bridge wing. Away from their deadly toys they seemed pleasant-enough representatives of the upper class, relaxed and informal in their inbred assurance of superiority, but hardly of presidential caliber.

If our seer had further prophesied that the future Commander-in-Chief would be Lieutenant Kennedy, we would have recommended that he be locked up for mental observation. If a man couldn't keep a 45-knot PT-boat out of the way of a Japanese destroyer, we would have reasoned, how the hell could he ever conn the ship of state? That possibility exceeded even the elastic bonds of reality which governed our perilous operations in the Solomon Islands.

While the forepart of *PT-109* was lodged on a reef in Ferguson Passage and the survivors prayed for deliverance from Olasana Island, one of the real heroes of the Solomons took his 6 destroyers into Vella Gulf. We did not know it then, of course, but Commander Moosbrugger, detached at last from the umbilical cord of the cruiser admirals, fought a nearly perfect surface action.

The Japanese long-lance torpedo had twice the explosive charge and three times the range of American tin fish. Surprisingly, no one in the South Pacific was fully aware of its deadly superiority. Sometimes, the "fog of battle" caused our commanders to greatly exaggerate enemy losses and claim unwarranted victories which seemed to justify our losses. At other times, sinkings were falsely attributed to Japanese submarines. Moosbrugger's tactical plan—coupled with a measure of the good luck which is always a factor in naval warfare—nullified the Japanese advantage in night surface engagement. He used radar skillfully to exploit the vital element of surprise; withheld torpedo fire until the salvos would lash out at right angles to the targets; turned away quickly before the enemy could counterattack with the long lance; followed up the initial advantage with radar-controlled gunfire. His Task Group 31.2 sank 3 of 4 destroyers without receiving so much as a near-miss. The scarlet looms of destruction we saw from Ferguson Passage that night of 6–7 August had come from the *Hagikaze*, *Arashi* and *Kawakaze*.

Moosbrugger was the first of the tough, smart, new-breed officers to emerge from the crucible of the Solomons. In the native tongue, Kolombangara, whose towering volcanic cone dominates Vella and Kula Gulfs, means "king of the waters." At last we had found a real combat commander, and another was following close behind: Captain Arleigh Burke of Destroyer Squadron 23.

I remembered what my late friend M. G. (Johnny) Johnson had told me six months before Pearl Harbor: "There's gonna be a war soon, and the Navy will weed out all the lousy COs and send them back to shore duty, where they belong. Then they'll bring up some real salty skippers who don't give a shit about personnel inspections and writing reports and firing salutes and running general court-martials—but know how to fight a ship."

He had added, a somber expression on his face: "The trouble is, Ted, there are a lot of peacetime misfits and they're gonna get a lot of guys killed before the Navy wises up."*

Before the war was an hour old, he had been one of them. Many others had followed him, here among the feral islands of King Solomon.

From our anchorage in 24 fathoms of water off the Marine airstrip, we men of the *Pawnee* considered ourselves friendless and nearly alone in the forward area. Only "Ping" Wilkinson, commander of III Amphibious Force (Task Force 31) and his eager-beaver subordinates at Koli Point paid us any heed, and they seemed determined to get us sunk in Blanche Channel or Ferguson Passage or the Slot.

The Navy's offensive in the South Pacific resembled an extended pyramid, broad at the base and narrow indeed at the apex, the combat cap. Only 2,000 sailors had participated directly in the victory at Vella Gulf. Fifty times that many were manning an ever-lengthening string of bases that projected northward from Halsey's headquarters at Noumea through the New Hebrides to Guadalcanal, Tulagi, the Russells and, since 30 June, Rendova. Blissful in our ignorance of logistics, we wondered what most of them did to justify their safe, if boring, shore duty. We could use some help in the fire zone!

One group of "coconut-grove commandos" escaped our general censure. The personnel of the Fleet Post Office, by whatever sleight of hand, were performing a service absolutely essential to our morale: maintaining our tenuous links with home. Periodically, we received a visual message that mail had arrived. Within minutes Flash Aposhian, our mail orderly, was under way in the whaleboat.

Long before he returned, off-duty crewmen began assembling in the mess hall. The 15- by 25-foot compartment was soon filled to capacity and overflowing onto the weather-deck passageways outside. When the boat came alongside, eager hands hoisted aboard the canvas mail pouches heavy with letters, packages and periodicals.

---

* See *Battleship Sailor*, p. 185.

Standing on a mess bench, Aposhian began calling names: "Flowers . . . Knott . . . Primozich . . . Smith, H. I. . . . Brady . . . Englehardt . . . Billau . . . Schmidt, 'Pappy' . . . Taylor . . . Swan . . . Cantley . . . Wolcott . . . Newcomb . . . Thomas . . . Zimmer . . . "

The letters were snatched from his outstretched hand and ripped open at once. Later they would be reread and savored again and again, along with the hometown newspapers and the overseas edition of *Time* magazine (printed on lightweight stock and carrying no advertisements). On 11 August the first V-mail arrived. Instead of intimate billets-doux written with real ink on perfumed stationery and sealed with lipstick imprints, some crewmen received half-size photostats which were one step removed from the originals. V-mail letters supposedly had the advantage of being speeded to servicemen by air, but we quickly decided they would never fly. They were too damn impersonal.

Some of the men shared their letters and snapshots. (They also shared crumbled cookies, stale gingerbread, rich chocolate fudge and fruit cake pungent with rum.) A shipmate was expected to listen with interest to excerpts from the letters and to offer envious praise over photos of girl friends, sisters and wives. There were diplomatic limits to this admiration: one was complimentary—lavishly so, if possible—but never lascivious. Of necessity, I developed a repertory of phrases to cover every occasion.

For the obvious Plain Jane: "She has a very nice face. I'll bet you're proud of her." For the routinely attractive: "Say, she's very pretty. I'm sure she's very nice, too." And for the occasional beauty: "She's a lovely girl. You're a lucky man, buddy!"

Some young ladies sent photos of themselves in form-fitting bathing suits or tight sweaters and shorts. Here one treaded warily: "She has a great figure, doesn't she? By God, she reminds me of Carole Landis (or Alice Faye or Ann Miller or Claire Trevor or Rita Hayworth)!"

Finally, some girls did not qualify even as plain. Perhaps they were too skinny or too heavy or too homely. Then one said: "I like her. My sister Beverly worries because she can't put on any weight. I tell her she'll be damn glad later." Or: "I like her. Some guys go for beanpole women. Personally, I prefer them with some flesh on their bones." Or: "I like her. Her face shows real character."

A few shipmates did not share. They retreated to the most private place they could find—no easy task in a ship as small and congested as the *Pawnee*—for an hour or two of memory and introspection. The champion correspondent was the ship's yeoman, Le Roy Zahn. At every mail call he received dozens of letters, as well as packages and papers. His fiancée in his home town in Kansas wrote to him nearly every day. Each letter was numbered: the total soon passed 100, then 200 and 300.

Tall, wavy-haired and good-looking, our yeoman was something of a mystery to his shipmates. He had no close friends, so far as I knew, and did not share in the noisy, profane camaraderie of the mess hall, the head and the crew's quarters. A Methodist of deep religious conviction, he read his Bible, attended church services whenever a Protestant chaplain was available, wrote his letters, and did his duty. From the viewpoint of the officers he was an ideal yeoman: earnest, polite, diligent, never in trouble, properly secretive. The crew soon learned that trying to get the latest dope from Zahn (who typed the action reports and other secret documents and, after 1 December 1943, the deck logs) was an exercise in futility. He walked among us, ate chow with us, used the same head, slept in the same compartment, but he was not one of us. Being a young man of unquestioning patriotism, he gave the Navy his loyalty and his dedicated service, but his heart and soul remained in Kansas. And that is where, after the war, he returned.

For most of us, the loneliness, deprivations, constant tension and nagging fear of sudden or anguished death would have been unendurable without the close bonds of friendship. What was not possible for the solitary one was attainable by the two or three or four together. In unity there was strength, each sacrificing some of his individuality to a group resistance against the tyranny of the officers and the threat from the declared enemy. Aposhian, Gerber and I had allied ourselves in such a fellowship. I called us "The Three Musketeers," after the book that had mightily impressed me as a boy of fourteen.

But Zahn was a man who walked quite alone with his God as he understood Him. It was not a posture that made a man loved, but it did earn him the acceptance which strength of character warrants.

Since I had deliberately severed all romantic ties, my own correspondence was both less demanding and less satisfying than that of many crewmen. More than once on a midwatch, which lent itself to such speculation, I wondered why I was writing to some people rather than others I could have chosen. It was considered patriotic to send cheery, morale-boosting letters to servicemen, so there was no shortage of possible correspondents.

I wrote to my foster-parents, the Masons, not because I felt close to them but because they were the only real family I had. My father, Bayard Bowman of San Francisco, was occupied with his second family, as was my mother, now Lilah Murray (nee Dale) with hers in Santa Cruz. I sent the Masons an allotment from my pay because I felt it my duty to help them in their chronic poverty. Mrs. Mason, a devout Christian Scientist, believed I had had divine protection in the mainmast of the *California* during the attack on Pearl Harbor. She was "working" (the Christian Science term for goal-directed prayer and meditation) every day to ensure that protection would continue. I rubbed the shrapnel scar on my left knee and remembered how I had escaped death or maiming by an inch or two. Who was to say she was wrong?

I wrote my great-uncle, the Rev. Lyman R. Bayard, because it was good for me. In long, inspirational letters he reminded me of my antecedents (especially the Chevalier de Bayard, "the knight without fear and without reproach"), my obligation to posterity ("People will not look forward to posterity, who never look backward to their ancestors," he wrote, quoting Edmund Burke), and my duty to God, country and conscience. All three duties were part of the same seamless, indivisible whole, he counseled. I admired him greatly.

In a lighter vein, I kept in touch with a sailor's girl I had known well in Seattle, San Francisco and Long Beach. While June was not in close communication with God, she was performing certain services for the Navy in the lights of conscience and survival. Those services included, but were not confined to, sustaining the morale of three petty officers, all of whom were contributing to her survival with allotments. As a sinner she was quite unashamed but, like so many women who followed the fleet in prewar days, she was gay, generous and kind-hearted. I thought even my principled great-uncle would have found it possible to forgive her.

Another correspondent, Floyd C. (Bill) Fisher, had been a high-school pal in Placerville. Together we enlisted in the Naval Communication Reserve in 1939, volunteered for active duty in 1940 and, after boot camp and radio school at San Diego, served in the *California* until the "day of infamy." Following a short period of duty in the Hawaiian Islands, we were selected for the flag radio complement of Vice Admiral William S. Pye in the *Pennsylvania.** In mid-summer of 1942 our paths had at last diverged: mine to the receiving station at Yerba Buena Island to await the *Pawnee* commissioning, and Fisher's to the prestigious California Institute of Technology at Pasadena for officers' training. Although I sensed from his letters that my old friend and I were drifting apart—a natural result of his concentration on radio engineering and mine on survival—the bonds between us were still strong.

I wrote also to Cora Baker in Placerville, and here my reasons were

---

*   For a full account of these adventures, see my *Battleship Sailor* memoir.

more obscure. It certainly wasn't because she and her husband Perry owned a photo studio on Main Street and were true patriots, which they were. It was because they had a daughter named Betty Jane, a kittenish brunette with eyes of the most opaque green I had ever seen. Once I lost myself in their depths while she quoted some lines from Poe ("All that we see or seem / Is but a dream within a dream . . ."). I kissed her upturned oval face and went away quite infatuated with this fifteen-year-old whose Nile-green eyes reflected sometimes the innocence of a child and sometimes the knowledge of a woman. She had written to me for a time, but her boy friend was there and I was here. So I wrote to her mother. What I really was doing, I reflected, was cheating on myself with some vague, unshaped dream of an even more uncertain future. I didn't believe in cheating, especially on myself, but I did it regardless.

At every mail call I received copies of Placerville's weekly *Mountain Democrat.* I read them avidly with mingled pleasure and pain. They contained news of people I knew, of births, marriages, accidents and deaths, of the victories and defeats of the high-school athletic teams. But increasingly they reported casualties, the dead and wounded from the ranks of school chums and classmates in every war theater. It seemed to me that small-town America was being asked to sacrifice its sons out of all proportion to their numbers. But that was the way it always had been, the history books told me.

In the photo album I kept in my locker was a snapshot of my eighth-grade graduating class at Missouri Flat Elementary School: four boys and one girl. Already, the number had been reduced by 40 percent.

Hardy Tatum, always a better athlete than student, was dead. After lettering in football and baseball at high school and junior college, he became a fighter pilot. He was shot down in North Africa.

Stanley Thiele was dead, too, killed in a logging accident in the El Dorado National Forest. He had majored neither in sports nor studies but rather in riding, shooting, drinking and driving too fast. Since he had been teamstering in an essential industry, I supposed he also could be considered a war casualty.

I didn't know the whereabouts of Wilbur Daniels, the third boy. Already sixteen when he finished eight grades (not uncommon during the Great Depression), he had soon dropped out of high school to go to work. Not a student, athlete or hell-raiser, he was the kind of sincere, loyal young man who would have quickly volunteered when war came. (The girl, whose name I had half-forgotten, dropped out of school, too, in favor of marriage. Perhaps she was a casualty of a different sort.)

The odds were fair if not even, I guessed, that World War II might make a clean sweep of those four boys in the class photo.

Not all the casualties were from my age group. On my last visit to Placerville I had seen Ray Nichols, the Signal Oil distributor who had been my supplier when I ran a small service station on the outskirts of town. A former merchant sailor, Ray had accepted with surprise a commission in the Naval Reserve and soon was shipped out as engineering officer in an oiler. Just as promptly, the oiler had been torpedoed and sunk in the Atlantic. The experience had left him a shadow of his once-robust self, gaunt of frame and haunted of face. Wars are planned and directed by old men but are fought by young men. Middle-aged men, unless they be professionals, have no business getting involved in them.

Another artifact from my album which I looked at often on a midwatch was nothing more than an oversized nickel postcard. The black-and-white aerial view followed the east-west progress of the "diggings" once known as Hangtown down a narrow, twisting valley between the surrounding foothills. The meandering wagon trail which had become the Main Street of my home town ran like a golden thread through the tapestry of my reveries.

Each landmark along the street evoked its own weave of memory: the whitewashed granite county courthouse where Judge Thompson had pronounced me legally adopted; the Christian Science church upon whose Puritan pews I had twisted and squirmed on many a Sunday morning; the Masonic Temple where I had been initiated into the order of De Molay; the city library that had introduced me to Balzac and Sabatini, Maugham, and Nordhoff and Hall. In the postcard I could identify the old pyramidal bell tower in the center of town, where the tocsin had rung out against the fires which periodically leveled the wood and tarpaper shacks of the roaring mining community. On the south side of the tower was the Empire Theater, which offered two Westerns, a serial and a cartoon at Saturday matinees for the dime admission. On the other side was Mac's Jumbo Fountain, where teenagers gathered to flirt, make dates and play pool, and where a hamburger, French fries and a milkshake cost fifty cents. Just down the street was the Hangman's Tree Cafe, site of the great white oak where robbers and murderers had been summarily executed without reference to the law's delays. On its hill to the north, overlooking all, was the red-brick campus of El Dorado Union High School. It enrolled only 500 students, offering me the chance for limited glory I couldn't have hoped for in a larger school: an "E" in sports, election to student office, a role in the senior-class play, a school column for the other local weekly, the Placerville *Times*.

I needed no photo to recall my visits to the Mother Lode country during the months at Yerba Buena Island, that strange and glorious interlude of peace in war. The dust of the long hot summer coated the sumac leaves and lay heavy in the unpaved road to the Mason's tin-roofed cottage in Missouri Flat, five miles from town. Indian Creek was only a trickle in its wide, stony bed. But robin, linnet and sparrow still called their territorial imperatives from the live oak and pine trees, the blue jay scolded from the thickets of toyon and manzanita and the acorn woodpecker continued his assault on the stately white oak.

There were no Cap and Dixie to greet me in ecstasies of tail-wagging joy: they slept where I had laid them, in a high bank above the creek, four years before. I visited the place and thought of my youth and of my shipmates Johnson, Reeves and Gilbert, who were buried 2,500 miles away in Honolulu.

I took a .250–3000 Savage rifle and a Colt Woodsman pistol from the gun rack in the living room and went target-shooting in the woods. That skill might prove useful in the South Pacific, where I was likely to go. At the angry burr of a diamondback rattlesnake, I instinctively brought up the .22 pistol and prepared to fire. At home was a boxful of rattles I had collected on many another summer and fall.

Then I remembered the promise I had made in the maintop of the *California* during the Japanese attack, when I had felt like one of the helpless hunted. If I were spared, I vowed, I would never again shoot an animal. A rattlesnake, I must assume, was an animal. I lowered the handgun and moved away, feeling curiously relieved. Rattlesnakes were morally superior to my enemy. They gave warning before they struck.

At dusk I sat on the terrace above the creek and looked across the meadows and fields and wooded hills to the familiar lonesome peak. The setting sun burnished it with molten fire. Past the burning mountain was the Pacific, and we would blaze a path of fire and blood across it to Honshu and Tokyo Bay. Some of the blood would be ours. More would be theirs, despite the bungling of some of our commanders.

Now, a year later, I wondered if I would ever see those places again, drive the Missouri Flat Road, swim in the South Fork of the American River, drink at the town's most popular bar, the Rainbow Club, park in that lane overlooking Weber Creek which was known to generations of lovers. From the vast distance of the Russell Islands, these things seemed as unattainable as capturing a fistful of air.

On the interminable watches of early morning, the ship was dark and heavy with the sleep of a hundred men. Hardly a ripple disturbed the pondlike surface of Renard Sound. I had to strain to hear the muffled rumble and hum of the 60-kilowatt generator around the remorseless piping of Morse code. And I wondered whether I had made my town of Placerville, old Hangtown of the Mother Lode, a substitute for something else. Something gone but impossible to forget, something which rang louder in mind than the thrum-thrum-thrum of the diesel-powered generator. Something like love.

It had been something like that with Dorothy Harvey, she of the Nordic face, thick blonde hair and Junoesque figure. Before I joined the Navy I had danced with her often but she was only fifteen or sixteen and strictly chaperoned. When I returned in the late summer of 1942, she was a grown-up eighteen.

I took her to the Empire Theater to see an Andy Hardy film. In the hush of early evening Placerville dozed and dreamed fitfully in its long, slow decline from the golden days of the 1850s. Afterward, we parked in that lovers' lane. I could hear the monolog of the crickets and the occasional falling whoooo of a hoot owl. In a nearby pasture a cowbell tinkled and a bullfrog croaked his hoarse mating call.

For a while I too was lost in a dream of the past and thought I had fallen in love. Here where I had grown up, young men courted and married girls like Dorothy Harvey, who soon swelled with child as small-town girls were supposed to do. Even when they swelled before they were supposed to, the marriage followed. It was a very old tradition, and one I respected.

A car sped by on the Mother Lode Trail. I had remembered in that moment that Placerville was not very far from San Francisco and that my country, like England in Lord Nelson's day, expected every man to do his duty. My duty would take me far from Dotty Harvey, far from Helen Hazelton in Oakland. Even if I did not come back to marry one of them, it was necessary to ensure that some young man did. Women were more important than men in God's scheme, anyway. They conceived and bore the children. Regretfully, I drove Dorothy home, and out of my life.

Had I been right, had I been wrong? It was not easy to sustain one's resolve on midwatch in the Solomons.

As the brutal months passed in their varying combinations of tedium and terror, the States receded into a misty remembrance of Eden for many of my shipmates as well. The boundaries of their lives became fixed at the precise hour they had left their farm, town or city, caught in the unchangeable vision of the snapshots they carried. The women in the photographs were Sleeping Beauties, waiting to be awakened by a kiss when they returned. While they did not put it that way in their brave conversations, I knew that was what they believed, perhaps forced themselves to believe.

But this was America's first total war, and few were permitted to sleep the crisis away. Everyone who was physically able was expected to work, producing the goods which were enabling the United States to fight a many-fronted war while serving also as President Roosevelt's "arsenal of democracy." In factories, shipyards and offices, in restaurants, bars and shops, our women met men of all classes and conditions. Even among the armed forces, only a small percentage of the men were overseas; most were concentrated at stateside camps, ports and bases. The plaintive wartime song about the shortage of men—"They're either too young or too old"— was simply not true in most parts of the country.

In an atmosphere charged with feverish patriotism and the no-tomorrow morality war always brings, romance often was fired between the working women and the 4-Fs, 1-As and servicemen they encountered. The "Dear John" letters began to arrive in the *Pawnee* mail pouches. Then my services might be needed.

On an evening watch, a shipmate would slip through the open door to the radio shack. Glancing all around to make sure he hadn't been seen, he would say:

"Mason, have you got a minute? There's something I want to show you."

"Sure thing." I would turn up the gain on the receiver and hang the earphones around my neck so I could still hear the NPM Fox signal.

A letter much the worse for wear would be produced from a hip pocket. "I just got this 'Dear John' from my sweetheart. How do you like that shit?"

In flowing feminine handwriting, usually with little circles dotting the *i's*, the trite phrases would leap off the pages at me. "This is the hardest thing I've ever had to do." . . . "I waited and waited all these months." . . . "You've been away so long and I've been so blue." . . . "I've met someone else." . . . "I didn't mean for it to happen but it just did." . . . "He's a really nice guy and treats me just swell." . . . "I hope you'll find it in your heart to forgive me." . . . "We were married last week." . . . "But I'll always have a special place in my heart for you, Joe."

"Jesus, I'm sorry, buddy." Each letter served as a sharp reminder of my cruel-kind reasons for breaking an engagement before we departed San Diego. "Is there anything I can do?"

"Well, yeah. Will you help me write her a letter, Mason? Christ, what else can I do?"

"I'll be glad to. Now?"

"Thanks a million, Mason. She really shafted me—but this'll make me feel a little better, anyhow!"

Chapter Seven

COURAGE
IS CONTAGIOUS

"Hey, we got an F4U in trouble!"

That shout from a bosun's mate brought me out of the mess hall, where I was reading the Hemingway-edited *Men at War*. All day long planes had been taking off from the Marine fighter strip on Banika Island and heading north. This one probably was "Comin' in on a Wing and a Prayer."

The gull-winged Corsair came down the channel low and fast, landing gear up and engine coughing asthmatically. I saw the pilot slide his canopy back; he had decided he couldn't reach the strip and was going to ditch.

He passed the *Pawnee* at superstructure height and skimmed the water. I held my breath. Water was unforgiving. Unless the plane was set down as gently as a falling feather, the impact was similar to a head-on crash into a brick wall.

With engine nacelle up, the wings and fuselage of the F4U skated the surface of Renard Sound for a couple of hundred feet. Then they intercepted the backwash of a passing motor launch. Abruptly, the propeller bit into the water, the large tail flipped up and over and the Marine was catapulted from his cockpit. The Corsair filled and sank almost at once, but he remained afloat in his yellow "Mae West" lifejacket and was soon on his way ashore in the duty picket boat.

I was glad to see that he apparently was all right. Most of the participants in modern naval warfare seemed little more than pawns upon a chessboard, their freedom circumscribed within narrow limits, their lives a possible forfeit to the strategy of the remote chessmaster. Only the fighter pilot retained a measure of individual initiative and control over his destiny. Alone in his cockpit, he went aloft to engage the enemy in combat that was always intensely personal. He was our sole link with the knighterrant of old, and I envied him his freedom and honored his daring.

I was no knight, only a member of a craft guild in the Navy's medieval hierarchy. Still, I was an important one, for the fate of my ship and the lives of her crew well might hinge on the performance of my specialized duties. When I relieved the watch at 1545 on this 14th of August, I brought along my helmet and lifejacket and an extra package of cigarettes. I had a feeling we would be under way soon.

In the fast-deepening twilight, the signal from NPM's transmitting station at Lualualei, Oahu, began fading badly. I shifted from 26.1 kc to 4235 kc and then to 8470 kc, the next-higher harmonic band. NPM finished a long message and immediately started another. The Fox schedule was saturated and ran continuously, twenty-four hours a day.

No. 161 B̄T̄ Z COLX 141428 QRYL Q GYMP OP GR 48 B̄T̄

QRYL was the encoded call sign of the *Pawnee;* the originator was Commander Task Force 31. I cranked a message blank into the typewriter.

"Bridge!" I shouted through the voice tube even as I copied the text. Each five-letter code group was repeated, as was the heading.

"Bridge, aye."

"Operational priority message for *Pawnee.* Stand by!"

No sooner had I finished copying the dispatch than Ensign Moodie appeared. Since he left the running of the radio gang to Proctor and me, he had proved quite acceptable as a communication officer. As the ship's censor, he had given me no trouble with my letters or those I had ghostwritten for shipmates.

"Will it be Blanche's Sna—er, Channel or the Slot?" I asked. (After the *McCawley* sinking the crew had given the former a suitable epithet: "Blanche's Snatch.")

With only a nervous smile as reply, Moodie took the message form and raced down the ladder two steps at a time on his way to the coding cubicle in the wardroom. Within a few minutes the decoded orders had been delivered and the captain and exec were on the bridge. The port anchor was weighed and we departed Renard Sound for Blanche Channel.

In the first application of "leapfrogging" strategy in the Solomons, Admirals Nimitz, Halsey and Wilkinson had decided to isolate the large Japanese garrison on Kolombangara by "hittin' 'em where they ain't." A small expeditionary force of destroyer-transports, LSTs and LCIs (infantry landing craft) screened by twelve destroyers was already under way from Guad-alcanal. Passing through Blanche Channel and Gizo Strait, the three transport groups would land troops at Barakoma Bay near the southern tip of Vella Lavella early the next morning. *Pawnee*'s assignment in this out-flanking of Kolombangara was to stand by at the entrance to Gizo Strait in case any ships or landing craft were hit.

Patrolling "Point X-ray" under a molten full moon, we expected a distress call on this or any of the following nights when reinforcement echelons were approaching Barakoma. But several air attacks from the enemy base at Kahili in lower Bougainville, 90 miles away, were repelled. Our only loss was *LST-396*, the result of the gasoline-vapor explosion and fire, and most of the crew were saved. Again, the "knights-errant" of Air Solomons proved superior by day to the enemy's once-invincible "sea eagles." At night-into-day, good ship-handling, radar-controlled shooting and well-laid smoke screens—plus a measure of what we called "*Pawnee* luck"—prevailed.

The operational-priority dispatch of 14 August was the prologue to two of the most grueling months in the history of the *Pawnee*. It was a period memorable not so much for dramatic events like our escape from PT Squad-ron 9 off Rendova, as for sustained night operations under conditions of privation, discomfort and constant peril. During daylight hours the Amer-icans were masters of the waters of the Central Solomons. When the sun set, the balance tilted to the Japanese, who enjoyed close support from their nearby bases on Bougainville and the Shortland Islands.

Almost every afternoon around 1700 hours, an "OP" message was copied in the radio shack: our orders for that night's sortie. Within half an hour we were under way up the Slot or Blanche Channel to patrol another Point X-ray, Yoke or Zebra, close at hand if Admiral Wilkinson's forces needed towing or salvage services.

The Japanese were withdrawing some 10,000 men from Kolombangara to Bougainville, using *Daihatsu* diesel-powered barges screened by the Tokyo Express. Destroyer Squadrons 22 and 23, augmented occasionally by a cruiser task group, were assigned the mission of sealing off Kolombangara. When our destroyers were under way, so was the *Pawnee*.

Just north of our lonely sector, gun flashes shimmered often on the horizon, along with bursting flak, flares and floatlights. Back at Renard Sound, scuttlebutt informed us that our destroyers were intercepting the barge traffic despite harassment from the Express and "Pete," the night-fighting Zero float plane. The results were a carnage which was soon dubbed "the Central Solomons turkey shoot." The *Pawnee* gunner's mates rigged extra .30- and .50-cal. machine guns along the boat-deck rails, anxious for a chance to join in the annihilation of Nipponese soldiers and sailors.*

Some of the more cautious, or squeamish, among us counseled prudence. They had heard that the *Daihatsu* mounted machine guns and 37-mm. field pieces, supplemented by the weapons of the troops. Already they had bested our PT-boats in several encounters. If we ventured too close, the Japanese might be the ones shooting the turkeys. With destroyers of the Express also removing soldiers, the evacuation route between Kolombangara and the staging point on Choiseul, across the Slot, was no place for the *Pawnee* to be.

Still, the macabre connotations of "turkey shoot" bothered few crewmen. After three months in the Solomons we well understood that this was war without pity; quarter would neither be asked nor given. It was the enemy who had established the barbaric rules of the conflict at Pearl Harbor and in the Philippines. Now they were being repaid in kind.

I paraphrased a line from *Hamlet* that was greeted with harsh, approving laughter by my buddies. "We will," I said, "hoist the bastards by their own petards." They assumed petard meant penis, not a medieval engine of war. Nor did they hear me add, under my breath: "If they don't hoist us first."

Many of us, myself included, let our hair grow long and wore knives in our belts. If we had to take to the water, we would have some defense against sharks and the unthinkable: capture by the enemy. In the ship's small machine shop, Gerber turned out a handle of multi-colored plastic for my G.I. knife. I honed the blade to a razor edge and longed for a sidearm.

For the nights of the *Pawnee* were 10 or 12 hours of nerve-racking uncertainty. Each one might bring a call for help from a battle-damaged destroyer. Or it might bring an aerial attack by a Pete fighter, an underwater threat from a prowling submarine, or a surface contact with an enemy tin can. While we might dodge Pete's bombs and tracers or elude a sub in one of the many coves and inlets of the heavily indented New Georgia coastline, a destroyer would make short work of us. We didn't have enough guns to fight back with any hope of success and we were too slow to run away. Our best defense was not our limited firepower, our sonar gear and

---

* The blockade of Kolombangara was far less successful than we thought at the time. It succeeded in destroying less than 1000 men. Japanese barges and destroyers extricated some 8,400 troops. See Morison, Vol. VI, pp. 242–43.

depth charges or our night lookouts with their binoculars. It was, I thought, the rigid authoritarian mind of our adversary.

The Americans, as befitted their national character, were opportunists, willing to assault any available target rather than return home empty-handed. Had the *Pawnee* been flying the flag of the Rising Sun, she and her crew would not have lasted a week in the Solomons. If the PTs hadn't sunk her (as indeed they very nearly had on 30 June), a dive- or torpedo-bomber, a destroyer or cruiser would have painted another ship silhouette on fuselage or bridge wing. The Japanese, on the other hand, repeatedly ignored easy targets to concentrate on combat ships. It was, I believed, a very foolish policy and one for which I devoutly thanked Emperor Hirohito and the militarists who ran his government. My fear was that, on one of those 12-hour nights, we would encounter an enemy pilot or ship commander who thought like an American.

Considering the number of vessels involved in supplying our troops on Vella Lavella and blockading Kolombangara, the calls for assistance were few. The employment of *Pawnee*-class ships for close support of combat operations had never been attempted by the fleet of any nation, so far as we knew. It was in its infancy here in the Solomons. Before *Pawnee* joined the Third Fleet, a number of ships had perished that could have been saved by the timely arrival of an ocean-going tug. The most striking example was the carrier *Wasp*, torpedoed off the Santa Cruz Islands on 15 September 1942. Burning fiercely, she was abandoned and given the coup de grace by destroyer *Lansdowne*. Her engineering plant was still intact. *Pawnee*'s sister ship *Navajo*, then stationed in the New Hebrides, might have overcome the fires and towed the invaluable carrier back to Espiritu Santo.

The failure to employ the *Navajo* was also a factor in the loss of the *Yorktown* following the Battle of Midway in early June 1942. Abandoned prematurely, the carrier could have been towed to safety if AT-64 had been operating with the fleet. But *Navajo* was then at Canton Island locked onto the old, slow converted troopship S.S. *President Taylor*, which had run aground in February. The effort to salvage this antiquated Dollar liner, built in 1921, had to be abandoned and the ship was later destroyed by Japanese aircraft. Only the little mine-sweeper *Vireo* was available to take the *Yorktown* in tow. She was inadequate to the task of moving the 20,000-ton carrier and was barely making headway when *Yorktown* was closed and sunk by Submarine I-168. Piling tragedy upon tragedy, the sub's torpedoes also sank the destroyer *Hammann*, which was alongside the carrier with a salvage party. Eighty more lives were lost. All for want of one stout litter-bearer of the seas, properly deployed.

In the summer of 1943, the Navy base commanders were still clinging to peacetime practices of using ATs as jacks-of-all-work: moving ships around within a harbor, towing barges, and salvaging hulks which might bring a few thousand dollars on the San Francisco or San Pedro scrap market. Afloat, the cruiser and destroyer officers were still suffering from the go-it-alone, limp-into-port-without-crutches syndrome first noted by the *Pawnee* crew when the *Honolulu* and *St. Louis* spurned our offer of assistance. Usually we got under way from Renard Sound before dark, patrolled our assigned sector without incident, and returned to our anchorage sometime the next morning. Often we would weigh anchor again within an hour or two, ordered to tow a yard oiler to Guadalcanal. At 1700 the dreaded "Oboe Prep" message would sent us north again. After a few weeks of this merciless routine, the crewmen were utterly exhausted, performing their assigned duties with the slow, mechanical precision of zombies.

Once a helmsman fell asleep at the wheel and was roused by alert Quartermaster Miller just before we ran off course into a coral reef. "I didn't have the guts to put him on report," Miller said, revealing a quality of compassion unsuspected by most of his shipmates. "Hell, there's a limit to human endurance."

One notable departure from routine made us feel there was some purpose to our "milk runs" beyond obedience to orders at the risk of our necks. On the morning of 25 August an urgent message on the Fox sked sent us coursing up Blanche Channel at 15½ knots, west into the Solomon Sea and north to Gizo Strait. The *Montgomery*, a World War I destroyer converted to a fast minelayer, was leaking badly and listing to starboard. Her thin old plates had been scalpeled open in a turning collision with her sister ship *Preble* as the venerable flushdeckers and another sister, the *Breese*, retired from a minelaying operation off Vella Lavella.

We took the *Montgomery* in tow alongside, our port to her starboard, rigged our powerful 1200-gallon-per-minute dewatering pumps and began building up shaft revolutions. Overhead, a few P-39s provided air cover.

"By God, I've never been so glad to see anyone in my life!" the minelayer skipper shouted across from his bridge wing.

"Glad to be here, captain," George replied. "Is there anything else we can do?"

"Just keep those pumps going and get our butts back to Purvis."

We gathered along the weather passage to exchange greetings and action reports with the *Montgomery* crew. Their ship had been under continuous surveillance from enemy "snoopers" based on Kahili since 0100 that morning. Flares and bombs were repeatedly dropped as they withdrew at a scant 10 knots. All the bombs were near misses which pockmarked the ship with flying shrapnel, slightly injuring one steward's mate. But they had opened wider the gash in the starboard side and increased the list.

"If you guys hadn't come along when you did, we'da never made it," one *Montgomery* sailor rejoiced.

"Thank God," John Day told me. "Did you see the look of relief on their faces? I tell you, that was worth a thousand words!"

We moored the minelayer to the floating dry dock in Purvis Bay eighteen hours later. Long after that, I remembered one deckhand on her forecastle. His face was still immature: he was no more than eighteen or nineteen. His hair was falling out in great tufts, exposing areas of sunburned scalp. What remained had turned snow white.

Back on our nightly runs, we wondered why the *Pawnee* was the only AT assigned to Task Force 31. Where the hell were all the Indian-class ships being turned out at United Engineering, Charleston Shipbuilding and the other yards? Above all, where the hell was the *Menominee*?

All during the weeks stretching into months of our nightly sorties to the Central Solomons, the *Menominee* was lying at anchor in Halavo Bay, Florida Island, operating under direct orders from Admiral Halsey and exempt from all but emergency salvage duties. Still under the command of the redoubtable Emile C. Genereaux of "Dirty Dell" memory, our sister ship was raising the Japanese destroyer *Kikutsuki* from 12 fathoms of water. Anchored there in the lee of Halavo Peninsula, a spit of densely wooded land lying athwart the entrance to Tulagi Harbor, the *Kikutsuki* had been heavily damaged by our SBD dive-bombers during the air strike of 4 May 1942. She was beached but later slid back into the water and sank. Now Halsey wanted her.

In his revealing memoir, *The Captain Loved the Sea*, Genereaux described his first meeting with Halsey at Commander South Pacific's Noumea headquarters. He gave no date but the reference below places it as mid-March 1943.

"As I entered, he got up from his chair and greeted me warmly and right away I felt at home so to speak and he questioned me as to how in hell was I able to get that destroyer off in such a hurry when he had all the local talent fail." (Halsey was referring to the *Shaw*, which *Menominee* had freed from a reef in Bulari Passage and *Pawnee* had put in dry dock at Noumea on 11 March 1943.)

"After I had described the incident, he said, 'Now I have a real job for you. During the Coral Sea battle one of my planes sank a Jap destroyer and I promised her to Nimitz and I want you to get her. We intend to fix her up and use her as a decoy for future attacks.'

"I asked him where she was sunk and he said somewhere around Guadalcanal. I asked if he could be more specific and he said that is for you to find out. Well, that was a big order, but now that I had established myself I felt that this is a 'must' and the next day I was on my way."*

Following his seaman's instincts, Genereaux soon located the wreck in Halavo Bay and set about raising her with no more resources than his ship, a 500-ton lighter and salvage gear scrounged from all over the South Pacific. When the word finally reached the *Pawnee*, our experts jeered. The *Menominee*'s assignment was impossible under such primitive conditions, they said. Then what would Halsey think of his so-called salvage genius? Having seen "Black Jack" Genereaux in action at Nomobitigue Reef, where he easily accomplished the salvage of the *Delphinus* after we had failed, I wouldn't have described any project he tackled as impossible.

Aposhian, as usual, got to the heart of the matter:

"The raising of this beat-up tin can is the most hare-brained scheme I've ever heard of. Halsey must have been in his cups when he got this insane idea."

"Maybe the Bull should change his brand of Scotch," I added. Because the top admiral in the SoPac had promised an enemy ship to Nimitz essentially as a war trophy, we had lost the services of the *Menominee* and her superlative C.O. during the critical months of the New Georgia and Vella Lavella campaigns.

Although it was winter in the Southern Hemisphere, the sun continued to glare down at us from a nearly vertical position. There are no seasons in the Solomons, which lie between 5 and 10 degrees south latitude. The weather is always the same, like the world's largest outdoor sauna. The climate is called "equatorial," with constant heat, high humidity and rainfall of 100 inches a year or more. We called it several other things, especially when we developed symptoms of prickly heat, more popularly known as "the crud." They began with sharp, tingling sensations, as if one were being punctured with needles, followed by an irresistible urge to scratch. Soon, large areas of the body would be covered by a fiery red rash. Then we lined up at sick bay for the treatment, which consisted of painting the affected areas with a purple tincture. As Doc Ortalano wielded the brush, a lecture was part of his ministrations:

---

*   "Salvage in the South Pacific," Chapter 14 of *The Captain Loved the Sea*. Copyright 1970, Emile C. Genereaux. Published in the *Nautical Research Journal*, Vol. 18, No. 3 (Autumn 1971), Bethesda, Md.

"Don't scratch your balls. Shower twice a day. Drink a gallon or two of water. And take your goddam salt tablets." He left the clear impression that prayer wouldn't hurt.

Athlete's foot, too, was endemic in the steamy climate. And some of us had recurring bouts with a mild ear infection that caused an intense itching where it couldn't be scratched.

"Goddam it," Doc would pontificate as he operated the syringe, "I told you bastards not to go swimming in that coral lagoon. Now you got an ear fungus that's gonna be with you for the rest of your lives."

"Let's look on the bright side, Doc," I said. "You don't have a single case of clap or syphilis in the whole ship."

"The only reason I don't," he retorted, "is that the cannibals took all their broads into the jungle when they heard the Navy was comin'. Some of you swabbies would screw a snake if someone held its head!"

Many men joined Aposhian, Gerber and me in sleeping topside. Some agreed with us that the airless crew's quarters were intolerable at night. Others feared being trapped belowdecks if the ship was torpedoed or bombed. The devastation that one torpedo could inflict on the unarmored *Pawnee* was nearly unimaginable. Even a 500-pound bomb, if it exploded in a vital area, would disable the ship and kill many of the crew.

Our sister ship *Seminole* had been sunk by three Japanese destroyers off Lunga Point the past October. The casualties were light only because the foe was using armor-piercing shells which passed through her hull without exploding. While we were still playing lifeguard for the reluctant destroyer squadrons, the *Navajo* was rocked by an explosion of unknown origin, mine or torpedo, off the New Hebrides and went down like a stone. The salvage ship which might have saved the *Wasp* and *Yorktown* was towing a gasoline barge from Pago Pago to Espiritu Santo.

Death by torpedo, bomb, shellfire or mine—or death by our own armament turning against us like Dr. Frankenstein's soulless monster—were all possibilities. When the *Navajo* headed for the bottom her depth charges had detonated, killing a number of men in the water. Dwelling on these chances was worse than futile; it was condemning myself to a future conditional. I brought myself back to the very hour with the great lines from *Hamlet:*

> Not a whit, we defy augury; there's
> a special providence in the fall of a sparrow.
> If it be now, 'tis not to come; if it be not to
> come, it will be now; if it be not now, yet it
> will come: the readiness is all . . .

Lying across three lifejackets on the fantail, I derived more comfort from the soliloquies of the Melancholy Dane than the preachments of the Holy Bible and *Science and Health,* whose vest-pocket editions I kept in my locker. The *Pawnee* was a dark, noisy shape advancing across a silent gray sea, her progress marked by a phosphorescent trail of marine organisms that lingered like an afterglow. Ahead, astern and on either beam were the black masses of the brooding islands with exotic, prosaic and bizarre names: Choiseul and Wana Wana and Nusatupi, Plum Pudding and New Georgia and Gross, Bambanga and Ranongga and Giiunabena.

Overhead, the stars and constellations of the Southern Hemisphere shone down brilliantly and coldly. Many had been unknown to me until John Day pointed them out eight months before. Even when they were familiar, they hung in strange, upside-down positions in the sky. Among the star groupings were many fanciful predators that seemed to reflect our purposes in the South Pacific: Orion the belted hunter; Leo the lean and hungry lion; Canis Major and Minor, the greater and lesser dogs; Hydra the sea serpent; Centaurus the monster, half man and half horse; Lupus the wolf.

The ancient astronomers must have been gifted with vivid imaginations, I thought. Few of these constellations bore any resemblance to the creatures they were supposed to represent. Only Scorpio, rising now above the 5500-foot peak of Kolombangara, looked like its namesake of the venomous stinger. Even the benign Southern Cross was leaving the *Pawnee* to the hunters and killers as it sank toward its refuge below the far polar horizon. There did not seem to be much consolation in this firmament, even for the astrologically or metaphysically inclined. I thought of the quartrain from Omar Khayyam:

> And that inverted Bowl they call The Sky,
> Whereunder crawling coop't we live and die,
> Lift not thy hands to *It* for help—for *It*
> As impotently moves as you or I.

With remarkable swiftness the clouds that were always present in the Solomons coalesced and thickened and blotted out the cold constellations. Now the only light in all our world came from our glittering evanescent wake. Without warning the rain came pelting down, heavy and cool and sweet-tasting on my face. I and the other men who had been sleeping or reflecting topside gathered our lifejackets and mattresses and hurried below to the still and musky air of the crew's compartments, where long thoughts of God's inscrutable purposes seemed vain and absurd.

Our food was as predictably bad as the weather. Nearly everything came from a can or carton: Spam and chipped beef, anemic small peas, clingstone peaches, sour grapefruit juice. The eggs, milk and potatoes all were powdered. The Rice Krispies in their individual-serving boxes were stale and tasteless. Occasionally we received a side of frozen "ox meat" from Australia or New Zealand. Once it may have been beef. By the time our cooks had quite finished with it, the resemblance to roasted shoe leather was unmistakable. When the Navy didn't know what to do with a rank foulball, we grumbled, it made him a ship's cook.

Jim Sewell, the seaman who had gone ashore with me in San Diego, was now one of them. His incentive, the Musketeers suspected, was a desire to avoid hard labor on the deck force. As we passed through the cafeteria line with our metal trays, we enjoyed taunting him:

"Where'd you learn to sling hash, Sewell—in a C.C.C. camp?"

"No, he had the food concession for one of those Rebel chain gangs."

"Is it true, Jim, that you were a goddam embalmer in civilian life?"

One day Warrant W. O. Armstrong went ashore and told it to the Marines. He returned with a whaleboat piled high with K-rations. We cut the heavy foil wrapping with our knives, ate the canned stew, savored the chocolate bars and smoked the Old Gold cigarettes. Loudly we proclaimed, so the cooks would be sure to hear, that K-rations were a helluva lot better than our own chow. Once we ran out of sugar and had to sweeten our coffee and dry cereal with molasses. Indignant over this shortage of a basic staple, we sent a leading petty officer to the exec's stateroom in a mast for requests. It probably was coincidental that 100-pound sacks of sugar were hoisted aboard shortly afterward.

If we had run out of coffee, the exec would have been visited by a delegation of angry petty officers in defiance of regulations. Fortunately for morale and good order, we never did. The crew could not have endured the endless sleepless nights in Blanche Channel without this necessity. During our few free hours at anchor in Renard Sound, coffee was the essential social lubricant. We swallowed salt tablets from the dispenser above the mess hall scuttlebutt (although they sometimes came back up as fast as they went down) and sweated and scratched our prickly heat infestations and drank hot coffee and talked longingly of food. Of huge top-sirloin steaks broiled medium rare, baked potatoes piled up with butter, sour cream and chives, salads awash in Roquefort dressing, side orders of artichokes and asparagus served with mayonnaise, all accompanied by pitchers of ice-cold milk.

By the time we finished with supper, we were ready for breakfast. We started with three or four glasses of freshly squeezed orange juice while we waited for giant platters of bacon, country-style potatoes and eggs basted to a golden promise.

"Don't forget the toast," someone would be sure to add. "It'll be served with real strawberry or red raspberry preserves, not this goddam grape jelly." If we ever found the war profiteer who had the Navy's grape-jelly concession, we swore, we would cast him adrift in a leaky life raft.

Exhausting the subject of food at last, the conversations turned always to the inexhaustible one of girls. Our connoisseurs of sex spun out epics of erotica, spiced with vivid anatomical detail. These I equated with the tales of Baron von Munchausen: amusing but wildly improbable fictions. I had had fairly good luck with women but I certainly did not rate myself a Don Juan or Casanova, and I doubted that my lustful shipmates qualified, either. Conquest, I had discovered, was seldom easy. When it was, one had better examine motivations and proceed with caution.

Whether fact or fancy, the sea stories of the seducers sprang from a very real fear that was shared, secretly or loudly, by all of us. What effect would this long period of enforced abstinence have on our future lives as husbands and fathers? Would we even be able to perform? The persistent scuttlebutt that the Navy added saltpeter to its food as a suppressant of sexual desire was the subject of much agitated conversation. The ship's cooks were queried: did they or didn't they? All vehemently denied it. They were in such disfavor, however, that no one believed them. Even if they were telling the truth, one skeptic noted, it didn't make any difference. The stuff was probably added to the flour or sugar long before the supplies came aboard.

Within the radio gang I had to deal with an even more alarming rumor: that constant exposure to high-frequency radio and radar transmissions made one infertile at best and impotent at worst. Chief Proctor scoffed at this suggestion, but he lacked credibility. Since he spent most of his time apple-polishing on the bridge, it was obvious he was bucking for warrant or a commission and the truth was not in him.

"How about it, Mason?" I was asked.

I hated to deceive my radiomen, but a considerable morale factor was involved and that took precedence over candor. The last thing we needed off New Georgia or Vella Lavella were radiomen worried about becoming eunuchs. I began naming chief radiomen and senior firsts I had known in the *California* and *Pennsylvania* who not only were married but also had produced numerous "Navy brats."

"Now take Flag Chief Reinhardt," I concluded. "He's been around Navy radio for thirty years. The old bastard has a wife who's twenty-five years younger than he is. Good-looking, too. And he has a son by his first marriage who was an All-American football player at the University of California."

The radiomen were more satisfied with this explanation than I was. I knew that some of the career radiomen in the battleships were married but I didn't have the vaguest idea whether any children had resulted. So far as "Pappy" Reinhardt was concerned, I had met his young, attractive wife but doubted his story about the football-playing son. The All-American tackle at Berkeley spelled his surname differently.

As always when placed in an ambiguous ethical position, I wondered whether the end justified my means. In elementary school I had been taught that George Washington never told a lie. I still believed in a rigid code of personal honesty. But how, in the middle of a war, could one live up to it without possibly endangering one's ship and shipmates?

Modern war was waged not only by force of arms but also with words. The words were double-edged, designed to sustain morale on the home front while concealing the truth from the enemy. That meant deceiving your own people, too, with the additional benefit of shielding commanders who lost battles from the public consequences of their blunders.

On the night of 30 November 1942, Rear Admiral Carlton H. Wright led five cruisers and six destroyers into Ironbottom Sound against eight enemy destroyers engaged in a reinforcement mission to Guadalcanal. Lacking knowledge of the exceptional range of the long lance, he closed into torpedo waters behind his destroyer van—and a devastating defeat off Tassafaronga. The heavy cruiser *Northampton* was sunk; the heavies *Minneapolis*, *New Orleans* and *Pensacola* suffered extensive damage with severe loss of life and were out of action for nearly a year. The public was told that we had sunk four destroyers and damaged three others. Even the sailors who fought Tassafaronga accepted this claim, for it made their defeat less humiliating. (Later it was learned that the Japanese lost only the *Takanami*.) Admiral Wright was quickly and quietly shipped back to the States to become commandant of Treasure Island, the largest naval base on the West Coast.

Under the pressure of military necessity, or because they believed the action reports of their subordinates, the fleet commanders often misled the correspondents. The journalists, responding in turn to the demands of their publishers for good news, passed along the exaggerated claims to the American people. Indecisive actions, even defeats like Tassafaronga, were turned into victories. The first casualty in war was not some hapless enlisted man. It was truth.

At such times I headed for the fantail and the forgetfulness of disciplined violence. Most of the crew did nothing more strenuous in their off-duty hours than wash clothes, write letters or shuffle a deck of cards. Only a dozen or so of the hardiest (or, in the opinion of some, the most "Asiatic") cared to exert themselves in that awful climate. By now, however, I had grown accustomed to being a little different. Not many of my shipmates read the books in the library or wrote poetry either. So I ran in place for a few minutes, did fifty pushups, punched a heavy bag Gerber and I had improvised from a seabag, and boxed with any of the crew who cared to put on the 12-ounce gloves. It was not unusual for me to box twelve or fifteen untimed rounds in late afternoons at Renard Sound or Tulagi.

Among my sparring partners was George Tahbone, an Oklahoma Indian with a shy, engaging smile, a slightly deviated septum and a potent punch in either hand. He had gone to the finals of the Golden Gloves eliminations in Chicago; the war interrupted another try for a national championship. Despite the fact his boxer father had died in the ring during a brutal match, he still planned eventually to turn professional. Obviously, few in the *Pawnee* cared to provide him with a moving target. When I did, I quickly discovered how good he really was. I also found out he had never learned to pull his punches, for even routine jabs stung and snapped my head back. By boxing with him often, I soon improved my skills. It was a choice between that or going about my duties with a permanent black eye, swollen nose or cut lip.

Tahbone's relentless stalking attack was punishing but not malicious, more a test of manhood than a desire to hurt. When you laced on the gloves with him, you had better be prepared to stand up and fight and, if necessary, take a beating without complaint or excuse. If you could do so, you earned his respect and possibly his friendship—and those were not things George Tahbone gave lightly.

Boxing with him and the others meant a good deal more than physical conditioning and increasing proficiency in a rugged sport. I considered it a mental and emotional toughener as well. Where the chance of death sudden or slow had to be faced daily, those who had inured themselves to it in every respect had the best chance of survival.

During the first two weeks of our nightly operations in support of the landings on Vella Lavella, we had lacked a full complement of crewmen. In the United States the most massive shipbuilding program in the history of the world was now in full production, and several of our skilled petty officers had been transferred off the *Pawnee* for new construction. When we returned to Renard Sound on a morning in late August, a Higgins boat came alongside and deposited ten replacements on the fantail.

"My God," someone said. "They're all boots. Only a couple of 'em look old enough to shave."

Reporting for duty with bag and hammock were Seamen Second Class Adams, Atterbury, Baker, Bell, Bishop, Bissler, Bittle, Blair, Bozynski and Compton.

"I don't believe it," Papoose Evans told me as we watched these green hands being shepherded down the ladder toward the forward crew's compartment. "We need four or five POs and half a dozen seamen firsts. The Navy sends us ten boots with cowshit still on their shoes. They just pull out ten warm bodies. Did you notice all the names begin with 'A' or 'B', except for one 'C'?" The detailing practices for the Service Force, we decided, had been devised by an 80-year-old "retread" captain with a crew of dissolute yeomen still celebrating their escape from the defunct Asiatic Fleet.

All through the furious roundelay of the Central Solomons, Captain George's quiet, poised leadership inspired the crew. There were exceptions: those who noted with alarm his frequent trips to the beach, certain he was volunteering our services for ever-more-hazardous assignments. Soon a rumor of mysterious origin began circulating through the crew's quarters: the captain had woman troubles. That explained his eagerness for action up Blanche's Snatch. He had joined the ranks of the "Dear Johns" and didn't give a shit what happened.

I didn't believe this for a moment. On the built-in desk in George's cabin I had seen a framed color photograph of his pretty wife and two handsome children. They looked like a typical upper-middle-class American family from a magazine advertisement. If his marriage was failing, I didn't think the captain would keep such a painful reminder in sight. I knew I wouldn't.

The man who abandoned hope over a lost love and secretly sought death by reckless adventure was a stock figure in fiction and folklore. Perhaps the scuttlebutt about George was an attempt by those of conventional courage to explain the inexplicable: the man whose sense of duty propels him above and beyond a due regard for his life. Four of my *California* shipmates—including my esteemed chief radioman, Thomas J. Reeves—won the Medal of Honor at Pearl Harbor for deeds of almost unbelievable heroism and sacrifice. Three of the awards were posthumous. No one of ordinary virtue could possibly understand why the three enlisted men and one ensign had acted as they did—it defied all logic. Heroes do not have to be entirely admirable men, but they are always extraordinary men.

The captain, I told the worriers, was accepting the principle of calculated risk in carrying out his mission. It was better to have a commanding
officer who was too bold than one lacking in intestinal fortitude. At Pearl
Harbor the *Nevada* had been the only battleship that got under way. Her
Acting C.O. was a Reserve lieutenant-commander, just like George. Despite taking two torpedoes, the *California* could have got under way but
didn't because, in my opinion, our four-striper captain and three-star admiral lost their nerve. Although the *Nevada* was hit repeatedly in mid-
channel and had to be beached, she suffered fewer casualties than my ship,
which was abandoned and sank at quayside.

To clinch my argument, I related my favorite anecdote about George.
Once during our first days in the Russells, I copied an air-raid warning
before the 0600 reveille. I went to the captain's cabin less than fifteen feet
away and knocked on the door.

"Good morning, captain," I said after I had received permission to
enter. "Condition Red. Enemy planes approaching."

George sat up in his berth and looked at his watch, an elaborate wrist
chronometer of the type favored by navigators and pilots. I noticed he slept
in his T-shirt, like the enlisted men. He seemed wide awake.

"Well, Ted, they're a little early this morning, aren't they?" he said
casually. "I think you'd better have the bridge sound general quarters."

"Most C.O.s would have leaped from their bunks and raced up the
ladder shouting orders," I finished. "But George was calm, cool and collected. There was no sweat. Now that's the kind of skipper I want up here!"

A couple of weeks later I witnessed an even more striking example of
George's panache. One murky night in Blanche Channel, I happened to be
standing beside him on the port wing of the bridge. As usual, *Pawnee* was
operating alone. The ship was in condition of readiness two and materiel
condition Baker, with lookouts posted and the 20-mm. and .50-cal. guns
manned and ready.

Without warning, a Pete night fighter came diving at us out of the
broken cloud cover. I heard the whine of its powerful radial engine before I
spotted it, a dark shape hurtling down from an altitude of less than 2,000
feet. We had just met a Japanese pilot who thought like an American.

"Open fire," the captain ordered. Nothing happened. Our gunners,
taken by surprise, were trying desperately to get the target in their sights.

The seconds passed, each one stretched as long and taut as a bow-
string just before the release. At such moments, time is relative.

"Do you think he's going to get us, Ted?" George asked in a noncha-
lant tone.

"Yes, sir, I think he will," I replied in the same tone. From the angle of his dive, I judged the Pete's wing bombs would hit in the pilothouse area. My stomach tied itself into the old familiar knots. I could visualize my broken body, torn apart by shrapnel.

At the penultimate moment, we were saved like the heroine in the old *Perils of Pauline* serials. One of our new P-38 Lightning fighters came rocketing down on the tail of the Pete, its machine guns spewing red-hot tracers. The enemy plane pulled out of its dive and fled north with the twin-fuselage P-38 in close pursuit.

The captain and I looked at each other. I shook my head and gave a low whistle of relief. He smiled briefly and shrugged his shoulders. Then he went into the pilothouse.

We had been very close in those elastic seconds, not a ship's captain and one of his petty officers but two men looking together into the face of death. It was probably only my imagination that I saw his legs trembling a little. I hoped he hadn't noticed mine.

Departing the Russells at dusk not long after the Pete's aborted attack, Gerber and I stood near the fantail roller chock smoking and watching the ship's boiling wake. All at once a new sound penetrated the high-pitched rackety-rack of the four diesel engines.

Instinctively, Gerber hunched over in his boxer's crouch. Straightening up, he said:

"We got us a visitor—and I don't think he's no friend."

A plane was approaching fast, flying just above our wake. Now I could see an engine cowling on either wing, the plexiglass gun position in the nose.

"It's a Jap Betty," I said.

Lacking armor and self-sealing gas tanks, the long-range Mitsubishi bomber had been dubbed "the flying coffin." But it carried four 7.7-mm. machine guns, two 20-mm. cannon and a payload of more than a ton of bombs or long-lance torpedoes. It was as dangerous as a hooded cobra, for it had struck many an American ship and sailor in the struggle for the Solomons. If the pilot of this Betty thought like an American, he could cut down many of our topside crew in a strafing run.

I should have dived for cover immediately. Instead, I waited for Gerber to make the first move.

He didn't make it. We kept up a desultory conversation as the plane passed low over the ship without opening fire. The last thing I saw were the guns projecting from its bulbous tail enclosure. Again, our gunners had failed to find the target. Not for the first time, nor the last, Gerber and I and numbers of our shipmates probably were alive because a Japanese officer had lacked the initiative to depart from his explicit orders.

"God damn it, buddy," I told Gerber. "Why didn't you take cover?"

"Why didn't you, you crazy bastard?"

It was a show of what some might term a foolish bravado. Others might think it a demonstration of our regard for the Pawnee's intrepid skipper.

In early October several events hinted at renewed action to the north. Radio traffic from III Amphib to the destroyer groups increased. Pawnee took on 14,000 gallons of diesel fuel from a yard oiler. After our nightly patrol of 5–6 October we anchored in Rendova Harbor instead of returning to Renard Sound. At 1730 on 6 October we got under way and headed west into the Solomon Sea. The first-quarter moon was already descending and we sensed it would be a long night.

An hour before midnight, three of our destroyers (three others steaming to the scene arrived too late to join the action) engaged six destroyers of an enemy evacuation force off Marquana Bay on northwest Vella Lavella. The Chevalier was torpedoed and abandoned in a sinking condition with a loss of 51 men. A single torpedo from the LaVallette finished her off at 0300. If she could have been kept afloat, Pawnee would have dashed in to put a tow wire on her.

The Selfridge was torpedoed at frame 40 and most of her forecastle structure was destroyed. The forward bulkheads were shored up and she eventually was able to make 10 knots by turning up 16. Probably, she should have been taken in tow, but her C.O. was another graduate of the limp-proudly-into-port school. The O'Bannon suffered a damaged bow in a collision with Chevalier, which had sheared out of control after the first torpedo hit.

At dawn G.Q. of 7 October, the two cripples, escorted by Ralph Talbot, Taylor and LaVallette, were still off the west coast of Vella Lavella, far from Purvis Bay. Pawnee was still standing by to the south, off Ganongga Island, in case of an SOS. What we copied instead was an urgent-priority message reporting a large formation of Zeros closing to attack. The destroyers went to general quarters again, and so did the Pawnee, at 0727. Our knights-errant of Air Solomons galloped to the rescue and routed the dastards.

The commander of the destroyer group, Capt. Frank R. Walker, claimed he had sunk three destroyers and damaged others in the Battle of Vella Lavella. The Chevalier seemed a reasonable price to pay for this coda to the Central Solomons Campaign. (Actually, the enemy lost only the

Yugumo while successfully completing his mission of evacuating troops from Vella Lavella with a subchaser-transport group which slipped through unnoticed during the engagement. Rear Admiral Matsuji Ijuin was the real victor. Not all of the destroyer commanders had yet adopted Moosbrugger's bold but prudent tactics for surmounting the Japanese edge in torpedoes, optics and night-fighting skills.)

By the afternoon of 11 October we had worked our way from Blanche Channel to Renard Sound to Purvis Bay to Lunga Roads. About dusk two low-flying Betty bombers slipped in under the radar surveillance and transited Ironbottom Sound before Condition Red could be sounded. Ignoring *Pawnee* and the other ships anchored in the roads, they headed for nearby Koli Point, where two Liberty ships were unloading. Both merchantmen were torpedoed. Soon the *George H. Himes* was taking on water and the *John H. Couch*, carrying aviation gasoline, was afire.

Early the next morning a belated call for assistance sent us to Koli Point. The *John H. Couch* was burning fiercely now, flames leaping up from No. 2 and No. 3 holds forward of the midships house. The Seabees had a pontoon lighter alongside and were directing streams of salt water at the hatches. As we rigged our fire-fighting gear and prepared to moor starboard side to the lighter, we could see the *Menominee* a few hundred yards away. She had a line on the sinking *George H. Himes* and was towing her away from the anchorage stern first.

"There's 'Black Jack' Genereaux," one bosun's mate muttered, "playin' hero again."

"Yeah," a second boats agreed. "Notice he took the easy towin' assignment. He's gonna leave the goddam fire-fighting to us."

"He'll beach that Liberty," the first said. "By this afternoon he'll be back at Tulagi, messin' with that Jap tin can."*

When I went to the bridge to check our progress, four streams of water from our 2½-inch hoses were playing on the two holds. Supplied by our

---

* If the bosun's mates (and the rest of the crew) had known how the resourceful Genereaux used this occasion to restock his ship's food lockers, they would have been even more disgruntled. He writes in *The Captain Loved the Sea:* "In those hectic days out there, food was scarce and of very poor quality. We had to scrounge food from any ship that put in and this was one big chance to really pay off. I told the Captain of the Liberty Ship that inasmuch as his plant was out of commission that all his food would spoil and that we should transfer it to my ship where I had ample refrigeration space but no food. So he fell for the idea and we filled our lockers with very fine merchant seaman's food. We had roast turkey that night and prime ribs the second night and so on for some time to come. The crew on the ship were taken ashore and had a taste of K rations. It's an ill wind that blows no good."

salvage pumps through the manifold on the boat deck, the hoses were disgorging nearly 1,200 gallons a minute at a pressure of 80 pounds per square inch at the nozzles. The deluge of water seemed to have little effect. In fact, the smoke got thicker and the orange-red flames leaped higher, as if angered by our interference. The searing dry heat pulled at my face as I stood on the starboard wing. I thought about the burning battleships on Pearl Harbor day. Was the *Couch* about to explode, as the *Arizona* had?

The captain leaned against the splinter shield nearby, a thin smile on his face. Seemingly, he was oblivious to the ovenlike temperatures and the danger. Turning to the OOD, he gave terse orders. Two hoses were secured and rigged to six lengths of 1½-inch hose through a pair of three-way dividers. Soon all six hoses, half fitted with foam nozzles and half with applicators, were directed at No. 3 hold. The two larger ones continued to play on No. 2.

Within half an hour we seemed to be gaining some authority over the fires. The licking tongues of flame were subsiding into rising pillars of dense black smoke. Another order from George and all eight hoses were aimed at No. 3 hold. From the lighter, the Seabees concentrated their attention on the forward one. The captain's strategy obviously was to extinguish the larger fire first while keeping the other under control.

It might have succeeded but for mechanical failure and the caprice of nature. The lighter's water-supply line sprang a leak and the pressure failed. The fire in No. 2 hold vaulted up again. Before we could bring this new threat under control, the wind shifted. Flames began blowing across the lighter and scorching the paint on the *Pawnee*. I felt as if I had stuck my head into the open hearth of a blast furnace. The wind increased; the flames snapped eagerly at the bridge.

"Captain!" a lookout shouted from the searchlight platform. "There's a goddam DE on the other side, sir. She's opened fire on us!"

Lying to off the *Couch's* starboard beam, the destroyer escort was pouring 5-inch projectiles into her hull at point-blank range. Apparently this rash intruder hadn't seen the *Pawnee* in the pall of smoke. A couple of officers who had remained aboard the Liberty hastily joined their shipmates on the lighter.

All eyes were fixed on the captain. We were now in peril from two sources: fire and our old nemesis, "friendly" fire.

A flicker of annoyance crossed George's face. He was a man who didn't like to lose. Then he put on his impassive mask of command.

"Secure all fire-fighting operations," he said in a pleasant voice. "Let's haul ass with Halsey."

As we got under way with the lighter alongside, Miller grinned down at the sweaty, apprehensive sailors in blackface clustered on its lee side.

"Hey, you merchant sailors," he bawled. "Don't forget to put in for your hazardous-duty pay!"

Looking back as *Pawnee* moved slowly toward Lunga Roads, I could see that the Liberty was ablaze from the forward 3-inch gun to the midships house. Fresh explosions from the DE's methodical fire put her well down by the head. Great masses of hissing steam rose as fire met water.

The *Couch* began a long, shallow death dive, her prow pointed toward the palm groves of Guadalcanal. Very soon only her after mast and cargo boom were visible. Then she gave a convulsive lurch and was gone, leaving a boiling cauldron of bubbles and circling flotsam to mark her resting place.

The death of a ship is a sobering experience for any sailor. So long as she remains afloat, he can fancy himself master of that thin, bright rind of water upon which he skates. When she plunges into the dark, alien depths below, he knows he has lost his authority and he feels humbled and afraid.

We had lost the *John H. Couch*. She rested on the coral bottom under a few fathoms off Koli Point. Soon the coral polyps would invade her shattered hull, encrusting every surface with a rainbow of brittle limestone. Steel is made by man but coral is made by nature, an aspect of God no theologian had yet explained to my satisfaction. Another of nature's creations, the mindless fish, would now claim the compartments man had thought were his. Man didn't really own anything, I thought as I toyed with a cup of coffee in the mess hall: not the land, not the air and especially not the sea. Only in his arrogance could he imagine that he did. It was all on loan from nature and would all be reclaimed by nature in her own good time. Just as she had reclaimed the *John H. Couch*.

The date was 12 October 1943. It was an anniversary of a sort. On 12 October 1940 I had reported on board the U.S.S. *California* at Pearl Harbor. On 12 October 1941 I had steamed under the Golden Gate Bridge in that great gray battleship for "strength through love in the States." A year later I was again in San Francisco but waiting for a new ship. My old one had just been raised from the silted bottom of Pearl Harbor and rested in dry dock, oil-smeared, patched and pathetic. Today, Guadalcanal in the *Pawnee*. A year from today, where would I be? Quite possibly with the *John H. Couch* in the cold and loveless embrace of the sea. Considering the frequent communication foulups in the Solomons, if the Imperial Japanese Navy didn't get me, my own might.

Dick Garrett, the muscular black officers' cook, came into the mess hall.

"Hey, Ted," he said. "Let's go a few rounds."

"Okay, Dick," I agreed. "Get the gloves and I'll meet you on the fantail."

Sparring with Garrett, a former Golden Gloves lightheavyweight boxer from Philadelphia, meant that I would spend most of each round slipping and ducking whistling left hooks and straight rights and trying to counterpunch at close quarters. I didn't worry about losing face in front of my shipmates. I was giving away nearly fifty pounds and years of experience. I wasn't concerned about getting hurt, either, only stung. Dick was a fine fellow and a good sportsman who didn't take undue advantage of his size and skills.

In the Solomons, it seemed to me, almost any kind of action was preferable to introspection.

Chapter Eight

EMPRESS AUGUSTA BAY:
SOLOMONS FAREWELL

"Hey, Ted, you heard the latest scuttlebutt?"

I looked up from the motor-generators I was servicing in the lower level of the engine room. My good friend C. J. Aronis was standing beside the dismantled No. 4 diesel, a serious look on his face.

I grinned. "Why do you think I'm down here in motor-mac heaven?" For the past week, the *Pawnee* had been moored starboard side to the hoary repair ship *Prometheus* at Ile Nou in Noumea Harbor. After five months of continuous operations in the Solomons, our always temperamental main engines had been driven to the point of insurrection. Now they were being overhauled by diesel technicians from the *Prometheus*.

"Well, what's the straight scoop, old buddy?"

"Here it is, Ronnie. The old man called me into his cabin last night and laid out his operations plan. He's heading directly for the Philippines. If the rest of Halsey's Navy wants to tag along, okay."

But Aronis wasn't in the mood for my black humor. "No kidding, Ted. I hear we're heading north soon in a big hairy invasion. You know where we're going?"

It so happened that I did. Chief Proctor had passed the word along to me as a way of ensuring that our radio equipment was in the best possible condition. The three motor-generators I was working on provided power for our receivers and TBL transmitter. Without them, the *Pawnee* would be playing the naval equivalent of blindman's buff. Since the chief had neglected to swear me to secrecy, I saw no reason to keep the "straight scoop" from trusted friends like Ronnie. The Navy was entirely too secretive with its enlisted crews. The men who were going to be sticking their necks out deserved to know the truth.

"You ever hear of an island called Bougainville?"

Aronis thought about it. "That's way to hell north, clear beyond the Slot, isn't it?"

"Just as far north as you can go and still be in the Solomons. In fact, it's only about two hundred miles from the big Jap base at Rabaul. We're going to hit Bougainville—but keep it to yourself, Ronnie."

He grinned wolfishly. Being in the rear area made Aronis nervous, and he spent most of his time fussing over our machine guns. Earnest and resolute, he longed for action, not to win medals and glory but so "we can get this shit over with and go home." He was, in truth, precisely the kind of young man America had always depended upon to win its wars after the politicians and diplomats had failed to keep the peace.

I didn't exactly share Ronnie's enthusiasm. Pearl Harbor had made me a reluctant realist. One could look at a map of the Pacific and quickly determine that 58 degrees of latitude and 27 of longitude yawned between Noumea and Tokyo. After Bougainville we would invade another island of the thousands in the Western Pacific. And another and another. Near one of them, inevitably, *Pawnee*'s auspicious star would blink out.

The luck, she has been very good, I thought. So far. Still, our eight months in the South Pacific already had exacted their price.

Even before our move to the Solomons, a seaman first and an electrician's mate third had been transferred to the hospital ship at Noumea, one for "mental observation" and the other for "asthma." The opinion of many crewmen was that they were suffering from combat fatigue before they ever saw combat. I thought that was too easy a judgment. While I knew little about emotional disorders, I had an acquaintance with anxiety and fear. Too much of the latter could easily result in the former. But I also understood why my shipmates seemed to lack compassion. It was a virtue they could not afford.

On our first round trip to the Solomons, the Henderson Field air raid of 18 May had taken a once-valorous petty officer over that tenuous line that segregates the fit from the unfit, the survivors from the casualties. A week later, our young Filipino steward's mate developed war-neurosis symptoms of a more direct kind. Arming himself with a butcher knife in the wardroom pantry, he headed aft, brandishing his weapon and screaming in Tagalog. His meaning was clear, even if his language wasn't. As he raced through the mess hall, one of the ship's cooks stepped from the galley and landed an overhand right behind his ear. The steward's mate dropped as if he had been shot.

There being no hospital ship at Espiritu Santo, the man was transferred to the destroyer tender *Dixie* for safekeeping. He would be perfectly safe in the *Dixie*, even if his shipmates weren't, according to one South Pacific humorist. The tender had been anchored in Segond Channel for so long that she was high and dry on an artificial reef of garbage and beer cans.

A fortnight later one of our seaman-second plank owners was transferred off, apparently for reasons of morale—although some wondered whose morale was being served. He had got into a fight with a black steward's mate I shall call Jackson. A Southerner and a staunch racist, the deckhand found it offensive to share the forward crew's compartment with "niggers."

While the Navy was still totally segregated, it was not possible to provide separate quarters for the officers' cooks and steward's mates in a ship as small and congested as the *Pawnee*. They were lodged in the cul-de-sac formed by the ladder up to the main deck, the forward transverse bulkhead and the portside shell plating. A bank of lockers provided for the further isolation of these third-class Navy citizens, who were virtually ignored by most of the crew. Only the bland, worldly Arsenio Albano, a veteran of the San Francisco restaurant scene, was allowed to sit in on the poker games and otherwise fraternize with the white enlisted men.

Dick Garrett, the boxer, was a Navy regular who understood the system and operated within it. He was given a measure of respect, partly because he made no waves and partly because he would have been a formidable opponent for anyone. Greatly to Bill Miller's credit, risking as he did the disapproval of some shipmates, he voluntarily occupied one of the bunks closest to the cul-de-sac and often carried on friendly conversations with Garrett and the other occupants.

But even he had trouble communicating with Jackson. The steward's mate was tall, thin and very black, with a small head and a pendulous lower lip. He looked like Stepin Fetchit, the film comedian whose specialties were mouthing "Yassuh, Boss!", looking foolish and sprinting past graveyards—the very caricature of an illiterate black Southern sharecropper. Jackson lived in constant terror of his two enemies, one recent and one lifelong—the Japanese, and the whites of the nearly all-white crew. He literally oozed fear from every pore. His life on board the *Pawnee* must have been a purgatory, eased only by Garrett's solicitude and protection.

One day he had the misfortune to find himself alone and friendless in the crew's quarters. The Southerner mimicked his dialect, commented unfavorably upon his appearance and I.Q., and taunted him with racial epithets. Goaded beyond endurance, Jackson retaliated with some choice invective centering on the seaman's relations with his mother, and the fight was on. The assistant master-at-arms broke it up and put both men on report. They were given a stern lecture by George at captain's mast and many hours of extra duty. Within ten days, the Southerner was on his way to the Advance Base, New Hebrides, where the only blacks were the native Melanesians.

"It's obvious that a foulball steward's mate rates higher in this ship than a Rebel seaman second," Aposhian commented. "It's a matter of priorities. Who the hell would wait tables and swab out the officers' heads?"

In September our plank-owner chief quartermaster was transferred to the States, probably for the commission Captain Frank had recommended months before. There were few long faces when Earl Clark went over the side. A taut, cold careerist, he was unpopular even in the CPO quarters. Like all too many senior petty officers I had observed in two battleships, his concept of leadership seemed limited to threat and reprisal. We had conveniently forgotten that it was Earl Clark who passed the cool, crisp orders from the flying bridge which had saved all our lives off Rendova.

Several other chiefs and senior firsts, all Regular Navy and some survivors of the *Yorktown*, were no longer with us. Their orders for the States would arrive at Santo or Tulagi or the Russells in the arcane fashion of Navy personnel transfers. Then they would empty their lockers, pack their bags, shake hands with their friends and leave the ship. Junior petty officers would assume their responsibilities and the daily routine would continue with scarcely a pause.

I had a theory that some of these 30-year men may have adroitly stage-managed their transfers through peacetime connections and the cooperation of the exec. Operating in the Solomons under a skipper who seemed determined to go "in harm's way," the *Pawnee* hardly qualified as good duty. What was the advantage of making warrant or jaygee if one didn't survive to enjoy the privileges of rank?

Bill Miller, who had suffered his share of abuse from the chief quartermaster but who still planned to make the Navy a career, had a kinder explanation. He said the detailers realized they had made a mistake in assigning survivors of carriers sunk during the Coral Sea and Midway Battles to a ship like *Pawnee* in the forward areas and were bringing them back to the States for months of easy precommissioning duty. His theory made sense if one assumed the anonymous detailers gave a damn. I remembered the *California*. After she was sunk at Pearl Harbor, Secretary of the Navy Frank Knox allegedly instructed the Bureau of Navigation to give the crewmen their choice of duty. Instead, hundreds of them were shipped off to the heavy cruisers. Many went down with the *Quincy*, *Vincennes* and *Astoria* at Savo Island and the *Chicago* in the Santa Cruz Islands.

In the case of O. P. Spann, a motor-mac second, there was no doubt whatsoever about his transfer. In the tropics the heat generated by the four big diesels made the engine room nearly untenable, even when all the exhaust blowers were running. At sea under Materiel Condition Baker, temperatures hovered around 110° F. With the ship "buttoned up" in Condition Afirm at battle stations, they soared to 125° F. or above.

Doyle Saxon, a freckle-faced Tennessean whom I had first noticed at Treasure Island because of his skill on the mandolin, drew on his readings in comparative religion to describe duty in the engine room. "It is," he said with his customary good cheer, "like being consigned to the sixth circle of Hell."

No sooner had we crossed the Equator the past January when Spann passed out on watch and had to be treated for heat prostration. After that, his visits to Sick Bay had been frequent. Before our invasion of the New Georgias, it became obvious that Spann was risking his life every time he pulled an engine-room watch under way. He was transferred to shore duty in the New Hebrides.

About the same time, another transfer had a profound effect on my future. *Pawnee* received orders to send one qualified crewman to San Diego for Officers' Candidate School. As a Pearl Harbor veteran, former flag radioman in a battleship, and first-class petty officer known to be preparing for college on my own time, I had to be considered for this coveted assignment. I was passed over in favor of a personable young soundman third class named Norman Hilburn.

One of the officers with whom I had a good rapport was delegated to give me an explanation. Until ordered to stop fraternizing with enlisted men, Ensign E. E. Willson had often dropped by the radio shack for nostalgic conversations about girls, parties and school days. He had grown up in Stockton, not far from my home town, and was a graduate of the College of the Pacific in that city.

"We know you're the one who should have gone," Willson said with a rueful smile. "But you're also a damn good radioman. Chief Proctor will be leaving one of these days, and we just can't afford to lose you."

If I had been sitting in the wardroom, I had to admit that I probably would have agreed with the decision. A soundman third could be replaced easily, but a radioman first who had been in combat could not. The welfare of the ship had to take precedence over that of one man.

The repair ship to which we were moored met the enlisted men's definition of a true "rust bucket." The *Prometheus* had been commissioned at Mare Island Navy Yard in 1910 as a fleet collier (coal carrier). Converted from a coal-burner to oil and fitted out as a repair ship in 1913–14, she had spent most of her life in the Reserve Fleet at Bremerton. Obviously, she considered herself too old for recall to the service, for she creaked and groaned in the wake of every passing ship, as if afflicted with terminal arthritis. How she ever made the South Pacific with floating dry dock ARD-2 in tow on her balky reciprocating-steam engines was a mystery even to her crew. But every night she screened open-air movies of later releases and better print quality than the ones we received in the Solomons. Some of the *Pawnee* crew went on a veritable movie binge.

Most of the films were pure escape fare, approaching the ways of lads and lasses with a song, a leer and a double entendre. In this category were *Lady of Burlesque*, starring Barbara Stanwyck; *The Cat and the Canary*, with Bob Hope playing his customary brash and lascivious coward opposite Paulette Goddard; *Coney Island*, featuring Betty Grable, George Montgomery and Cesar Romero; and *Alexander's Ragtime Band*, with Alice Faye, Tyrone Power and Don Ameche. The blonde Miss Grable was a special favorite of servicemen. She looked like a glamorized version of everyman's girl next door, and she acted as if she might be available. Her famous pin-up photo, displaying her trim derriere and "million dollar legs," was taped inside many a locker door. Personally, I thought she was a trifle coarse. I preferred the equally blonde Miss Faye, who looked and acted like a lady. Perhaps I was prejudiced; she reminded me of my ex-fiancée.

A few films, invariably solemn and inspirational, fell into the biographical genre. We saw *Young Tom Edison*, with Mr. Ameche and Mickey Rooney; *Pride of the Yankees*, with Gary Cooper playing Lou Gehrig, the great first baseman who had died in 1941 of a wasting disease; and *Knute Rockne, All-American*. The famous coach of the Notre Dame "Fighting Irish," killed in a 1931 plane crash, was born in Norway and was not even a Catholic—facts well known to me from daily reading of the San Francisco *Chronicle* "green sheet" as a youngster. The studio moguls solved this casting problem by giving the role to Pat O'Brien, the professional Irishman.

Occasionally, Hollywood roused itself from its dream world to produce a war film with a message. The point was driven home with the heavy-handed finesse of circus roustabouts pounding in the stakes for the "big top." *Mrs. Miniver* waded its sticky way through a sea of broad-A treacle. Apparently there would always be an England to stand gallantly against the Huns while Mr. Miniver sailed off to rescue the troops from a place called Dunkirk and Mrs. Miniver smiled bravely and tended her rose garden.

"Yeah, there'll always be an England," Gerber gibed. "Just as damn long as there's one American left to finish her wars!"

Casablanca was another film where the Musketeers dissented from the general approval. The story of refugees, agents and Nazis in Vichy French territory seemed contrived as slick war propaganda; the characters were mere stick figures, cartoons of real people. The scene where Humphrey Bogart indulged himself in an orgy of boozy self-pity while Dooley Wilson crooned "As Time Goes By" was painful to watch.

"God damn," Gerber shouted. "This guy ought to see a head-shrinker!"

"It's easy to see that the problems of three little people don't amount to a hill of beans in this crazy world," Bogart said as he sent Ingrid Bergman off to do her duty at the denouement. It was not difficult to extract a moral from this fake dialogue: in wartime it is necessary for the "little people" to sacrifice themselves to the common good. We doubted that our ruthless Axis enemies would find any fault with this preachment.

While we were still tied up to the *Prometheus*, a destroyer moored to our port side. I paid no attention. Even in the rear area, our heavy work schedules left little time or energy for intership socializing. So I was surprised when a seaman came looking for me one morning while I was making the latest corrections to the communications manual.

"Hey, Mason, you're wanted on the fantail. Something about a boxing match with that tin can next door."

As I went by the galley I spotted Garrett. He was teaching our cooks something about food preparation, I hoped. "Dick, some guys want to arrange a little boxing exhibition. Why don't you join me?"

We found a delegation of three sailors from the destroyer. Their leader was short, stocky and swarthy. His sharp, nasal accent told me immediately he was from New York. He was, he said, a former Golden Gloves "champeen" and was looking for a little competition.

"You got anyone around featherweight, lightweight who's pretty good? Maybe boxed in the amachoors?"

Garrett smiled thinly. "Yeah, we got someone."

"His name is George Tahbone," I said. "He's from Oklahoma but I think he made it to Golden Gloves in Chicago." I didn't mention he had gone to the finals in Chicago. "Of course, he's out of shape," I added disarmingly. "We've been in the Solomons. But I'm sure he'll go for a little workout with the 12-ounce gloves."

The delegation exchanged satisfied smiles. So did Garrett and I. With the quick agreement of Tahbone and Captain George, the match was arranged for late afternoon.

After supper most of the crew gathered on the fantail. The destroyermen found points of vantage on their fantail and after gun mounts. George appeared and briskly cleared an area roughly 10 feet square for the ring.

"Sit on that bitt, Ted," he said. "You'll be a ringpost." He would referee and keep time from another bitt. "Now if Tahbone can't defend the honor of the *Pawnee* against this Dead End Kid, you're up next."

"You bet!" I said. Then I remembered myself. "Aye, aye, sir!"

I showed more confidence than I actually felt. If Tahbone wasn't good enough, I certainly wasn't. I planned to study the style of this "amachoor champeen" and map a strategy that would keep me from disgracing myself and my ship.

My concern proved baseless. The destroyer sailor charged out when George called time, throwing left jabs and hooks and overhand rights. But Tahbone, as I had long since learned, was a counterpuncher. He slipped some blows and parried others, stepped inside his opponent's extended arms and landed short, jolting punches to his now unprotected head and body.

Beyond a couple of softball games in the Russells, the *Pawnee* crew for months had had little to shout about. They shouted now as the New Yorker gave ground, obviously surprised. He returned to the attack, only to be stung by another series of perfectly executed counters. The captain never had to move from his bitt. Occasionally he would order "break" when one of the swarthy boxer's lunges carried him into a clinch with Tahbone, and the two would step back obediently.

By the second round, the exhibition began to assume the aspects of a bullfight. The New Yorker charged straight ahead, pawing the air with his gloves. Our shipmate, standing erect and unblinking, a faint cruel smile on his gladiator's face, let the punches whiz by within an inch or two of his head and responded with tattoos of gloved fists: one-one-two, left-left-right. Soon blood was trickling from one nostril of his *toro*; his skin was disfigured with reddish blotches. Like the bull, he seemed too dull-witted to change his tactics. The only way to box the Oklahoman was to force him to lead, taking a few blows to get inside the combat zone. One simply couldn't give him punching room.

Captain George was enjoying the spectacle no less than his crew. He let it go into a fourth round of punishment. Tahbone landed a whistling right cross to the jaw, perfectly timed and accompanied by a noisy exhalation of air. His opponent went down, shook his head and got up slowly. "A slip," he muttered.

"Clean knockdown," the captain ruled. "Resume boxing." But for the 12-ounce "pillows," the match would have ended in a knockout.

George and I were the first to reach Tahbone before he was engulfed by a mob of happy shipmates. "Well done, Tahbone," the skipper said.

"That was a beautiful job of boxing, George," I said, hugging him. "You took him apart and put him back together again. You were really good."

Tahbone smiled shyly. "Not quite good enough to win at Chicago," he said modestly. "Maybe after the war . . . "

Dick Garrett approached the defeated boxer and his silent entourage. "Say, men," he said, "we've got several other boxers aboard. Mason here and Gerber over there and me. Maybe we can arrange some more matches."

"Yeah, sure," one of them said. "We'll be in touch." It was apparent they wanted nothing to do with the *Pawnee* boxers after the humiliating defeat of their "champeen."

As we tested our rebuilt engines and made preparations for leaving Noumea, the men were in a cheerful, even playful mood. They had been buoyed up by Tahbone's victory in the impromptu smoker despite the rumors, now shipwide, of the Bougainville operation. Our captain was a damn fine leader, I reflected. When action was indicated, as in the boxing match, he played an active role and earned the respect of the crew. Where inaction was advisable, as in my near-altercation with the junior officer at the softball game, he earned the crew's respect by not interfering. Whatever he did, I was sure, was with the single objective of molding the *Pawnee* crew into an efficient, cohesive and valiant unit. Despite the fact he had probably cast the deciding vote to keep me aboard and send the soundman to OCS, I devoutly hoped that there were many more like him in the Navy.

On the morning of 1 November, the reinforced Third Marine Division stormed ashore at Cape Torokina, Empress Augusta Bay, on the southwest coast of Bougainville. In the face of determined enemy resistance, we learned from odds and ends of scuttlebutt, 14,000 men and more than 6,000 tons of supplies were landed before nightfall.

Faced with the loss of their last important bastion in the Solomons and the subsequent outflanking of New Britain and New Ireland in the Bismarck Archipelago, the Japanese sent two heavy and two light cruisers and six destroyers toward Cape Torokina to break up the landings. They were intercepted in the early hours of 2 November by the four light cruisers and eight destroyers of Admiral A. S. ("Tip") Merrill's Task Force 39. In the resulting Battle of Empress Augusta Bay, Admiral Sentaro Omori's force was turned back with the loss of light cruiser *Sendai* and destroyer *Hatsukaze* and damage to several other ships. On our side, the cruiser *Denver* and destroyer *Spence* received minor shellfire damage and destroyer *Foote* lost her stern to an enemy torpedo.

Pawnee's sister ships *Apache* and *Sioux* served as the salvage group for both the III Amphib invasion force of troop transports and Task Force 39.

Sioux took over the tow of the *Foote* from destroyer *Claxton* and brought her safely into Purvis Bay on 4 November.

"Well, whaddaya know," was the reaction when this intelligence reached our mess hall. "The Navy finally found out we're not the only AT in the South Pacific." We were celebrating the *Pawnee's* first birthday with a festive dinner of roast turkey, candied yams, fruit salad and mince pie. We had almost as much cause for a Thanksgiving as the Plymouth Colony did in 1621. The Pilgrims had survived their first year in savage New England—and we had just survived our first year in the savage Pacific.

Perhaps it was a premonition, the sixth sense which men who live with danger sometimes develop, that awakened me. Or perhaps it was only the moon shining on my face. I sat up on my mattress of lifejackets and looked at my watch. It was 0315 on the morning of 17 November 1943. All around me were the ships of Task Group 31.6, a reinforcement echelon for the Marines at Cape Torokina.

I got a cup of coffee from the galley and went up two ladders to the bridge. The convoy was steaming across a dead-calm sea under a radiant, nearly full moon. In the center were eight LSTs in three columns, encircled by a shield of eight destroyer-transports. On the flanks of the formation, five destroyers provided an outer screen. In the van, six or seven miles ahead, destroyer *Saufley* was formation guide. *Pawnee* was the last ship in the center column of "large slow targets."

Bill Miller had the quartermaster watch. "Look at that goddam moon," he said. "What a time for a night torpedo attack."

I nodded. "Where the hell are we?"

"Twenty-five miles due west of Cape Torokina."

"Any of our night fighters around?" I asked hopefully.

"Should be some operating from Barakoma to cover our perimeter, but I sure haven't seen 'em," Miller replied.

What we did see, very shortly, was a bursting white light that painted the convoy in a cold and ghostly radiance.

"Holy smoke!" Miller exclaimed. "Why do I have to be right all the time?" Turning to the OOD he snapped, "Permission to sound general quarters, Mr. Willson?"

Some of our deck officers were fearful of making a decision without the captain's approval. This one didn't hesitate. "Permission granted."

Before the words were out of his mouth, Miller was pushing the button that activated the G.Q. klaxon. I dashed down the ladder to the radio shack. Using the advantage of being wide awake, I soon had Proctor's permission to observe the drama from the boat deck rail.

Several Betty torpedo-bombers were boring in from astern at low altitude. The lead plane peeled off in a dive toward the *Pringle*, the screening destroyer off *Pawnee*'s port quarter. Not a ship had opened fire as yet. But one of those unaccountable fortunes of war saved the *Pringle*. Instead of leveling off for its torpedo run, the Betty continued in a twisting dive and plunged into the sea just off the destroyer's bow in a tumbling cascade of white water.

The Japanese pilots were not as good as they had been. Or else the planes weren't. "Praise the Lord and pass the ammunition," I intoned.

The second Betty made a wide turn around the convoy's flank and approached from our port bow. The destroyer *Conway* and three LSTs opened fire with their 20-mm. and 40-mm. batteries. No order to shoot was passed from our bridge—a prudent decision since *Pawnee*'s range was fouled by several ships. Boring in through a fussilade of tracers, the plane dropped two torpedoes, was hit, reeled out of control and burst into flames. Plowing a furrow of ocean with one wing, it cartwheeled and sank almost at once.

The torpedoes launched by men now dead passed through the boisterous wake of destroyer *Renshaw* and twenty yards ahead of the leading LSTs. By that margin the outboard one escaped the fate of *LST-342*, "the nightmare 'T'," at Oloana Bay.

The Bettys were indeed "flying coffins," I thought, and the men who flew them were brave to the point of foolhardiness. When the Americans or English performed rash deeds, we celebrated them with poems like "The Charge of the Light Brigade" or the posthumous Medal of Honor. When the enemy sacrificed himself, we called it "Oriental fanaticism." Perhaps raw courage always contains an element of fanaticism.

Approaching again from the left flank, the third Betty changed its tactics. It crossed over our formation astern of the *Pawnee*, flying very low and offering only an intermittent and difficult target, and aimed itself at the starboard side of the last ship in the column, the destroyer-transport *McKean*.

Hit by gunfire from the *McKean*, the Betty's unprotected gasoline tanks flared up. The plane fell into the sea in a consuming orange fireball. But again the scorpion had struck with its deadly stinger, and this time it did not miss. The torpedo detonated well aft, setting off a secondary explosion and a fire that sent up a tall plume of oily black smoke. From across the water came the thin Banshee wail of the *McKean*'s siren—a signal of doom for the brittle old converted four-stacker.

As *Pawnee* moved toward Empress Augusta Bay with the rest of the formation, the destroyer *Sigourney* and destroyer-transport *Talbot* were detached to pick up survivors. The five or six remaining Bettys swooped to attack the three ships but were driven off again and again by well-directed gunfire that splashed two more planes.

By 0430, *McKean* had gone down stern first, and even the smoke was drifting and dissipating above her watery tomb. Since she had been transporting a company of Marines, there was little doubt that many men had perished with her.*

When I stepped out onto the boat deck after breakfast, I found the *Pawnee* under way at slow ahead in the open roadstead of Empress Augusta Bay. The body of water named for the consort of German Kaiser Wilhelm was a large, semicircular indentation in the coastline, anchored by Cape Torokina just to my left and the jutting thumb of Mutupina Point 15 miles south. Overhead, cumulus clouds puffed themselves up into fanciful shapes of beasts and men, just as they had when I daydreamed the hours away from a fishing pier on Monterey Bay during my summer vacations. But one look toward shore reminded me sharply that I was a long way from Santa Cruz.

Tropical rain forest so dense that it seemed a solid mass of interwoven roots and boles and branches began at the very edge of the black sand beaches. Passing swamps and lagoons, it climbed foothills and arêtes to the peaks of a mountain range that formed the spine of the island. Off the port bow, a mighty volcano in the rhomboid shape of the Bent Pyramid of Egypt rose up nearly 9,000 feet high. Against the still-lingering colors of a salmon sunrise, the mountain was emitting a column of gray smoke that drifted northwest with the prevailing winds.

For a moment I wondered whether Bougainville and Mount Bagana were real, or only figments of an imagination fevered by too many midwatches and too many nights up Blanche Channel. They looked almost two-dimensional, like a painted backdrop for the greatest Cecil B. DeMille epic ever filmed. Except that no landscape artist could possible capture the untamed sweep and majesty of this scene. The physical details, perhaps,

---

* In an unaccountable failure of discipline, some of the Marines began jumping overboard before the abandon-ship order was passed. Most of them burned to death in flaming oil from ruptured fuel tanks. According to Morison (Vol. VI, p. 351), 52 of the Marines embarked were lost, along with 64 *McKean* crewmen in what the Japanese called the "Fifth Air Battle of Bougainville."

but not the immensity nor the intimations of death sudden and violent that clung to it. These fetid mangrove swamps and clammy jungles concealed 40,000 Japanese soldiers and 20,000 sailors. Even as I looked toward them, many were looking toward the *Pawnee* and the other ships of Task Group 31.6 with loathing and fear. And with the hope of our annihilation, for through the cloud-smudged skies over this incredible island their "sea eagles" would surely come.

They did, at about 1000 hours. The blaring alarm sent me double-timing to the radio shack. With a lurch and a roar of engines, *Pawnee* increased speed and heeled over in a 90-degree turn. We were heading for deeper water, away from the many uncharted shoals near the landing grounds. At the port rail outside the captain's cabin, Aronis was checking the action of his .50-caliber machine gun. I punched him lightly on the shoulder as I passed by.

"Give 'em hell, Ronnie," I said.

"I'm ready, buddy," he said grimly.

Chief Proctor left me in charge of radio communications and departed for the bridge.

"The chief missed his calling," Howard Murphy observed sardonically. "He should have been a war correspondent."

"He's practicing up for the States," I said, partly to relieve the growing tension. "He'll be sashaying around with all his ribbons and battle stars, giving interviews to the Florida newspapers."

Now every gun in the *Pawnee* opened up on the enemy planes. I could distinguish the loud staccato of the .30- and .50-caliber machine guns and the whump-whump-whump of the four 20-mm. Oerlikons, overridden at short intervals by the sharp, barking report of our 3-inch rifle. At the receiver, See turned up the gain and hunched forward in concentration on the Fox sked transmission.

Leaning close to his ear phones, I could hear the faint signal from NPM, roiled now and again with bursts of static. "Are you reading okay?" I shouted above the din.

See gave a V-for-victory sign. The air attack swirled above us, but we could not see it and were powerless to influence its course. Our lives were in the hands of the captain and our shipmates manning the guns. Once again, as had happened so often in the Solomons, we must endure those endless claustrophobic minutes that tested a sailor's resolution. Death was overhead and could strike at any moment, just as it had struck at the crewmen and Marines in the *McKean* a few hours ago.

I thought about the damage a bomb would wreak on the tiny radio compartment and its occupants. We would be shoveled out in bloody pieces of unidentifiable flesh and organ and bone, just as Ortalano's working party had disposed of the dead of *LST-342* off Vangunu. You are getting morbid, Mason, I told myself sternly. You are supposed to be a leader like the late Chief Radioman Thomas J. Reeves of the *California* had been.

I forced a smile. "Say, we should be getting an action report from our war correspondent any time now," I told the other radiomen.

Fortuitously, the tempo of the aerial battle slackened and fell off to a few isolated bursts of gunfire. The door opened and Proctor came in, flushed with excitement.

"It was a hell of a show, men," he exclaimed, removing his helmet and lighting a cigarette. "Aronis got one of theirs, but the other gunners got one of ours!"

As Proctor recounted the events of the air raid, I had to admit that he did possess the instincts of a reporter. "Condition Red" sent all twenty-two ships of the task group maneuvering independently in the spacious waters of Empress Augusta Bay. When the Bettys, Val dive-bombers and escorting Zeros approached the roadstead, they were "tallyhoed" by the Corsairs of Air Solomons. Those that broke through were greeted with shifting curtains of flak and geysers of tracer bullets. Some of the Corsairs recklessly followed the bandits right through the A.A. fire of *Pawnee* and other ships. One fighter in hot pursuit of a Zero crossed the *Pawnee*'s bow from port to starboard at low altitude and point-blank range. The Corsair intersected the tracers from our bridge 20-mm. guns and a burst from the 3-incher, and nose-dived into the sea. Proctor doubted that the pilot could have survived.

"About then Aronis got a bead on a Betty that was coming in on us. It went down flaming like a haystack!"

At least one other enemy plane was shot down. Disconcerted by the fierce resistance, the Japanese airmen did not score a single bomb or torpedo hit. Soon, landing craft were again ferrying guns, ammunition and food from the LSTs to the Marine beachhead.

When the order to secure from general quarters was passed, I hurried toward the portside weather passage. Aronis was coming through the door, an exultant grin on his face.

"Good shooting, Ronnie. I hear you got one!"

"You're goddam right," he said. "I stitched a row of tracers right into the cockpit!"

We embraced emotionally, as if he had just scored the winning touchdown at a high-school football game. What is football, after all, but a pale imitation of the real thing? The elation was short-lived. All of us, especially the men on the guns, had to deal with the sobering knowledge that we, however inadvertently, had caused the death of a fellow American.

"So far our score is one Jap plane, one U.S. plane," Aposhian reflected at the evening meal. "Ammo is neutral. It doesn't give a shit who it kills."

A few days earlier the new light cruiser *Denver* had received her own baptism of blood. Operating off Empress Augusta Bay with Admiral Merrill's Task Force 39, she had been boxed in by four Bettys and torpedoed in the after engine room, with casualties of twenty dead and eleven wounded. Our sister ship *Sioux* was called up to tow the *Denver* to Purvis Bay.

Arriving at Purvis with the rest of the transport group on 20 November, we watched George heading for the beach in the whaleboat and predicted we would be returning to Bougainville soon with another convoy. But the *Sioux* drew this onerous assignment. We were ordered to take the *Denver* to Espiritu Santo. Following temporary repairs there, the cruiser was scheduled for a five-month "vacation" at Mare Island.

When we put grim, scabrous Guadalcanal on our starboard quarter, the listing *Denver* astern on 1200 feet of 2-inch tow wire, it was in a sense our farewell to the Solomons. We would return a number of times, either on routine assignments or passing through for operations to the north, but the Solomons Campaign had been won. Now, only mopping up remained.

In sixteen months, American forces had occupied the Solomon Islands and now threatened enemy strongholds in the Bismarck Archipelago. It had been one of the most savage and bitter campaigns in U.S. history, waged under incredibly primitive conditions. For half that time, the *Pawnee* had been there and had played her small but important role with distinction.

Behind us we left thousands of our own dead. They had been blasted by bomb and torpedo and gunfire, burned or suffocated in sealed compartments, scalded to death by pressurized steam, drowned or eaten by sharks. A Navy ship in wartime presents an infinite variety of ways to die, few of them glorious, most agonizing and untidy.

The hulks of our ships—carriers, heavy and light cruisers, destroyers, transports, freighters and one of *Pawnee*'s sisters—littered the bottoms of bays and sounds, or lay broken in the abysses of the deep ocean.

The reputations of some admirals, captains and commanders lay there, too, never to be salvaged by history. They had been tried in the Court of War, their chosen profession, and had been found guilty of want of skill, want of preparation and, in a very few cases, want of that most fundamental requisite of a naval officer: valor. But others, the resolute and bold and ambitious ones like Halsey, Moosbrugger and Burke, had found the Slot a pathway to fame and glory.

Despite "kicking our ass" in night combat on numerous occasions, the enemy had suffered far more grievously. The Japanese, brave and tough and merciless foes, had been sacrificed too often by incompetent leaders. Instead of sweeping us out of the Solomons in late 1942 with their much stronger fleet, their admirals and generals had arrogantly underestimated American capabilities and resolution. They had committed their ships, planes and men piecemeal, only to see them chewed up through attrition. They still might have prevailed, but we could replace our losses and they could not.

The slow and lightly armed *Pawnee* had led a charmed life. She had had a superb commanding officer. He had been given the time and the hazardous assignments that together had coalesced some ninety-five men, gathered at random from all backgrounds and all parts of the nation, into a spirited ship's company. Luck and skillful handling (and, perhaps, the notoriously defective American torpedoes) had spared us off Rendova. At other times, the enemy had saved his ammunition for bigger game, or had missed us, as in the Russell Islands, or had been foiled in the last seconds, as in Blanche Channel.

My performance had, I hoped, been up to the standards of the service. Always I had remembered Tom Gilbert of the *California*, a radio gang protégé sleeping now in the military cemetery at Honolulu, and the promise I had made to his memory: that not one man in my ship would be lost through any dereliction of duty or temporary failure on the part of me or my radio gang. And so far not one man had.

From San Cristobal to Bougainville, death had crouched in waiting, as it did in all the war theaters. But here it assumed an aspect so brutal and alien that King Solomon's Islands might have belonged to another age, or another planet altogether. Here among the jagged coral heads, the dripping rain forests that marched up mountain slopes toward towering thunderheads, the smoke-breathing volcanoes, here under the implacable sun, there was nothing to relate to, nothing to remind one of home. Only the 100,000 ebony-skinned aborigines seemed to have some tenuous identification with the place, and that only as squatters tolerated indifferently by Nature.

Here the vastness of scale reduced man and his engines of destruction to insignificance. Steaming up the Slot against the huge cyclorama of ocean and islands and sky, our warships were plastic toys, our weapons popguns, ourselves Lilliputians led by posturing popinjays. The phosphorescent blue water swallowed our toys, the crawling green jungle quickly covered the scars gouged by our petty disputes, the voracious fauna of both stripped the flesh from the bones of our dead in a wink of time.

Here amid these savage beauties, this bursting chaos of Nature, we and our enemies were the aberration, as out of place as the first man in the first garden. I thanked "whatever gods may be" that I had not died here, where death was so commonplace—and so unmourned. Here the individual counted for no more than a falling leaf; here only life en masse had value. Perhaps the islands were as much a state of mind as an actual location in the South Pacific.

Whatever they were—a gateway to hell, a last paradise, a fall from grace—nothing was ever like the Solomons.

Chapter Nine

STORM FRONTS

"Now ain't that a beautiful sight?"

Gerber, Aposhian and I were lying on the creamy sands of a wide, crescent-shaped beach in the New Hebrides. A mild breeze rustled the fronds of the palm trees in the jungle just behind us. The surf, its force broken by an offshore reef, rolled up with a gentle murmur. On the horizon to the north and south were the sentinel shapes of densely wooded Ile Toutouba and Ile Malo. A few cumulus clouds sailed by in a lapis lazuli sky.

I agreed that this beach on Aore Island made Waikiki look like something hammered together on a back lot for a Jon Hall South Seas movie.

"That ain't exactly what I mean, buddy," Gerber snorted. "Take a look down yonder."

Fifty yards away on the nearly deserted beach I saw something I had not seen for seven months: a white woman. Three white women, to be precise, in bathing suits. They were surrounded by a cordon of six or seven males. One of the women laughed, shook out her blonde hair and ran into the surf, closely followed by three of the men.

We observed this scene with the keen interest of starving men peering through a window at a banquet.

"Navy nurses," I said.

Nurses were considered officers. Hence, they were off-limits to enlisted men. To ensure that they stayed that way, commissioned escorts accompanied them everywhere. We discussed the great pleasure it would give us to rout the palace guard and take over the women. The odds didn't bother us: most of the officers looked older and out of shape.

"It's the damndest operation I've ever seen," Aposhian complained. "The white hats get two cans of beer, if they're lucky. The 'braid' get bourbon and Scotch. We get the Pink House in Noumea. They get the nurses and the Red Cross broads."

"They keep telling us we are defending Mom, apple pie and democracy," I said. "No one mentions we are defending them with one of the most undemocratic organizations in the world—the United States Navy."

"R.H.I.P.," Aposhian agreed. "Rank hath its privileges. In the South Pacific, the rankest seem to have the most privileges."

"By God, they've taken away our booze," Gerber roared. "They've taken away our women. They won't even give us any 'R and R.' We're supposed to live like monks in a monkery!"

"But of course," I said. "The enlisted men are Galahads, pursuing the Holy Grail. I wouldn't mind that so much if the officers applied the same high standards to themselves."

Gerber looked down the beach at the nurses cavorting in the water with their entourage. "Holy Grail, hell," he exclaimed. "What I'd like to be pursuing is right over there."

That was a pursuit which could lead only to a general court-martial. We had to console ourselves with the latest Santo scuttlebutt. One of those uppity Navy nurses had been shipped home in disgrace. Taking advantage of an unparalleled economic opportunity, she had been renting her body for one-hundred dollars per brief encounter. The huge money orders she was sending home aroused the suspicion of a postal clerk—an enlisted man, we were pleased to note—who reported her to his superiors. We hoped the enterprising "officer" was doing well in the States. Maybe she had opened a bordello.

For the past week we had been moored alongside the *Dixie* or anchored in Segond Channel. Our duties were light: retrieving practice torpedoes launched by our TBF Avengers or towing gasoline barges to Pallikulo Bay. On other days we sent half a dozen men to the fleet recreation center on Aore with chits allowing them to purchase two cans of beer at "Duffy's Tavern." Additional chits were available from nondrinkers among the mob of sailors for a dollar or two. By following a jungle trail, liberty-goers also could laze on the beach and admire the nurses from afar, as the Three Musketeers had done. At night we had our choice of movies in the *Dixie* or poker in our messing compartment.

Gambling had long been taboo in Navy ships. But in the SoPac it was tolerated as a necessary evil by successive *Pawnee* skippers when the ship was in port. Unfortunately, we had several "card sharks" in the crew. There were a few habitual winners and many losers. Although I often played, with indifferent results, I really didn't approve of the high-stakes games that left some crewmen broke from one payday to the next.

After it was too late to do anything about it, I learned that three of the winners had acted in collusion. They employed an ingenious system to signal their hands and shared the profits. I was appalled that shipmates would stoop so low. It confirmed my earlier opinion that gambling should have been banned, or confined, at least, to penny-ante limits.

Aposhian, a non-gambler, was less indignant.

"We're talking about a human failing that's universal," he commented. "The cheaters and their 'marks' richly deserve each other. They have one thing in common. Simple goddam greed."

The second anniversary of the attack on Pearl Harbor passed without official notice by our new executive officer-navigator, Lieutenant (junior grade) Warren R. Hughes, a relaxed, easy-going Reserve with a ready smile. We considered him so great an improvement over the taut "Jessie" Lees, who had departed the ship two months before, that we forgave him the oversight. But Papoose Evans and I remembered. (So did survivors John Day of the *Argonne*, flagship of the Base Force, and Bill Miller of the new cargo ship *Castor*.) For an attentive audience of crewmen, Evans and I relived the events of 7 December 1941.

As the proud flagship of the Battle Force, the exemplar of Battleship Navy "spit and polish," the *California* should have been the best prepared of any of the eight capital ships present at Pearl Harbor. Instead, she was the worst prepared. Many of her officers—including her admiral, captain and executive officer—were ashore. Many manhole covers to the voids of the torpedo defensive system were off or not tightly secured because of a pending materiel inspection. With her watertight integrity violated, two torpedo hits she would otherwise have shrugged off with minor flooding sent her to the bottom with heavy casualties. The confusion of her officers had been so great that I abandoned ship three times in one day and Papoose twice.

Joining our ship on the bottom were the battleships *Arizona*, *Oklahoma* and *West Virginia*, the overage battleship *Utah*, which had been converted to a target ship, and the minelayer *Oglala*. Heavily damaged were the *Nevada*, the light cruisers *Helena* and *Raleigh*, the repair ship *Vestal* and the destroyers *Cassin*, *Downes* and *Shaw*. Battleships *Pennsylvania*, *Maryland* and *Tennessee*, light cruiser *Honolulu* and seaplane tender *Curtiss* received lesser damage. Regardless of where the ultimate responsibility lay—with Admiral Kimmel and General Short in Oahu, as some thought, or with President Roosevelt, scheming diabolically to get us involved in a war to save Western Civilization, as others believed—one thing was certain. Pearl Harbor was the most devastating defeat in the history of the United States Navy, one that left its indelible mark on every man who was present.

Two days later, only a few crewmen who dealt with logs and calendars remembered another anniversary. Just a year before, on 9 December 1942, we had taken the newly commissioned *Pawnee* outside the continental limits of the United States, bound for Hawaii and the South Pacific.

When the word was passed in the mess hall, I realized that some sailors were existing in a sort of timeless vacuum. They had adapted so completely to the ship's two stultifying daily routines, one for port and the other for sea, that only the repetitive events of reveille, mealtimes, watches, turn-to for ship's work, knock off and taps had any relevance. Something like that happened, I supposed, to convicts in prison.

"Hell," one seaman said, "I don't even know what month it is, let alone what day." Another thought we had been away much longer than a year. "Christ, it seems like five!" Others wondered if we would return to San Francisco or San Diego before a second anniversary was necessary.

A career bosun's mate observed caustically that there was no reason to send the *Pawnee* stateside. Nowadays, even badly damaged ships were patched up in dry docks at Santo or Noumea so they could proceed to Mare Island or Bremerton under their own power.

"This work boat is going to the Philippines," he said. "When we take the slanteyes, she'll end up in Japan. She may never get back to the States."

"That's right," another career pessimist chimed in. "There are only two ways you V-6s are gonna make the States—get a transfer to new construction or go over the side in a pine box."

If some crewmen were ignoring the passage of time, that implacable adversary was not ignoring them. More than a few had aged noticeably. Long exposure to the tropic sun had etched furrows in foreheads and crow's-feet around eyes. Hairlines were receding; gray hairs were being pulled out and examined with disgust. " 'Darling, I am growing old, / Silver threads among the gold'," Doyle Saxon sang before beating a hasty retreat from the crew's head.

Our months in the Solomons had exacted other, less obvious tolls. Dale Gerber periodically threw up blood. Doc Ortalano gave him some chalky tablets and told him to quit smoking and drinking coffee. Naturally, this advice was rejected.

"Imagine that goddam pill-pusher tellin' me to give up the two things that keep me goin'," Gerber shouted. "He might as well ask me to stop thinkin' about a piece of ass!"

The most startling casualty was Tom Peters of Mississippi, one of our whaleboat and motor-launch coxswains. The fair-haired Peters was about six feet tall and as sturdily built as a wrestler. He looked indestructible, the kind of man who had probably worked as a roughneck on an oil-drilling rig. He was about his duties on the fantail one muggy gray morning in Segond Channel when, without warning, he went into convulsions and was soon on his way to the base hospital at Santo. Although Peters was a serious young man who seldom smiled, he was well liked and respected by the crew. We hoped he was only suffering from heat exhaustion, not an epileptic seizure triggered by our perilous "milk runs" up Blanche Channel and the Slot.

With the arrival of the summer monsoon season, the climate of the New Hebrides declined from barely sufferable to intolerable. The prevailing winds hauled around from southeast to northwest. They brought tumultuous downpours, broken by days of oppressive calms. The calms were worse than the storms, for the slightest physical exertion left one bathed in sweat and struggling to wring oxygen from the saturated air. Out of the swamps came clouds of *Anopheles* mosquitoes.

We were anxious to depart this pernicious place, a breeding ground for malaria, dengue fever, dysentery, tuberculosis, poliomyelitis, yaws and even leprosy. Scuttlebutt had us going to Noumea for the long-delayed installation of a search radar and a battery of 40-mm. Swedish Bofors A.A. guns. But Comseronsopac (the Navy acronym for Commander Service Squadron, South Pacific) had a better idea. He ordered us to tow YOG-42, a 10,000-barrel gasoline barge, to the Treasury Islands just south of Bougainville.

C. J. Aronis smiled wolfishly and got to work on his machine guns. The two islands that form the Treasuries, Mono and Stirling, had been occupied on 27 October by 6,300 troops, mostly New Zealanders. A PT base had been established and the Seabees were hacking out an airstrip, but the islands were not yet suitable for picnics and moonlight swimming parties.

As we approached Blanche Harbor, the channel between Mono and Stirling, in the early morning hours of 18 December, a Japanese snooper dropped a yellow flare off our port quarter and we scrambled to battle stations. But no attack developed. By that afternoon we had anchored YOG-42 and were headed south past Vella Lavella, Ganongga and Simbo Islands.

We hoped we were going far south: Sydney, for example. The natural beauty of the Treasuries was wasted on our jaundiced eyes. By now we had seen the tops of too many drowned volcanoes, smelled the rotting vegetation of too many verdant islands, dropped anchor in too many iron-bottomed bays. The very name that the captain of H.M.S. *Blanche* had given the picturesque harbor was anathema to us.

"If I had a woman named Blanche, which thank God I don't," Bill Bowser said with a steely grin, "I'd make her change her name—or I'd kick her ass out."

By Christmas Eve we were in torpedo waters off the New Hebrides in a convoy officially designated as Task Unit 35.2.1 but quickly dubbed "the slow boats to Noumea." Steaming at less than 10 knots in two columns headed by *Pawnee* and the refrigerator ship *Octans* were merchantmen *Thunderer, Glenn Curtis, George Ross* and *Fred Turner.* Screening this oddly assorted group were fleet minesweepers *Shelldrake, Swallow* and *Zeal.*

We celebrated Christmas at sea with the Navy's standard holiday dinner. Captain George provided presents for the crew: candy, peanuts, cigarettes and cigars. We had occasion to remember this gesture of appreciation by our skipper. It was the last time any *Pawnee* officer would treat the crew as other than enlisted functionaries.

Entering the Great Roads, we moored to the ship-repair-unit dock at Ile Nou where an SO-8 search radar and four 40-mm. guns in dual mounts were waiting to be installed. The Bofors would replace the two inadequate 20-mm. A.A. guns at the aft end of the boat deck.

"A day late and a dollar short," one crewman complained. "We should have had this stuff when we were getting shot at in the Solomons."

"Never fear, my boy," Cy Hamblen said. The old Marine was grinning like a nine-year-old with his first Daisy air rifle as he examined the guns. "There's plenty of war left. Stick around and you'll see these beauties in action."

While specialists in gun and radar installation swarmed over the ship, new officers and men began reporting on board for duty. Sourly the Musketeers noted that all the enlisted men—seven seamen, one of them radar striker William P. Smith, and two third-class firemen—were green and unproven hands. The Navy was following its standard personnel policy, which we cynically defined as trading men for boys, skill for ignorance, and the known for the unknown at the cost of morale and leadership. We understood that every new ship required a cadre of experienced officers and petty officers which must come from the fleet. But the consequences for the *Pawnee,* from the narrow perspective of her crew, might well be tragic.

The first officer to report was James S. Lees, our former exec. He could be returning with a promotion to full lieutenant for one reason only: to take over the ship. At 1300 hours on the last day of 1943, he read his orders to the officers and men assembled on the fantail. There were many long faces among the crew, and mine must have been as long as any. Usually the ancient change-of-command ceremony gave the ship's company a chance to evaluate the new captain, whose humanity determined whether the ship would be happy or unhappy, and whose competence might spell the hair's-breadth difference between life and death. But we already knew what kind of C.O. Lees was likely to be.

I recalled another change of command on another 31 December, three years before at San Pedro. Captain Joel W. Bunkley had relieved Acting C.O. Robert B. Carney as skipper of the *California*. Within a year the ship had been sunk and Bunkley was shortly transferred back to shore duty. I hoped the coincidence of dates was not an augury.

Although officially relieved, George stayed on board for another week, presumably to impart some of his knowledge to his successor. On the morning of 7 January 1944, he made his way from the captain's cabin to the starboard bulwarks amidships. Some two dozen crewmen were on hand to see him off.

"Well, good-bye men," George said with a wave of his right hand that was half salute.

Bill Miller stepped out from the group of sailors. "Let's give Captain George a real Navy send-off with three cheers," he roared. *"Hip hip hooray!"*

The traditional three cheers was now so rare that I was taken aback for a moment. I had never seen this honor performed. I had had only two commanding officers who, in my opinion, rated it. Frank Dilworth was one and Flave George was the other. I joined the rest of the men on the second and third *"Hip hip hooray!"*

George almost lost his customary composure. He half-frowned in surprise, recovered quickly with a smile and another wave. "Thank you, men," he said. Then he went over the side and down the sea ladder into the waiting whaleboat.

"God damn it," Flash Aposhian said in an emotional voice. "This ship will never see another old man like Commander George." Many heads nodded in agreement.

Doyle Saxon put his fingers together in a prayer pyramid.

"Men, let us give thanks that the Lord sent George to us. He has delivered us from 'the snare of the fowler, and from the noisome pestilence'."

"Amen, Doyle," I said. "We've had two great skippers. One showed us what duty in a Navy ship should be like. The other was right for the Solomons."

"That leaves just one little problem," Gerber added. "What is Lees right for?"

Our acting exec, the smiling Warren Hughes, was the next to go. The consensus was that he had done pretty damn well for a former Los Angeles Chamber of Commerce official. His replacement was Lieutenant (junior grade) Howard C. Cramer, USNR. Some said he was a former Merchant Marine officer, others that he had "run a charter boat out of some Florida port." It was not easy to like Cramer, a rather small man with an oversized ego to compensate. I found him somewhat slack of face and coarse of voice and manner, a long way from the Annapolis ideal of officer and gentleman. On the other hand, he was no typical ninety-day wonder. The word soon came down from the bridge that he seemed a competent seaman and navigator.

The radio gang was directly affected by two other changes in leadership. On 5 January Chief Radioman Proctor was appointed warrant radio electrician, just as I had predicted.

"I want you to know it's been a pleasure serving with you, Ted," he said, all smiles. "I know I'm leaving the radio gang in good hands."

"Well, I was trained by two of the best chief radiomen in this or any fleet—you and Tommy Reeves," I replied as we shook hands. "Damn it, Mister Proctor"—emphasizing the "Mister" he now rated—"I'm sure going to miss your guidance—and those action reports from topside!"

One of my first, if hardly official, duties as radioman-in-charge was to break in a new communication officer. Ensign Moodie had been reassigned. His replacement was Calvin Rempfer, a tall, dark-haired engineer from Oregon who spoke with a trace of a Scandinavian accent. I was sure Proctor had passed the word that I was competent to run the radio gang with a minimum of supervision. One thing I had learned from the late Thomas J. Reeves was that the proper place for communication officers who didn't know the code was the electric cipher machine. In small ships, happily, comm officers also had to qualify for officer-of-the-deck duties, limiting the time they could spend in the radio shack.

No sooner had our new officers settled in when three petty officers and five seaman firsts, all plank owners, were transferred off for new construction. Among them were my friend George Tahbone and another seaman with the noteworthy name of Delbert Eudell Schrimsher. They were soon followed by another of our able commissioning crew: career boatswain's mate G. R. (Stinky) Higgins.

I was very sorry to see Tahbone go. He was a young man who talked little and smiled often, but his words were always to the point and his smile concealed much: a certain shyness, a pain at growing up Indian in a white-man's culture, and a controlled rage that he expressed best with a pair of boxing gloves. Above all, the smile overlay a valor that was bottomless, too deep for anxiety or fear. In my mind there had never been a doubt that he would do his duty and beyond, if necessary, for to him the only alternative was death. "Meeting the highest standards of the service" was the Navy phrase, but Tahbone would have smiled at that, too. He performed to those standards because his sense of honor would permit no other course of action.

To say any of that when we embraced by the sea ladder would only have embarrassed him. Instead I said:

"I hope you'll keep in touch, buddy. You'll be fighting the main event at the Olympic Auditorium in L.A. one of these days and I want to be there with you."

He smiled his bottomless smile. "Yes, my friend, we will meet again."

The Three Musketeers said goodby to another fine shipmate that day—Motor Machinist's Mate Edward Harris. He would soon be seeing the wife who meant more to him than anything in the world save his duty to God and country. He was a man who believed in such simple verities. That made him, to some of us, a simple man indeed. Aposhian and Gerber had often pointed out that his patriotism might well cost him his wife. In their view, exaggerated for satiric effect, no woman accustomed to regular sexual relations could possibly remain virtuous while her man was gone for a year or more, as Harris had been. Sooner or later, they opined, she would be out with a shipyard worker.

"Women just don't have men's loyalty and sense of values," Flash told Harris. "In the Arab countries the men are smart. They isolate their women in harems guarded by eunuchs. Even in Europe in the old days, the knights locked their women into chastity belts before they went off to the wars. What is that verse you quote, Ted, about women's weak character?"

" 'Between a woman's Yes and No / There is not room for a pin to go.' Cervantes."

"You see, Harris, that's the way women are," Flash finished triumphantly. "They may mean to say no. They may even say no a few times. But sooner or later they're going to break down and say yes!"

"When you get transferred, Harris, I wouldn't let the wife know you're home," Gerber added with sham solemnity. "I'd just drop in on her, say about midnight. Never can tell what you might find." He broke into loud laughter at his own wit.

"Yeah," Aposhian said, grinning broadly. "Be damn sure to look under the bed!"

Harris endured this ribbing with remarkable good humor. Like many large and powerful men, he was slow of speech and slower still to anger. But he adamantly maintained that he would find his wife just as he had left her.

Now, as I shook hands with Harris on the fantail, I regretted that I had acquiesced to my friends' barbed humor. The big lumberjack, whose name had been anglicized from the Slavic, was solid in belief and dependable in duty, a good man in a hard and testing time. I hoped his idolized wife appreciated his virtues.

"We were only kidding about the shipyard workers," I said. "Actually, we're just envious. We wish we had a woman like yours waiting for us."

"Damn right," Aposhian concurred. "We're glad you're getting a chance to prove us wrong. Hell, there are a few good women around."

"Sure," Gerber said. "I met one once." He laughed and punched Harris lightly on the shoulder to show he didn't mean it. "I gave her a cab ride to the convent."

We watched the whaleboat head for the fleet landing at Noumea with the eight plank owners. Tahbone, Harris and the others were looking back at the ship, and we waved a last good-bye. The overcast above brushed everything in shades of gray: the dirty waters of the Great Roads, the somber warships at anchor, the bare high hills behind Noumea. The air seemed to press down with moist hot hands. Many sailors insulated themselves against the inevitable loss of shipmates by maintaining a frosty impersonality. Since I could not do so, would not if I could, I was saddened by the departure of men with whom I had shared so much. Life in the *Pawnee* would go on, but it would never be quite the same again.

"Do you think George will make it if he turns pro?" I asked Gerber.

He shrugged. "A fighter's gotta have guts. He has too much. If he gets hurt bad, he won't have sense enough to quit. His father was killed in the ring, wasn't he? Like father, like son."

"George is damn good. Maybe he won't get hurt that bad."

"Maybe. Then the booze and the broads will get him. There won't be any shipmates around to look out for him—just leeches and bloodsuckers. I've been there, buddy."

He was probably right, I reluctantly agreed. "How about Harris?"

It was Aposhian's turn to shrug. "You can be sure of one thing, Ted, and that's what I tried to prepare him for. It's never as good as you thought it would be."

When a popular skipper leaves, his replacement has an especially onerous burden. He has inherited the title and the perquisites, but he must prove his ship-handling ability and he must earn the respect of the crew. Until then he is, in effect, on trial. Despite his customary mask of self-assurance, Lieutenant James S. Lees must have been keenly aware of that the first time he took the *Pawnee* out. He must have felt the many appraising eyes that were watching his every move and known that many more ears would soon be hearing what the eyes saw. Ordinarily a new commanding officer is given the benefit of every doubt by his crew, who are anxious to see him succeed. But Lees, during his previous tour of duty, had deliberately distanced himself from the enlisted men. Now as he took the captain's chair forward and to the left of the helmsman and passed his orders to the bridge watch through the OOD, he must have realized that he was very much alone—and very much on trial.

The evolution was simple enough. The port director ordered him to get under way from the repair base at Ile Nou and moor the *Pawnee* to the port side of the *Prometheus* at Berth A-6.

As we approached the repair ship at two-thirds speed, I stationed myself by the starboard life-line outside the radio shack. This I didn't want to miss. Lees's ship-handling experience was limited. As exec in the *Pawnee*, he had stood very few OOD watches under way. In the old ocean tug *Cahokia*, he had been boatswain and exec. According to bridge scuttlebutt, he had never had command of anything larger than a yard tug. But *Pawnee* was a deep-sea vessel. She bore about as much resemblance to one of those small, dirty harbor workboats as a fleet oiler did to a self-propelled fuel-oil barge.

My ship was 205 feet long over-all, with a beam of 38 feet 6 inches and a mean draft of 13 feet 10 inches. Her standard tonnage of 1,450 approximated that of all but the newest destroyers. From the pilothouse where Lees sat, it was 28 feet to the waterline. In addition to her substantial superstructure, her bow rose up more than 20 feet from the water at the stem. Both of these surfaces acted as sail areas in the wind. Moreover, she had but a single four-bladed propeller of manganese bronze, 12 feet in diameter, which had been especially pitched for towing. Consequently, I had been told, the *Pawnee* was much more difficult to handle when going alongside or clearing a pier or mooring than were ships with twin or multiple screws.

Two vessels were already tied up to the *Prometheus*—the 165-foot minesweeper *Dash* and the YP-292, a 130-foot wooden-hulled yard patrol craft. We would have to go alongside the "yippee" and moor to her port side.

We closed the YP-292 at a speed which seemed excessive to me, considering that the tide was running and a brisk breeze was blowing from port to starboard. Apparently the captain was going to make a close landing rather than stop his ship with open water between and let the current set her onto the YP. He's either damn confident, I thought, or he's in trouble.

Now the wind took our bow, which began sheering off inexorably to starboard and making a collision angle with the port quarter of the patrol craft. At the same time, our stern was swinging to port. Lees had underestimated the effects of wind and current on his ship.

"Back full speed!" he ordered.

But it was too late. Our bow struck the YP-292 a mighty slashing blow which carried away a section of her bulwarks and opened up her timbers from the gunwale to well below the waterline. Noumea Harbor began pouring into her hull.

The resulting scene took on the aspect of a Laurel and Hardy comedy. The skipper of the Yippee was beside himself with rage at the possible loss of his command but dared not express it too openly, since Lees outranked him. Checking a flow of invective just in time, he was reduced to stomping the deck and shouting orders at his subordinates.

From the Pawnee's bridge wing came a babble of directives, concerned principally with our two three-inch portable pumps, which were soon passed across to the YP, and with preparations for putting the latter into ARD-2, the floating dry dock. The shutters of our signal searchlight clattered as messages were sent to the port director. The steel ladders to the bridge vibrated and rang with the impact of many feet at double time. On YP-292 the enlisted men, as usual, paid the heaviest price. They had to sacrifice their mattresses and pillows to plug the breach at the port quarter.

I indulged myself in the all-too-human failing of rejoicing at the misfortunes of the arrogant. I went into the radio shack, still laughing, and said: "Chalk one up for our new skipper. He's just bagged himself a yard patrol craft."

Many shipmates shared my belief that Lees would not be with us long. We were wrong. Any possible consequences of his foul-up were overtaken by two events which followed almost immediately: the salvage of a French merchant ship and a hurricane at Noumea. Far from being censured for nearly sinking YP-292, Lees emerged with a commendation. Gerber delivered an admirable summing up: "I'd rather have his luck than a license to steal!"

In the case of the S.S. Polynesian, which had gone aground on the Great Abore Reef adjoining Bulari Passage, we were fortunate that salvage operations were directed by Emile Genereaux, now promoted to "brass-hat" commander in charge of the Salvage Depot at Noumea.

Arriving at the reef on the morning of 12 January, we found that the Polynesian, a medium-sized passenger and freight vessel engaged in supplying the Navy from Australia, had broached and was portside to the beach. We put our 2-inch tow wire aboard, paid it out to 225 fathoms, veered the anchor chain to 50 fathoms and took a strain. The stranded vessel wouldn't budge, even though her captain was ordered to pump fuel oil overboard.

The next morning the Locust, a 560-ton net-laying vessel with the elevated proboscis typical of her kind, arrived and put a tow wire aboard the French ship. Together, she and *Pawnee* began taking a strain on the starboard bow. Around 0930 the *Polynesian* gave a sudden lurch. Our tow wire shifted and carried away all the lifelines along the merchantman's starboard side. To the accompaniment of profanity in two languages, the wire was cast loose. We heaved it in and secured the main engines and the special sea detail. So far, Lees's debut as a salvage expert was hardly auspicious.

Four hours later a PT-boat came alongside and Genereaux scrambled up the sea ladder and strode toward the bridge. Making full commander hadn't changed him a bit. He still was scowling, he still looked as if he needed a shave, and he still seemed ready to tackle any officer or man who gave him any lip. No one did.

Within an hour and a half, we had heaved in our anchor and were maneuvering into position to pass our tow wire to the starboard quarter of the *Polynesian*. By 1900 we were taking a strain from seaward while the *Locust* pulled from the cripple's starboard bow. Meanwhile, a small French tug had stood in with two barges and longshoremen began discharging cargo on the inshore side. The next morning the *Polynesian* floated off the reef, and we towed her to a safe anchorage. She soon departed for Noumea under her own power.

As *Pawnee* threaded Bulari Passage toward the Great Roads, I wondered what Lees thought of "Halsey's fair-haired salvage boy." Genereaux was a hard man and a vain one, but a sailor sensed also that he would bring a ship safely to port if it was humanly possible. His competence seemed as awesome as his confidence. He had what most officers never attained: an elusive quality of leadership that the Navy called "command presence." I thought about Chief Reeves, the benevolent autocrat of the *California* radio gang. He, too, had had that quality. No matter how good a radioman and petty officer I became, I knew that Reeves had been twice as good.

The timely arrival of a hurricane on 18 January gave Lees another chance to prove that the near-loss of YP-292 was pure mischance. For the *Pawnee* it was an occasion to demonstrate what we already knew, that she was a well-designed, stout and seaworthy ship.

During the early morning hours an easterly wind developed from a strong breeze to gale velocity. At 0500 the crew was broken out, the special sea detail was set and *Pawnee* was shifted to a more sheltered location in the Great Roads.

When I paid a visit to the bridge around 0600, the wind had increased to whole gale force of 55 knots, or 63 mph. With a mighty moaning and howling, it was ripping and tearing at every exposed surface of the ship. Signalman Third J. E. Newcomb, small and wiry with a face already wrinkling despite his mere twenty-one years, was at the helm. One engine had been left on propulsion, making 10 turns ahead, to ease the strain on the port anchor chain.

"You-all hold that line," I told the Southerner. Newcomb was a special favorite of mine, for he sometimes let me take the wheel at sea when the captain and exec weren't around.

I found Papoose Evans in the charthouse, catching up the quartermaster's notebook. "What's Mother Nature trying to do to us?" I asked.

Papoose closed the notebook. "Take a look for yourself."

We stepped out onto the port wing of the bridge and were assaulted by the still-rising wind. We had to stand with feet wide apart, each with one hand gripping the splinter shield, or we would have been thrown backward into the 20-mm. gun. Fine rain, blown in furious, nearly horizontal sheets, stung our faces as if the drops had been tiny grains of sand. Overhead, the sky was pearly gray with thin high cirrus. The rising sun was encircled by a prismatic halo ranging in hue from baleful red inside to violet-blue at the outer diameter.

Evans pointed to the northeast. "See that cloud bank? That's the storm front." He had to shout in my ear to make himself heard.

Just above the horizon, the solid purple mass of the cloud bank looked as substantial as land. I would have thought it an island where no island should be, except for the ropelike filaments of rain squalls that were breaking off and radiating out from the center.

Papoose pulled me inside the pilothouse. "Take a look at the glass," he commanded. The barometer needle stood at 29:30. "It's dropped half an inch in the last couple hours, and it's still dropping."

I whistled. "Hurricane?"

"One hellacious hurricane. This one is right out of the book—and we're right in its track." He grinned defiantly. "Maybe it'll level that crummy convict city and take the Pink House with it."

"Remember, Bull Halsey and his Comsopac staff are over there, too."

"Shit, no hurricane would dare screw with the Bull. He'll have Carney issue an executive order. If that doesn't work, he'll stand out in front of the Jap consulate where he lives and wave the storm around him!"*

---

* Actually, Halsey was in Washington for consultations with Admiral King (and to receive a Gold Star in lieu of a second Distinguished Service Medal) at this time. Doubtless he would have enjoyed a good laugh at Evans's remarks.

By 0830 the full might of the hurricane was upon us. The winds rose to a shrieking crescendo at more than 100 knots. The noise was a vast bedlam, like all the stadiums of the world aroar at one time. We had to increase shaft revolutions simply to maintain position. The captain ordered two more engines warmed up and alerted the special sea detail in case we dragged anchor and had to get under way in a hurry.

An hour later the barometer had fallen to 29:11. The clouds of misty rain that boiled around the ship were as thick as smoke from a prairie-grass fire. Visibility was reduced to a hundred feet or less. The normally placid harbor was whipped into a froth of whitecaps which buffeted the *Pawnee* from every point of the compass. We were informed that several ships had gone aground, or were about to, but it was impossible to attempt their rescue until the center of the hurricane had passed over.

Concern showed on the faces of the men assembled in the radio shack. Some were, like me, precariously balancing handleless Navy coffee mugs as the ship pitched, lurched and rolled.

"Any chance of us going on the rocks, Ted?"

The question came from Bill Bates, my new striker. It was more than coincidence that he reminded me strongly of Tommy Gilbert of the *California*. A quiet, polite Arkansan, Bates was as happy to be free of the deck force as his predecessor, Bill Bowser, had been. He would have practiced the code sixteen hours a day if I could have provided relays of instructors. He assumed that a salty prewar sailor like me had been through hurricanes before.

I hadn't but this was no time to admit it.

"Hell, no," I said confidently. "This little ship keeps the sea better than any destroyer. All Lees has to do is hold her head into the wind and feed her some gas so we don't snap an anchor chain."

"Well, it scares the shit out of me," John See said. "Imagine trying to abandon ship in the middle of a typhoon."

"It's not acts of nature that worry me," I replied. "It's the acts of men—especially Japanese men. Bill, go up to the bridge and check the barometer reading. I'll bet it's rising."

It was a good guess. The barometer stood at 29:15 and would soon go higher. The wind diminished by scarcely perceptible degrees. At 1140, under orders from the port director, we began heaving in on the anchor and were soon under way in the Great Roads.

Near Beacon K we found subchaser *PC-1128* in a sinking condition and the *Noa*, a destroyer-transport, hard aground. The small, steel-hulled patrol craft needed help fast; she had dragged anchor and been driven onto a coral outcropping. We moored alongside, quickly rigged salvage pumps and a collision mat, and sent a shipfitter aboard to plug the hole in her side with mattresses. As soon as the subchaser was able to proceed toward the floating dry dock, we put our tow wire on the *Noa*—one of the last of the World War I-era destroyers—and began taking a strain. She finally came off the rocks at 1300 the next afternoon.*

Our next salvage operation took us to Ducos Peninsula, where the *YAG-25*, a yard auxiliary craft, had been driven onto the beach. With our 1⅛-inch tow wire secured to the stern of the vessel, we began building up speed, only to have the wire part and wrap itself around our propeller. Much to our surprise, the captain came aft, got into a shallow-water diving outfit and helped Shipfitter H. I. Smith clear the wire with an underwater cutting torch. But we were not successful in pulling *YAG-25* to deeper water until we had rigged beach gear and had the honor of another visit from Commander Genereaux.

During these lengthy operations we were joined by visitors of an even more unwelcome kind. The residents of the nearby leper colony assembled at the shoreline to act as "sidewalk superintendents," New Caledonia style.

My knowledge of this loathsome affliction was confined to what I had read in the New Testament and seen cosmetically depicted in the film *Ben Hur.* From a hundred yards offshore, the lepers looked almost normal. Their disfigurements didn't show, except for an occasional missing limb. But I felt a surge of fear. I was sure that Hansen's disease was highly contagious and wished to be far away.

"You were worried about abandoning ship in a hurricane," I told See. "What about being cast ashore and finding yourself in a village full of lepers? You know, this whole goddam South Pacific is inhospitable to human life."

But not necessarily unfriendly to commanding officers, especially when they enjoyed the benefit of Genereaux's supervision. Soon after the "big wind" at Noumea, a letter arrived from Rear Admiral C. H. Cobb, Comseronsopac, addressed to Lees:**

---

* Commissioned in 1921 as DD-343, the *Noa* would remain afloat for only eight more months. She was sunk in a collision with the destroyer *Fullam* off the Palau Islands on 12 September 1944.
** Ironically, this same officer supervised the revisions of *Modern Seamanship* for the Tenth Edition of June 1941 when he was a captain and Head of the Department of Seamanship and Navigation at Annapolis. The volume contained no references to the beach gear (or Liverpool bridle) which Genereaux employed so successfully in the South Pacific.

Subject: Commendable Performance of Duty.

1. The hurricane which passed through Noumea, New Caledonia on 18 January 1944 caused several ships and harbor craft to go aground or adrift in the harbor. The PAWNEE very promptly came to the aid of all of these distressed vessels. In a comparatively short time, the PAWNEE hauled clear and reberthed safely all of these vessels with a minimum of damage incident to their salvage or rescue.

2. The performance of the PAWNEE in this emergency was excellent and the Commander Service Squadron, South Pacific Force takes great pleasure in commending the Commanding Officer, the officers, and the crew for their demonstrated ability, efficiency, and devotion to duty in rendering such outstanding service under very difficult conditions. I bespeak a continuance of this fine record.*

When a copy of Admiral Cobb's letter was posted on the crew's bulletin board, the reaction was mostly amused. We had done no more than our duty, employing a ship designed for that kind of work. But our rescues had been performed in the full sight of the admirals.

"Now if we'd got a commendation for hauling the *Montgomery* out of the Upper Solomons, it would have meant something," Flash Aposhian observed.

"Yeah, but the brass wasn't around," Cy Hamblen said with his usual worldly grin. "If they don't see it, it didn't happen. You old swabbies oughta know that."

We "old swabbies" (meaning anyone who was in the Navy before Pearl Harbor) did know that. We dismissed the letter and chuckled over a poem that Murphy had retyped on the radio gang's all-cap mill and posted on the board. Written by an anonymous Marine on Guadalcanal, it had been widely circulated from hand to hand through the South Pacific. In a crude but effective way, the doggerel expressed the resentment the gyrenes felt at the Army "dogfaces" who often arrived after the Marines, at bloody cost, had secured a beachhead.

---

* In his memoir, *The Captain Loved the Sea*, Genereaux devoted only one paragraph to this event, which he remembered as occurring in the fall of 1943. He did not consider the *Pawnee's* role worthy of mention: "Later that fall a typhoon of moderate velocity [sic] hit the harbor and a total of five vessels were grounded, all of which were rescued in the course of time. I had taken three of my key men off the salvage ship that I had been in command of [the *Menominee*] and placed them in charge of the salvage base. They were available to me at all times for salvage work and to maintain the base" (p. 183).

Our Fighting Men

A Marine told his buddy on Guadalcanal,
  "The Army is coming, just think of it, pal!"
"All right," said the corporal, "let's get busy then
  "And build a fine clubhouse for 'our fighting men.'

"They'll have entertainment and maybe a play,
  "Recreation advisors from the W.P.A.;
"They'll have sexy hostesses and movies galore,
  "For the Army's morale must have high score."

"Oh boy!" said a chow hound, "we'll eat better now,
  "You can depend on the Army to drag in the chow,
"They'll start post exchanges and serve ice cream,
  "For life must be pleasant for 'our fighting men.' "

A Seabee awoke and asked, "What's the score,
  "With cruisers and battleships lying off shore?
"A bunch of destroyers are sweeping the bay—
  "God! The Army is landing today!"

Out on the beach when the men hit the sand
  With fixed bayonets and rifles in hand,
Said a Marine scrubbing clothes, "Where you headin' for?
  "Oh! Did you guys finally hear there's a war?"

"Shut up," said the sergeant. "Go limber your legs,
  "And trade that Jap helmet for a case of fresh eggs.
"All this razzing of soldiers must come to an end;
  "We must show respect for 'our fighting men.'

"Their officers outrank us, so they'll take command,
  "New rules and orders will govern the land;
"They'll have their MPs to push us around—
  "When the Army takes over, they sure shake the ground."

"Cheer up," said a Raider, "it won't be long.
  "Old Halsey will bellow and we'll shove along.
"We'll head on north and hit the beach again,
  "And make Bougainville safe for 'our fighting men.' "

The poem was given a special poignancy by the progress of the war in the Central Pacific. On 20 November 1943, the Marines landed on a remote atoll of the Gilbert Islands—Tarawa. It was secured after four days of the most savage fighting yet seen in the Pacific, but at a shocking cost: 980 Marines and 29 sailors killed and 2,101 wounded. Nearly all of the 4,000 Japanese defenders had preferred death to surrender. When the casualty figures were released, the Navy and Marine commanders were harshly criticized by the public and the usually docile news media for sacrificing American lives in frontal assaults on worthless pieces of coral.

The high costs of amphibious warfare were brought home by events in Italy, as well. On 22 January 1944 Allied forces stormed ashore at Anzio, south of Rome. A delay in consolidating the beachhead allowed Field Marshal Albert Kesselring to ring the high ground around the perimeter with troops and artillery. A long and bloody stalemate followed, one that brought General Mark Clark under increasing fire for suffering maximum casualties while achieving minimum results. On the Russian front, however, an ally that did not have to consider public opinion captured Novgorod and opened a new offensive in the Leningrad and Baltic Sea areas.

Most of the crew were hardly aware of these momentous battles and campaigns. Perhaps wisely, they chose to ignore events they did not understand and over which they had no control. It took a choice item of scuttlebutt which raced through the ship on 25 January to get their full attention. *Pawnee* was going to Sydney, Australia, for R and R!

Even after we got under way for the fuel dock at Dumbea Bay, where we took on 27,776 gallons of diesel oil, we could hardly believe our good fortune. This would be our first visit to civilization since departing the States nearly fourteen months before. Neither Honolulu nor Noumea was considered civilized.

But we had all heard about Sydney and its friendly people, grateful to the "Yanks" because we saved them from a Japanese invasion. Especially had we heard about its superlatively friendly women, starved for male companionship because most of the eligible Aussies were serving in the jungles of New Guinea or in the Middle East with the British Eighth Army. We knew we would be greatly outnumbered but vowed to do our best to alleviate that problem.

Chapter Ten

"STRENGTH THROUGH LOVE"
DOWN UNDER

We for a certainty are not the first
Have sat in taverns while the tempest hurled
Their hopeful plans to emptiness, and cursed
Whatever brute and blackguard made the world.
A. E. Housman

"Australia dead ahead!"

This report from the bridge at 0830 on 29 January 1944 sent me hurrying topside for my first look at the island continent. The southeast coastline unfolded in dozens of headlands, misty purple from twenty miles out, which plunged into the sea like dolphins in line abreast.

Half an hour later we crossed the 100-fathom curve and changed course to 310 degrees true. Now I could see the real colors of Australia: not the obscene green of the Solomons but pastels of beige and pale gold, much like Southern California. A spume of surf was breaking at the feet of the headlands and on the sugary sands of the deeply indented beaches between.

The first Europeans to sail the eastern littoral I was now admiring were Captain James Cook and the crew of His Majesty's Bark *Endeavor* in 1770. Cook claimed everything he could see, and a good deal more, for Britain, and the claim was later extended all the way to the Indian Ocean 2,500 miles to the west.

In 1788 the first settlers arrived at Sydney Cove—788 convicts and 450 soldiers, sailors and dependents. The fair land discovered by the "Columbus of the Pacific" became a dumping-ground for British prisoners more than half a century before France established its notorious penal colonies at New Caledonia and Devil's Island. By the time the cruel system was abolished in 1840, 75,000 convicts had been shipped to Australia and another 27,000 to the island of Tasmania. They were followed by many free settlers, and the colonies prospered on sheep and the gold rush of 1851. With prosperity came respectability, and Australia joined the British Commonwealth in 1901. But the country in 1944 was a nation of colonists still. One-quarter of its population of 8,000,000 was concentrated around the two cities of Sydney and Melbourne. Except for the coastal enclaves of Adelaide, Brisbane, Darwin and Perth and a few remote towns and villages, the continent slept in its ageless isolation.

Knowledge of a more useful kind came from sailors who had visited Sydney. Australians, they told me, spoke a strange harsh version of English but it was possible to communicate if they didn't fall into their colorful but incomprehensible slang. Their aptly named Tiger-brand beer was better and stronger than ours but it was served warm. The hard stuff was available only at a high price on the black market, as was anything else one might need. Cigarettes, clothing, tea (but not coffee) and sweets were rationed. "If you want to make friends fast, take along a carton of fags and some Hershey bars," I was advised.

The women were not quite as pretty or stylish as ours but were more candid and straightforward. It was not uncommon for one to take a sailor home for the night. The next morning they would have breakfast with her parents. I was not sure I believed that.

If the Australians' sexual mores were more permissive than ours, their official attitude toward drinking was not. The pubs sold nothing but beer and ale. They were open for only a few hours a day and never on Sunday. "You gotta get there early and drink fast."

One of the luxuries available in Sydney was fresh milk at the soda fountains, called "milk bars." Another was the plain but delicious food. The sailors' favorite entree was steak and eggs. Since none of these staples was part of the Spartan Navy diet in the South Pacific, some enlisted men gorged themselves on four or five meals a day. For the satisfaction of another basic need, the place to meet girls was Luna Park, a permanent carnival on the other side of Sydney Harbour. But a young lady might boldly stop a sailor on the street. The entire city was one happy hunting ground.

Australian money, I learned, was based on the English system of pounds, shilling and pence. One didn't have to bother learning about tuppence, thrippence and sixpence, however, since very few people would cheat an American sailor.

"Just hold out a handful of coins and they'll make change for you. And don't try to tip an Aussie, either. They believe everyone is equal and take it as an insult." That was, I agreed, a revolutionary idea.

Street cars were called "trams," gasoline was "petrol," and sidewalks were "footpaths," as in England. A friend was a "mate," a casual acquaintance was a "bloke" and a dishonest or disliked person was a "mug." The primitive black aborigines, of whom less than 100,000 remained, were called "Abos." They were considered nearly subhuman and accordingly were treated even worse than we treated our American Indians and Negroes. Australia was 97 percent British stock, and the dominant majority firmly intended to keep it that way.

In matters of etiquette, I was jokingly warned about one taboo word. The Aussies didn't mind the strange way we ate, shifting the fork from one hand to the other. But one never asked for a "napkin" in a restaurant. The word meant a sanitary napkin. The proper phrase was "table linen."

By 1030 hours the mile-wide entrance to Sydney Harbour was just ahead. It was framed dramatically by sheer, flat-topped cliffs of stratified sandstone nearly 300 feet high. "Outer North Head" and "Outer South Head," I was told. The only thing lacking to make this harbor entrance as breathtaking as San Francisco's was a Golden Gate Bridge.

A pilot boat painted in orange and yellow came speeding toward us, throwing up sheets of spray. We stopped our engines and a tall, lean pilot was soon on board. At eight knots we passed between the great, sun-splashed cliffs, went through the submarine net gate and anchored in calm waters between two landmarks with the picturesque names of Shark Point and Chowder Head.

A long delay ensued. To the west we could see the gray girders of a mighty steel-arch bridge. The sight completed some vague identification I had already made between this place and San Francisco. But my shipmates had left no fiancées in "the City." To them the bridge meant one thing: liberty. Already, some were shifting into their dress blues.

"Say, why are we anchored in this God-forsaken spot?" one seaman asked.

"Because we're flying the yellow quarantine flag, you boot," Chief Ortalano replied. "The Aussies ain't gonna let us ashore till they're damn sure we didn't bring along leprosy or elephantiasis or Old Joe from Noumea or the Solomons."

At last the crew were mustered on the fantail. A boat came alongside and the port quarantine doctor appeared. With the exception of the

French pilot and a couple of war correspondents, he was the first civilian I had even seen in the *Pawnee*. He was dressed in a gray tweed suit and had the bland, expressionless face I associated with medical men. Somehow, I had expected an Aussie doctor to be different. We were instructed to hold out our hands, first the backs and then palms up, for his inspection. He passed quickly down the ranks, adding a brief but probing look at each face, and soon gave us a clean bill of health. The yellow flag came down and *Pawnee* got under way on all four engines.

"Now the liberty party lay aft to the fantail!" someone shouted hopefully. But the growing numbers of men in dress blues were again frustrated. We cut in our degaussing gear and made two runs on the degaussing range off Bradley Head. It was 1350 before we got our prow aligned with Sydney Harbour Bridge.

The city spread out before us on both sides in a riot of red tile roofs and flowering gardens that began at the hilltops and spilled down the slopes to the water's edge. Off the port bow the business district occupied an irregular rectangle of building blocks interspersed with broad green parks.

"I feel like one of the wandering tribes of Israel who has seen the Promised Land," Doyle Saxon said, rubbing his hands in anticipation.

Just before reaching the bridge, we veered hard left into narrow Wool-loomooloo Bay. A large graving dock was under construction on the east side. We eased right and moored alongside the destroyer-transport *Dent*, a battle-scarred veteran of the Solomons Campaign, at Berth 11. The only other Navy ship present was the destroyer *Pringle*, another Solomons survivor we well remembered, which was snubbed to the finger pier across the channel. The few crewmen on board waved a friendly welcome.

"Glad you're here to lend a hand, *Pawnee*," one of them shouted. "We need help!"

Meanwhile, I was faced with a difficult decision. I was allowed to secure the radio watch, but someone had to remain on board until the captain made official arrangements for a shore guard on the Fox schedule. I looked from one anxious face to another. All the radiomen were in dress uniform for the first time since San Diego.

"All right, you guys can go ashore. I'll secure this operation when the old man returns. See you later on the beach."

"By God, Mason, you're all right!" Bill Bowser cried, fervently shaking my hand.

"What I am, probably, is island-happy," I said. "You'd better shove off before I change my mind."

I had the crew's head to myself as I shaved and showered. In the empty living compartment I put on my tailor-made blues. I didn't wear my campaign ribbons: that was for shore-duty types and repair-ship sailors. In the silent radio shack, now free of the driving rhythm of Morse code, I waited impatiently for the captain to return.

And waited and waited. The minute hand of the 24-hour clock on the bulkhead seemed hardly to move. I got out my Vibraplex "bug" (a semiautomatic keying device that was much faster than the standard brass key) and hooked it up to the oscillator for a practice session. The only radiomen permitted to use speed keys were those assigned to fast circuits in flagships or shore stations, but I might need this skill if I were transferred. Then I switched to the hand key, which I used daily at slow speeds in training my strikers, but seldom at 20 to 25 wpm for transmitting official dispatches. Forced to maintain radio silence except for emergencies, seagoing operators lost the fine edge of their skills unless they practiced constantly.

Still I waited. I opened Jack London's *Sea Wolf*, but my thoughts were fixed on the streets and pubs and girls of Sydney and I kept reading the same lines over and over. I cursed the captain for acting like Wolf Larsen, and I cursed myself for impersonating Jack Armstrong, the All-American boy. By now my friends were probably scattered from one end of the city to the other, and I would never find them.

At last I heard heavy steps on the ladder. I closed the book and got to my feet. Lieutenant Lees came through the door.

"What you doing here, Mason?" he demanded. His voice was slurred, his face was flushed. Obviously he had been drinking at the officers' club. Drinking quite a lot.

"Waiting for your permission to secure the radio shack, captain."

"That's a job for a third class like Murphy."

"I didn't have the heart to do it, captain."

"That's very noble of you. I don't suppose you have the heart to put your radiomen on report when they foul up, either."

"Captain, they have their choice. They can face you on the gun deck at captain's mast, or me on the fantail with the gloves."

"You're non-reg all the way, aren't you, Mason?"

That was, I thought, an unfair accusation. "I'm never non-reg where duty is concerned, captain. My methods are a little different, that's all, sir."

The captain and I measured each other. "I know all about you, Mason, and I'm not afraid of you. You're the one who should be afraid of me."

I was astonished. It had never occurred to me that Lees might consider me a threat of some unspecified kind. He must have sensed, or even heard, that I did not consider him in the same league with Dilworth and George.

But my personal opinion had nothing to do with the way I ran the radio gang. Why should he care?

"Captain, you don't have any reason to be afraid of me. You're the commanding officer of this ship. I'm well aware of that, sir."

"Good. You keep on being aware of that. Now secure your shack and go ashore."

"Aye aye, sir!"

The captain paused in the doorway. "Mason, the poetic boxer," he mused. "You get squared away and start operating by the book, and I'll promote you like I did Proctor."

"Thank you, captain." I could see that Lees rather liked and respected me. What I did not see, and should have seen, is that he may have made a request for help in meeting his heavy responsibilities. Sometimes two men want to talk, but neither one can find the words.

I crossed Cowper Wharf Road and struck out for downtown Sydney through a broad, tree-lined park called the Domain. The sun was shining and the temperature was in the low 80s, for it was mid-summer down under. The few people I met nodded and smiled. I smiled in return. This was a long way from the cold hostility and language barrier of Noumea. These people spoke my tongue; their ancestors had come from the same country as mine. I felt almost at home.

After a brisk walk I skirted another extensive park and emerged into the commercial district along Castlereagh and Pitt streets. These thoroughfares were narrow and not quite straight: they must have begun as wagon tracks. Despite being converted to one-way traffic, they were congested with double-decker buses, taxis and private autos. The latter were mostly Fords and British Hillmans. The buildings were drab Victorian and Edwardian sandstones, with a sprinkling of other architectural styles, even a few modern office buildings in polished stone, glass and concrete.

But I was not on a sightseeing expedition. The bars and cafes were where I would find my buddies. I went into a large hotel and changed some of my money to Australian currency. I asked about pubs and was directed to King's Cross.

"It's rather like your Greenwich Village, I fancy," the woman behind the counter told me. "But do be careful, Yank, about showing your money. You're carrying a lot of it, you know."

As I walked down Pitt Street looking for a cab, I became aware of a young woman approaching on clicking high heels. She was wearing a tight-fitting dark suit and scarlet blouse that set off her raven hair and milky skin. My God, she looks like Vivien Leigh! I thought. Our eyes met. Hers were almost as green as Betty Baker's. To my surprise, she stopped in front of me and smiled invitingly. What I had heard was true.

Now I felt awkward and afraid, like a high-school sophomore at his first prom. What could I possibly say to this dangerously feminine woman? My mind went blank. I had been too long in the hard male world of the ship, living in the enforced celibacy of Santo, Noumea and the Solomons. The transition to grace here on a Sydney street was too abrupt. I hesitated, smiled sheepishly, stepped around Miss Leigh and walked quickly away.

Her disgusted voice followed me. "Well! What kind of a sailor are you, Yank?"

I felt ashamed of myself. What kind of sailor indeed? The first thing you need, Mason, is a drink, I told myself. And then another.

The cabbie who took me to King's Cross drove with abandon on what seemed the wrong side of the road. He dropped me at a pub on Darling-hurst, near the intersection of five streets that formed a wayward cross, with an admonition to "mind your money, Yank."

My first Aussie pub was a far cry from an American cocktail lounge. The walls were painted white, the floor was tiled in white and the over-head lights were bright. At the bar, drinkers were lined up four or five deep, some with a glass in each hand. Neither an American sailor nor a woman could be seen.

"Joinin' the 'six o'clock swill', mate?" a rough, friendly voice asked. "It takes a bit o' doin'. Here, let me get you a pint." The man, middle-aged and dressed in working clothes, plunged into the mob and soon emerged with a foaming glass of warm beer. It was delicious.

Over a second pint, which I was not allowed to pay for, I learned that the pubs were legally required to close by six o'clock, hence the picturesque phrase. Under wartime conditions, they shut down as soon as the day's ration of beer was exhausted. I could understand the frantic haste of the drinkers. I also learned that Scotch whisky and even American bour-bon were available from many cab drivers. The going rate was four or five pounds.

All too soon the barman called, "Time, gentlemen!" and the boister-ous crowd was herded out the door. My companion directed me to a nearby hotel. I gave him a couple of packs of Chesterfields. We parted with firm handshakes and fervid affirmations of the undying friendship between our two countries.

The proprietor of the small hotel, a bluff, red-faced Irishman, gave me his best room, just off his own quarters. He also produced a bottle of Black & White Scotch for four pounds and the usual warning against flashing my roll of bills, especially if I brought a "tart" home. I had a couple of iceless drinks in my room. This, I thought darkly, is a hell of a way to spend my first of six precious liberties in Sydney.

Night had fallen when I ventured out into King's Cross. The wartime brownout was in effect and the neon lights were off. All of the restaurants and shops seemed to be closed. The streets and buildings looked worn and shabby, badly in need of a field day and paint. If this was Sydney's Bohemian quarter, what must the rest of the city be like after eight or nine o'clock?

An auburn-haired woman wearing a sailor's peacoat was walking slowly down the street toward me. As she came near, she smiled. I smiled, my best John Barleycorn smile. She stopped, just as the woman in the scarlet blouse had done. This time I stopped, too. In the murky light we appraised each other. I saw that she wasn't more than nineteen or twenty years old. She wasn't Vivien Leigh, but she was not unattractive. And I wasn't exactly Clark Gable.

"Where are you going, sailor?" she asked.

"I'm going wherever you are, Ma'am," I said boldly if not gallantly. "But first, would you like to join me at my hotel for a drink?"

She looked at me searchingly. "Well, you seem like a proper gentleman," she said, laughing now. "All right."

Remembering all the warnings I had received, I slept with my billfold between the pillow and its slip. I didn't think it was really necessary. She was, I discovered, as lost as I, fleeing her own secret fears, groping for the warmth that might shorten the long nights. I was glad I had met her.

The next day I went ashore with Aposhian, Gerber, Hamblen, Aronis and a couple of others. While no one would admit he hadn't done well the first night, we all agreed that planning and organization were called for. The first requirement was living quarters.

We found them on Goulburn Street in the Haymarket, a graceless but vibrant working-class district. "This is the place," Aposhian said, convinced by a solicitous landlady who offered to serve our tea and draw our baths. We engaged a number of rooms on the third floor.

Next, liquor. A scouting party found a cabby, a Cockney who hailed from London's East End. He came calling with a suitcase full of whiskey. The bargaining was conducted by Aposhian, who got the price lowered from 5 pounds to 4, with a keg of Aussie beer thrown in and an assurance that the next lot would cost but 3 pounds and some odd shillings.

I complimented Flash on his acumen and drew one of his long, slow grins.

"It's in the blood," he said. "I've told you about the Armenians. They're the only ones who can beat a Jew in a business deal."

Although it carried a lower priority, food was a consideration. To drink as much as we intended to, it would be prudent to eat at least twice a day. Around the corner we found a small restaurant in a decor of gloomy dark woods and hard, high-backed booths. We had steak and eggs, accompanied by many glasses of fresh milk, and pronounced it the best meal we had had since leaving the States.

Our only disagreement was where to look for the women who would make all these preparations worthwhile. Aronis and I favored Luna Park, where girls outnumbered sailors by two or three to one, according to reports from shipmates. The others considered the source, mostly young seamen. The park, they scoffed, was full of school girls and other "San Quentin quail." They set off to find the cafes and nightclubs, hangouts the world over for older, more practiced women.

Ronnie and I wished them luck and went to Luna Park anyway. A cab took us across the Sydney Harbour Bridge and deposited us in its very shadow on the north shore. We passed into the fun fair through a huge, grotesque laughing face and soon discovered that the seamen had exaggerated but little. That meant we could afford to be selective. We talked to various young ladies, looking for two who met our vague qualifications of attractiveness, availability and ardor.

"What you guys waitin' for?" one shipmate demanded. "Jesus, this is like turnin' a little kid loose in a candy store!" He was soon claimed by a seventeen-year-old who had decided, after five minutes, that he was her "myte."

Eventually we spotted two very pretty girls. One was petite and copper-haired. The other was taller, blonde and possessed of a fantastic figure.

"Hey, they're up to L.A. standards," Aronis exclaimed. "Which one do you like?"

"The blonde, I think."

"Great. I like the redhead. Let's go."

Our overtures were refused, but politely and without finality. We followed them. Again we were rejected but with giggles and feminine whisperings as they withdrew. Obviously, they wanted us to know they were not casual pick-ups. Aronis and I conferred. Luna Park was awash with girls but these two seemed special. We took up the trail and found them in the crowd. This time they stopped to talk.

That is how I met Yvonne (Pat) Leckie. Her long hair was the color of wheat at the harvest. Her eyes were as blue as the deep ocean. She did not have the typical Australian accent, which I heard as a variety of Billingsgate, or Cockney, but spoke with a hint of a Scottish burr. She was eighteen years old, she told me. She worked in Sydney but lived in Manly across the harbor. Her father was serving with the Eighth Army in the Middle East.

We rode on the ferris wheel and the merry-go-round and the roller coaster. That gave me a good excuse to put my arm around her and hold her hand. We ate ice cream and drank American Cokes and for a little while I was not a war-weary veteran of Pearl Harbor and the Solomons. I was eighteen years old again, visiting the carnival at the California State Fair with Bertha Morton, my first love. Which was probably why I had come to Luna Park at all. Substitute Venice Pier for the Sacramento fairgrounds and my friend's reason was most likely the same. Later, the four of us took a cab back across the bridge to the ferry station at the Circular Quay.

"Ted, what is your last name again?" Pat asked. We were sitting on a wooden bench in the dimly lit terminal building waiting for the Manly ferry. Aronis had kept the cab so he could take her friend Betty home.

I told her.

"I was right," she said in a pleased voice. "I just knew you were English."

"Well, in a way. Some of my ancestors got kicked out of England in the 1600s."

Now she was brightly curious. "Were they, well, political prisoners?"

"You mean convicts?"

She blushed. "It's all right, you know. Australia was settled by convicts. Many were political prisoners, really. Were yours?"

"Even worse than that," I said, pretending embarrassment. "They were Puritans."

She looked at me blankly for a moment, then burst into laughter. "You see, even your sense of humor is English!"

"I'm afraid it gets me into trouble. Americans like broad humor. Mine isn't always appreciated."

"It will be in my country."

"I like your country, Miss Leckie. And I like you."

"I like you, too, Mr. Mason."

Across eight thousand miles and different cultures we had met. The miles and the differences fell away and we were simply a young woman and man who spoke the same language with slightly different accents. It was a very fine feeling. Public displays of emotion were not considered good form in this country where male matehood reigned supreme, but I kissed her anyway.

I stood watching as the ferry gave a mournful blast of its whistle and eased away from the slip. Pat stood near the counter on the after deck. Even in the brownout there was no mistaking that long, tawny-blonde hair with the large blue bow that matched her eyes. Half shyly, she blew me a kiss.

I could hardly wait for tomorrow evening, when I would see her again. But the night was still young and I had some catching up to do. I returned to the rooms on Goulburn Street to find the expected party at the jocose stage. My buddies had met several of those older, more practiced women and had brought them along.

The moon danced a pathway of silver across the water as the double-ended steam ferry headed east past Farm Cove and Woolloomooloo toward the Sydney suburbs. Eons ago the sea had flooded a complex of river valleys to create this magnificent harbor. The high ground now formed a hundred peninsulas and lesser promontories that divided Port Jackson—the official name bestowed by Captain Cook—into as many bays, reaches and sheltered inlets. Here land and sea met and merged in a harmony that was complete unto itself. The works of man faded and were lost in the shadows of the brownout.

Sitting on a bench outside the main-deck passenger cabin, I felt at one with it all. My left arm cradled my peacoat, which held a bottle of Black & White Scotch. My right arm cradled Pat Leckie. I will probably wake up at any moment and find myself back at Tulagi Harbor, I thought. This was as near to heaven as a sailor of the South Pacific Force was likely to come in early 1944!

Fifteen or twenty minutes out, the ferry changed course to north-northeast. It rocked gently as it crossed the rougher waters of the harbor entrance, between those great jutting Sydney Heads. Entering Manly Harbour, it passed an enclosed salt-water swimming pool on the right and made a landing between the terminal building and an amusement park on the adjacent pier.

As we disembarked, I saw a wide beach bordered by tall Norfolk Island pines and heard the faint lullaby of the breaking sea. Manly occupied a neck of land not a mile thick between the harbor and the Pacific. Along the ocean strand stood another, longer row of pines. This night they were sighing gently in a mild easterly breeze. But in the winter, Pat told me, they protected the village from storms which came beating in from that direction.

It scarcely mattered that the business district around the tree-lined Corso seemed almost as salt-burned and seedy as Redondo Beach's in Southern California. Manly looked out to ocean and surf at first light and back to the graceful curve of the bay at dusk, and always up to the great sentinel ranks of pines.

"It must be very quiet and peaceful here," I said.

Pat smiled. "Not on week ends. Lots of people come over to swim and surf and visit the fun pier."

"Do you swim?"

"Oh, yes. And bike, too. I like the outdoors."

I grinned. "I can tell."

"Is that some more of your English humor, Mr. Mason?"

"Oh, no. That, Miss Leckie, is American humor."

Hand in hand, we walked dark, quiet residential streets. We stopped at a modest wooden cottage whose walls were aflame with climbing bougainvillea. "Here," she said.

Inside, her younger sister and an Aussie lad of pre-military age were occupying the sofa. After introducing me, she tersely instructed them to go elsewhere. They left rather sulkily, I thought, and we took their places for some heavy necking.

But it went no further than that. Her mother was asleep nearby. This Australian household did not practice the permissive sexual customs sailors had told me about. Without even meeting Pat's mother, I hadn't expected it would, so I left with as much good will as I could muster.

On the ferry back to Sydney, I got out the bottle of Scotch. I seemed to be going back and forth between different cities: the one Pat Leckie inhabited and the other of King's Cross and the Haymarket. My shipmates would hardly understand why I bothered with the first, since it lacked immediate tangible rewards. I was not sure I understood why, either, except as a reprise of a youth I had left incomplete when I joined the Navy. Could one ever really leave that kind of youth behind? I joined my buddies on Goulburn Street, determined to try.

With most ship's activities secured, nearly all of the crew had daily liberty and a few resourceful sailors, including the Three Musketeers, managed 48- or 72-hour passes. Only a skeleton watch was maintained at the gangway, in the motor room to keep a generator running for lighting and power, and in the galley (where fresh eggs, milk and vegetables were served now that few but the married men cared). From the bridge, several unauthorized messages were exchanged with the *Pringle* by semaphore. On our fourth day in Sydney, a group of crewmen from DD-477 were our guests on Goulburn Street.

"Hot damn, this is some lash-up!" one of the destroyer sailors exclaimed as he and his shipmates noted the bottles of Scotch and bourbon, the large punchbowl on the fireplace mantel filled with wine-dark Australian beer—and Gerber's roommate. She was a pleasingly rounded redhead of outgoing personality whom he had met on that first foray to the night-clubs. Since then the two had spent most of their time in bed.

When our landlady popped in to announce that Mr. Aposhian's bath was ready (and to accept a double Scotch), the men of the *Pringle* were nearly speechless.

"Damn all," one finally managed. "Even back home Mom sure as hell didn't do that!"

We soon settled down to strong drink, using the potent beer as a chaser, and war stories. For a new audience, the *Pawnee* sailors told of the torpedo-boat attack off Rendova, the bombs in Renard Sound, the narrow escapes in "Blanche's Snatch" and the Slot, the destroyer-minelayer we had rescued in the Central Solomons, and the plane Aronis had shot down at Bougainville.

The *Pringle* sailors had some tales of their own. Arriving at Purvis Bay on 30 May 1943, they had participated in many of the destroyer patrols and sweeps for which we had played lifeguard. They considered the *Pawnee* their special good-luck charm: when we were operating in the area, the *Pringle* never even got her paint scorched. Two events in particular confirmed their almost superstitious regard for our ship and her crew. On the approach to Empress Augusta Bay the past November, a Japanese Betty had their ship dead in its sights. Before the plane could be brought under fire, it had crashed without launching its torpedo. *Pawnee* was in the formation; I had witnessed this attack. Three months before, however, in Gizo Strait with a support echelon for Cape Barakoma, Vella Lavella, *Pringle* suffered damage from a near-miss bomb and was heavily strafed, with casualties of 27 dead or wounded. That time, we were salvaging two disabled landing craft in the Munda Bar area. If *Pawnee* had been around Gizo, in the opinion of our visitors, it wouldn't have happened.

Far into the evening we drank and cursed and laughed and shared the almost mystic camaraderie of combat. At last we remembered how little time was left of our Sydney "rest and rehabilitation" and disbanded with some reluctance. For we had been in the Solomon Islands together. We were among the comparative few who had taken their ships up the Slot and through Ferguson Passage and Blackett Strait and on to Bougainville, and the even fewer who had returned to tell about it.*

Following the *Pringle* party it was necessary to replenish our liquor stocks. The Cockney arrived with his suitcase and the announcement that

---

* The *Pringle's* luck ran out on 16 April 1945. She was sunk off Okinawa by a direct hit from a Kamikaze. Casualties were heavy. *Pawnee* was not in the area.

the price had gone back up to 5 pounds per bottle. The destroyer escort *Williams* and the *Yuma*, a sister ship of the *Pawnee*, had just arrived at Woolloomooloo.

"Supply and demand is what it is," the cabby said with an apologetic smirk. "You blokes understand that, don't you? Supply and demand."

Aposhian had been sitting on his bed in shorts and T-shirt, hunched over in a morning-after melancholy. Now he gave the black-marketer a baleful glare.

"What I understand is that you reneged on a business deal, you Limey bastard. I ought to pitch you down the ladder on your head."

I could see my buddy was getting so angry he might do exactly that.

"If you know what's good for you, Tommy, you'll shove off," I suggested. "Let's haul ass with Halsey." He did.

The Three Musketeers and a couple of our coterie sallied forth into downtown Sydney to find a new supplier. On George Street, not far from the Italian Renaissance Town Hall, we came upon a well-dressed man of early middle age who looked properly worldly. I explained our problem to him.

The civilian favored us with a faint, ironic smile. He extracted a billfold from his coat pocket and opened it. I could see a badge and official-looking identification. Behind me, the two shipmates began edging away, prepared to make a dash for freedom. I wasn't worried. What could he do to us?

"As you can see, I am hardly the one to ask," the plainclothesman said in a cultured voice. He smiled again and let his glance shift toward a scruffy-looking man lounging against a building. "All I can offer is a Biblical injunction. 'He who seeks shall find.' Good hunting, gentlemen."

We sought, and we found.

Back at the rooms, drink in hand, I should have felt good. Tonight Aposhian, Hamblen, Aronis and I would go out and do what sailors on liberty are supposed to do. Instead, I felt depressed. The face of Pat Leckie kept returning to my mind. It was a face that fell just a little short of beauty, but it had something better than that: character.

"Damn it, Ronnie," I said. "I wasn't intending to see Pat again. But I miss her."

"That makes two of us, good buddy. I kinda miss Betty."

"Let's go see them. I know where they work."

"Let's go!"

We found them in the shipping department of a clothing factory near Darling Harbour. When Pat saw us, she let out a little shriek.

"Ted, you shouldn't have come here. If they see you, I'll get sacked!"

"We'll leave," I said placatingly. "But we want to see you and Betty when you get off. All right?"

"Why didn't you ask the other night, Ted? Of course we'll see you."

Joined by Aposhian, Gerber and the latter's roommate, we had dinner at the restaurant off Goulburn Street. I presented Pat with two pairs of genuine silk hose purchased on the black market: I had noticed she and the other girls of Sydney painted their legs. The Scotch flowed freely. Pat and Betty didn't join in but made no objection. Heavy drinking by males was accepted in their culture.

Over after-dinner coffee, Flash got to his feet and made a speech to the diners. We were happy to be here, he told them. We loved their country. It was very much like America had been fifty years ago. We were glad the United States Navy had played a major role in saving them from a Japanese invasion. The bonds between our two countries were strong and would only get stronger in the future.

It was a good speech. Aposhian sat down to scattered applause and a few cries of "Here! Here!"

Pat was embarrassed. Impromptu orations, except in the Domain on Sunday afternoons, were not an accepted part of the culture. She hid her face behind my shoulder. "You crazy Yanks!" she whispered.

Once again we took the steam ferry from the Circular Quay, sitting exactly where we had before. This time I held Pat a little closer. My precious hours in Sydney were running down the glass, and I doubted if I would ever again ride this ferry past Sydney Heads to Manly. That knowledge made the night seem dark with something more than the brownout and the overcast which blocked the moon.

We had scarcely settled on the living-room sofa when Pat's sister came in. She was not sulky this time. She had brought three Aussie sailors with her.

"The black-haired one has a crush on me, but I won't go out with him," Pat said in my ear. "Oh, Ted, please be nice!"

"I didn't come here to fight with my allies," I whispered back. Not only was I badly outnumbered but also I didn't think there was another American within twenty miles.

The sailors eyed me without pleasure and did not offer to shake hands when introduced. I didn't blame them. How would I feel if the situation were reversed?

"Men," I said, "I have a bottle of Black and White. Let me offer you a drink."

Pat's admirer was sitting tensely on the edge of his chair, as if awaiting a cue to spring into action. He was about my size and, like me, had a deviated septum. I felt sure it had been acquired as mine had been, in a brawl over a woman.

"Scotch is very dear these days," he said coldly. "How can you Yanks afford it?"

Even as I got my feet in position to leap up and fend off an attack, I gave him a smile that I hoped was ingenuous. "I've been in the Solomon Islands for a year. Then I got lucky in a poker game. Please let me share with you."

Pat got four glasses and I poured generously.

"A toast," I said, "to Australia and the Australians. You have a wonderful and friendly country."

"Do you find our women friendly?" the broken-nosed one asked.

"I find them beautiful and ladylike," I said, staring back at him.

One of his companions began to laugh. "Aw, Jim, don't be a wowser. You can't blame the Yank if he met the prettiest girl in Manly, can you now? Let's all drink like mates."

That broke the ice. Surreptitiously, Pat squeezed my hand. We sailors talked about our two navies and the war. After another round of drinks, the pugnacious one leaped to his feet.

"Time for beddie-bye. Come on, Yank, we'll see you to the ferry."

I looked at Pat. She shook her head slightly.

"It's my last night in Sydney," I said, lying like a diplomat. "I want to stay a few minutes and say good-bye to Pat."

"Mind you don't forget to be 'beautiful and ladylike'," Jim told her as he left unwillingly.

She didn't forget. But I missed the last ferry to Sydney and had to wait for an electric tram. By the time it completed its circuitous route and crossed the Harbour Bridge, a false dawn was breaking. Even in the rooms on Goulburn Street, everyone was asleep. What could I tell my buddies in any event? That I was showing all the symptoms of falling in love? I had almost got a young lady fired, had spent hours riding ferries and trams and had barely avoided a fight that might have resembled Custer's last stand. My reward was an interlude of romantic but essentially frustrating lovemaking on a sofa. My shipmates knew, even if I didn't seem to, that there was no time for such folly. Perhaps I really was island-happy, after all.

"What fools these mortals be!" the sly and goatish Puck had proclaimed from the top of the Sunday comics in the San Francisco *Examiner* all the years of my growing up. Until now I had thought the words from *A Midsummer Night's Dream* applied to parents and foster-parents and some Navy officers, certainly not to me.

"Will I see you tomorrow?" Pat had asked when she kissed me good-night at the front gate.

"Yes," I had said. "It will be the last time."

If a mortal insisted on being a fool, he should have the pride to do a thorough job of it.

A two-note wolf whistle shrilled through the small park in downtown Sydney. Aronis and I, walking arm in arm with Betty and Pat, had just passed Chief Ortalano, seated idly near a fountain.

"How the hell you two white hats rate?" he bellowed after us. "Those are the best-looking dollies I've seen in this city!"

Passers-by stared. The girls blushed and giggled. Aronis and I grinned.

"I'll bet the Aussies are sorry they ever let you into their country, Doc," I replied over my shoulder.

We were on our way to the cinema district along Pitt and George streets, where we saw an old Buster Keaton film. Pat thought the bald, deadpan comedian was very funny, as did the others in the crowded hot theater. I was bored. I fidgeted in my seat, went out for a smoke and a drink, came back to hold Pat's hand and think about the months ahead. Being with her had reminded me of home, made me apprehensive about the thousands of miles of Pacific Ocean which had to be traversed for the invasions to come. Once again, as at San Diego, it would be necessary to turn my back on things soft and feminine, "suspend the functioning of the imagination," as Hemingway advised in Men at War, and live in the very hour. This time I would have a commanding officer who was very different from Frank Dilworth and Flave George, one who had announced his intention to rule "by the book."

After the movie and dinner, it was time to be alone with Pat. We strolled through Macquarie Place at the crossroads of the city. Nearby was an obelisk of weathered sandstone, built long ago by masons from England. The grass under the spreading trees was thin and patchy. Sydney was a comparatively young city, but tonight it looked worn and faded, as old as I felt. The breeze that whispered past brought the faint smell of eucalyptus and acacia and the even fainter one, dry and dusty, of the outback.

We sat close together on some eroded stone steps. She asked where I was going when I left Sydney, and I told her "somewhere north of Bougainville." She asked about my postwar plans. I told her it was a long way to Tokyo, and reminded her what Bobbie Burns had written about "The best laid schemes o' mice an' men." Again, she asked whether anyone was waiting for me in the States, and I shook my head. "Would you like me to wait for you, Ted?"

That was a difficult no. "You would have to wait too long. Your destiny is here, with some deserving Aussie back from the wars—and he will be a very lucky man. And mine? I don't know where mine is, God damn it."

We clung to each other in that sad and certain knowledge. The war had brought us together for a few days; now it was tearing us apart, probably forever. All over the world that was happening to young lovers, who would never know whether it was love or not. Very slowly, we walked to the Circular Quay station in Sydney Cove, where the first convicts had landed 156 years before. They had founded this big, casual, hospitable, sinful but essentially British city; this city of the girl in the scarlet blouse and the one in the sailor's peacoat, and the one with the deep-ocean eyes who had graced my days in Sydney with her luminous presence.

I shouldn't have asked, but I did. Maybe it was the Scotch. Or because I wasn't enough like Papa Hemingway. "You will write to me, won't you?"

"Of course. Give me that photo we had taken at Luna Park—the one that's so awful of me—and I'll send you a better one."

"When you send me a better one, I'll do it."

I kissed her. "Good-bye, Pat Leckie. I will never forget you."

"I shan't forget you, either. Good-bye, Ted Mason."

I watched her as she boarded the gray old ferry and made her way to the counter at the after deck. For the last time I saw the straight proud figure, the long wheat-blonde hair with the bright blue bow. She touched a handkerchief to her eyes and tossed her head and waved. I waved and saluted. As the ferry began to move away from the slip, she blew me a kiss.

Four decades later, I can feel it still.

When I returned to Goulburn Street I found Aronis, who had just said his own good-byes. Our emotions were private and words were inadequate, in any event, so we shook our heads and made small, futile gestures.

"Was it worth it, my friend?" he asked with surprising acuity.

Later I will think it was, I thought. Many shipmates had found a woman to make love to. But I had found a woman worthy of love.

"It would have been, Ronnie," I said. "But time was our enemy. Let's go see how the enlisted men are living."

We filled our glasses and made the rounds. Gerber was with his inamorata; we paused for bedside conversation. Aposhian had come back with a bizarre tale of seduction in a graveyard; we marveled at that. Cy Hamblen was wandering the hallways with a woman companion, dispensing cynical good cheer; we laughed and felt better.

Gerber's redhead had told us about this young lady, so we got Hamblen aside.

"Your little playmate has the clap, we are told."

Hamblen only grinned, a cigarette dangling as usual from one corner of his mouth. "Nothin' to worry about, men. You see, I'm immune to them bugs for some goddam reason. Found that out when I was a twenty-one-dollar-a-month buck private at the International Settlement in Shanghai."

That was even more of a marvel, if true, than Flash's activities in the country churchyard. Two women who were moving toward or into their thirties joined us for drinks but Pat and Betty—and Hamblen, no doubt—had spoiled us for such easy conquests.

"You know, buddy, it won't be this way when I drink you under the table at the Zamboanga," I told Aronis. For some months we had had a standing date to meet in friendly liquid combat at the well-known Polynesian nightclub in Culver City.

Aronis reached for his Scotch. "We don't have to wait for the Zamboanga, matey."

I reached for my Scotch. "I accept your challenge, Sir Aronis."

The word was quickly passed and several shipmates, Aposhian included, joined us. But most of them either had started drinking too soon or lacked our motivation. One by one they fell and were unceremoniously dragged to one corner of the room, where I mockingly saluted them with the favorite toast of the Musketeers:

> Not drunk is he who from the floor
> Can rise alone and still drink more;
> But drunk is he who prostrate lies,
> Without the power to drink or rise.

Finally, only Aronis, Aposhian and I were upright. Some time later a dense fog invaded the room. Visibility decreased to near zero. Our vision blurred. Our movements were impeded. Our voices seemed to come to each other across a vast distance. Still we raised our glasses and shouted of great deeds past and future, and of loves mortal and immortal. I think I quoted Shakespeare, the *Rubaiyat* and Sara Teasdale about springs that never came before we were engulfed in swirling mist and Stygian darkness.

When Gerber and Hamblen held reveille, they found Aronis collapsed across one chair, Aposhian another and Mason half on and half off the bed. The others, Gerber reported with some trivial exaggeration, were "stacked up in the corner like so many lengths of firewood."

"By God," Hamblen added, "I'd rather have the clap than be in the shape you swabbies are in." Our hangovers were epic in proportion. But once on our feet, dosed with aspirin and black coffee and navigating shakily, we agreed it was only fitting and proper we depart Australia in that condition. The only thing we couldn't decide was the victor in the big drink-up at the Sydney Zamboanga. Each of the three survivors claimed the honor.

We cleared Woolloomooloo Bay at 1230 hours and held quarters for muster. Signalman Evans, Bosun's Mate Wilson and two others had missed the ship. On the port wing of the bridge, Lieutenant Cramer and John Day were taking land bearings for our position in the channel. Cramer turned to look back at the skyline of the city and quoted:

> Ah, Sydney, the land of my dream!
> I met her; I loved her:
> God, I hope she was clean!

"He sure changed my sad mood," Day told me later. "I realized we'd had a beautiful time, with beautiful memories we can have again when we get back to Uncle Sugar."

We began a wide turn to port and lost that great, coathanger-shaped bridge which would always be our symbol of Sydney. Then, as we passed between North and South Heads, the red tile roofs of the suburbs faded from sight. We steadied astern of the U.S.S. *Dent* on course 049 degrees true for Noumea, nursing our various hangovers and memories.

Already the past six days had assumed a floating, unreal quality, as if they existed not in Cramer's pragmatism but in Poe's "dream within a dream." I stood on the fantail with a mug of coffee straining for a last look at Manly by the ocean. When it was gone, I turned and started forward. Soon the *Pawnee* would have business "somewhere north of Bougainville."

Chapter Eleven

"ROCKS AND SHOALS"

Passing through the forward crew's compartment in mid-morning soon after we reached Noumea, I heard loud curses and sounds of a struggle.

A seaman named Schleppi, who had reported aboard a month before, was muscling Shipfitter W. T. Adams against a bank of lockers near the starboard ladder. He whipped a hunting knife from a belt scabbard.

"You bastard," he shouted. "I'm gonna carve you up!"

I moved over quickly. Schleppi had the knife at the other's throat and was applying pressure. The swarthy Adams had turned pale with fright. The only sound he could utter was a gurgle of desperation.

I could see that the tall, whip-slender seaman was half drunk. Moreover, he handled the knife like an expert. I had better employ the tactics I had refined on Shore Patrol duty in San Francisco, where my purpose was to prevent trouble, not punish sailors.

"What's going on, men?" I inquired in a conversational voice.

"This Bohunk from Caponeville threatened to put me on report," Schleppi snarled without looking around. "He'll be carrying his head in his hands when he does!"

Schleppi was probably the handsomest man in the ship. His thick, jet-black hair and heavy eyebrows contrasted dramatically with a fair skin and eyes of porcelain blue. Right now the eyes were glittering with a maniacal fury. He was, I decided, one of those men of always uncertain temper who becomes positively dangerous under the influence of alcohol.

"It's all right, mate," I said soothingly. "He's not putting anyone on report. He's still a boot seaman for my money. You can let him go."

Schleppi turned and impaled me with a few blue thunderbolts. "How about you, Mason? You're a first class."

"I'm not turning anyone over to Lees unless I have to."

Slowly he removed the knife from Adams's throat. "Shove off, Bohunk. Go and count your blessings."

"Forget this ever happened," I told the fleeing shipfitter. "Everything's okay."

"Hey, you're four-oh, Mason," Schleppi said, sticking out his hand. "Call me Al. How about a drink?"

That was my introduction to Harley Alexander Schleppi of Houston, Texas, a man fit for a bottle or a brawl, a game of chance or a seduction. He was not a man you could trust with your wife but you could, if he were a friend, trust him with your life. He had joined the Navy in a rage of patriotism following the sinking of the heavy cruiser *Houston* in the Java Sea early in the war. Unfortunately, patriotism was far down on the Navy's list of desirable qualities for a petty officer. Since Schleppi lacked most of these virtues, save valor, he was not likely to ever wear a rating badge.

The next morning I came across my new friend on the fantail. Although he had just been relieved from coxswain duty, he was so intoxicated he was weaving. Greeting me warmly, he pulled several five-dollar bills from his pocket.

"Poker winnings," he said. "You think I give a shit? The way these guys play cards, there's plenty more where that came from."

He crumpled the bills into a wad. "What good are a few measly fins in the South Pacific?" Winding up like a baseball pitcher, he hurled the money overboard.

Doyle Saxon, the music-loving motor machinist's mate who often served as a boat engineer, was horrified.

"Let's go, Ted," he said, sprinting for the accommodation ladder. He assumed I could handle a small boat.

I never had, but I had observed many a coxswain. Saxon started up the whaleboat engine and I took the tiller, remembering that I had to push it to starboard to go port, away from the ship. The wad of bills was still afloat and Saxon scooped it up as we passed by. I approached the ship on a slightly converging course, Saxon stopped the engine and we coasted to a perfect landing.

We were just climbing the ladder when Schleppi appeared above us. He had torn off his shirt and was balancing precariously on the fantail bulwark.

"I'm going ashore and get laid, goddammit!" he shouted. He dived into the murky green water and started swimming for Noumea, at least two miles from our anchorage off Ile Nou in the Great Roads.

"Sweet Jesus," Saxon intoned. It was as close to profanity as the religious Tennessean ever came. "Let's rescue him before he drowns."

Again we manned the whaleboat. Schleppi was swimming strongly and waved us off. But the ebbing tide began carrying him toward the northern end of Ile Nou and the sea beyond. We idled alongside until he tired and pulled him aboard, somewhat sobered by his immersion.

This time I couldn't save Schleppi from a captain's mast. He had been observed by a number of idlers, including our junior master-at-arms, an officious, skinny coxswain the Musketeers had dubbed "Jessie Junior." He got twenty hours extra duty for being under the influence of liquor aboard ship. Scrubbing bulkheads in the mess hall, he laughed off the incident. But I sensed a certain loneliness and vulnerability beneath the bravado. He was not a man who made friends easily. Some feared him, with good reason, and others who made overtures had been summarily rejected. He needed friends who did not fear him and whom he would accept as peers. Their influence, I thought, might rein in his rash and impulsive nature. I invited him to go ashore with the Three Musketeers.

With enemy forces in the Solomons defeated or isolated on blockaded islands, the focus of the Pacific War had shifted to the Bismarck Archipelago and the Marshall Islands. New Caledonia was now a backwater thousands of miles behind the lines. But a military buildup acquires a momentum of its own, unrelated to necessity. Instead of being rolled up and moved forward, the large naval bases like Noumea and Espiritu Santo continued to demand huge quantities of shipping and supplies, even as they tied up the services of many thousands of men who were needed for close mobile support of the fleet. Only America could have afforded such extravagance and waste in its war effort.

When the Musketeers and our acolyte went ashore, we found Noumea straining at its frayed seams with rear-area sailors and soldiers who lacked a mission. Our own mission was clear—finding something to drink.

Dividing our forces, Aposhian and I visited the bistro while Gerber and Schleppi reconnoitered the other side of the Place des Cocotiers. Yvette was no longer behind the bar and the owner raised his hands in Gallic ignorance when we inquired about her. Without her, his prices were much too high. But, as we had learned in Sydney, the key to getting along in Noumea was communication with the natives in their own language. Our halting French drew many smiles of appreciation, corrections of our mispronunciations, directions in a sort of Pidgin French, and finally, a rough map which directed us to a house on the hill behind the Rue Paul Doumer.

A pink-cheeked Frenchman in his mid-thirties chuckled over our execrable accents, as the others had done, and remarked in passable English that he was pleased to see two Americans who were learning the language of their host city. He took us to his basement and pointed to shelves lined with bottles.

"You will find my cognac *très excellent*," he said. "I myself make it."

He poured two dollops into wine glasses and we agreed it was excellent brandy. It bit and burned all the way down, as brandy should, and left an agreeable after-taste. The price was ten dollars a bottle.

By South Pacific standards that was a bargain. Some time before, a New Zealand corvette had come alongside for emergency refueling. While our fuel oil was being transferred to her tanks, a reverse transfer was taking place: bottles of grog for twenty-dollar bills. A number of green *Pawnee* seamen and even a few petty officers who should have known better participated in this demonstration of *caveat emptor*. When our sailors sampled their purchases, they found the rum had been so heavily diluted it was little more than colored water. The corvette uncoupled and departed before we could organize a boarding party.

Aposhian and I purchased two bottles of brandy and promised to return. We joined Gerber and Schleppi at an open-air lemonade stand on the waterfront. The charming matron who ran the place was bilingual and glad to help us with conversational French.

"By God," Gerber said, "I never thought I'd see the day I'm spiking pink lemonade with bootleg brandy. You know, it ain't half bad."

A mild breeze from the Great Roads tempered the summer sun. The brandy soon went to our heads, blurring the outlines of Noumea's militant reality. For the fifth or tenth or twentieth time we talked about our adventures in Sydney and wondered why we couldn't have stayed longer. Except for two days in *ARD-2* dry dock for inspection and painting, we had done nothing but swing around the hook. If Dilworth had still been skipper he would have tried to get us an extension. George probably would have organized a ship's party. But "Jessie" Lees, in our opinion, had little concern for the welfare of his crew. All he thought about were commendations and a rapid promotion to lieutenant commander.

Sydney introduced the subject of girls. We were reminded that just down the street was the Pink House; we could see its faded paint and the long line of men undulating back toward us. We debated about sampling its wares.

I thought about the prewar bordellos of San Diego, Bremerton, and Honolulu. There, at least, one could sit in a waiting room and make a selection. Some essential illusion was maintained. Here in Noumea, commercial sex had been dehumanized and stripped of the last vestige of dignity. I doubted that even the primitive Melanesians of the Solomon Islands would couple under such conditions. If I patronized the Pink House, I would feel soiled where no prophylaxis could reach.

"I've done a few things I'm not too proud of," I told my shipmates. "But I've never stood in line to pay a prostitute—and I'll be damned if I'm going to start now."

Even Schleppi agreed with this position. As I had thought likely, he had been on his best behavior. Obviously, membership in the Musketeers was a thing he badly wanted. We diverted ourselves with the latest Eleanor Roosevelt story.

On a visit to Halsey's headquarters the past August, the peripatetic First Lady had insisted on inspecting all the military facilities in the Noumea area. It was hardly possible to conceal the line before the Pink House or its purpose. Nor could Mrs. Roosevelt be dissuaded from halting her limousine to lecture the servicemen she found there.

"Your wives and sweethearts are waiting for you in your home towns," she allegedly scolded in her high-pitched, patrician accents. "How can you justify these tawdry encounters? Have you considered the dreadful infectious diseases you may bring back with you?"

We howled at the possibly apocryphal reaction of the sailors and GIs. A few men had fallen out of line and slunk away, shamefaced. The rest quickly moved up to fill in the gaps, delighted that their waiting time was shortened.

I laughed as loudly as the rest. I knew about the Puritan mindset: my foster-mother had one. The Puritans thought it perfectly proper to send men out to die for their country. They didn't want them to do anything sinful in the process. The ultimate tawdry encounter was not with a prostitute but rather in the act of war itself. I disagreed not with the purpose of the Pink House but with its demeaning, assembly-line operation. My rejection rested upon a personal, not a moral, choice.

I soon became concerned that our discovery of the liquor supply had opened what Gerber called "a can of worms." Several shipmates began smuggling brandy aboard in their peacoats. Each pocket would accommodate one pint bottle if the coat was artfully folded over an arm.

"I'm sweatin', fer crissakes," said a petty officer of the watch. "What's this crap with the peacoats?"

"Don't you know it's still hurricane season?" the quick-witted Schleppi replied. "You'd better batten down all the hatches, mate."

"Thin blood," said another. "Spent so much time up Blanche's Snatch I'm freezin' my ass."

Ashore, the open-air stand was crowded with *Pawnee* sailors spiking their lemonade. They returned to the ship with uncertain gait and voices raised in off-key melody. The brandy was cached in cargo and engineers' stores, the paint locker and shaft alley and among the hawsers and lines stowed in the after hold. The tense months and hair's-breadth escapes in the Solomons were still heavy on our minds. The brief visit to Sydney seemed a reward that had been proffered, then snatched away. The future promised nothing but variations on a theme, or worse.

To think too much on these things was to risk psychosis ("cracking up" or "going Asiatic," the sailors called it) or falling into a kind of despair that sought temporary oblivion at all costs. At 1300 hours on 21 February, the whaleboat was called to the fleet landing by the Shore Patrol. It returned with Flash Aposhian comatose in the footlings. He had gone to Noumea that morning in his capacity as mail orderly, visited the bistro and fallen in with a French planter of prodigious capacity for alcohol. We had to rig a sling and bring my friend aboard hand over hand, using one of the starboard davits. He was put into his bunk to sleep it off.

As if in atonement for secret guilt, Aposhian had delivered himself up to the Navy's feudal and unforgiving penal system. His principal sin, I thought, was in being a sensitive and thoughtful man at a time when callousness and blind obedience were the rewarded qualities. If a shipmate had been along to remind him of the difference between a reasoned and a foolish rebellion, he wouldn't have tried to blot out his world pain with rotgut bourbon at the bistro.

The *Pawnee* officers "threw the book" at him in the ensuing summary court-martial. He was reduced one rating, to electrician's mate second class, and heavily fined. Broke for months afterward and refusing all offers of a loan, Aposhian had to wear old, patched dungarees and forego minor luxuries like Old Spice after-shave lotion. Among the Musketeers he was known affectionately as "the rag man".

At 1435 hours on 21 February the whaleboat left the ship again, this time with two armed police petty officers. The mission of John Day and Motor Mac Paul Rydman was to pick up Al Schleppi and his drinking buddy, Soundman Second Class Martin Hansen, and return them to the ship as prisoners-at-large.

Once aboard, the two proved very much at large, roaming the ship in loud and drunken abandon. Fearful that Schleppi might attack the two PPOs, I coaxed him into turning in. My shipmates marveled that he actually did so. Together, Day and Rydman put Hansen, a 6-foot 2-inch giant weighing at least 235 pounds, into his bunk. But the usually sunny-natured soundman refused to stay there. Within a few minutes he was prowling the ship in search of a bottle. The OOD decided to send both prisoners to the brig in *ARD-2* until they sobered up.

Day came back shaking his head. "Schleppi was passed out, thank God. But Hansen was really belligerent. A couple of times I nearly had to take out my forty-five and bend it over his blond skull. Christ, I'm only five feet nine and weigh 160 pounds. That big Dane towered over me like King Kong!"

Both men had gone ashore without permission. Hansen got a deck court-martial for being "under the influence of intoxicating liquor while on duty." Schleppi got a summary court-martial for the same offense, in addition to "leaving his station of duty without being relieved." The fines were substantial.

"We got some bad booze from a goddam slant-eyed Tonkinese near the waterfront," Schleppi reported. "The stuff must have been loaded with fuel oil. Ted, I sure wish you'd been around."

Amid this turmoil, three of the four men who missed the ship in Sydney—Signalman Evans, Bosun's Mate Wilson and Electrician's Mate Paul Whatley—reported on board in the custody of the Shore Patrol. The fourth ship-jumper never did return, so his fate remained a mystery.

Experienced in the ways of the Navy, the petty officers had had the good sense to report to the authorities the day after the ship departed. They were treated with surprising leniency by Lees. All three were reduced one rating at captain's mast, but no fines were levied and no courts-martial went into their records. The captain obviously drew a sharp distinction between being under the influence on liberty, even if you missed your ship, or while on duty. The distinction drawn by the crew was that Lees, in less than two months, had held more captain's masts and passed out more courts-martial than both his predecessors combined.

"Sonar contact, sir, bearing two eight five degrees, range one eight double oh!"

This report from Soundman Hansen sent the crew double-timing to general quarters. We were off Bangon Point, Malekula Island, two hours from Espiritu Santo on the sun-splashed morning of 24 February 1944.

As soon as the radiomen were on station, I went to the bridge. We had made a submarine contact, I was certain. The directional sound beams were ricocheting from a large object on our port bow and returning solid, sharp echoes. They were different from the lower-frequency, mushier returns from whales, shrimp and schools of fish.

The captain thought so, too. He ordered the depth charges cradled in their four fantail Y-gun projectors reset from safe to standby and began closing the range. At last we might have a chance to fire our ashcans. Although they looked like 50-gallon oil drums, each was packed with 600 pounds of TNT. They were safe enough, theoretically, until the firing mechanism was set and activated by the hydrostatic pressure of seawater.

For the next forty-five minutes we played a game of cat and mouse. The bridge was filled with sonar pings and returning echoes at various ranges and bearings. The submarine was zigzagging ahead of us, moving toward deeper water. Operating in three dimensions, she could change directions, speeds and depths at will. Before we could get into depth-charge range, we would lose contact. By the time we regained it and started another run, the sub again was a thousand or more yards away. Obviously, her skipper was very good at his profession.

In the pilothouse Hansen was bent over his echo-ranging gear in fierce concentration on the sounds coming through his large, padded earphones. The captain paced back and forth behind the helmsman and annunciator operator giving an occasional change of course or speed. At the bridge wings and flying bridge, quartermasters and lookouts scanned the waters with their glasses for the telltale feathery trace of a periscope. On the fantail men stood by with depth-setting wrenches and the impulse charges which, when loaded into the projectors and detonated from the bridge, would hurl the ashcans out and away from the ship.

The enemy had sonar, too, and was tracking us. He was no mouse at all, more like a grizzly bear that occasionally circled back and turned the tables on the hunter. If so, my TBL transmitter was warmed up and tuned for an emergency message to Base Button.

I thought about our sister ship *Navajo*, the first of the *Pawnee*-class of modern deep-sea tugs. When she went down in two minutes off Espiritu Santo the past September, her depth charges began exploding. Seventeen men were lost. Although details were sketchy, we surmised she had been stalking a submarine with depth charges on standby, just as we were now. In the haste to abandon ship after the torpedo struck, someone had failed to reset them to safe; they had fired when their setting depth was reached. It was not the first time this had happened—and would not be the last.

But off Malekula Island the enemy declined to engage. We lost contact and with it our chance for glory—or the fate of the *Navajo*. Once again we wondered at the unaccountable failure of Japanese U-boats to sink more of our ships. How many times, between Noumea and Santo and the Solomons, had one had us in her sights and let us pass: fortunes of war?

"Testing," I said. "One, two, three, four, five. Five, four, three, two, one. Fire Chief One from Mohican. How do you hear me? Over."

I was in the pilothouse again on 8 March, holding the microphone of our new voice transceiver. The *Pawnee* now had a "talk-between-ships" rig, even though it was only a low-powered SCR-610 we had scrounged from the Army Signal Corps.

"This is Fire Chief One, Mohican," came a gravelly baritone from the yard oiler we were towing between Tulagi and Blanche Harbor in the Treasuries. "I hear you strength five, readability five."

The SCR was on frequency and working perfectly. "Roger, Fire Chief One. Maintain a guard on this circuit. Over."

"Roger, wilco and out." A simple "wilco"—meaning that the order had been received and would be complied with—was sufficient, but few adhered that closely to voice radio procedure.

The captain had been standing by impatiently while I tuned and tested the SCR. Now he favored me with a faint, pleased smile. He was a man who devoutly believed in establishing clear lines of communication. Except, I thought, with his crew.

At 0300 the next morning I was awakened by a messenger and summoned to the bridge. Our SO-8 search radar, installed at Ile Nou the past month, had gone out near Vangunu Island. Our sole escort was radarless subchaser 1046, and Captain Lees wanted his eyes back. Immediately.

For a long time the *Pawnee* had had a radio technician who couldn't copy code and no radar. Now the situation was reversed. Trained as an operator, I had little schooling in radio materiel and less knowledge of radar circuitry. But I had had the foresight to study the instruction manual for the SO-8 and to stock a supply of replacement parts. I brought up a boxful of spares from the storage locker on the second platform deck, got out my manual and rudimentary test equipment and began checking vacuum tubes, the cause of most radar failures. All were functioning. So were the resistors, condensers and inductance coils laid out in bewildering array on the chassis for the receiver and pulse transmitter. That left the rotating-beam antenna atop the foremast.

At dawn's early light I climbed the mast, using the flimsy ladder welded alongside, and emerged onto a small railed platform which housed the fore-and-aft, speed and aircraft-warning lights. Just above was the concave shape of the now-motionless antenna. Below, with each half roll of the ship, I was looking down nearly one hundred feet to the waters of the Slot. With one arm locked around the top of the platform railing, I examined the seal between the antenna and the coaxial transmission lines to the transmitter and receiver. Wear and tear at the joint, I had read, could allow the inert gas in the seal to bleed out and moisture to enter. If that was the problem, nothing could be done until we returned to Tulagi. In disgust, I made a few swipes at the connection with my wrench.

Back in the pilothouse, I turned the power on. To my considerable surprise, the oscilloscope lighted up in the familiar grassy green. On the scope's plan position indicator were the partial outlines of Vangunu, New Georgia, and the other islands of the Central Solomons.

"The radar is now operational, captain."

"Set the radar watch," Lees instructed the OOD. He looked at his wristwatch. It was 0630.

"Well done, Mason," he said in a tone faintly edged with sarcasm.

"Thank you, captain," I said.

Gerber had observed my scaling of the foremast. "This Mason is a goddam genius," he remarked facetiously at breakfast. "He can copy the code, read *Time* magazine, and carry on a conversation all at the same time. When the radar craps out, he hangs by one hand from the top of the foremast and by God fixes it!"

"I used the old Henry Ford method," I said with a wink. "Learned it on my first Model A. When it wouldn't start I'd rap it across the hood a few times, just to teach it who was boss."

When we returned to Purvis Bay on 13 March with the now empty YO-162, we moored alongside our sister ship *Menominee*. The motor launch was called out to pick up a passenger from PC-584.

"My God, it's 'Black Jack' Genereaux," someone muttered as the launch approached. That square-jawed face and dark stubble of beard were unmistakable under the gold leaf of a commander's cap.

Only a year ago, although it seemed much longer than that, we had begun our ill-starred salvage of the U.S.S. *Delphinus* at Nomobitigue Reef.

" 'Beware the ides of March'," I quoted.

"If Genereaux's involved, I'll buy that."

No sooner had the commander clambered aboard than we were under way for Koli Point, Guadalcanal, to pick up several of his salvage party. Something was afoot, probably an invasion in the Bismarck Archipelago.

All doubts were dispelled when *Pawnee* weighed anchor on 17 March and joined a two-column formation departing Lunga Roads with a screen of destroyers. We fell in astern of two landing ships of a strange new type in the left column and increased speed to 14.5 knots on a course almost due north.

From the forecastle I pointed to our companions. "They look like a shotgun marriage between an LST and a floating dry dock," I told Doyle Saxon. He had just emerged from the airless after hold, where he spent hours every day practicing on the "fiddle" he bought in Sydney.

He chuckled. "Back in the Great Smokies, we really do have shotgun weddings. From this angle, Ted, that ship up ahead looks like the whale that swallowed Jonah."

We were talking about the dock landing ships *Gunston Hall* and *Epping Forest*. They were designed to transport loaded LCMs (landing craft, mechanized) and smaller craft to invasion beaches. When the dock well—which extended clear forward under the superstructure—was flooded, the LCMs could leave the mother ship through stern gates under their own power.

In column one was another LSD, the *Lindenwald*, astern of the attack transport *Callaway*. Our sister ship *Apache* brought up the rear. We were glad to note that our destroyer screen included the *Pringle*, along with the *Eaton*, *Fullam*, *Saufley* and *Sigourney*. Genereaux was commander of Task Unit 31.2.8, the salvage group. Perhaps the Navy had learned how to properly deploy its *Pawnees* and *Apaches*. Now it was attaching them directly to the invasion force rather than having them operate independently, as we had in the Solomons.

On 19 March we rendezvoused with eight destroyer-transports and their screen to form Task Group 31.2, commanded by Commodore Lawrence Reifsnider in the destroyer *Terry*. We were now well north of the enemy base in Rabaul, on a course that roughly paralleled the needle shape of New Ireland. Our destination, we learned, was an insignificant island named Emirau in the St. Matthias group, located at 150 degrees east latitude just south of the Equator.

I sat alone on the fantail watching the gray silhouettes of the converted transports wax and wane as a high half-moon passed through scudding cloud cover. No sound could be heard but the ceaseless metallic pounding of *Pawnee*'s diesel engines. The other ships seemed as silent and unreal as ghosts, Flying Dutchmen of the Bismarcks. Would the landing on Emirau be opposed? If so, many of the young men of the Fourth Marine Regiment (First Provisional Brigade), sweating now in their overcrowded troop compartments, would themselves become ghosts, sentenced never to return from this remote archipelago named for Germany's Iron Chancellor.

Music drifted up from the open hatch to the after crew's compartment. Someone had put "There Will Never Be Another You" on the record player. I thought of Bertha Morton, my childhood sweetheart. She was now a wife and mother but I still carried her photo in my billfold. I regarded it as a talisman, a sort of occult protection against the random lightning bolts of war. The photo had been with me when I swam through the burning waters of Pearl Harbor and when I rode the *Pawnee* through a Blanche Channel boiling with torpedo wakes. Wherever I went, it would go with me. To the bottom of the sea, or to the States.

I thought of Pat Leckie. What was it I had told her that last night in Sydney? "We will go somewhere north of Bougainville. Then the Philippines. After that, who knows?"

We had been corresponding but this knowledge fell like a shadow across every page. Her letters were bright and cheerful and insubstantial. Mine already were heavy with nostalgia. I knew I would not, could not return to Sydney. Assuming survival, it was a choice between her and college and career in my own country. She knew it, too. I must stop clinging to foolish song lyrics, like a man overboard grasping at flotsam, and let her go, as I had let Helen Hazelton go.

At 0530 on 20 March the klaxon sent the *Pawnee* crew to general quarters. I had expected to awaken to gunfire but heard none. As soon as the radio shack was manned and ready I went to the bridge to check the performance of the voice radio and radar.

We were lying to off an island of modest size which might have served as a prototype for all South Pacific islands: a white-sand beach behind its guardian coral reef, a coconut plantation, a tangle of tropical flora rolling like surf across the low interior hills. Emirau was green, beautiful and perfectly without character.

While our destroyers patrolled the seaward approaches, the mother landing ships began disgorging their "guppies"—LCMs and LCTs that went wriggling toward the shore. Overhead, friendly fighters and bombers from a nearby carrier task force darted and swooped and climbed in layer upon layer of air screen. By 1940 we formed up with Task Group 31.2 in a cruising disposition and departed Emirau.

From the viewpoint of the *Pawnee* crew (and, no doubt, the Fourth Marines) it had been one fine little invasion. The landing was unopposed and there were few, if any, casualties. We had fitted the last link in the chain of steel around Rabaul and broken through the Bismarck Archipelago into the Caroline Islands. Best of all, there would be no telegrams to American families from the Navy Department: "We regret to inform you . . . "

For the next month we were under way almost continuously. Twice we returned to Emirau's Homestead Plantation Beach with supporting echelons of shipping. When the attack transports, cargo ships and LSTs finished unloading, the island was groaning beneath the weight of 18,000 men and tens of thousands of tons of supplies. Since Emirau's only future role was that of a torpedo-boat base and secondary airstrip for the surveillance of enemy forces, we learned later, it seemed a classic example of overkill.

For a third of this time the *Pawnee* continued as the flagship of Task Unit 31.2.8. But Commander Genereaux could find nothing to salvage. He was reduced to holding court in the wardroom and stalking the bridge, where he was treated by our officers and men with the deference he demanded and no doubt deserved. All hands were greatly relieved when we anchored at Koli Point just long enough to send Black Jack ashore in our motor launch. We felt sure we would see him again. The *Pawnee* seemed to attract him as a magnet does iron filings. The betting was that next time he would be a four-striper. (Events proved us only half right. Genereaux did not return to the *Pawnee*; he was promoted to a captaincy.)

"We got a B-24 in trouble!"

That report sent all the idlers scrambling for topside vantage points. The *Pawnee*, tucked safely behind a column of LSTs, was just north of the Green Islands with Task Group 31.6, the second echelon to Emirau.

A four-engine Liberator bomber, easily recognizable by its two slab-shaped tails, was crossing ahead of the convoy at about 3,000 feet. Its engines were coughing and sputtering and it was losing altitude. Off our port bow they quit altogether. In an eerie silence the thick-bodied bomber started dropping toward the sea. One by one, white parachutes unfurled and blossomed. We counted ten, the entire crew of a heavy bomber. Out at the line of the horizon, a faint plume of spray marked the plane's demise.

On our bridge a signal lamp blinked Morse code. We requested, and received, permission from the task-group commander in the *Terry* to rescue the airmen. As the convoy steamed on, we set sonar and radar watches, changed course to 250 degrees true and launched the whaleboat. Within half an hour, all ten fliers were being helped over the bulwarks from the sea ladder. Miraculously, none was seriously injured.

Following a trip to sick bay for Doc Ortalano's gruff ministrations, they were given clean skivvies and dungarees and plied with sandwiches and coffee in the mess hall. Their bird, they said, had been hit by flak over Kavieng, New Ireland. Some were still pale and shaken by their ordeal while others were voluble and expansive in the euphoria that follows a brush with death. I knew both reactions well.

The calmest of all was a tall, fair-haired sergeant, a waist gunner. "Say, what kind of a boat is this?" he asked in the accents of the Confederacy. "What's its name?"

I told him.

"Injun tribe," he said. "Well, we shorely won't forget you-all. There's a heap of water out here and it's damn deep. No, don't think I'd cotton to being a bluejacket."

"Well, there's a heap of air up there and it's damn thin," I said, laughing. "Parachuting down is not my game."

"Nothin' to it," he shrugged. "These twenty-fours are easier to bail out of than your B-17s. Hell, this is the second time I've hit the silk."

The sergeant had lost two planes but still preferred the Air Corps. I had lost a battleship but still preferred the Navy. It is a good thing for the military, I thought, that men are tribalists at heart. Secretly, they believe their own village is best and choose the known evil over the unknown.

The next day I had reason to question my choice. I found myself standing with Seaman Tom Peters at captain's mast, charged with sleeping during the routine general quarters at 0550. After standing the midwatch, I hadn't heard the Junior MAA make his rounds. I awakened to an empty compartment and double-timed to the radio shack, but "Jessie Junior" already had put me on report. He was one of the few shipmates I had learned to dislike as a petty despot swollen with his own importance, and he disliked and feared me in turn. His failure to awaken me might have been deliberate, but I had no proof. Peters was charged with the same offense.

With *Pawnee* in a forward area, I could give no excuses that Lees would find acceptable, least of all an hour and a half of sleep. Standing watch eight hours a day while still supervising the radio gang and training a striker were not sufficient. Nor was the fact that the morning G.Q. was simply precautionary. The klaxon, which would surely have roused me, was reserved for emergencies, and the *Pawnee* had no public-address system, relying upon the master-at-arms to sound reveille.

"I'm going to let you off with a warning, Mason," the captain said. "I'd advise you to spend less time with your buddies and your books." I bit my lip and said nothing.

Peters's defense was obvious from his appearance. His hands were shaking and his face had an ashen pallor. Hospitalized the past November at Espiritu Santo, he had been returned to the ship as fit for duty three months later. He was not fit for duty, a fact that was known to every enlisted man and should have been to the officers. To humiliate a sick man at a mast for punishment, even though he too was let off with a warning, seemed to the crew an abuse of a commanding officer's authority.

When, we asked, would the "Articles for the Government of the Navy" be revised by Congress to afford some minimal protection to enlisted men? We answered our own question: not until the war had been won. We understood that a military organization was not, and could not be, a democracy, with civilian-type law courts where a man was presumed innocent until found guilty by a jury of his peers. The authority of a ship's captain must, especially in wartime, approach the absolute. In the interests of order, discipline and combat efficiency, he or a court-martial board answerable to him served not only as judge and jury but also as jailer. In the hands of commanding officers who tempered justice with mercy, there were few complaints from the enlisted men. But under "sundowner" captains, the Articles often proved an instrument of guilt assumed, mitigating circumstances ignored, and harsh penalties without recourse. The Articles, in fact, had been known to generations of sailors as "Rocks and Shoals," or "Death and Greater Punishments." The problem, it seemed to me, was that the Navy assumed its captains to be nearly perfect human beings, nautical versions of Plato's philosopher-kings. Some enlightened commanders I had heard about—Daniel J. Callaghan of the *San Francisco* and Ellis M. Zacharias of the *Salt Lake City* and *New Mexico,* among them—approached that ideal, but they were the rule-proving exceptions. The Navy was rightly concerned with the competency of the autocrats selected to command its ships. I wished it was also concerned with their humanity.

When we got under way for Guadalcanal and Purvis Bay with our task group ten days later, we left the airmen and Tom Peters behind. Shortly after his captain's mast Peters had another seizure and was transferred to the cargo ship *Adhara* for treatment. Our question here was why the Navy doctors sent men back to their ships when they belonged in a hospital bed? With thousands of idlers on shore duty, they no longer could plead a shortage of personnel. We hoped Peters would get a medical discharge before he suffered a fatal attack and was buried and forgotten in some jungle cemetery.

Chapter Twelve

SCAVENGERS OF WAR

Now began five months of mopping-up duties around the Solomons, a period which brought us two meaningless commendations and came close to breaking the spirit of the crew. While newer sister ships supported the Fifth Fleet in the Central Pacific, *Pawnee* became what I called a "scavenger of war."

Our first operation took us to Pavuvu Island in the Russells. An LCT had gone aground on the reef off Cape Baloka, Sunlight Channel, where the First Marine Division was rehearsing for its next invasion. We anchored in 38 fathoms, put our tow wire aboard the tank landing craft and took a strain while heaving around on our anchor chain. When we built up our speed to 112 rpm, the LCT slued to port and floated off the reef. With a yard tug standing by, the craft was soon proceeding to Renard Sound on neighboring Banika Island under its own power.

Before returning to Purvis, we moored to a buoy in the sound for the night. The fighter strip off which we had anchored so often the past eventful summer was nearly deserted. The Russells had made a brief stage appearance in the spotlight of war and now could return to the farming of coconuts. (We could not know then that they would be remembered chiefly because a Reserve lieutenant named John F. Kennedy had based his *PT-109* at Wernham Cove, Banika, in that same summer of 1943.)

To our considerable amusement, the ship's company received a commendation from Commander Naval Bases, Forward Areas, South Pacific, for this humdrum salvage exercise. Lees's ability as a ship-handler was still in question, the Musketeers decided, but not his skill at writing glowing reports to his superiors.

Daily by Armed Forces Radio and at every mail call we received reports of the momentous events which were reshaping the world and altering our futures. By comparison, our pull-and-push assignments seemed utterly without significance, as meaningless as schoolboys playing at Cowboys and Indians.

To our north, Kwajalein and Eniwetok atolls in the Marshall Islands had been taken against the typical fanatic resistance of the Japanese. From Great Britain, thousands of Allied bombers were reducing German cities to rubble in almost continuous air raids. In Italy, General Clark's Fifth Army at last had broken out of Anzio, and Rome had been abandoned by the enemy. To the east, Russian armies were pushing the Wehrmacht back upon the fatherland with offensives in Poland, Romania and the Crimea. The biggest news of all came on 7 June, East Longitude date. Mounting the greatest seaborne invasion in history, the Allies sent 600 warships and 4,000 other vessels across the English Channel to land 155,000 men on the beaches of Normandy. Hitler's *Festung Europa* had been breached, and the end of the Third Reich now was only a matter of time and blood.

While the American and British soldiers were consolidating their foothold on the French coast, the *Pawnee* was ordered out on another scavenging job. At Govanna Inlet on Florida Island, midway between Tulagi Harbor and Purvis Bay, we anchored near the derelict Japanese destroyer *Kikutsuki*.

We would earn no plaudits here. Many months before, Commander Genereaux had rightly taken the credit for raising the *Kikutsuki* from 72 feet of water in Florida Island's Halavo Bay, where the seaplane base was located, and putting her into dry dock. Admiral Halsey, the originator of the plan to present the enemy ship to Nimitz, had decided she could not be made seaworthy without enormous expense. She was towed to Govanna Inlet and beached. Now, with Halsey preparing to leave the South Pacific for his new command, the Third Fleet, someone had revived his "hare-brained scheme," as Aposhian described it. The 34th Seabee Battalion was ordered to pump out the *Kikutsuki* and prepare her for a second dry-docking.

When *Pawnee* arrived on the scene on 10 June, the Seabees were swarming over the hulk. Our principal contributions to the resurrection of this war trophy were passing a welding machine across by pontoon barge, followed by a few shipfitters and seamen, and providing a mooring for two assisting yard tugs, YT-312 and -313. With the exception of brief periods away for our own dry-docking at Port Purvis and test runs in Ironbottom Sound, we remained there for the next twenty-four days.

Govanna Inlet was a rancid lagoon behind Carter City, the site of the Navy's landing-craft repair unit. Anything that couldn't be fixed was beached or moored upstream. The inlet was fast becoming a graveyard for war-crippled vessels.

Only the daily ebb and flow of the tide gave any indication that Govanna was connected with the sea. Even the breeze that rippled the dull green waters was an occasional thing. The inlet was girdled by steep hills solid with a choking growth that fought for light and space right to the water's edge.

In the *Pawnee* we fought to extract oxygen from the soupy air and tried to avoid the sun. But the belowdecks compartments were as hot as the engine room and we were driven to the mess hall, where we spent hours drinking coffee, swallowing salt tablets, sweating and cursing.

"I've been in some real hell holes," said one well-traveled Regular. "Lunga Point was the worst, as you guys know. Then Honolulu and Norfolk, Virginia, with T.I. running a close fourth. But none of 'em can compare to this slimy slough."

As if to make the difficult nearly unbearable, the captain began holding quarters for muster on the fantail at 0750 every morning. Under his predecessors, we usually had been mustered at our work stations. Following the roll call by the senior petty officer of each division—communications, gunnery, first lieutenant, engineering and stores—and the report, "All present or accounted for, sir," the executive officer would step forward.

His remarks could hardly be dignified as an address: harangue would be an apter description. Lieutenant (junior grade) H. C. Cramer had a loud voice and, apparently, a low opinion of enlisted men. His concern was that we were not following the ship's Organization Book, written by Lees when he was exec, to the letter. His method was to impugn our dedication, skill, integrity and, on occasion, our patriotism.

"Day after day this feather merchant stands there and insults us," I said angrily. "When he's hiding behind his uniform, he's really tough. Where was this flag-waver when I was at Pearl, when we were making our nightly runs up Blanche Channel and the Slot?"

"Safe in Florida is where he was," Schleppi said contemptuously, "and that's where I'll find him after the war. I'm gonna stomp him into the deck and then I'm gonna carve my initials in his hide with this knife! Hey, maybe he'll come out on deck some night when we're under way. How many officers been lost at sea down here?"

"More than one," Aposhian replied. "But you'll never see Cramer after dark. He knows what the crew thinks of him."

On 1 July *YT-312* brought the *Kikutsuki* along our starboard side, where she was moored with bow, after bow spring, forward quarter spring and stern lines. Her draft was near normal and she had only a slight starboard list. But that condition was temporary, the Seabees told us. Some of her transverse bulkheads were made of wood and were permanently warped and sprung. They had been heavily shored up but there was no way they could be made water-tight. We had better get this relic into dry dock *pronto*.

Before we moved the ship to *ARD-14* in Purvis Bay, I went aboard. She had a short forecastle with a pronounced break to a well deck forward of the superstructure but the rest of her was conventional destroyer. Some of her 12-cm. guns in their shielded mounts were still in place, but the tubes for her long-lance torpedoes were missing. I was sure our experts were studying them most carefully, along with any tin fish salvaged from the bottom of Halavo Bay. Her foremast was gone but the pilothouse was still intact, equipped about as our destroyers were except for the Japanese inscriptions and the lack of any radar gear.

Despite the diagonal stains on her bow from changing waterlines as she was raised, I could make out the faded white numerals 23. If the enemy followed our numbering system, she must be a rather old ship, dating at least to the 1920s.* On the starboard side of the main deck, above the after engine room, was a large steel patch placed by Genereaux. That was where the 500-pound bomb dropped by one of our *Yorktown* dive bombers had hit on 4 May 1942. One smallish bomb had been sufficient to sink this eggshell destroyer.

I wondered how the Japanese could fight so well with such mediocre ships. One reason, of course, was their superlative torpedoes. Many an American sailor had died before Moosbrugger showed the Navy how to employ radar to counteract them. Another must be the skill and valor of the enemy crews. It was a service axiom that superior crews in inferior ships often defeated superior ships manned by poorly trained, unblooded crews. The British had done this often in the Mediterranean against the Italian Navy.

Treading the decks my enemies had trod gave me an odd feeling of déjà vu. I was uncomfortably reminded of our common humanity. I had

---

* On this assumption, the Navy originally identified her as the *Yayoi* of the *Mutsuki* class. For at least the first six months of the war, however, Japanese destroyers carried the number of the division to which they belonged. The bow numerals indicated destroyer division 23, destroyer squadron 6. The ship was the *Kikutsuki* (also spelled *Kikuzuki*). Like the *Yayoi*, she belonged to the *Mutsuki* class of 1926.

heard, and believed, that the enlisted men of the Imperial Japanese Navy were pawns of a discipline fiercer and a tyranny more absolute than my captains and admirals dared enforce. Their culture was authoritarian, and ours, we liked to think, was not. When they took their ships on suicide missions or machine-gunned helpless survivors in the water, they were simply following orders. We had had our own suicide missions, like that Bloody Friday the Thirteenth off Guadalcanal, and we too had had our "turkey shoots." Even their Bushido code, which equated surrender with dishonor, was understandable, for had I not made essentially the same commitment? Probably, they were men not very much different from me. They knew fear, anxiety, doubt, exaltation. They had left wives and sweethearts behind in Osaka, Kobe, Hiroshima. Some doubtless had renounced love for duty, as I had done. And they had families who would grieve at their deaths in battle. Knowing these things, it was not easy to hate them. But in war hate is a defense against debilitating fear. In the interests of both survival and country, it was necessary to go on hating.

We were not to leave Govanna Inlet without another reminder of the cost of war. As we prepared to anchor off the beach near Carter City, Bill Miller put his glasses on what appeared to be the forward end of an LST. "God damn," he intoned. "There's the 'nightmare T'." Many months before, we had brought the remains of *LST-342* to Carter City. The forward end of the torpedoed landing ship had been beached here and forgotten. From that top deck, red now with more than blood, we had shoveled and hosed the bodies into Oloana Bay while our officers' steward read the burial service.

She came off the beach easily at the end of our 2-inch tow wire, as if glad to be leaving Govanna Inlet. I hoped we were going to give her a decent burial at sea. But a PT-sized Higgins boat came up with a deep-throated growl and took her over when we heaved in our wire. That is the last we ever saw of *LST-342*.

"They're prob'ly gonna use her for target practice," Gerber guessed.

"How quickly the admirals and their strikers forget," I said. "The men went over the side like dog meat—make that shark meat—and now they're using up the ship, too. Hell, Kaiser has turned out fifty more like her by this time."

"There's one consolation" Aposhian said. "After the war who's going to remember the shore bases like Carter City or Koli Point or Lunga Roads, or any of the third-stringers who commanded them?"

We found that a sentiment worth holding to. We had forgotten about the military historians and the writers of war memoirs.

Without fuel oil, every piece of machinery in the Solomons, from a

Jeep to a cruiser, was so much useless scrap iron. The PT-boats alone burned thousands of gallons of high-octane gasoline a day (for a very poor return on the investment, in our opinion) and the aircraft much much more. The forces afloat consumed millions of gallons of "black oil" every month. All this fuel had to be transported from the States in fleet oilers and redistributed to Navy ports and bases the length of the Solomons chain and into the Bismarcks.

Pawnee's contribution to this massive exercise in logistics came at the end of our 2-inch tow wire. Having run out of scavenging jobs, we returned to hauling yard oilers and gasoline barges as far as Seeadler Harbor in the Admiralty Islands, a hundred miles southwest of Emirau.

Between towing assignments, we were often under way on "busy work" which could have been performed more economically by a yard tug. Tinkering with words one midwatch, I coined a phrase for these chores: "A pot-pourri of piddling pursuits." Some shipmates thought it rather humorous, once I had explained what pot-pourri meant. For we were realizing the aptness of the cliché that war is 1 percent sheer terror and 99 percent utter boredom.

One of the few who was not bored was our captain. He was busy, in the opinion of the Musketeers and others, "polishing apples" and amassing "Brownie points." Typical was our repair of the submarine fuel line between the storage tanks at Kukum Beach, Guadalcanal, and the offshore fueling buoys. When the line sprang a leak we picked it up from 10 fathoms of water with our seaplane winch and replaced the damaged section of hose with a new one. Commander Naval Bases, Forward Areas, rewarded us with another letter of commendation.

"The key paragraph is number four," I told the men grouped around the mess hall bulletin board. " 'A copy of this letter will be attached to the Commanding Officer's next fitness report.' "

"Ah, so," said Aposhian. "That's how you make lieutenant commander."

During these tedious months, the Marines took Saipan, Guam, and Tinian in the Marianas Islands of the Central Pacific, and the Navy sank three enemy aircraft carriers in the Battle of the Philippine Sea (popularly known as "the great Marianas turkey shoot"). Now only naval surface forces and land-based air could oppose MacArthur's return to the islands he had fled in defeat more than two years before. In the *Pawnee*, far from the action, the only breaks in our routine were unpleasant—saying good-bye to valued shipmates and friends.

The first to go, on 19 April, was John Day. Reporting as a signalman first, he had changed his rating at the request of his superiors and been promoted to chief quartermaster. Recommended for a commission by

Captain George, he was appointed instead to the broken stripe of a warrant boatswain. In the opinion of most crewmen, a ship scheduled for invasion duty could ill afford the loss of his dedication and competence on the bridge.

Day was followed the next month by Ensign Moodie, now a lieutenant junior-grade. Remembering our conversation in San Diego, I wondered if his woman had waited for him. Next to depart were my sparring partner, Dick Garrett, and a first-class baker named Aaron Flowers.

In August the radio gang lost John See. Leaving with him for new construction were Boatswain's Mate Wilson, Storekeeper First Bernard Cantley and Electrician's Mate First William Knott. All eight men were plank owners.

"I've been a lucky man to have had a first class like you," See said effusively as we gripped hands and arms.

"You made your own luck, buddy," I said. "We're sure going to miss you." In his twenty-one months on board he had seldom complained, never been late relieving the watch and, most importantly, had never garbled a message for the *Pawnee*. Like Aronis, he was the kind of dutiful young man the nation always had called upon in time of crisis. The Navy "brass hats" usually took the credit but their accomplishments and rewards were made possible by unheralded, unsung enlisted men like Aronis and See. (The sardonic service joke was that the only white hats who won medals were the dead ones, and those in defeats the officers were pleased to forget.) My striker Bill Bates, now standing watch on a Fox schedule which had gradually increased from 18 to 25 words per minute, was of the same breed. I was very glad of that.

Three more plank owners left the ship in August: Chief Boatswain's Mate Paul Campbell, Officers' Cook First Arsenio Albano and Chief Pharmacist's Mate Samuel Salvadore Ortalano. They were joined by Signalman First Bernard O'Donnell, who had been transferred from the cruiser *Helena* less than a month before she was sunk in Kula Gulf.

We would rather miss Doc Ortalano, the Musketeers decided. At the morning and afternoon sick call he could always be found in his chief's chair, his hands folded across his ample stomach like some dyspeptic Buddha. Rising reluctantly, he would accompany the taking of temperatures and application of medicines and bandages with a grumbling monolog. He liked especially to lecture Schleppi and me on the harmful effects of exercise. It was something he was opposed to at any time, but in the South Pacific it could lead to nothing but heart and lung disorders.

"Only mad dogs and Englishmen . . . " he would say. "You can excuse a guy with a name like Mason. But you, Schleppi, oughta know better. Not that you look Italian, fer crissakes. Who ever heard of a Dago with blue eyes?"

"Northern Italy, Doc," Schleppi would counter.

"Yeah, yeah. Your family musta got mixed up with them goddam Krauts."

Even Campbell, a gruff and uncommunicative man who seldom smiled, drew a few kind words. In his function as chief master-at-arms, he had seemed only too willing to bring men up before the captain. But at the mess hall poker games he had been a generous, if reluctant, contributor.

His favorite ploy, after an hour or so of steady losses, was the raise before the draw. "I'm drivin' all the shoe clerks out," he would rasp, throwing greenbacks onto the table. "It'll cost ya ten bucks to stick around."

We soon learned that he was probably holding no more than a pair and a "kicker." Those who called and improved their hands raised Campbell in turn. Several raises could leave a couple of hundred dollars in the pot. Almost always, the chief lost. Slamming his cards down, he would depart in a cloud of profanity. The next payday he was back at the table.

With the exception of Ortalano's replacement, a first class named Joe Manning, all the baker's dozen of new men were seamen or firemen fresh from boot camp. (Among them, I noted wryly, was one Jesse James Howard, Jr.) The training had to begin all over again. Every department of the ship except the radio gang was affected. When we went back up the line our lack of experience on the bridge, in the engine and motor rooms and at the guns might cost us dearly. The response of the captain and exec was the promulgation of new regulations, diatribes of increasing rancor at morning muster and frequent captain's masts.

"At boot camp the petty officers were like little tin gods," Aposhian observed. "On this bucket every enlisted man is treated like a boot, regardless of his rating."

The first to crack under the strain was the luckless Jackson, our black steward's mate. Given a deck court-martial for "disobeying orders, talking back to a superior and shirking duty," he allegedly armed himself with a knife from the wardroom pantry and issued dire threats against the officers. He was soon recommended for a general court-martial and shipped to the brig of the repair ship *Whitney* for "safekeeping." There was little doubt whose care and protection the captain had in mind. And little doubt, either, that Jackson would do hard time in a naval prison. It seemed an unnecessarily severe way to treat a man who had earned several campaign ribbons and battle stars.

Dick Garrett hadn't yet been transferred.

"What happened, Dick?" I asked.

His face became an impassive ebony mask. "You know about the three wise little monkeys, don't you? 'See no evil, hear no evil, speak no evil.' That's how I get along in the Navy."

The loss of the steward's mate resulted in an order which heaped insult atop indignity in the eyes of the crew. As one of Jackson's duties, he had carried officers' chairs from the wardroom to the fantail for the evening movies. Lees's solution to the servant shortage was to have the ship's duty section, seamen and petty officers alike, perform this menial task.

His action provoked a near-rebellion. For a change, the principal opposition came from Regular Navy crewmen who were aware of their few rights under the regulations.

"I consider this an unlawful order," Bill Miller said with great indignation. "The next step would be to have the duty section make up the officers' bunks and shine their shoes."

At an unusual request mast, several petty officers asked the captain to rescind his order. The matter was fortuitously resolved when a new steward's mate reported for duty. Lees may have avoided a loss of face, but even his later actions in the Luzon Strait did not entirely erase the enmity that he had incurred. As I had once feared she might under a commanding officer less considerate of his crew than Frank Dilworth, the *Pawnee* had become a hell ship. Thousands of miles from any hope of redress by senator or representative, the crew were without influence or power beyond a hat-in-hand "mast for requests." Nor could we look to our junior officers and warrants. They seemed no more than dutiful aye-aye sayers, unable or unwilling to oppose the captain. Even to go over his head to Commander Service Force, South Pacific, would be an exercise in futility which would provoke only retribution. My country was at war, and everyone and everything—including that most prized attribute of American citizenship, freedom of the individual—had been subordinated to victory. We all were prisoners of circumstance, caught between a necessary goal, the preservation of the Western democracies, and the force of arms which must be used to achieve it. By now I had read enough history to pray that the means did not, at last, become the ends.

I was reminded of that tension between ends and means when I stood at captain's mast on 22 June, charged with "late hammocks."

"In the *California* and *Pennsylvania*, Captain, the radiomen who stand 24-hour watches are allowed to sleep in after a midwatch," I said. I had already made this request of Cramer and been summarily refused.

"In my ship you radiomen get no special privileges," Lees replied. "The sooner you learn that, Mason, the better for you. I'm letting you off with a warning, this time."

Newly commissioned USS *Pawnee* (ATF–74) boxes the compass on shakedown cruise in San Francisco Bay in November 1942. (Navy Department photo.)

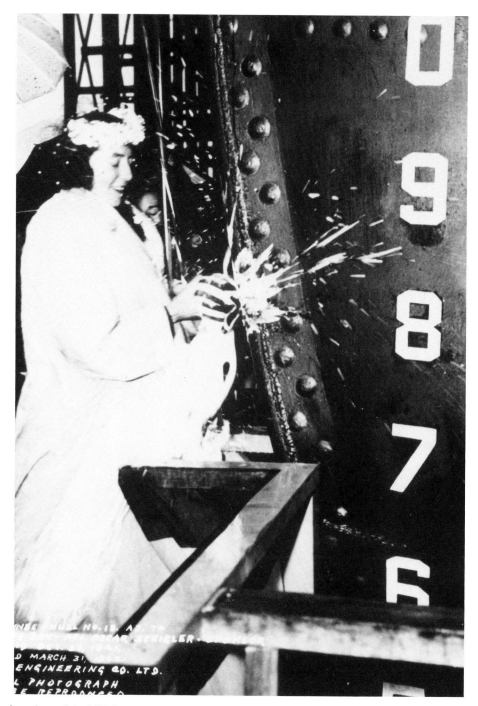

Launching of the USS *Pawnee* on a rainy day in late March, 1942. The charming sponsor is Mrs. Oscar Stiegler, wife of a naval officer (USNA, Class of 1926) attached to the 12th Naval District, San Francisco. (U.S. Navy photo.)

Grumman F4F Wildcats on patrol over San Francisco Bay in 1942. Below the fighter planes are Treasure and Yerba Buena (Goat) Islands, attached to "the City" by the thin umbilical of the San Francisco-Oakland Bay Bridge. (Photo courtesy of the National Archives.)

Noumea, New Caledonia, a former French penal colony and now, in early 1943, the headquarters of Admiral William F. (Bull) Halsey, Commander South Pacific. Chimneys of nickel smelter on peninsula in middle distance are belching "flames and foul smoke." Beyond are ships at anchor in the Great Roads. (Photo courtesy of the National Archives.)

Pawnee maneuvers radically to evade torpedoes fired by PT Squadron 9 on night of 30 June 1943. At right attack transport *McCawley*, hit by two torpedoes, has suffered a powder magazine explosion and starts toward bottom of Blanche Channel. Patrolling destroyer *McCalla* can be seen in the background. Painting by marine artist Richard DeRosset was meticulously researched and captures the event with photographic accuracy.

Attack transport *McCawley* offloads troops at Rendova Island around noon of 30 June 1943. During the withdrawal of the landing force a few hours later, she was torpedoed in the engine room by a Japanese plane. That evening, as *Pawnee* was coming alongside to take her in tow, she was sunk by American mosquito boats of PT Squadron 9. (Photo courtesy of John A. Hutchinson.)

Pawnee's sister ship *Menominee* (right), under the command of the redoubtable Emile C. ("Black Jack") Genereaux, salvages the Japanese destroyer *Kikutsuki* from Halavo Bay, Florida Island, in summer of 1943. (Photo courtesy of the National Archives.)

Unpublished photo of Navy's infamous "recreation center" on Aore Island, New Hebrides. At "Duffy's Tavern" (right), sailors could purchase two cans of uncured beer. (Photo courtesy of Le Roy E. Zahn.)

Gunners in LSTs stand by to repel enemy air attack during reinforcement echelon to Empress Augusta Bay, Bougainville, in November 1943. (U.S. Navy photo.)

During operations in the Solomons, sailors in the *Pringle* (DD–477) considered the *Pawnee* their special good-luck charm. VOS seaplane on catapult abaft no. 2 stack was an experiment which was abandoned before *Pringle* reached the war zone. (U.S. Navy photo.)

From this unnamed offshore island, Japanese brought a murderous enfilading fire upon the Marine landing force on Peleliu. (U.S. Navy photo.)

Fleet oiler *Mississinewa* burns furiously at Ulithi Atoll, the first victim of the Japanese *Kaiten*, the one-man suicide torpedo. (U.S. Navy photo.)

Author compares cruisers like the *Houston* and *Canberra* to the overage battleship *Pennsylvania*: "Powerful punchers with glass jaws." Above, frail *Pennsylvania*, sister of the *Arizona*, nearly sinks from effects of one torpedo at Buckner Bay, Okinawa, in 1945. Only determined salvage efforts by *Pawnee*-class fleet tugs saved her. (U.S. Navy photo.)

Old battleships *Pennsylvania* (left) and *New Mexico* somewhere in the Western Pacific in 1944. Author served with Admiral W. S. Pye's flag complement in the "Pennsy" in 1942. (U.S. Navy photo.)

As enemy surface force approached, *Houston* appeared in imminent danger of breaking up or capsizing. Her main longitudinal beams had been buckled by the impact of the first torpedo. All four engine rooms and both firerooms were flooded, and she was laden with more than 6,300 tons of salt water. (U.S. Navy photo.)

In June–July 1944, *Pawnee* helped the Seabees prepare Japanese destroyer *Kikutsuki* for a second drydocking. She was later beached and abandoned again; her rusted hulk can still be seen in Tulagi Harbor. (Photo courtesy of the National Archives.)

Units of Task Group 30.3, also known as CripDiv 1, head for Ulithi Atoll on an east-southeast course. In middle distance *Canberra* is towed by *Munsee*. Just abaft *Canberra*'s stern is *Pawnee* towing severely damaged *Houston*. Photo was taken from light cruiser *Birmingham*, shooting across her escorting *Fletcher*-class destroyer. (U.S. Navy photo.)

H174 V CCO   -A- C DIV 9   160227   H174 BR 50 BT

THIS IS PART PARAPHRASED X C T G 30R3 BATTLE PLAN EFFECTIVE
WHEN ORDERED X PLAN ABLE FOUR DDS TWO TUGS REMOVE PERSONNEL
SINKQCRIPPLE RETIRE REVERSE ENEMY BEARING X PLAN BAKER SIX
DDS REMOVE PERSONNEL CRIPPLE CONTINUE TOWING X PLAN CHARLIE
X SIX DDS REMOVE PERSONNEL CRIPPLE AND TUGS THEN SINK THOSE
SHIPS BT

TOR BY VIS: 0140 MIL/FL
TWU BY RDO: 0015 BATES

Date: 16 OCT 1944						DATE-TIME GROUP	160227			
Originator			Action Addressee				Info. Addressee			
COMMANDER CRUISER DIVISION			USS PAWNEE ATF 74							
X: Information A: Action	Capt.	Exec.	Nav.	1st Lt.	Eng.	Supply	Repair	Medical	Gun.	Comm.	O.O.D.

Task Group 30.3 battle plan, as copied by Radioman Bates in *Pawnee* radio shack and deciphered by Communication Officer Calvin Rempfer. Message was repeated an hour and a half later by flashing light and copied by Quartermaster William J. Miller. (Message decode courtesy of Calvin Rempfer.)

(BRISBANE FROM C. T. GL 30.3)

I WANT TO THANK ALL HANDS FOR THE SPLENDID JOB AND WELL DONE
TO OUR PILOTS AND THE PERSONNEL OF OUR INJURED FRIENDS AND TO
MUNSEE AND PAWNEE FOR GETTING US OUT OF THE DANGER AREA

TOR: 2240/TBY/
TWU: 0530/TM/RDO

Date: 18 OCT 1944						DATE-TIME GROUP	BLANK			
Originator			Action Addressee				Info. Addressee			
COMTASKGROUP 30.3			ALL SHIPS							
X: Information	Capt.	Exec.	Nav.	1st Lt.	Eng.	Supply	Repair	Medical	Gun.	Comm.	O.O.D.

Initials "TM" after time group indicate that author copied this message on the Fox schedule. It was originated by Admiral DuBose, Commander Task Group 30.3, decoded by Lieutenant (jg) Calvin Rempfer. Message had been sent earlier by voice radio to all ships of the task group. (Courtesy of Calvin Rempfer.)

Much as I disliked my condition of servitude, and on occasion disliked myself for accepting it, I must endure Lees and Cramer a while longer. I was sustained in this necessity by news from the nation's capital. On the very day of Lees's gun-deck lecture, the President had signed a historic "GI Bill of Rights" that included funds for a college education for any qualified veteran. The many hours spent in the mess hall with my books had ensured my qualifications, and now I knew how I would spend the first four years of peace. If the luck continued good.

Meanwhile, in newspapers and magazines from the States I found a way to remind the *Pawnee*'s tyrants junior grade that they had temporary custody only of my body; they did not own my soul. With the 1944 general election approaching, the government was encouraging the millions of overseas servicemen to register and vote. The various states had simplified their cumbersome procedures for casting absentee ballots.

I remembered the words of Thomas Jefferson: "A little rebellion now and then is a good thing." And I remembered a conversation with a hulking longshoreman on the San Francisco Embarcadero in 1942.

While waiting for the *Pawnee*, I had the pleasant problem of financing numerous liberties and leaves. The solution was a permit issued by the International Longshoremen's and Warehousemen's Union which allowed me to work on the waterfront. After a 10-hour shift unloading freighters at the then-princely wages of $1.75 an hour, I drank beer with the stevedores. They told me about the maritime workers' strikes of 1934 and 1936 which had broken, at the cost of several lives and great financial hardship, the corrupt labor practices of the shipping moguls.

The strikes had been led by Union President Harry Bridges, a tough one-time seaman from Melbourne, Australia, whom the Government was trying to deport as a Communist alien.

"Is Bridges really a Communist?" I had asked.

The 6-foot 5-inch longshoreman had fixed me with a cold eye. "I dunno. So what if he is? We need more socialism, not less, in this country. All Roosevelt did was save the lousy goddam system for the capitalists. Now he has to bribe 'em with cost-plus contracts—that means cost plus whatever you can steal—so they'll produce the stuff we need. They're gonna get filthy rich while you're fightin' their war for 'em. Hey, you gonna be old enough to vote in the '44 election?"

I had encountered radicals in books but never before in person. I nodded.

"Well, vote for Norman Thomas, the Socialist Party candidate. If you're still in one piece, that is. He's an egghead preacher, not militant enough for my money, but he's the best we got."

Thanks to great good fortune and Commander George, I was "still in one piece." I decided to accept the advice of Jefferson and the long-shoreman. I registered as a Socialist. Aposhian, Gerber and Schleppi were delighted with this expression of defiance and constitutionality. They, too, registered as Socialists. So did several other shipmates. With much merriment we all cast our ballots for Norman Thomas, the pacifist Presbyterian minister.

Here was an instance where Lees and Cramer were powerless to act. The drive to get out the service vote was sanctioned by the highest civilian authorities, and the Navy had no choice but cooperation. The whole crew, even those who disapproved of our politics, joined in the laughter. Assembled by choice just outside the open portholes of the wardroom, the Musketeers laughed loudest of all. We had tweaked the noses of the naval personages, from Lees to "Iron Pants" Ernie King, and won a memorable if brief victory at psychological warfare.

The captain, according to the scuttlebutt, laughed not at all. In his eyes the Musketeers were "the terrible foursome," and Mason was their insurrectional leader. The burly San Francisco stevedore would, I thought, have been cynically amused. So would the author of *The Iron Heel*.

The case of a new seaman second I shall call Kapette gave the crew more sorely needed laughter. He must have been one of the very few men ever to go "over the hill" at Espiritu Santo.

He was a freckle-faced bricktop of muscular physique. He seemed, at first glance, a typical small-town boy from Anywhere, U.S.A. But a closer look discovered small mean eyes of a dull China blue and a swagger unbecoming a boot seaman. He gave the impression of having been a schoolyard bully and we had quite enough bullies already. He immediately antagonized Radioman Third Bill Bowser, apparently unaware that my protégé had grown up in a section of Denver where learning how to fight was a necessary condition of survival.

"Well, today's the day," Bowser told me. "Kapette has agreed to meet me on Aore Island and we'll settle our differences."

"He has more intestinal fortitude than some members of this crew," I said. As Bowser knew, I was referring to "Jessie Junior," who declined to meet me ashore and had, in consequence, been restricted to the ship for some months. "Think you can take him?"

"I'm sure going to try. I don't think he's as tough as he pretends to be."

I nodded. "Need a referee?"

"Naw. He wants to fight dirty, I can do that, too."

A few hours later our whaleboat returned from Aore with the recre-ation party. Bowser took the ladder two rungs at a time. He was grinning and unmarked except for a bruise or two.

"I took him, Mason!" he exulted. "We went off under the coconut trees and had at it barefisted. I punished him good. Pretty soon he'd had enough. He quit."

"I thought he might. Where is he, by the way?"

"By God, he took off. Didn't come back with the rest of us. I think he's embarrassed to show his ugly face around here." Bowser laughed. "I tell you, it's a little uglier now!"

Four days later a police petty officer picked up Kapette from the Shore Patrol at Santo and returned him to the ship for a summary court-martial. The seaman refused to explain how he had made his way from Aore to Base Button and eluded the patrol for all that time. One popular theory was that he had fled into the bush with the intention of turning native, but the reformed cannibals refused to have anything to do with him.

In late August we got under way for Ironbottom Sound, rendezvoused with the attack transports of Task Group 32.3 and began four days of ma-neuvers as one of the inner anti-submarine screen. The impending invasion which would break the *Pawnee*'s five-month-long doldrums was not the long-awaited "main event," the assault on the Philippines. It was, I heard, a sort of six-round semifinal: the seizure of one of the Caroline Islands on the approaches to the Philippines. By the last day of the month we had refueled and were anchored in Supply Cove, Purvis Bay.

I was in the mess hall when a messenger approached. Thanks to the free pocketbooks of the Armed Services Editions, I was on a reading spree ranging from Budd Schulberg's *What Makes Sammy Run?* to Carl Sandburg's biography of Abraham Lincoln and Will Durant's *The Life of Greece*.

"Mason, the captain wants to see you in the wardroom."

Lees, Cramer and one of the other officers were drinking coffee at the oval table in the wardroom mess. Standing before them was Ray Figlewicz, who had been advanced to radioman first class some months before.

"Glad you could join us, Mason," the captain said in that bland voice which can turn a pleasantry into a veiled judgment.

He held up some documents. "I have good news. I've received orders to transfer one first-class radioman to the States for new construction."

The officers looked at me, trying to gauge my reaction. I half-smiled and said nothing.

The captain's smile became broader. He seemed to be enjoying this tableau. "Now the question is, who will go and who will stay?"

So that's it, I thought. You people shafted me before on OCS and you're going to try to shaft me again.

"Since you and Figlewicz are both plank owners, I think the fair course is to cut cards. High card goes to the States. Is that agreeable?"

"Yes, sir!" Figlewicz said.

In the background Officers' Steward Head, the minister, gave me a faint smile and the barest of nods toward the table. Together, they managed to convey encouragement for me and rebuke for the officers. He disapproved of cardplaying, I had heard.

"If you think that's the 'fair course', captain." Half a chance was better than none.

"Mr. Cramer will shuffle the cards."

The cards were already on the table. Cramer shuffled adroitly and placed the deck squarely in the middle of the green baize tablecloth.

"You're senior petty officer, Mason. You go first."

It was one of those random chances upon which a man's life and destiny hinge. The one who cut the high card would shortly be on his way home. The low man would invade the Caroline Islands in the far Western Pacific. Thinking about the incident later, I recalled the lines from the Rubaiyat:

> The Ball no question makes of Ayes and Noes,
> But Here or There as strikes the Player goes;
> And He that toss'd you down into the Field,
> *He* knows about it all—HE knows—HE knows!

I reached for the deck. I turned a black nine.

Figlewicz stepped forward, hesitated, leaned across the table. He turned a red jack.

"Very well," the captain said. "Figlewicz goes."

I refused to give these officers the satisfaction of observing my disappointment. I shrugged as if it did not matter, and walked jauntily from the wardroom.

"A goddam nine," Schleppi said at dinner. "A knave of hearts! If I'd cut for you, buddy, you'd be packing your seabag right now, instead of that Polack from Caponeville."

"Like hell you would have!" Gerber shouted, wrapping a brawny arm around my neck. "If we've got to stay on this prison ship, Mason's got to stay, too. We're the Four Musketeers, ain't we?"

Aposhian looked thoughtful. "You had the seniority, so you should have gone. On this ship you play by their rules, or you pay the price."

I hoped my public smile wasn't too rueful. "No one ever said there wasn't one."

Secretly I wondered just how high the price might be. I went to the fantail that afternoon and boxed many rounds with Gerber, Schleppi, Murphy and anyone else who would volunteer to put the gloves on.

Chapter Thirteen

"ONCE MORE UNTO THE BREACH": PELELIU

To commit brave men to a needless struggle was criminal; to consign them to oblivion is profane.

William Manchester, *Goodbye, Darkness*

A rising cloud of gunsmoke and coral dust covered the southern half of the seven-mile-long island of Peleliu in the Western Carolines. Sheets of flame flickered like heat lightning at the turrets of the three battleships and five heavy cruisers steaming slowly offshore, followed by the double and triple thunderclaps of the salvoes. Watching from the gun deck of the *Pawnee* in the brilliant sunshine of early morning, I could follow the flights of the high-explosive projectiles until they slammed into the island in great gushers of scarlet and gray.

Slowly the cloud of destruction spread as the ships "walked" their fire toward a rugged spine of dark gray coral which dominated one claw of the pincer-shaped island. By 0730 of 15 September, Peleliu had disappeared from view. After four days of this terrifying bombardment, alternated at two-hour intervals with dive-bombing and strafing by carrier aircraft, it was hard to believe that very many of the 10,000 defenders were still alive. But I knew about Tarawa from sailors who had been there. The Japanese had survived a heavy bombardment, emerged from their concrete and coconut-log fortifications and met the Marines at the landing beaches. I was very much afraid they would be waiting here, too.

Gerber joined me at the lifeline. "By God, it sounds like a summer storm in the Rockies! What are the names of them battlewagons?"

216

"The one with the cage foremast is the *Maryland*. Sister of the *West Virginia*, sunk at Pearl. The two with the tower superstructures are the *New Mexico* class. Probably the *Idaho* and *Mississippi*. Some admiral's riding in style in the *New Mex*—she's fitted as a force flagship."

"Where the hell are your old ships?"

"The *Pennsy* is a few miles south. She and the *Tennessee* are hitting Angaur Island. The 'prune barge,' God bless her, is probably milling around Saipan and Tinian, up north."

"Say, what's it like on one of those wagons when all the guns are firing?"

"Like being locked up in the brig while the gyrenes pound on your cage with sledgehammers," I said with a grin. "The whole ship is shoved sideways in the water. Light bulbs shatter. The cork insulation falls down from the overhead and the paint peels off the bulkheads—that's when they still had paint. You pray your radio gear holds together. You also pray you're not stone deaf before you're twenty-five."

"You must have been glad when you drew the *Pawnee*, buddy."

"I was until Lees came along and began running her like a battleship."

Gerber laughed. "Well, we're safe from the horseshit for a while. He's got more important things to worry about now."

"And Cramer's busy in the chartroom. No time to insult the crew at quarters for muster. Let us give thanks for that."

The *Pawnee* was under way at 10 knots as an inshore screen for the attack transports and dock landing ships of Task Group 32.3, which we had accompanied from Guadalcanal in a huge convoy. The troopships were lying to just outside the range of enemy artillery. The thirty LSTs that carried the Marines of the 1st Division who would make the initial assault had moved in to 4,000 yards and were disgorging their LVTs (amphibious tractors). The skies were cloudless, the surf was down and a fitful breeze barely ruffled the waters west of Peleliu. Conditions were ideal for an invasion.

I thought of my former shipmate, George Tahbone.

"Before they took the warpath at the Little Bighorn, the Sioux and Cheyenne braves told each other, 'This is a good day for dying!' " he had said as we approached Empress Augusta Bay. On this 15th of September 1944, I was certain many brave men would die.

The thunder of the guns ceased and an eerie silence fell over the beleaguered island. As the smoke drifted up and away, I had my first good look at Peleliu. Behind the white-sand landing beaches at the southern end, an X-shaped airstrip had been hacked out of the rain forest. The four-day bombardment had snapped off or leveled nearly every remaining tree, revealing the rough coral of the broken terrain. The 300-foot-high series of ridges that ran along the western claw of the pincers had been stripped of ground cover, too, and stood stark and ominous. I didn't claim to be a military expert, but I had been a hunter. If I were the Japanese commander, I would have fortified this high ground. When the Americans advanced upon the airstrip, I would make them pay dearly.

I heard a thin Banshee wail and recoiled instinctively. I had first heard that sound at Pearl Harbor; it had very nearly been my last one. Out of the sun came our Dauntless dive bombers, ripping at the sky in near-vertical descents. They pulled out at a thousand feet, their bombs falling in graceful arcs upon the enemy installations and pillboxes. Fresh explosions reverberated across the water, but I waited in vain for the double detonation and fountain of flame which would announce a direct hit on an ammunition or fuel dump. Now I was sure the Japanese were well prepared for another desperate defense to the last man.

The SBDs were followed by squadrons of gull-winged Corsair fighters. The F4Us peeled off and fell away in sections, just as I had seen planes do in the Hollywood war films. As they hurtled across the island, the orange tracers from their 20-mm. cannons stitched orderly patterns of coral shrapnel. It was a brave show, except that I couldn't see any Japanese. Doubtless they were belowground, holding their fire so as not to reveal the gun positions.

Now the transports were offloading the men of the reserve forces and their equipment into LCV(P)s. The 36-foot landing craft began circling the ships in a kind of martial Maypole dance as they awaited orders to head for the line of departure just outside the fringing reef. There they would transfer their troops to LVTs returning from the beaches.

The first assault waves were already at the reef, preparing to make the last perilous dash through the surf and into the guns of the enemy. What were they thinking, these fellow countrymen who faced death or maiming within a few minutes? Most likely, as I knew from my own experiences at Pearl Harbor and in the Solomons, very little. With the body mobilizing its defenses against danger, all orderly thought processes were blocked out. The stomach twisted into ever-tightening knots, the blood pounded in the temples, the hands and legs trembled as a cold sweat chilled the body and the scalp tingled atavistically. Against the whirling unreality of the moment, one offered only a brief incoherent prayer or a curse that was itself a prayer. One was sustained not by that but by the presence of one's buddies, the greater fear of showing cowardice before them and, finally, by an inability to accept the fact of one's imminent death.

A dozen or more LCI gunboats fitted with 4.5-inch rocket launchers moved in close to the reef. The rockets whooshed out at the shore like flights of flame-tipped arrows. I thought about the words of the Star-Spangled Banner. Had we really made so little progress from "the rockets' red glare, the bombs bursting in air" of 1814?

Promptly at 0830 the first wave of tracked LVTs began moving toward the beaches. I could see that it was in trouble immediately. The Japanese emerged from their concealed fortifications in the high denuded ridges, the shell-pocked area behind the landing grounds and a small offshore island to the south and caught the Marines in a murderous cross fire of artillery, mortars and automatic weapons. Great white spouts of shrapnel-laced water erupted among the LVTs. Machine-gun fire flayed the water. Some of the amtracs were hit and burst into flames. I could see tiny figures leaping and falling into the lagoon. Not all of them came up to struggle on toward the dubious shelter of the beach. Soon the entire mile-long landing area was hidden in a thick pall of smoke.

I cursed the admirals and generals who sent Americans into the massed gunfire of an enemy-in-waiting. Hundreds, more likely thousands, would die to capture fourteen square miles of coral outcropping that few had heard of before the war and no one would care about afterward. Our military leaders, pompous and arrogant again after their humiliating defeats at Pearl Harbor, in the Philippines, the Java Sea and the Solomons, seemed almost as contemptuous of human life as their counterparts in Tokyo and Berlin. In Washington my once-admired President, now a sick man, was evidently relinquishing the reins of government to the Joint Chiefs of Staff. The nation's industrial capacity, the greatest in the world, had been turned entirely to the service of the gun. The war, judging by the carnage unfolding before me, had assumed a mad momentum of its own, beyond the reach of civilian supervison and restraint. Who was controlling the men who controlled the Pacific Fleet?*

"Four days of bombardment and I'll bet we didn't knock out half a dozen Jap positions," I told Gerber and Aposhian as we watched the dive

---

* Finding no air opposition to his carrier strikes of 6–8 September on the Palaus, Admiral Halsey proposed bypassing the islands in favor of an immediate assault on Leyte in the Philippines. He was overruled by Admiral Nimitz, Commander-in-Chief Pacific. The latter's decision to proceed with the landings on Peleliu and Angaur as a preliminary to Leyte was quicky approved by the Combined Joint Chiefs of Staff of the United States and Great Britain. At the time, 12–16 September, they were meeting with Roosevelt and Churchill at Quebec for the Octagon Conference. (Morison, Vol. XII, pp. 13–15.)

bombers and fighters continue their assaults. "I can't believe it. Now the Marines are going to have to dig 'em out with M-1s and bayonets."

"You can say one thing for Dugout Doug," Gerber commented. "He knows one of the first rules of boxing: hit 'em where they ain't expectin' it. The Marines just charge in swinging."

Morse code blinked out at us from a signal searchlight on the *Mount McKinley*, the amphibious command ship for the Palau Islands Operation. The flagship's derricklike foremast bristled with radio and radar antennas.

"You ought to see the Comm Op Plan for this invasion," I said. "At least fifty radio frequencies to guard from that AGC over there. I hear they've got a vice admiral, a rear admiral and two major generals on board. In fact, we've got enough gold braid floating around out here to form a couple of platoons. Just think of all the medals they're going to award themselves."

Pawnee increased speed and moved inshore to the LST staging area. We spent the next few hours circulating among the LSTs to pick up the skids used in launching their tank landing craft. Ashore, the smoke of battle had partially lifted. Wrecked amtracs, some still burning, were strewn like discarded toys along the entire landing area, from White Beach 1 to Orange Beach 3. Just to the south, "Elsie Item" rocket gunboats were attacking the nameless offshore islet from which the Japanese were interdicting the beaches.

The 1st, 5th and 7th Marine Regiments had now tied their lines together and held a tenuous beachhead a few hundred yards deep extending to the edge of the airstrip. They were forming up and moving out in company strength to reduce the enemy pillboxes from their blind sides with rifle grenades and flame throwers. From beyond the reef, I could make little order of the confused struggle but I could hear the sharp crack of artillery, the crump of mortar fire and the ceaseless popping of machine guns, like endless strings of firecrackers at this range. Every land breeze brought the musky stench of burning jungle, the acid sting of cordite and another, quite unmistakable smell: putrefaction. Already the dead were beginning to decompose under a remorseless sun which had driven the temperature to 115 degrees Fahrenheit.

"It's a goddam blood bath," I told my friends. "We're towing skids around like a harbor tug, and over there the Marines are getting knocked off like clay pigeons in a shooting gallery."

Aposhian looked as shaken as I felt. "I wish someone would tell me why we landed on this island. Have you seen one Jap aircraft up there? I tell you, this is nothing but a criminal waste of good men."

"Say, what's the name of this fouled-up operation?" Gerber asked.

I laughed, a short laugh. "Some flag officer had a great sense of humor or a lack of imagination—I can't figure which. It's called Stalemate II."

Towards dusk of D-day the transports and their screen retired to sea, but *Pawnee* spent the night lying to off White Beaches 1 and 2, the sector where Colonel Lewis B. ("Chesty") Puller had landed his 1st Regimental Combat Team. Puller, an ex-private who owned a chestful of decorations for action in Haiti, Nicaragua, Guadalcanal and Cape Gloucester, New Britain, was rightly renowned as the toughest Marine in the Corps. All that night we heard intermittent fire as the Japanese tried to infiltrate the American lines. Periodically, star shell from the cruiser *Honolulu* and three destroyers burst over the enemy positions. In the sinister cold light, the battered island looked like a moonscape. I thought of the photos I had seen of no-man's land during the trench warfare of World War I.

The next morning we transferred the LCT skids to a passing landing craft, got under way and began closing White Beach 1. When we stopped engines and laid to, we were very close indeed: perhaps a hundred yards.

Just to our left, off the port bow, the land ended in a jumble of fissured spires and boulders some fifty feet high. For the past twenty-four hours, "the Point" had been the focus of desperate action. From pillboxes blasted into the solid coral, the Japanese had brought down an enfilading fire upon Puller's exposed flank at White Beach 1. A company of Marines had fought its way to the crest, overrunning the pillboxes and decimating the enemy infantry. What was left of Company K still held the isolated Point in the face of incoming mortar, grenade and sniper fire. On the ship's bridge and flying bridge, all the binoculars were aimed at this rocky outcropping, a battlefield in microcosm.

Papoose Evans looked down from the flying bridge. "Hey, Mason, take a look at that point, just above the water. Friend of yours?"

Fifteen feet above the lapping surf were the head and torso of a helmeted Japanese soldier. From the forecastle, where I was standing with Aposhian and Gerber, I could see him clearly. He was holding his rifle in a port arms position, as if on a parade ground, and looking toward the *Pawnee*. He must have infiltrated during the night and now was marooned in a "spider hole." The Marines' attention was directed toward the danger from the east. As soon as they noticed him, his life would be measured in minutes, perhaps seconds.

I decided to shorten it before he could take any fellow Americans with him. The promise I had made in the main top of the *California* at Pearl Harbor was to kill no more animals. It did not include men. I requested permission to draw a Springfield service rifle from the armory and open fire on the soldier.

Permission was denied by the captain. He also denied permission to send a few rounds from our port 20-mm. gun toward the Point.

I could understand not hazarding cannon fire for fear of hitting the Marines directly above the sentry. But sniper fire was hardly a risk, unless I missed my first shots. I didn't think I would miss: I had been shooting a rifle since I was eight years old.

"Damn it all," I said. "We might have saved some poor gyrene's ass. If the old man doesn't trust me, why doesn't he let Hamblen or Aronis try?"

"Suppose you'd only wounded this Nip," Aposhian said. "Why, the bastard might have fired back!"

"Maybe Lees never read Halsey's sign at Tulagi," I replied. If I was secretly relieved, I was too furious about Peleliu to admit it even to myself.

Whatever the reason for our presence at the Point, we were ordered to return to the transport area in late afternoon. The lone Japanese soldier had disappeared. I looked back at bloody Peleliu and thought about him. He had seemed calm and resolute, fully prepared to perish in battle. Or perhaps what I interpreted as resolution was only a numb acceptance of his fate. Did he really believe that dying for his "divine" emperor would transport him into some Oriental Valhalla? Or was it only a shadowy hope one clung to, as some of my shipmates clung to a hope of salvation through their Christian God?

What had sent the Marines of the 1st Division into a firestorm of lead and steel on the beaches of Peleliu? What had sustained Company K in its assault on the pillboxes of the Point, and now was sustaining those other companies as they began their reduction of the fortifications in depth on the Umurbrogol (already named Bloody Nose Ridge)?

Partly it was God and Country, Old Glory and the National Anthem. But these were abstractions, unlikely to long sustain men looking moment by moment at death. Partly it was Family, Home Town and the Girl Next Door, but even these became abstractions when viewed from the stinking coral limestone of Peleliu. Ultimately, the Marines fought for their squad, their platoon and their comrades, just as sailors fought for their ship, that shard of home they took with them, and the men who shared its close and boisterous confinement. Especially for the true friends, those whom Shakespeare called, in *King Henry V*, "We few, we happy few, we band of brothers." I knew I would risk my life for the Musketeers, and I was sure any of them would risk his life for me. I supposed the enemy picket had felt the same way. I was sorry for those shipmates who would never know the brotherly love—for that it surely was—which sustained a man when all else failed.

By D-day plus 3 we had done very little to justify our presence in the Palaus. We returned to White Beach, took a crippled LVT in tow and passed it to *LST-127* and moved some pontoon barges to Orange Beach, where a causeway was under construction. We laid to off Angaur Island, where the 321st Regimental Combat Team of the 81st Army Division had landed the previous day, provisioned ship from the *Mount McKinley*, refueled from *LST-687* and resumed patrolling.

Ashore, the 3rd Battalion, 1st Marines, was scaling the dead dark coral of convoluted Bloody Nose Ridge in the face of mortar barrages and raking machine-gun fire from above. The Japanese were entrenched in multiple bunkers, caves and defilades and there they fought to the death. Against the fanaticism inspired by their Bushido code, the Marines brought fixed bayonets, hand grenades, flame throwers and a matchless valor.

I felt almost ashamed that I could do so little to help them, that the Navy could do so little. Only our carrier aircraft were of any value. They swooped low and engulfed enemy positions with the terrible searing fire of jellied napalm.

"Pearl Harbor was one level of hell," I told Aposhian. "Peleliu is another, even worse because it's sustained. I tell you, Flash, I take back everything I've ever said about the Marines. They're the ones who are really winning the Pacific."

"No doubt about it," Aposhian agreed. "They held Guadalcanal when Frank Jack Fletcher hauled ass with his carriers and left them in the lurch. They took Bougainville and Tarawa—and they'll take Peleliu, too. All we did was get them here."

A part of me shrank from the violence I was witnessing at a safe distance. Another part had a fierce impulse to take a gun and join my valiant countrymen on Peleliu. I wondered if I was a good enough man to endure the horrors of Bloody Nose Ridge. I hoped that I was.

On 19 September, D-day plus 4, we closed the *Mount McKinley* for new orders, came alongside the heavy cruiser *Louisville* (my transportation from Pearl Harbor to San Francisco a decade or so before, in the spring of 1942) to embark three aviation specialists, and headed north-northwest. Scuttlebutt spread through the *Pawnee* with the speed of sound. We were going to Kossol Passage, where no American ship had ever been! The Japs had sowed more mines in the passage than there was corn in Kansas!

I went to the bridge, ostensibly to check out the voice radio and radar gear but actually to sneak a look at the charts. The Palau group, which extends some 110 miles in a roughly north-south direction, comprises half a dozen main islands and hundreds of smaller islands and islets, mostly steep-cliffed and all choked with rain forest, as Peleliu had been before we arrived. A broad, unfriendly reef with few navigable channels girdled the entire group. At the northern end was the 10-mile-wide strait named Kossol Passage.

Making an end run around the barrier reef, we passed Malakal and Koror Harbors, now empty of Japanese shipping, and Babelthuap, largest island of the group. Some 25,000 troops were isolated there and unable to reinforce the garrison at Peleliu, I was told. At the west entrance to Kossol we were met by the minesweeper *Competent*. To the great relief of the crew, she led us into the passage with paravanes streamed.

"She's one of the new *Raven*-class sweepers," Bill Miller remarked, "A trim-looking ship, about 900 tons. She's got a high freeboard and a shallow draft—less than 11 feet."

"If I were serving in one of those things I'd want a very shallow draft," I quipped. "In fact, I'd want to be clear out of the water."

"Hit a mine and you would be," was his cryptic reply.

Part of the scuttlebutt proved untrue. We had been preceded into Kossol by seaplane tenders *Chandeleur*, *Mackinac*, *Pocomoke* and *Yakutat*, which already were servicing three squadrons of PBM patrol and search planes. The *Grapple*, a new-type salvage vessel equipped for air-sea rescue, was waiting to receive our passengers. I wondered if taxi service was our only reason for venturing into this inhospitable strait, whose muddy waters were continually roiled by strong winds and currents from the west.

With due allowance for American exaggeration, the rumors about the mines were true. Before abandoning Kossol, the Japanese had planted it with hundreds of contact mines. Our sweepers were passing slowly back and forth in formation, their torpedo-shaped paravanes rigged out from sweep cables that cut mines loose from their moorings. When the mines floated to the surface they were destroyed by gunfire. An occasional booming detonation and a trunk of boiling white water supporting a tree of black smoke announced success in their nail-biting work. But failure could be fatal. A few hours before we arrived a wooden-hulled sweeper, YMS-19, had passed over a mine. The entire stern end disintegrated in a cascade of timbers. Within seconds, the 136-foot-long vessel had heeled over 90 degrees and slid below the surface. Nine men of the crew of thirty-five were lost.

"Friendly" mines posed an additional threat. During a carrier air raid on the Palaus the past March, specially equipped Avenger aircraft from the *Lexington*, *Bunker Hill* and *Hornet* had laid dozens of "eggs" at both entrances to bottle up enemy ships at anchor in the passage. Sent to demolish swept mines on D-day plus 1, the destroyer *Wadleigh* was herself nearly demolished by an unswept one at the east entrance. She limped away with four dead and fifteen wounded.

Many of the *Pawnee* crew remembered our own near sinking by "friendly" torpedoes off Rendova. The question we argued to no conclusion in the mess hall was: if your "number is up," is it better to go by friendly fire or at the hands of the enemy? I believed there were many fates worse than death in honorable combat and few more futile than being sacrificed to our own armaments. Others more pragmatic than I thought it didn't matter.

We anchored near a boomerang-shaped atoll, set a Condition III gun watch and stationed a mine lookout at the forecastle. A few hundred yards off our starboard beam was the ammunition ship *Mauna Loa.* Aposhian and I took a long look at this gigantic floating bomb, rolled our eyes heavenward and spread some lifejackets on the forward hatch cover. Kossol Passage was less than 8 degrees north of the Equator. At 2000 hours our living compartment was still as hot and damp as a Turkish bath and smelled worse than a chicken coop.

The food in the *Pawnee* being as barbaric as the quarters, our conversation turned nostalgically to San Francisco. If we had our choice of three restaurants we could visit during one glorious evening of dining, which would they be? We decided on appetizers at Bernstein's Fish Grotto, whose entrance on Powell Street was shaped like the prow of a ship. Under a clock that sounded the bells in the nautical dining room, we ordered steamed coo coo clams and mussels Bordelaise. These whetted our appetite for the cable-car ride to North Beach. At Vanessi's on Broadway we enjoyed a full Italian family dinner: antipasto, minestrone with sourdough bread, salad with oil and vinegar, homemade ravioli and chicken cacciatore, the whole lubricated with dry red Chianti served in wicker-covered bottles. Passing up dessert, we took a cab and hurried to O'Farrell Street for our reservation at Omar Khayyam's, the famous Armenian restaurant. We were greeted by owner-chef George Mardikian, who remembered Aposhian well, and escorted to the best table in the house. Over a glass of slivovitz, the fiery plum brandy of Eastern Europe, Aposhian began leading me through the mysteries of sarma, shashlik and various exotic lamb dishes.

Without warning, the waters between the *Pawnee* and *Mauna Loa* erupted like the volcano. A fan-shaped geyser of dirty gray climbed and hung against the horizon, followed at once by the deep, dull rumble of an underwater explosion. The *Pawnee* shivered all over in the shock waves, as if she were a sailing vessel headed too close to the wind.

"What the hell is——?" I started to exclaim. Before I could finish, Aposhian had shoved me off the hatch cover onto the forecastle deck and fallen protectively on top of me.

I heard another eruption in the same area. I thought about the *Mauna Loa.* If she were hit—whether by mine or bomb—she would disintegrate into a fireball and possibly take us with her. At the very least, we would be riddled by missiles of whining shrapnel. Flat on the deck behind the bulwark with Aposhian's body shielding mine, however, I had a good chance of survival. His had been an instinctive gallant gesture.

The general alarm clanged. We got up and ran to battle stations. Then we learned that "Washing Machine Charlie" had moved his act from the Solomons to the Carolines, dropping two bombs with the usual results. The reaction of his audience was likewise predictable: "If Charlie represents all the air power in the Palaus, what the hell are we doing here?"

Afterward I found Flash in the mess hall. I shook his hand with feeling.

"Thank you, my friend. I won't forget what you did."

"Think nothing of it, Ted." He smiled. "Charlie sure ruined our dinner at George Mardikian's, though."

"By God, you're a real true Aramis."

"Aramis? With that name he must have been a Greek like Aronis, not an Armenian."

"You're right. Athos and Porthos won't do, either. I guess we'll have to call you D'Artagnan."

"That's better! Let's have some joe."

The next morning we took on a cargo of twelve extra depth charges from the *Mauna Loa,* stationed mine lookouts in the bow and on the flying bridge and headed west through the swept channel, fighting a strong tidal current.

"Floating mine one point on the starboard bow!" a voice sang out. The mess hall emptied in seconds as idlers scrambled for points of vantage or safety.

The barnacle-encrusted mine was very nearly the color of the disturbed waters of Kossol Passage and not a hundred yards ahead on a collision course. If it ripped open our shell plating forward, *Pawnee* would fall off to starboard, flood and dive to the bottom. If it struck us aft, where those dozen depth charges were lashed to the fantail deck, we would go up like the world's largest Roman candle. Either thought, my stomach reminded me, was not pleasant to contemplate.

After what seemed an interminable delay but was probably only a few seconds, we altered course to port.

I watched the mine pass swiftly along our starboard beam, a ball of destruction yawing in the choppy waters and showing its many triggering "horns." To contact one of them was to close the firing circuit, as the unlucky YMS-19 had done. But the mine passed safely astern, bobbing like a cork in our wake, an ideal target for our aft 40-mm. battery. Again, no order to fire came from the bridge. I assumed the captain had used our voice radio to alert the other ships present in the passage.

"Surface contact," said Radarman Bill Smith. "Bearing oh oh five degrees relative, range one five oh double oh."

Lees got out of his captain's chair and examined the SO-8 scope, which was mounted on the bulkhead above the pilothouse portholes. "It's closing fast, sir," Smith said. There was an edge of tension in his voice.

"Very well. Quartermaster, alert the 3-inch gun crew and prepare to challenge."

We were somewhere west of the Palaus on our assigned patrol station, boxing in a 12- by 12-mile area and zigzagging at 15 knots. That afternoon we had watched Task Group 38.4, the carriers which had covered the Peleliu operation, fuel from a unit of oilers and depart to the west, toward Mindanao in the Philippines. The contact should be friendly, but in these waters I wouldn't care to bet my life on it. Which was exactly what I was doing, I reflected from my position near the voice radio transceiver.

With every sweep of the SO-8 antenna, the "blip" on the plan position indicator moved perceptibly. We were closing at a combined speed of something like 45 knots.

Our three-letter challenge for 23 September blinked out bravely into the starless night. The seconds ticked away like a time bomb set to explode at any moment. The ship was a man-o-war, I knew by her speed, and surely had all her guns trained on us.

From her bridge a hooded signal lamp flickered briefly with the correct response. Relief showed on the faces of the bridge watch as we ceased zigzagging off our base course and slowed to 5 knots. The other ship made a careening turn and came close aboard on our starboard side. The numbers "552" on her bow identified her as the *Evans*, a *Fletcher*-class destroyer identical in silhouette to our own favorite tin can, the *Pringle*.

Her skipper, a bulky figure in a leather jacket, lifted his bullhorn.

"New orders from Commander Third Fleet, *Pawnee*," he bellowed. He gave a position well to the northwest. "We're covering the movements of the fast carriers."

"Aye aye, sir," Lees acknowledged after verifying the coordinates.

"Let's get the hell out of here, *Pawnee*," the salty C.O. roared. He really didn't need a bullhorn. The *Evans* rocked us with her wake as she put on full ahead. We changed course to 348 degrees true and followed at best possible speed.

Miller and I chuckled over Admiral Halsey's method of relaying orders from his flagship, the new battleship *New Jersey*. Most commanders would have arranged to put the message on the Fox schedule. Instead, he had sent a new 2,100-ton destroyer chasing after us like a dispatch boat.

"I guess the Bull has forgiven us for the Dirty Dell," I speculated.

"Why not? He knows what we did at Rendova and Vella and Bougainville. There's always a chance one of his big ones will get hit. Then he'll need us more than he needs another tin can."

Pawnee spent the next week boxing in our new patrol station of 12-mile legs. Since we were now doing duty as a destroyer escort, we understood the presence of those spare depth charges on the fantail. We also heard that a regiment of the 81st Army Division had seized Ulithi Atoll, several hundred miles to the east, on the 23rd. The huge atoll, only 60 miles from enemy-held Yap Island, was to be developed as the Navy's advanced fleet base and anchorage in the Pacific. Despite this provocative move, the only contacts on our sound gear came from schools of fish and playful dolphins.

I had read that dolphins were highly intelligent, employing some kind of advanced sonar which made ours seem nearly as primitive as schoolboys clicking rocks together in the old swimming hole. They enjoyed the company of man, for some reason, and had been known to save shipwrecked mariners by nudging them ashore. Aposhian and I thought the dolphins were exercising very poor judgment in befriending man, the most vicious and dangerous of all animals. In our present sour mood, depressed by the blood bath at Peleliu, we envied the gregarious sea mammals for their perpetual "smiles" and *joie de vivre*.

The principal danger to the Third Fleet came not from enemy U-boats but from a tropical disturbance to the north which was developing rapidly into a full-blown typhoon. We were ordered (by radio dispatch this time) to refuel from the oiler *Lackawanna* at Kossol Passage—now free of mines and providing anchorage for at least 60 vessels—and report to the *Mount McKinley*.

When we reached Peleliu, the wind was howling in from the west at whole gale force. Across a fetch of hundreds of miles of open water it had built great disheveled waves twenty-five or thirty feet high, their turbulent surfaces nearly white with blown spindrift. Closer inshore, great walls of water were rolling clear over the reef and breaking against the landing beaches with the shuddering impact of naval gunfire.

Lying to near the amphibious command ship, *Pawnee* was unable to keep her head to the seas. Falling off steeply into yawning troughs and riding up again in a corkscrew motion, she was like a chip of wood adrift in a stream at flood stage. During supper we had to brace our knees under the mess tables and eat with one hand while gripping the trays with the other. Periodically, a soup bowl or coffee mug broke free and crashed to the deck, provoking shouts of:

"Get that man's pay number!"

"Grab that swab, swabby!"

Shortly after darken ship, the commander of the salvage unit instructed us by voice radio to go to the aid of *LST-278*, which had been driven onto Orange Beach.

When I looked aft from the bridge wing, salty rain blown in horizontal planes stung at my face, just as it had during the big wind at Noumea. A few hundred yards to the east, the LST was a shimmering spectral shape against the white sand. With every breaking wave she disappeared behind a curtain of foam, only to emerge again as if called up from a seance.

"I never heard such a stupid order," Miller complained. "If we went in there we'd be on the beach, too. The captain told those jerks in the *McKinley* we can't do a thing until this front passes."

By 2000 hours the wind velocity had increased. The *Pawnee* was rolling, pitching and yawing all at one time as the great seas collided, peaked and decayed in a chaos of random motion. Lurching into the radio shack, I discovered that Murphy had lashed his chair to the operator's position after it had repeatedly pulled his earphones from the receiver jacks in its violent gyrations. The carriage of our sturdy Underwood was sticking or sliding clear to the end stops; it was necessary to steady it with one hand while typing hunt-and-peck fashion.

"You copying the headings okay, Murph?" I shouted above the shriek of wind, the concussive blows of water and the groan of protesting metal.

Murphy grinned insouciently. "We've never missed one yet, have we, Mace? But it's a little like trying to ride a goddam Brahma bull!"

Faintly we heard a high-pitched rattle followed by the reassuring rumble of our main engines. The captain had put three on the line and was going ahead at 35 rpm to maintain steerageway and keep the wind and sea one point on our starboard bow. The ship's erratic movements were damped to a steady pitching and I could stop worrying about the Fox sked. I headed below, assured also of being able to stay in my bunk until called for the midwatch. I had to admit that Lees had read his book on seamanship.

Shortly after 0500 the next morning we edged in close to the reef. The center of the typhoon was now far to the north but it was still lashing us with its whipping tail. During the night *LST-129* had gone aground near her sister. The long, tunnel-like holds of the landing ships presented a large sail area to the wind. With only two diesel engines developing 1,800 horsepower, LSTs lacked the maneuverability to stay out of harm's way near any kind of shore. I watched the combers roll in eagerly, gather momentum, overreach themselves and fall heavily upon the cripples, sending up tendrils of spray fifty feet high. If the ships began to break up, we could do nothing but order our boats away to assist survivors.

The salvage commander apparently agreed. He ordered us to Purple Beach on the lee side of Peleliu, where the *Menominee* had her tow wire on *LST-661*. We passed her a 5-inch Manila messenger shackled to our 1¼-inch wire and rigged for a tandem tow. Together, we took a strain. Within two minutes the *Menominee* was "in irons," being set down toward the beach by wind and current, just as *Pawnee* had been at Nomobitigue Reef. Hastily, she cast off our towing cable. Two days passed before we were able to rerig and get the LST afloat.

"Our battin' average ain't nothin' to write home about," a bosun's mate observed. "It's a good thing ole 'Black Jack' ain't around."

But Commander Amphibious Forces was and sent us new orders on the Fox schedule. Leaving *Menominee* to worry about the two grounded LSTs, we towed a crippled LCT to Kossol Passage and refueled from the *Endymion*, an LST converted to a landing-craft repair ship. On 8 October we departed Kossol in company with our sister ship *Munsee* and headed north-northwest into intermittent rain squalls and heavy, confused swells that buffeted our port quarter. In the pilothouse the helmsmen fought to keep *Pawnee* on course. Going from the crew's quarters to the radio shack involved a sort of tiptoe ballet to avoid bone-jarring collisions with the bulkheads.

Our mission was to join Task Unit 30.8.16, comprising oilers *Schuykill*, *Tappahannock* and *Mississinewa*,* a "Jeep" carrier and five or six destroyers and destroyer escorts. It was one of nine or ten similarly composed units that stood by at sea to fuel the four fast carrier groups of Task Force 38 in echelon. From this forward position *Pawnee* or *Munsee* could be quickly dispatched to pass a tow wire to a crippled combatant. The Third Fleet no longer was tied to wasteful, immobile shore bases, as it had been in the

---

* The days of the *Mississinewa*, commissioned in the spring of 1944, were short. Lying at anchor in Ulithi lagoon, not far from the *Pawnee*, on 20 November 1944, she was rocked by a heavy explosion. Her cargo of 404,000 gallons of aviation gasoline and 99,000 barrels of fuel and diesel oil ignited, her after magazine detonated and she went down with sixty of her crew. She was the first victim of the *kaiten*, the one-man suicide torpedo. For the absorbing details, see *I-Boat Captain*, by Zenji Orita with Joseph D. Harrington (Major Books, Canoga Park, Calif., 1976). The *kaiten* that sank the *Mississinewa* was launched by Commander Orita from his submarine *I-47*.

South Pacific, and could remain at sea for long periods of time. It was a brilliant solution to the logistics problem of fueling and provisioning the fighting ships, made possible by America's enormous production of ships and planes.

At the same time, the creation of the At Sea Logistics Service Group made it "goddam tough on the TF 38 crews," as Miller pointed out. When the fresh and frozen supplies were exhausted, they existed largely on beans, Spam and coffee. Even their mail was delivered by destroyer or oiler from the new fleet anchorage at Ulithi.

By Columbus Day, we were squaring 12-mile legs at a new rendezvous. The fast carriers, we learned, had launched a series of air raids on Formosa. It was from Formosa bases in December 1941 that the Japanese had destroyed our entire air strength in the Philippines. Now we were exacting payment with interest. Soon General MacArthur could make good his vainglorious promise: "*I shall return.*"

Halfway around the world, the wartime confederacy of capitalism and communism was squeezing Nazi Germany between the jaws of an ever-tightening vise. The Red Army had invaded Yugoslavia, broken through to the Baltic Sea near Riga, Latvia, and occupied German soil in East Prussia. In the west, the Americans and British were attacking along a line extending from Switzerland to Belgium. On 14 September, as the *Pawnee* was approaching Peleliu, Aachen became the first large German city to fall to the Americans. By early October we were breaching the Siegfried Line, the deep zone of fortifications in West Germany.

In Holland, however, the Battle of Arnhem had demonstrated that British generals were quite as adept as ours at slaughtering their own men. An entire division of British paratroopers landed by Field Marshal Sir Bernard Montgomery had been surrounded by the Germans and cut off. Desperate efforts by Montgomery's armor to break through to Arnhem failed. When the 11-day battle ended, almost 7,000 troopers had been lost. Fewer than 2,000 were rescued by air.

On another Columbus Day four years before, I had reported for duty in the *California* at Pearl Harbor, a landlubber fresh from boot camp and radio school at San Diego. Was it only four years ago that I had climbed the mahogany accommodation ladder with my bag and hammock, saluted the national ensign and the JOOW and stepped onto the holystoned teakwood quarterdeck of Battleship 44? It seemed a great deal longer. Then I had been dressed in spotless whites, my black shoes shined to a mirror luster. The *California* herself was painted a pale peacetime gray and all her brightwork glittered in the Hawaiian sun. Now I was wearing faded, sweat-soaked dungarees and my shoes were shined only because that was a personal vanity. My ship was no mighty combatant, only a mere litter-bearer of the seas. In salt-stained wartime gray, battered and bruised by encounters with burning, drifting or stranded vessels, she looked weary, worn and vulnerable.

I may not have looked that way but I felt it. Twenty-seven months of wartime sea duty were enough for any man. Perhaps too much, I thought, fingering the agate ring I wore. It had belonged to my great friend Johnny Johnson. I had recovered it and our wristwatches from a Honolulu pawnshop after he was killed at Pearl Harbor. In San Francisco a few months later I gave his watch to Eleanor, his long-time mistress, but I couldn't bear to part with the ring. We were losing the Pacific War and it had seemed likely I would join Johnson and the other fallen comrades of the *California* at the military cemetery in Honolulu. Now that we were winning and the war had increased in scope and savagery, I felt I still might. Judging by what I had seen at Peleliu and heard about the amphibious operations in the Marianas, the Navy and Marine Corps high commands no longer cared about casualties, only victories. (Lieutenant General H. M. Smith, director of the bloody assaults on Tarawa and Saipan, seemed typical: his nickname was "Howlin' Mad.")

By Friday the thirteenth we had left the security of the oiler unit and were keeping station on the port beam of the *Munsee* at 4,000 yards. Our course was southerly, but I felt uneasy. I encoded the *Munsee's* call sign and told the radiomen to copy any messages addressed to her.

About 1745 I was summoned to the radio shack. Bowser had just typed an urgent dispatch for *Munsee* from Commander Third Fleet. I sent it to Calvin Rempfer, the communication officer, for decoding. Very shortly, our sister ship came about and departed to the northwest. I guessed one of the ships of Task Force 38 had been hit off Formosa.

All that night and the next morning *Pawnee* continued toward the Palaus. But shortly after dinner NPM broke into a routine Fox transmission with instructions to stand by for an urgent dispatch.

"Here we go, Murph," I said. "This one is for NUMA."

It was. I inserted a message blank into the typewriter over the rolled-up log sheet, copied the thirty or so five-letter code groups, filled in the heading from the log and handed the form to Murphy.

"Get this to Rempfer on the double," I said with a small smile. " 'Double, double toil and trouble', Murph."

At 1357 the *Pawnee* came about, steadied on course 323 degrees true and increased shaft revolutions to turn up 15.5 knots. Rempfer came into the radio room and, in the course of a brief conversation, held the decoded message so I could read the text. As soon as he left, all the radiomen arrived.

"What's the scoop, Ted? Where we goin'?"

"You guys know an enlisted man can't be trusted with that kind of info," I said with a straight face. "Especially when he's got a hot transmitter under his fist."

But I wasn't fooling anyone. "C'mon, Mace, give us the straight dope," Murphy pleaded.

"All right. If you check our heading, you'll see it puts us on a collision course with the island of Formosa. The new light cruiser *Houston* has been torpedoed about a hundred miles offshore. We're going in and drag her out of there."

Chapter Fourteen

"WE WILL
STAND BY YOU"

Great occasions do not make heroes of cowards; they simply unveil them to the eyes of men. Silent and imperceptible, as we wake or sleep, we grow strong or we grow weak, and at last some crisis shows us what we have become.

Canon Westcott

In the first light of an overcast dawn we found the *Houston* at the eastern approaches to Luzon Strait. Under tow from the heavy cruiser *Boston*, she was wallowing in long oily swells and listing at least 15 degrees to starboard. At the top of her stick foremast, the SK search radar hung down at a precarious angle, jarred loose by the impact of the torpedo that struck amidships. The long rifles of her four 6-inch gun turrets pointed at various inclinations, frozen there when power was lost. On the broad fantail which housed the seaplane hangar and crane, one of her OS2U Kingfishers was half on and half off the starboard catapult.

Far below, sealed in flooded engineering spaces, were her dead, past caring whether or not we saved the *Houston*. One long-lance torpedo had turned this 10,000-ton combatant into a helpless cripple lacking mobility or the means to defend herself. Modern cruisers and the carriers they escorted were as vulnerable as the wooden ships of the line in the days of Lord Nelson and John Paul Jones. Armor had been sacrificed for speed, range and armament: like my overage battleship *Pennsylvania,* sister of the *Arizona,* they were powerful punchers with glass jaws.

A mile off the *Houston's* port beam another wounded warrior, the new heavy cruiser *Canberra,* moved lethargically at the end of the *Munsee's* tow wire. The namesake of the Australian cruiser sunk at Savo Island had been torpedoed in the fire-room areas on 13 October but had only a slight starboard list and appeared much more seaworthy than the *Houston.* Ironically, the latter was hit shortly after replacing *Canberra* in Task Group 38.1 on 14 October. Both cruisers had "dazzle" paint schemes. So much, I thought, for the art of ship camouflage.

Circling around us a few thousand yards out were the three cruisers and nine destroyers of Task Group 30.3, commanded by Rear Admiral Laurance DuBose in the *Santa Fe.* On the bridge, our new TBY transceiver crackled with imperious voices. A fire in the *Houston's* after steering compartment early that morning had caused her to lose all rudder control; there would be a delay in taking over the tow. We fell in 6,500 yards astern of our charge.

I took a long look at my *National Geographic* maps of the Western Pacific and called a meeting of the radiomen. With Ray Figlewicz and John See long since transferred stateside, I was left with Radioman Third Bill Bowser, Seaman First Howard Murphy ("busted" from third class by Lees for disorderly conduct ashore many months before), Seaman First Bill Bates and a striker I was still training. The two radar operators under my nominal control couldn't copy the code, so there would be no help from that quarter if anything went wrong.

In my battleship days only Murphy would have been trusted with any circuit more taxing than back-up on the Fox sked. But I had selected Bowser and Bates from the deck force and had trained all three men myself. I had confidence in them and knew they would not panic under stress. Even if I were incapacitated, any of them could handle the key well enough for emergency messages: many drills at the practice oscillator had seen to that.

"Now we're going to earn all those perqs we have, like sleeping in after the mids and taking coffee with the comm officer in his stateroom," I began. That drew the expected laugh.

"We're speeding away from Formosa at three knots and the enemy must know where we are," I continued. "The *Houston's* leaving an oil slick fifty miles long and the *Canberra's* leaking, too. It's very important we don't miss any messages, so we're all going to be on the ball, aren't we?"

Heads nodded in agreement. The young faces looked serious but determined.

"I've started encoding a lot of call signs—including the two cripples, Task Group 30.3 and its two task units. When any of them shows up in a heading, copy the message for Rempfer to decode. If there's a problem, get me up here. Remember our slogan. If in doubt . . . "

"Yeah," they chorused. "Copy the goddam thing!"

At 1000 hours we began moving up along the *Houston's* starboard beam, her weather side in the prevailing southwest wind. Since she had no power on her winches or anchor windlass, it was necessary to lay our port bow right alongside her forecastle so the messenger line could be passed across. The delicate operation was planned, in Bill Miller's colorful phrase, "for a contact as light as a sisterly kiss."

So it might have been but for the typhoon of 2–3 October, which had created heavy groundswells which continued to roll unimpeded across the Philippine Sea. Just after we passed the messenger, one of those great rollers caught the *Pawnee* and drove her up against the *Houston* in a shuddering collision.

The flukes of the cruiser's starboard anchor fouled on the *Pawnee's* port bulwark, just abaft the 3-inch gun platform. With a mighty rending and grinding of metal the 1300-pound anchor sheared from its chain, tore away eight feet of bulwark and fell heavily to the main deck, where it gouged out a foot-square section before toppling into the sea.

Two chief petty officers were having coffee in the CPO mess one deck below the point of impact. Startled by the unexpected jolt, they looked up to find a new "skylight" in the overhead.

"Those two chiefs set what I believe is a Pacific Fleet record for the topside scramble," Miller reported. The response of the CPOs is unprintable.

Despite the collision (which caused our main chronometer to jump ahead by several seconds), our 2-inch tow wire was soon aboard the cruiser and shackled to her anchor chain, which was manually payed out to 90 fathoms. We ran out 275 fathoms of wire, rigged a chafing board at the roller chock, and began working up speed to 3½ knots. In approved towing fashion the catenary, or dip, in the tow wire extended about 50 feet below the surface of the water at midpoint. This provided a shock-absorber effect, easing the strain exerted on the wire by a 600-foot-long cruiser which rode unpredictably astern, veering first to one side and then the other in the absence of any steering control.

By 1300 hours we had all four engines on propulsion at 107 rpm, about 4 knots, and were inching up abeam of the *Canberra*. At this rate we wouldn't gain our assigned station, 2,000 yards on the starboard beam of the *Munsee*, for some hours yet.

Meanwhile, we faced the imminent possibility of air attack. We learned that the light carriers *Cabot* and *Cowpens* were keeping us company just over the northern horizon. Sooner or later, however, planes from numerous airfields on Formosa and Luzon were certain to penetrate the carriers' Combat Air Patrol. I decided to make a brief, informal tour of our A.A. batteries.

At the starboard 40-mm. mount I found Cy Hamblen, a cigarette dangling from one corner of his mouth as usual.

He gestured toward the fantail, where Bosun's Mate Winston (Pappy) Schmidt was standing by an acetylene torch. The oldest man in the crew, the phlegmatic Schmidt had the physique of an oak tree and sported a bushy Gay 90s mustache. If the *Houston* started to go down, he would burn through the steel tow wire quickly enough, with luck, to save the *Pawnee*.

"I hope Pappy doesn't hafta light off his torch," Hamblen said with a twisted grin. "Don't feel like swimmin' today. When are the Nips expected?"

"Any time now." I remembered my first conversation with the ex-Marine in San Francisco Bay. "I hope you've taught this new crop of 'hayseeds and range riders' how to shoot straight."

"Just give us a target that isn't fouled by our goddam ships for a change and you'll see."

He was as calm and unperturbed as if he were running his freshwater evaporator or conducting a loading drill in port. He was not a man who would show concern about anything, be it gonorrhea in Sydney or Japanese off Formosa. When his fantastic statement that he was "immune to them bugs" proved true after our week in Australia, his place in *Pawnee* lore was assured. That was the kind of Bunyanesque tale sailors took home to tell and retell at bars, poker games and reunions of shipmates.

My last stop was the No. 1 20-mm. on the bridge wing, where Aronis was giving last-minute instructions to the seaman gun crew. With him was his friend Clint Spooner, a burly but soft-spoken gunner's mate first who sometimes joined our fantail sparring sessions "just for the exercise." Since Spooner's specialty was small-bore destruction, I found it thought-provoking that he always pulled his punches so he wouldn't hurt anyone. Men of sensibility resisted easy analysis and classification; they were more than malleable pegs to be fitted into the Navy's round holes. My friend Aposhian, a peaceable man, had wanted to commit mayhem upon a deckhand who threw the ship's mascot overboard. Schleppi, a hostile man who nearly cut a shipfitter's throat, wept surreptitiously at sentimental films. Gerber, a rough-hewn roustabout, sent money home for his sister's Mormon mission.

"Clint, here's the man with the inside dope," Aronis said. "When does our company arrive, buddy?"

"I've just been chatting with Admiral DuBose on the TBY," I said. "I told him to get more fighter planes up."

"No kiddin'? What'd he say?"

"He promised to knock down every 'sea eagle' that came our way."

"Is that right?" Spooner said, adopting my mood. "Then what did you say?"

"I told him he'd better, with the gunners we've got."

The laughter was louder than my wit deserved.

"Ronnie, I reminded the admiral about our date at the Zamboanga, where I'm going to drink you under the table again. Guess what he said about that?"

"He's going to detach us and ship us home?"

"Not exactly. He asked if we'd mind making our liberty at the Manila Zamboanga."

We were still laughing when Captain Lees appeared on the bridge wing. I straightened and saluted.

"Good afternoon, captain." I wanted to say more but didn't. Lees and I still could not find the words.

He returned the salute. "Good afternoon, Mason," he said brusquely.

At 1348 the hoarse sound of the klaxon sent us to general quarters. I took a quick look astern before ducking into the radio room. The puffs of flak from our destroyer screen announced that one or more planes had broken through the Combat Air Patrol and were headed down the oil slick for the *Houston*. I was sorely tempted to emulate Proctor and monitor the attack but that was hardly the example I wanted to set.

For the radiomen, the next fifteen minutes replicated many another G.Q. in the Solomons. We were like blind men, trying to reconstruct the dramatic events around us from aural evidence only. At the boat-deck rail outside the radio shack and from the flying bridge, the .50-cal. machine guns reverberated like jackhammers. The beat was picked up in slower tempo by our No. 2 20-mm. on the port bridge wing. In the distance, other ships were firing their A.A. weapons in a dissonant chorus. I thought I heard an explosion, followed a minute later by another—whether from torpedo impacts or planes breaking up I couldn't be sure.

At the operator's position Bates had turned the gain up full and was calmly copying the Fox, ignoring the cacophony around him. I patted him reassuringly on the shoulder. All I had provided was training: he had done the rest. It was a good thing for the Navy, and the country, that patriotic young Southerners like Bates had volunteered in great numbers.

Gradually the gunfire abated to a few Parthian shots. *Pawnee* had not changed course or slackened speed. I stepped out on the boat deck and saw the *Houston* still riding astern. She had survived the attack, but not without more battle damage. From her starboard quarter a column of greasy smoke boiled up several hundred feet high. Caught by the prevailing wind, it had assumed the shape of the head and forequarters of a rearing horse. A few hundred yards astern, fire blazed on the water. That rising column seemed to me a death's-head symbolizing the demise of many of the *Houston* crew.

Amid a babble of loud conversations in the mess hall, I reconstructed the attack from the always conflicting eyewitness reports.

A twin-engine Frances torpedo bomber had bored in on the *Houston* at an altitude of only a hundred feet. The cruiser opened fire with her 20- and 40-mm. guns on manual control. The *Pawnee* could not fire for fear of hitting her tow; Cy Hamblen had stood helpless and cursing at his gun mount.

From a range of some three thousand yards the pilot of the Fran launched his torpedo in a narrow stern shot. Tied together by their 2-inch umbilical cord, *Houston* and *Pawnee* were unable to take evasive action. "All we could do was keep movin' and prayin'," one crewman reported.

Instead of breaking off to safety, the enemy pilot continued on toward his target. He passed to starboard, crossed her forecastle and came into range on the *Pawnee*'s port side. We opened fire with three machine guns and the bridge 20-mm. Both Aronis on his favorite 50-caliber and the bridge scored hits on the plane's upper fuselage.* The *Houston* gunners also were scoring, aided now by the *Canberra* and a couple of destroyers. The pilot was seen slumped over in his cockpit, either dead or badly injured.

The Fran emitted a single spurt of flame as it nosedived into the sea off the *Pawnee*'s port bow. But the wicked torpedo was running hot and true. It struck the *Houston* far aft, at the starboard counter. That was the first explosion I had heard. The resulting pillar of fire, gases and debris carried the hatch to the aircraft hangar with it. The hatch cover tumbled end over end before disintegrating into a shower of shrapnel.

---

*   In his endorsement to the *Pawnee*'s Action Report of 16 October 1944, Rear Admiral L. J. Wiltse wrote: "Commander Cruiser Division TEN notes with pleasure and admiration the valiant efforts made by the PAWNEE to defend the crippled tow."

The gasoline tanks in the hangar bulkheads went up next; the second explosion I had heard. Almost instantaneously, fire roared across the fantail and spread to the oil slick on the water.

Through his binoculars, Bill Miller now witnessed a macabre sight also seen by other topside crewmen.

"For a minute or two after the fish hit," the quartermaster said, "men took position on deck along the starboard side and leaped overboard—some fifteen or twenty of them. Flames were still pouring out of the hangar and burning on the water, and the sight of men hurling themselves near the flames and even through the flames to reach water was almost unbelievable. It was like films I've seen of penguins jumping one after another from an ice floe into the sea—but these were men. A lot of them must have burned to death. It was a horrible sight."

After two torpedoings in three days and more than fifty dead shipmates, some crewmen apparently were unwilling to chance another attack. Others must have been convinced the Houston was finished and shortly would plunge to the bottom. Only the most battle-hardened crew could have maintained discipline under such harrowing circumstances. Considering they had served together in the Pacific for less than six months and already had seen half the crew abandon ship to relative safety, the men of the Houston had done well. The ultimate price for the few who had not (and for a few others who were blown overboard) was death in the burning water.

On the Pawnee bridge, Captain Lees was faced with a fateful decision. If the Houston went down before the tow wire could be cut, the huge towing winch would be ripped from its moorings and carried away. Worse, the dead weight of the sinking cruiser might "trip" the ship—cause such a severe, sudden list that Pawnee would capsize and join her in the plunge to the bottom, nearly four miles down.

With little hesitation Lees made his command decision: he would hold on to his tow. Calling the duty signalman, Papoose Evans, he gave him a message for the Houston. The words blinked out by flashing light:

WE WILL STAND BY YOU

We had just participated in one of those memorable moments of naval history, but few if any among the crews of the Pawnee and Houston realized it. An air attack, with its potential for the long leap to eternity, narrows one's focus quite remarkably. When survival hangs in uncertain balance, the future scribblings of historians seem inconsequential. Miller considered our captain's message a matter-of-fact communication designed to show his immediate intention and to sound Captain Behrens on alternative actions, such as an abandon ship. There was no reply from the cruiser, indicating her captain concurred. The *Pawnee* continued at 107 rpm on course 130 degrees true and the *Houston* was saved.*

Meanwhile, a Kate torpedo plane came down the oil slick, swerved and made a surface-skimming run on the *Santa Fe*, several thousand yards astern of the towing group. Flak from the cruiser and nearby destroyers burst all around the Kate, joined by tracers from the *Houston*'s automatic weapons. Again Hamblen was thwarted; the plane was beyond the range of his 40-mm. battery. Two thousand yards off the *Santa Fe*'s starboard quarter, the pilot released his torpedo. The cruiser made an emergency nine turn and the long lance passed narrowly astern. Once again the enemy pilot failed to break off. He altered course with the cruiser, apparently intending a suicide crash. In the last seconds his plane burst into a ragged rising sun and plunged into the sea at the *Santa Fe*'s bow. The wreckage made an incandescent ring of fire through which Admiral DuBose's flagship steamed to safety—but, we soon learned, at the cost of one of her forecastle gun crews.

As we beat our way southeast the *Houston* appeared in little worse condition than before the attack, except for additional flooding. Fortunately, the force of the explosion had been directed upward and was largely dissipated in the empty hangar space. Captain Behrens requested, and received, permission to remove three hundred men, leaving a skeleton crew to bring the ship in. The same heavy swells that had made *Pawnee*'s approach so hazardous prevented destroyers from coming alongside the listing cripple. The men had to jump overboard in groups of one hundred and were fished from the sea by the *Ingersoll*, *Stephen Potter* and *The Sullivans*.

By now we knew that the sixteen ships of Task Group 30.3 had been nicknamed, with typical Navy humor, "CripDiv 1." That the division of cripples had acquired another sobriquet could be implied from a dispatch originated by Halsey and relayed by radio on the Fox and visually from the *Santa Fe*:

TWO ENEMY SURFACE GROUPS X TWO CHARLIE VICTORS
ONE CHARLIE VICTOR LOVE THREE CHARLIE LOVES ONE
CHARLIE ABLE FOUR DDS SIGHTED APPROXIMATELY
TWO HUNDRED MILES NORTH OF YOU X COMTHIRD

---

* In his history of World War II naval operations, Samuel Eliot Morison wrote that Lee's signal (which he altered slightly to "WE'LL STAND BY YOU!", apparently for dramatic emphasis) "deserves a place among the Navy's historic phrases." (Vol. XII, p. 102.)

FLEET SENDS ACTION COMTASKGROUP THIRTY POINT
THREE X TAKE SUITABLE DISPOSITION X DO NOT REPEAT
NOT DETACH CRUDIV THIRTEEN AND ESCORTS
TONIGHT X DONT WORRY X MORE LATER*

Papoose Evans receipted for the incoming visual while I speed-read it.
"What does the Bull mean, 'Don't worry'?" he complained. "The Japs
have sent their whole frigging Home Fleet out after us, and he says don't
worry about it. Goddam right I'm worried. The coyotes are moving in on
the chicken coop!"

"Yeah, with three carriers. Halsey seems very confident, though. He
must have something in mind."

"Whatever he's got in mind, don't forget we're still the chickens!"

Papoose's fears for CripDiv 1, now also known as "BaitDiv 1," were
shared by our admiral. In the radio shack Bates copied an urgent dispatch
from Commander Task Group 30.3 which was rushed to Rempfer for decoding. When I returned to the bridge Miller was taking down a visual
signal from Admiral DuBose, no doubt a duplicate of the one he had put
on the Fox schedule:

C T G 30R3 BATTLE PLAN EFFECTIVE WHEN ORDERED X
PLAN ABLE FOUR DDS TWO TUGS REMOVE PERSONNEL
SINK CRIPPLES RETIRE REVERSE ENEMY BEARING X PLAN
BAKER SIX DDS REMOVE PERSONNEL CRIPPLES
CONTINUE TOWING X PLAN CHARLIE X SIX DDS REMOVE
PERSONNEL CRIPPLES AND TUGS THEN SINK THOSE
SHIPS

I whistled. "That would be a hell of a way to lose the *Pawnee*,
wouldn't it? Deliberate friendly fire!"

"Better than deliberate enemy fire," Miller replied with his customary
aplomb. "Besides, it's only precautionary."

I looked back at the northern horizon. Out there at less than 200
miles and closing was a large enemy force intent on annihilating Task
Group 30.3. If the contact report was true, we could expect another air
attack at any time. Miller and I doubted the Japanese had three carriers

---

* Like many scouting reports, this one proved wildly inaccurate. There were no carriers
("Charlie Victors") or light carriers ("Charlie Victor Loves") in the area. The actual compo-
sition of Vice Admiral Kiyohide Shima's Second Striking Force was two heavy cruisers, one
light cruiser and four destroyers.

they could spare from the defense of the Philippines. In the Battle of the Philippine Sea on 19–20 June, Task Force 58 (essentially Task Force 38 with Admiral Raymond A. Spruance rather than Halsey in over-all command) had sunk 3 carriers and shot down nearly 500 planes. Echoing the savagery of the Central Solomons, the engagement had been dubbed "the great Marianas turkey shoot." But the enemy still had plenty of battleships and cruisers. If he was planning a surface attack, DuBose had a grace period of several hours before he was forced to execute one of his three battle plans.

For a moment, I had a vivid image of the Japanese striking force appearing hull down on the gray horizon. First, a squadron of swift destroyers in line abreast fanning out to press home a torpedo and gunfire attack. Then the battleships and cruisers in parallel columns opening fire at long range. I could hear the distant thunder of the turrets and the express-train rumble of the projectiles and see the geysers sprouting among our ships in dye-marked yellow, purple and red. Then it would be too late for Battle Plans Able and Charlie and much too late for Plan Baker. The *Cabot* and *Cowpens* already had beaten off several land-based air attacks. I sincerely hoped Halsey had moved up other carrier groups to reinforce them. Otherwise, his "bait division" might be swallowed whole. And what if the Japanese admiral attacked by night, as he probably would, nullifying our advantage in carrier aircraft?

There was nothing I could do about any of this. My fate was in the hands of the admirals, friend and foe. I stopped by the radio shack and saw a decode of the alarming message Miller had copied. I reassured the radiomen by quoting Halsey's words, "Don't worry." He must be planning to "bushwhack" the enemy force with his own carrier task groups.

For once, I had access to the latest intelligence from both the bridge and message decodes, and decided to share it with the Musketeers. Schleppi, on duty at the 3-inch gun, had heard scuttlebutt that the Japanese Home Fleet was only 75 miles away. It was double that distance, six or eight hours cruising time, I said. In the machine shop, Gerber was turning a knife handle on the lathe. Jokingly I told him there was nothing to worry about. There were only 90 million Japanese behind us, a few million more to starboard, and four miles of salt water under us. Seriously I added (with more confidence than I felt) that the Japanese would probably turn back when they sighted Halsey's carriers. They had to save their ships for our upcoming invasion of the Philippines.

My last stop was Flash Aposhian's domain, the small gyro room next to sick bay. Grouped around the massive Sperry gyrocompass in its binnacle were control panels for the power supply and the synchronous repeaters on the bridge, a motor-generator and a battery rack for emergency power. My friend was at the panel checking instrument readings.

"What's our heading, Flash?"

"One three oh, true and gyro."

"We're right on. The poor old *Houston*'s staggering around back there like a boot seaman on his first liberty."

I explained that we had become the unofficial guide ship for the entire group. When our helmsmen couldn't hold our base course because of the *Houston*'s frozen rudder, all the other ships deviated by a few degrees to follow suit.

"Right now, Flash, you're one of the most important men in Task Group 30.3. If your precious gyro goes down, we're on magnetic compass. We might end up at Yap Island, not Ulithi."

"Don't tell the old man that. He's got enough to worry about already. How bad is it, Ted?"

"The officers are getting chummy and showing me decodes."

"That bad, huh?"

I told him everything I had learned.

"Well," he said with a faint smile, "it isn't quite like being an Armenian in Turkey, but it'll do."

The *Cabot* and *Cowpens* had been our salvation so far. Of more than one hundred planes in the last attack, only three had penetrated the carriers' CAP. One had torpedoed the *Houston*, the second had narrowly missed the *Santa Fe*, and the third had been shot down by our destroyers. Had more planes got through, we would certainly have lost the *Houston*—and probably the *Canberra*, too. If we succeeded in snatching the *Houston* from under the noses of the Japanese, this single act would justify the *Pawnee*'s commissioning, and write a memorable finale to our own naval service.

Before relieving the evening watch, I stepped onto the fantail for deep breaths of salt air and grave thoughts about Task Group 30.3, also known as CripDiv 1 and BaitDiv 1. We still were in the Philippine Sea, moving across the approaches to the Luzon Strait at no more than a dog trot and facing four or five more days of unrelenting tension. Only the Combat Air Patrol of the *Cabot* and *Cowpens* stood between us and the continuing attacks by Formosa-based torpedo planes and bombers. Somewhere astern of the *Houston*, a morose dark shape deeply settled in the water, the enemy surface force was closing; it must be less than a hundred miles away. To make the threat three-dimensional, Japanese submarines doubtless were speeding to intercept. If they managed to penetrate our cruiser-destroyer screen, *Houston* and *Canberra* were doomed.

Living moment by moment with these possibilities was a sterner test of resolution than any sudden attack. It is difficult to be valiant when you are running away from the enemy. How many retreats had ended in panic and pell-mell flight? I must be careful to conceal my doubts, remembering that the withdrawal of CripDiv 1, if successful, would be a victory not a defeat.

I thought about our temperamental GM diesels. They periodically rebelled against the cruel demands of towing and salvage in the tropics, requiring extended overhauls while *Pawnee* idled alongside a repair ship. Still, they never had failed us in an emergency.

Gerber had given the Musketeers many lectures on diesel engines. Most of the technical details went over my head: the subject bored me. I did remember that diesel design eliminated the carburetor and spark plugs required of gasoline internal-combustion engines. Air was drawn into the cylinders and compressed to something like 500 pounds per square inch, about three times the compression ratio of a gasoline engine. When diesel oil was injected through special nozzles, the fuel ignited spontaneously.

The diesel, Gerber pontificated, produced more horsepower than a gas engine and occupied much less space than a steam-turbine unit with its bulky boilers. It didn't need a lot of cooling water, had a short warm-up period and was highly efficient at converting energy into work—driving the close-coupled DC generators which spun the propulsion motors in the case of the *Pawnee*.

"If our diesels are so damn efficient, professor, why are they always breaking down?" I had asked.

"Higher compressions and closer tolerances. They gotta be put together like a Swiss watch. Now if we had German-made diesels, we wouldn't hafta tear 'em down so often."

I was reluctant to abandon my schoolboy belief that anything built by Americans was superior to its foreign counterpart. "How can that be?"

"Cause they were invented by a German, old Rudolph Diesel. He patented the idea fifty years ago. Our goddam Detroit engineers still don't know how to build 'em. All they can do is throw together gas engines to loosey-goosey tolerances."

The performance of our main engines was by no means our only concern. We were towing a light cruiser of 12,000-ton full-load displacement which was additionally burdened with more that 6,000 tons of salt water. She maintained a pronounced starboard list, green water often washing across her main deck. Without steering control, she pursued her own erratic course 2,000 feet behind us, shearing out like a recalcitrant steer at the end of a cowboy's lasso. The strain on the *Pawnee*'s propulsion machinery was enormous. If anything went wrong—an engine, generator or motor breakdown, an electrical short at the power-distribution panel, a broken tooth in the reduction-box gearing, a burned-out bearing in the drive-shaft mountings, a cracked blade on the single 12-foot propeller—the consequences could be catastrophic. We well might lose a new light cruiser and more men from her already decimated and jittery crew.

Even the loss of face, to borrow a telling phrase from my enemy, was something I didn't like to think about. *Pawnee* would have failed at the ultimate task for which she was commissioned, failed before Task Group 30.3, the Third Fleet and the world; and I, along with every other member of her crew, would have failed with her. Once I had been a participant in a monumental failure, abandoning my battleship at quayside under orders, and the shame of it had never left me. Nor was it likely to, for historians would be judging and rejudging my bumbling commanders for generations, perhaps centuries, yet. Two ignoble failures would be almost too much for a proud man to endure.

The captain must be tossing restlessly in his berth as he considered these possibilities. Most of them were beyond his control. Regardless, he was the one who would bear the onus of our disgrace in the eyes of DuBose, Halsey, Nimitz and King. It was a price I would not want to pay for a commission and a captain's cabin.

It is too bad, I thought, that Lees's personality and concept of command made him hard to admire and easy to dislike. On this dark night of 16–17 October 1944, I would gladly have sympathized with him in his lonely burden. I could not do that but I could offer something: reluctant respect.

When the *Houston* was torpedoed while under tow, he had passed a sailor's test of valor. In those perilous seconds, while the death's head of fire and smoke boiled up over his charge, he had transcended his background, his natural caution and even possibly his ambition, and done what duty and honor demanded. He had hazarded his ship and the lives of his crew to stand by a comrade-in-arms in mortal peril. That was deserving of tribute.

In a long career an officer might have one golden opportunity, seldom repeated, to go beyond mere duty to country and reach for honor. Annapolis men thought and wrote a good deal about honor: the word was engraved on their class rings. Centuries before there was a naval academy, Shakespeare had said it best:

> By heaven methinks it were an easy leap
> To pluck bright honour from the pale-fac'd moon,
> Or dive into the bottom of the deep,

Where fathom-line could never touch the ground,
And pluck up drowned honour by the locks.

The leap was all or nothing, fame or shame, as the impetuous Hotspur and many another commander had learned. Captain Joel W. Bunkley and Vice Admiral William S. Pye of the *California* had their one chance at Pearl Harbor and failed utterly for want of preparation and resolution. Rear Admiral Carleton H. Wright took five cruisers against Japanese destroyers at Tassafaronga and came away with one: his failures were lack of knowledge and the resulting misjudgment of enemy capabilities. Commander Robert B. Kelly of PT Squadron 9 made his bold reach in Blanche Channel, but proved unlucky or too rash: the price was the *McCawley* and the near-destruction of *Pawnee* and her crew.

Some were not found wanting. Commander Frederick Moosbrugger of Task Group 31.2 had wrested honor from the contested waters of Vella Gulf one moonless night, and Captain Arleigh Burke of DesRon 23 found his on a night equally dark when he sent three enemy destroyers into the deeps off Cape St. George, New Ireland. Now Lieutenant James S. Lees, who wore no Annapolis ring, had reached for glory under a 10,000-foot overcast in the Philippine Sea, and it would be his—if we could only hold on.

That issue was very much in doubt when my relief arrived at 2345 and I went to the bridge. Under a hooded light in the chartroom, I read a dispatch Signalman Newcomb had copied from the *Santa Fe* a couple of hours before:

IN UNFORTUNATE EVENT HOUSTON IS LOST PLAN IS FOR
YOU TO TANDEM TOW MUNSEE X MUNSEE NOW READY
TO PASS YOU 100 FATHOMS TWO INCH WIRE BENT TO
HIS (sic) ANCHOR

The *Houston* was rolling ponderously in beam seas. All four engine rooms and both fire rooms were flooded to the overhead. Many hatches and doors were warped and leaking. Worse, her main longitudinal beams had been buckled by the impact of the first torpedo. If they gave way, the ship was certain to break up or capsize. On the positive side, bucket brigades and submersible pumps were keeping the flooding in check while damage-control personnel worked feverishly by battle lantern and flashlight to shore up weakened bulkheads and sagging decks. For most of the 16th, topside crewmen had been lightening ship, casting overboard everything which could be pried loose. Before the air attack, the starboard catapult and its damaged seaplane had been jettisoned. They were being followed by

A.A. directors, winches, davits, searchlights, ready lockers of now-useless 5-inch ammunition, even the radio gear and coding machines.

Assuming we could fend off the pursuing ships, planes and I-boats, the *Houston* would need good luck and weather to stay afloat. On our bridge, a signalman kept his long glass trained on the cruiser, as much to detect any signs of foundering as to copy her blinker-gun signals. Pappy Schmidt and our shipfitters stood a continuous watch at the acetylene torch, which would be used only if *Houston* threatened to take *Pawnee* to the bottom with her.

The 17th dawned grim and gray under the overcast. The seas were moderate but the *Houston* continued to roll uneasily in the ground swell. Back on the bridge, I noted that our heading remained 130 true and gyro-compass. We were making 106 rpm, about 4.3 knots. A mile off our port beam the *Munsee* kept station, her screw churning a frothy "rooster's tail."

Farther out, the dozen screening ships formed a rotating circle around us, steaming at 15 knots in a clockwise direction.

"What kind of formation is that?" I asked Miller.

"Admiral DuBose calls it 'Disposition 3-V,' our A.A. formation. The *Cogswell*, ComDesDiv 100, calls it our 'covered-wagon tactics.' "

"That's not quite right," I observed. "The prairie schooners made a stationary circle. It's the attacking Indians who were moving around them."

"Yeah," the quartermaster agreed. "How about this? It's sort of like a merry-go-round that's turning as it goes down the road on a flat-bed truck."

"The merry-go-round formation. That's good! Now all we need is some military music, maybe a John Philip Sousa march."

"Just like the movies, eh?"

War films always employed a musical background to set the mood, underscore the action and stir the emotions at critical moments. In real life men risked their lives in silence or a tumult of shouts and detonations. Taking battle stations to the martial sounds of "Stars and Stripes Forever" would add an exaltation of primitive spirit to the deadly proceedings.

But the best I could do for the ship's morale were corn-syrup ballads, courtesy of Tokyo Rose: "You'd Be So Nice to Come Home to," "I'll Walk Alone," "Long Ago and Far Away," "You Always Hurt the One You Love." Again she reported the sinking of most of the Third Fleet and the imminent destruction of the remnants. We would never return to our sweethearts and families, she told us with dripping regret. We laughed uneasily. This time the husk of her lies might conceal a kernel of truth. The radio reception from Tokyo was crystal clear, reminding us that we were still uncomfortably close to Japan.

There was no laughter at all when we half-masted our colors for funeral services in the *Santa Fe*. One of the dead was a young Marine gunner from the *Houston*, Lewis Cardozo. When his ship was torpedoed on 14 October he had joined some 750 officers and men in abandoning ship. (The order was soon rescinded by Captain William W. Behrens, leaving to history the question: had it been premature?) Transferred to the *Santa Fe* by one of the rescuing destroyers, Cardozo volunteered to man a 20-mm. gun. By a cruel jest of fate, his was the very gun crew which was incinerated in the ring of fire left by the burning Kate torpedo plane.

While Aposhian and I couldn't see the solemn funeral ceremony from 4,000 yards, we could reconstruct it from others we had attended. The bodies would be sewn into canvas shrouds weighted down with 5- or 6-inch shell casings and placed on tilt-boards draped with the national ensign. After the captain read the Protestant or Catholic Committal, the boards were lifted reverently and the bodies slid from under the flags and splashed into the sea.

To believe they would one day be miraculously resurrected from what I had called "the cold and loveless embrace of the sea" required a giant leap of faith. A realist knew the predators of the deep would first have their way with the corruptible remains. For these young Americans there would be no consecrated soil, no epitaphs carved in stone, not even a buoy to mark their final resting place 350 miles from Formosa and 250 miles from Luzon. I tried to remember the prayer I once had heard, which expressed a sailor's awe at the mighty rolling forces of nature upon which he moved, but got no further than: "O, Lord, the sea is so great and I am so small . . ." Aposhian and I did remember that mariners of old never harmed sea birds because they believed them to be the spirits of dead sailors. We preferred that superstition to any "sure and certain hope" of physical resurrection.

Having paid tribute to the dead, the ships of Task Group 30.3 two-blocked their colors and went about the business of survival. Beyond our line of sight the Combat Air Patrol of the escorting carriers tallyhoed enemy planes trying again for the cripples, shot down several and kept the rest at bay. Our inner screen shifted to cruising disposition 3-R: *Santa Fe*, *Mobile* and *Birmingham* zigzagging independently on either beam and astern of the towing group and the nine destroyers ranging ahead on assigned patrolling stations.*

---

* The destroyers were the *Boyd*, *Caperton*, *Cogswell*, *Cowell*, *Grayson*, *Ingersoll*, *Knapp*, *Stephen Potter* and *The Sullivans* (named for the five Sullivan Brothers lost in the cruiser *Juneau* after the Naval Battle of Guadalcanal, November 1942).

Pawnee sent her motor whaleboat to the *Houston* with one shipfitter, two 3-inch pumps, two "handy-billies" (small, gasoline-fueled portable pumps), hoses and spare parts. The *Cogswell* maneuvered off the lee side of the *Canberra*, now on a nearly even keel and rolling less than the *Houston*, and transferred 1,500 gallons of fresh water to her tanks. Some sailors in the heavy cruiser were less than grateful for this humanitarian act. In the absence of potable water they had kept their morale high by drinking the ship's supply of beer.*

At 1250 viscous smoke began curling up ominously from the *Houston's* counter. A fire had broken out in the wrecked hangar area, and all available hands rushed aft with handy-billies and foam generators. In ten minutes the fire was out and seamen were deep-sixing the cause, oil-soaked rags. At 1315 the *Pawnee* deck force began rigging a new chafing board at the roller chock. The first one already had worn through from the incessant abrasion of our tow wire. Forty-five minutes later we were startled when the *Houston* fired three rounds from her starboard 5-inch 38-cal. battery at no visible target. An explanation came by signal searchlight: her gunners were clearing mounts No. 3 and 5, which had remained loaded since power was lost three days before.

Looking back at the once graceful and formidable light cruiser, now a forlorn listing hulk bereft of power and purpose, I thought of the times I had been helped off the football field after a crunching gang tackle. My schoolmates had cheered my erratic retreat to the sidelines, just as I now was rooting, albeit silently, for the *Houston* and her crew. From my experiences in the *California* after the Pearl Harbor attack, I thought I knew what it was like for the 200 men still aboard of the original complement of 1300.

The topside decks would be a shambles of discarded shell casings, helmets, lifejackets, coffee gear and other debris of battle. Below decks, the compartments would be enveloped in a claustrophobic blackness, some flooded and others filling slowly with oil-contaminated water which sloshed back and forth as the *Houston* rolled. The smells of a wounded ship would be everywhere: sickly cloy of black oil, acrid tang of gunpowder, mephitis of decaying foodstuffs—and another, even more noisome:

> The ship is beginning to smell from defecation. There are no heads in operation, although they all have been used. After bowls are filled,

---

*   Interview with John L. Whitmeyer of Redondo Beach, Cal., 14 July 1984. Whitmeyer was a quartermaster first in the *Canberra* during the towaway. (He and shipmate Walter J. Raczynski, who also was topside on smoke watch, insist that their cruiser, having restored power to her A.A. batteries, shot down the Fran which torpedoed the *Houston*.)

the deck is used. Many men use helmets and then throw them over the side. The stench is terrific.*

With the crew's lower-deck compartments flooded or unlivable, men would be sleeping on steel topside. Some would be wearing the dungarees, now filthy and oil-smeared, in which they had gone to general quarters on 14 October. Others would be outfitted in any mismatched uniforms they could scrounge. Unable to shave or shower in the absence of fresh and salt water, they would be limited to the sprinkling of talcum powder and splashing of shaving lotion. If the ship's-service store had been submerged, they would lack even these amenities—and might be short of cigarettes as well.

The supply department has laid open their stores for general use. There are cigarettes all over the ship. Some men have mattress covers full of them. Toilet gear and cigarettes are available in the division gear lockers on the fantail. Much of the men's personal clothing has been lost and there is no way of cleaning what we have. The officers are wearing dungarees and Marine fatigue suits. Enlisted men are wearing anything they can find. Many are completely dressed in Marine clothing complete to hats and insignia. Marine shoes are in demand. Rice is wearing bright-colored shorts and a soft khaki cap.**

Probably, only two meals a day would be served. Until the seas abated, permitting destroyers to come alongside, the crew could expect nothing better than canned goods, canned fruit juice and coffee. If the galley ran out of coffee, the hot black liquid which fueled the seagoing Navy, that would be a real emergency.

No breakfast available. . . . Beans and pineapple juice for dinner in wardroom. . . . Vienna sausage and spaghetti for evening meal. Roll so bad that now and then someone goes sliding across the room or has a glass of juice flow into his lap. He's helpless as he must hold onto the table with one hand and his main dish with the other. The heavy seas are bad on the ship and there is danger that she may break in two. All the longitudinal beams amidships are bent.***

---

*   "Why Didn't Somebody Sink Her?" by Theodore C. Wilbar. Wilbar, a junior officer in the *Houston*, kept a daily journal as the saga of his ship unfolded. His candid, unpublished account offers a rare, valuable insight into life on board a crippled man-of-war. The above quotation is from his entry for 15 October 1944.
**   Ibid., 18 October.
***   Ibid., 15 October.

In the comradeship of combat and its aftermath a crew grew closer together, approaching for a little while the ideal of "all for one, one for all." Even the iron barrier between officers and enlisted men softened a little. But it was most unlikely that all the sailors, especially in a wartime crew, would live up to this Golden Rule of men-at-arms. A few would seek personal gain from the relaxation of routine and discipline. It had happened even in the *California* in a 1941 Navy where thieving shipmates were punished without pity, officially by the officers and unofficially by the enlisted men. "The men were given a long talk on looting. Nearly all personal lockers on the ship have been broken into and watches, knives, and money taken out. There seems to be no way to stop it even with security patrols.*

"Where the hell is that Jap task force?"

That was the question the Musketeers discussed long and earnestly over coffee in the mess hall. The enemy might be lying back to close under cover of darkness. He might have passed ahead to ambush us that night. Or he might have reversed course. The first two possibilities seemed remote in light of the morning and evening air reconnaissance conducted by our two carriers and Halsey's task groups. We concluded, fingers crossed, that the Japanese admiral had stopped believing his own government's propaganda, sensed a trap and returned to the Inland Sea. If so, we had only air and submarine attacks to worry about.

For the past twenty-four hours no enemy planes had been able to infiltrate our CAP. But where were the I-boats? With our position known and the *Houston* leaving a telltale oil slick, why hadn't they found us? They still might, of course. We were more than a thousand miles from Ulithi, edging away from Formosa at 100 miles a day.

Gerber reported that all four engines were on propulsion under bridge control and ticking over as smoothly as if Rudolph Diesel himself had built them. In *Pawnee*'s role as unofficial guide ship, our helmsmen and Aposhian's gyrocompass were holding course 130 degrees true. My radio gear and the temperamental SO-8 radar were performing just as flawlessly.

Schleppi and I rigged the heavy bag from a fantail davit, did our "dynamic-tension" exercises, beat a tattoo on each other's stomachs with bare fists and boxed a few rounds with the 12-ounce gloves. Some shipmates thought us slightly mad, but we laughed and ignored them. We

---

* Ibid., 18 October.

knew, without discussing it, that we were dealing with the anxiety of our snail's-pace retreat by expressing the anger and hostility which were always close to the surface in the Pacific.

When we pulled off the soggy gloves, Schleppi glanced toward the bridge, then north beyond the *Houston*. Admirably if enigmatically, he voiced a sentiment common among men at war:

"Ted, I'm thinking about a certain blonde B-girl in Frisco. You know what she told me? 'It don't have to be love, hon. Hate'll do just as well'."

At general quarters the next morning, 18 October, we discovered with some alarm that all three cruisers and four destroyers had vanished during the night. Now the remaining five destroyers were our sole escort.

Studying the bridge officers for subtle clues, I sensed a relaxation of the tension of the past two and a half days. I soon discovered why. Shortly after midnight Bates had copied a long operational-priority dispatch which was repeated by blinker gun from the *Canberra*:

SUMMARY X JAP FLEET RETIRED AFTER SIGHTING
HALSEY X TWO TASK FORCES HIT LUZON TODAY AND
THURSDAY OTHERS COVER US X CRUDIV 13 AND DESDIV
100 DETACHED LAST NIGHT X COMCRUDIV 10 NOW IN
CHARGE X HALSEY WILL NOT FURTHER REDUCE OUR
OUTFIT UNTIL NINETEENTH OR TWENTIETH OCTOBER X
LOCATION CRUDIV 5 NOT KNOWN TO ME X CINCPOA
COMMUNIQUE STATES WE RAISED HELL AND
MENTIONED TORPEDOES DAMAGED TWO MEDIUM SIZED
SHIPS

The excited, profane conversation in the mess hall reflected the relief and elation we all felt. The possibility of surface attack and the sinking of the *Pawnee* if Battle Plan Charlie was executed had wrapped the ship in an invisible shroud of menace. Air attack and submarines seemed threats of a lesser order which we often had overcome. For the first time my shipmates felt that Task Group 30.3 really would deliver the *Houston* and *Canberra* to Ulithi. Admiral DuBose, now detached as task-group commander, agreed. I was shown the decode of a message I had copied at 0530 that morning:

I WANT TO THANK ALL HANDS FOR THE SPLENDID JOB
AND WELL DONE TO OUR PILOTS AND THE PERSONNEL
OF OUR INJURED FRIENDS AND TO MUNSEE AND
PAWNEE FOR GETTING US OUT OF THE DANGER AREA

I wasn't sure we should start congratulating ourselves yet. We were probably at the outer limits but not beyond the range of land-based air on Formosa and Luzon. A typhoon was forming to the south, directly in our path. And both *Pawnee* and *Munsee* were getting low on fuel. Twenty miles away in the cruiser *Boston* the new task-group commander, Rear Admiral Lloyd J. Wiltse, faced a tough decision. Should the *Pawnee* and *Munsee* cut loose the cripples, leaving them adrift while they refueled—or should they attempt the precarious operation of fueling alongside fleet oilers while "in irons" from their tows and unable to keep station?

Wiltse's answer came at 1400 when *Boston* steamed up from the northwest escorting fleet oilers *Pecos* and *Kinnebago*. *Pawnee* hoisted and two-blocked the blue and white Afirm flag and put out the smoking lamp as *Pecos* came close aboard to port. Our seamen received the distance line, followed by the fuel hose, and made the hookup. While the oiler kept station alongside with delicate course adjustments in the heavy groundswell, we received 875 barrels of diesel oil. At the same time *Kinnebago* was fueling the *Munsee*. By 1730 we had let go the distance line and fuel hose and *Pecos* was easing away.

As soon as the smoking lamp was lit, the few old hands left among us got out their cigarettes with grins of satisfaction. This was the first time in naval history, they said, that ships bound to a tow and unable to maneuver had refueled by the alongside method. The COs of the oilers had done a sterling job of seamanship, and so had our bridge watch.

Before the oilers were hull down on the horizon we changed course to 180 degrees true, a maneuver which would bring us closer to unfriendly Luzon but away from the probable path of the typhoon. Thanks to the continued jettisoning of topside weights, pumping of compartments and shoring of bulkheads, the *Houston* seemed to be riding a little easier.

A handy billy with a hose has been rigged on the forecastle so we have salt water showers most every afternoon. Drene shampoo works very well with salt water. Though we still have [an] occasional bogie, the spirits on board are much higher. All the ships around are interested in our progress. Many of them have our men on board.*

As the morale of CripDiv 1 improved, so did the weather. The sun of 19 October rose off our port beam into cloudless skies and danced reflections on a sea of glass. An enemy snooper was spotted thirty miles out and

---

* "Why Didn't Somebody Sink Her?", 19 October.

chased by the *Cabot's* CAP. But where were the I-boats? Surely they had been given our exact position long before now.

The Musketeers wondered how eager they were to run the gauntlet of Task Force 38 and close the cripples. The enemy submarines were commanded by professional naval officers, not suicidal patriots. Their boats had been woefully misused by the high command of the Imperial Japanese Navy: our very survival in the Solomons and since testified to that. They must know it, too, and realize the war had been lost. In this Twilight of the Gods, they had to choose between annihilation and a prudent concern for the future.*

On board the *Houston* the half-dozen badly wounded were carried to the main deck aft, repeating the procedure of the previous mornings. Left on stretchers so they could be moved immediately if the ship began to break up, they must have suffered greatly. A motor whaleboat from *The Sullivans* at last was able to come alongside and the casualties were transferred to the *Boston* for urgent medical attention.

At 0807 our duty signalman receipted for a visual message from Admiral Wiltse:

FOLLOWING RECEIVED BY CTG 30.3 FROM 3RD FLEET
QUOTE YOUR CHEERFUL COURAGE SKILL AND
DETERMINATION THROUGH A TOUGH SPOT HAS (sic)
BEEN A CREDIT TO YOU AND YOUR COMMAND X WELL
DONE AND KEEP GOING X HALSEY

While we were savoring this praise and giving thanks that the author's bait strategem hadn't got us cheerfully sunk, the salvage vessel *Current* joined the formation. Her divers were soon aboard the *Houston*, closing hatches and scuttles which had been left open during the hasty abandon ship of 14 October.

---

* After the war it was learned that five submarines (I-26, -45, -53, -54 and -56) were dispatched to intercept CripDiv 1. In *Undersea Victory: The Influence of Submarine Operations on the War in the Pacific* (Garden City, N.Y.: Doubleday & Company, 1966), p. 378, W. J. Holmes offers an explanation for their failure—an inadequate one in the opinion of the author, since the location of the cripples was certainly known to Vice Admiral S. Fukudome, Commander of the Sixth Base Air Force, Formosa: "Eight I-class submarines were training in the Inland Sea, three of them with suicide weapons. Toyoda ordered the other five submarines out after Halsey. They straggled out the Bungo, as they became ready for extended operations. Information on the location of the Third Fleet was erratic and Japanese submarines were chevied around as new and contradictory reports reached Tokyo. They made no contacts. *Canberra* and *Houston* were towed with painful slowness across the Philippine Sea all the way to Ulithi, and Japanese submarines never sighted these vulnerable targets."

The next morning three more ships came up from the northeast: the destroyer-minesweeper *Trever*, merchant rescue tug *Watch Hill* and *Pawnee's* sister ship *Zuni*.

"There's our relief," someone on the bridge guessed. "Old ATF-95."

"I bet we'll be detached," Miller said with a taut smile. "There won't be any triumphant return to Mogmog."*

In our concern over becoming "a worm on a fishhook," in the colorful metaphor of Captain T. B. Inglis of the cruiser *Birmingham*, we had almost forgotten we were but an unplanned prolog to a drama of heroic scale. In the early hours of 20 October the most powerful armada yet assembled in the Pacific, more than 700 ships, entered Leyte Gulf. At 1000 hours the Central Philippines Attack Force began landing the first assault waves of some 132,000 troops on the beaches at Leyte.

General Douglas MacArthur was soon ashore to deliver a liberation speech directed to the Filipinos but aimed at the world.

"People of the Philippines," he said in tones vibrant with emotion, "*I have returned.*"

Listening to the "Voice of Freedom" broadcast over the mess hall loudspeaker, the *Pawnee* crew reacted predictably with whinnying horse laughs, thumbs-down gestures, erect middle fingers jabbed in the air and a couple of Bronx cheers.

"How about that bastard?" one shipmate asked. "It took a million sailors, GIs and gyrenes to get him there, and he says, '*I* have returned'!"

"I think he's got himself confused with Jesus Christ," I observed.

The Musketeers debated the respective qualities of MacArthur and Halsey. There was no doubt that the former was a brilliant commander, but his monomania and theatrics went beyond our understanding to verge upon the abnormal. Our own Bull Halsey was not so gifted, perhaps, but he had the virtues of his vices: drinking too much booze, driving too fast, and occasionally taking a swing at an obnoxious associate. Those were practices that he shared with reasonable men.

In midmorning of 21 October, under a sky nearly as blue as the ultramarine sea, the *Zuni* took over the tow of the *Houston* and the S.S. *Watch*

---

* Mogmog islet was the recently established fleet recreation center at Ulithi Atoll. Shipmate Miller later described it as "a ball diamond, beach, and pass-out-the-beer setup: a joke even then. It became part of the fleet lore. For years, when career sailors received a shore-duty assignment at some undesirable location, they would say: 'I've just been ordered to Mogmog.' "

Hill relieved the *Munsee.* By 1400 hours we had put our motor launch in the water, retrieved our salvage pumps and Shipfitter Adams from the cruiser, and hoisted the launch aboard. Miller had been right about our detachment. The only question now was our destination: the Palaus or Leyte Gulf?

We took station 4,000 yards on the starboard beam of the *Munsee* and were not disappointed that our course was 140 degrees true for Peleliu. By flashing light we wished the *Houston* "GOOD LUCK AND SMOOTH SAILING," and got a "WELL DONE PAWNEE!" in return.

Our association lasted less than a week, but it had been intense and personal. It began in mishap, was strengthened through air attack and sealed with five memorable words: "WE WILL STAND BY YOU." For five days our fates were bound together by 275 fathoms of *Pawnee*'s tow wire and 90 fathoms of *Houston*'s anchor chain. Now that we had delivered her from danger, the umbilical was an emotional one, and we knew that it would endure for all our lives.*

En route to the Palaus, the *Pawnee* officers and men agreed that we had rewritten the history of naval ship salvage with a least four precedent-setting achievements.** Never before had a crippled ship been kept in tow after she was torpedoed again. Never before had a ship been so flooded and survived: *Houston* was laden with more than 6,300 tons of salt water. We doubted these records would ever be approached, let alone surpassed.

We shared with *Munsee* two other honors, both won in enemy waters under threat of air, sea and submarine attack. We were the first ships to successfully complete a twin towaway, and the first ever to be refueled while towing. We didn't think these records would be equaled or broken, either.

---

* It has. The U.S.S. *Houston* Association created a special detachment for the *Pawnee* within its membership. Old *Pawnee* sailors are much in evidence at the annual reunions. The *Houston* returned to sea, but not to war. She arrived at Ulithi on 27 October for dewatering and temporary repairs. On 14 December she departed for dry docking at Seeadler Harbor in the Admiralties under the tandem tow of fleet tugs *Lipan* and *Arapaho.* On 16 February 1945 she stood out of Seeadler under her own power, bound for New York Navy Yard by way of Pearl Harbor, San Pedro and Balboa, C.Z., arriving 23 March. The war ended two months before her extensive rebuilding was completed. After training exercises in the Caribbean, she made an extended good-will tour of European and Mediterranean ports. She was decommissioned and placed in reserve in December 1947, stricken from the Navy list on 1 March 1950, and scrapped. The *Houston* received three battle stars for World War II service; the *Pawnee* earned seven.

** In his naval history, Samuel Eliot Morison wrote (Vol. XII, p. 95): "The story of towing these two severely damaged ships out of enemy waters—*Canberra* when hit lay 90 miles from the coast of Formosa and *Houston* only 80 miles south of the Sakishima Gunto—is one of the notable salvage exploits of the war."

One required a naval action which resulted in extensive damage to two ships far from a friendly port, and the other was too hazardous to be attempted under any but emergency conditions. (Later, the *Pawnee* and her crew received additional recognition from the Philippine Republic when they were awarded a Presidential Unit Citation.)

Quite properly, *Pawnee* had reserved her best for the last. We had had our successes, seldom easy, and our failures, chargeable mostly to the fog of war. We had taken the *Delphinus* off Nomobitigue Reef, lost the *McCawley* in Blanche Channel, salvaged the poor hulk of *LST-342* at Oloana Bay, saved the *Montgomery* near Vella Lavella, lost the *John H. Couch* off Guadalcanal, aided many vessels in distress at Noumea, Santo and throughout the Solomons. In scale and sustained drama, none of these prideful victories and bitter defeats compared to the rescue of the *Houston*.

Belatedly, *Pawnee* earned the plaudits of the admirals (and, in due course, the naval historians). In five days of nearly flawless performance by ship and crew, this namesake of a nation of Plains warriors had become the most renowned ship of her type in the Navy. Her new-found fame was an ironic reminder of one simple fact of life about military honors. *Pawnee* usually had operated alone, blamed unfairly for delays as at Nomobitigue, unsung in her solid accomplishments except by the crews of the ships she had saved. When she played her vital role in the Odyssey of CripDiv 1, the admirals were around by the numbers.

Another irony was not lost upon the Musketeers. We had completed our mission under a skipper we thoroughly disliked and about whose resolution we had had our doubts. We felt sure he would view the recognition *Pawnee* had won in its singular sense, seeing it not only as career-enhancing but also as a justification of his methods.

No such justification existed in our minds. He simply had been in the right place at the right time with a ship and cadre of skilled, battle-tested petty officers inherited from two previous commanding officers. He had treated his crew with contempt, subjecting them to prowling policemen and an arbitrary discipline more appropriate for San Diego Naval Training Station than a ship in a combat theater. But no one could deny that he had shown fortitude in crisis: a lesser man would have cut the *Houston* loose to sink. Had he done so, the pride of every *Pawnee* crewman would have gone to the bottom with her.

Maintaining his tow with no slack in the wire might have ensured his eventual promotion to commander, even captain. We didn't care. For it had ensured, of a certainty, that his crew could walk proudly in the knowledge they had made a significant contribution to victory. Looking back at

Pawnee's twenty-three months in the Pacific, we doubted that any other hundred men had made a more substantial one.

"A toast, fellows," Aposhian said with a half-embarrassed grin, holding his coffee mug aloft. "Lees, you S.O.B., here's to you!"

His gesture surprised me. He had more reason than most to remember the captain with bitterness. But my friend had also the virtues of liberality and tolerance.

I could do no less. "I'll drink to that," I seconded.

"Well, why not?" Gerber assented.

"Ted, are you really going to drink to him?" Schleppi asked.

" 'We will stand by you'," I quoted. "That's what the Musketeers do. Yes, Al."

"What the hell? Okay."

We clicked our mugs together and drank the bitter coffee.

Lees could never replace Captains Frank Dilworth and Flave George in our esteem. One truly cared about his crew, the other had saved us in the Solomons. Either would have stood by the *Houston* in the Philippine Sea, of that we had no doubt. But it was Lees who had seen the death's head rise over the *Houston* and made his decision to hold on. We didn't have to like him but we were obliged to admire his *beau geste*, that gallant act which had become ours as well.

Epilog:

QUO VADIS?

For want of me the world's course will not fail:
When all its work is done, the lie shall rot;
The truth is great, and shall prevail,
When none cares whether it prevail or not.

Coventry Patmore

From thirty-two miles south we sighted Diamond Head on a sullen sultry morning in December 1944. Three hours later we passed a black-and-white sea buoy, stationed the special sea detail and entered the serpentine channel to Pearl Harbor.

I watched without pleasure as the familiar landmarks came into view: the control towers at Hickam Field and Ford Island; the elongated hammer-head crane which dwarfed the ships in the dry docks and finger slips of the navy yard; the tall cylinder of the diving tower at the submarine base, and the tank farm on Makalapa Heights beyond.

In mid-1941, an English sailor I visited in the battleship *Warspite* had described Pearl Harbor as a "bloody awful hole." It was that and worse, I thought. From the *California*'s mooring at the head of the battle line, I had witnessed the Japanese attack, abandoned ship three times, lost ninety-eight shipmates and that part of myself which was young, naive and trusting of my leaders. To me, Pearl Harbor still stank of blood and always would.

Circling Ford Island—which the Hawaiians called Mokuumeume, the "isle of strife"—the *Pawnee* passed between battleship row and the supply

260

depot on Kuahua Peninsula, traversed the mouth of Southeast Loch and moored alongside Ten Ten Dock. A wooden brow was put across from the dock to the ship's port fantail, and the yard workers began dragging their heavy gear aboard. Our two-year tour of duty in the South and Western Pacific completed, we were scheduled for a complete ship overhaul.

To a casual observer, *Pawnee* showed little of the gross battle damage of some ships which limped into Pearl. We were still missing eight feet of bulwark from the encounter with the *Houston's* anchor but had put a temporary patch over the hole in the main deck. While pulling *LST-129* off Orange Beach, Peleliu, we had lost two depth charges and a davit when our 1¼-inch tow wire jumped the starboard roller chock. The next day Lees left the ship, turning over command to our exec, H. C. Cramer. Captain Cramer promptly lost both anchors in a 70-knot typhoon at Kossol Passage, making it necessary to rig a jury anchor.

Beyond the rust streaks in the salt-faded paint, the *Pawnee's* other deficiencies weren't evident. With two of the four main engines secured, we had struggled into Pearl Harbor at 8 knots on 80 shaft revolutions. Our 100-KW auxiliary generators were periodically breaking down, causing temporary loss of steering control and the gryrocompass. The distilling unit was out half the time; we were taking salt-water showers. And there was a disturbing vibration in our propeller shaft. *Pawnee* was as tired as her crew.

Before we left Ulithi for Pearl Harbor, we had witnessed the torpedoing of the new fleet oiler *Mississinewa* on the morning of 20 November. Burning furiously, she had capsized three hours later with heavy loss of life. At Eniwetok Atoll, where we had stopped over to refuel, I again was awed and appalled by the destructiveness of our island-hopping campaign across the Pacific. On the once-lush coral islands of Engebi, Eniwetok and Parry, stormed by the Marines the past February, not a tree had been left standing. Only the shredded stumps of coconut palms rose above the low profile of the islands.

Safe now in the rear area, we should have been grateful: no more gut-wrenching tension, long thoughts on life and death, muttered prayers valid only for the moment of peril. We were not. The past is mercifully screened by a selective amnesia, the worst forgotten or but dimly recalled, the best remembered with nostalgia. At the Pearl Harbor Navy Yard, dirty, noisy, stinking and sweaty, the present was inescapable.

Moored at Berth B 1½, Ten Ten Dock, *Pawnee* was no longer a proud, free, ocean-going ship, only a powerless aggregate of floating machinery in desperate need of repair. The yardbirds were everywhere, cluttering her decks with power cables, air hoses, oxygen tanks. The blue-white light of welding arcs burned our eyes. The stench of fusing metals stung our nostrils. The shriek of drills, drum roll of air hammers assailed our ears. Invading our home, the interlopers had destroyed what little privacy we had. I found them in the mess hall, living compartments, even the head. I felt diminished by the presence of these civilians who had never known the fear and fierceness of combat, the closeness of comradeship, the hundred nuances of the word shipmate. In the radio shack, secured now for the first time since Sydney, I elbowed a long-haired electronics technician away from the operator's position and started a letter to Betty Baker in Sacramento. Now that she was home from Catholic boarding school, her mother had written, Betty Jane could take over our correspondence.

During *Pawnee*'s first visit to Hawaii, I had moved a *California* shipmate's description of Honolulu from "armpit of the world" to a lower level of the anatomy. Now my vocabulary, despite the notebooks I had filled with word definitions, utterly failed me. The mean and narrow streets of downtown Honolulu were a beehive of servicemen with plenty of liberty and no place to go. The few women the *Pawnee* sailors saw were unavailable to enlisted men. The Army-Navy whorehouses had been shut down. The Musketeers thought of the Pink House and looked for a quiet cocktail lounge in Waikiki.

Even there, we were disappointed. With the exception of rum, few brand-name liquors were available. The principal bourbon was a foul native distillation of sugar cane named Five Islands. All the good stuff, we theorized, was going to officers' messes, private clubs and the black market around the world. We drank Ron Rico and Bacardi rum in taverns three deep with sailors and cursed Honolulu, its venal civilians and the Navy officer corps with impartial venom.

On Oahu, thousands of miles from the action, no distinction was drawn between seagoing and shoreside sailors. No one knew or cared that the men of the *Pawnee* had operated alone up the Slot, saved the *Montgomery*, rescued the *Houston* from the waters off Formosa, won the Philippine Republic Presidential Unit Citation. The bleak impersonality of an intrusive military presence hung over the island like a miasma which even the Hawaiian sun could not burn away. Squaring my white hat at the approach of the Shore Patrol—not men from the fleet but officious ex-cops who had never been west of Nanakuli Beach—I thought I knew what living in a police state was like.

Every excursion meant saluting squadrons of officers, most of whom had never served in a ship. "Shoe clerks" we called them with sailors' scorn for landlubbers. One day I took Radiomen Bowser, Bates and Murphy to a band-and-beer concert at the sub base. Near Merry Point Landing we encountered something we had never seen before, and never expected to see: a Negro officer.

"My God!" Bill Bowser exclaimed in shock. "A nigger with gold braid!"

I saluted as the junior officer bore down on us. He returned it with a suggestion of a smile. My shipmates stared stonily ahead.

"It's the uniform you're saluting, not the face," I explained. "I've saluted a lot of people I wouldn't give the time of day to. This one must have something on the ball, or the Navy wouldn't have picked him for a commission."

"They can lock me up and throw the key away but I'll never salute a nigger," Bowser said heatedly. He had grown up, I remembered, in a poor white district sandwiched between the Negro ghetto and the Mexican barrio. There, where colors and cultures clashed, equality was a meaningless abstraction.

"I'm sorry, Ted," Bates said with an embarrassed smile. "You know I'm from Arkansas. Down there we don't salute the coloreds."

"And you know where I'm from, Mace," Murphy added without apology. "Texas is a Southern state, too."

That attitude extended to the many WAVE officers we met around the sub base and here it was, with some reluctance on my part, unanimous. Remembering the Navy nurses of the South Pacific, we looked away as if the WAVES were beneath notice. I fully accepted the hand salute where men-at-arms, junior and senior, met briefly on common ground: it had originated in the days of my knightly ancestor, the Chevalier de Bayard. But I wasn't yet prepared to touch my white hat to an officer wearing hosiery and a skirt.

"What kind of a goddam Navy is this?" Murphy demanded. His rhetorical question was not easy to answer. We had left one country, a comfortable segregated one where minorities were largely invisible and women had had the vote for only a couple of decades. Judging by what we saw around Pearl Harbor, we had returned from war to find another, a country in jarring transition. Intellectually, I had to welcome this progress toward the democracy of merit to which Americans had long paid lip service. Emotionally, it was going to take some adjustment.

While the yard overhaul continued at our Ten Ten berth and in Dry Dock No. 3 just to the west, a score of shipmates were transferred to the States for school or new construction. Among them were a dozen plank owners. I shook many hands at the fantail brow and turned away each time gladdened at their good fortune and saddened by the loss of so many staunch comrades.

First to go were Cy Hamblen, Martin Hansen and Rodney Wolcott, soon followed by Papoose Evans, Bill Miller, Doyle Saxon, Winston ("Pappy") Schmidt, and others. Men of lower rating reported on board as replacements. We who were left behind surveyed them sourly and declared that the Navy was now scraping the very dregs from the manpower barrel. We were convinced that superb petty officers like the ones we were losing could never be replaced. When we returned to sea with a crew of misfits and a captain who had already been branded a Jonah, we avowed, we would wear our lifejackets twenty-four hours a day.

I rubbed my bad knee. It was astonishing that I had survived three years of war with so little overt damage: only a tracery of scar tissue on one leg. The other scars, like those of my ship, didn't show. No transfer orders had arrived for me, and I had a cold, desolate feeling that my luck at last was running out. Unwittingly, career petty officer Bill Miller didn't help.

"Well, Mason," he said just before he left the ship, "we haven't always seen eye to eye, but you were a good shipmate, anyway."

The feeling was mutual. Miller at the helm off Rendova very possibly had provided the split-second difference between life and death. A stickler for correct procedures, Miller made no effort to be popular, but his ability and fortitude could not be questioned. We had more in common, I realized at parting, than was apparent. In our differing ways we believed in Duty, Honor, Country, we despised carelessness and incompetence and, while he alone loved the Navy, we both loved ships and the sea.

"By the way, Mason, the last plank owner off this ship gets the commission pennant. I don't want any V-6s to have it. You stick around and bring it back, hear?"

"Thanks a hell of a lot, Bill," I said.*

In the inevitable letdown after so many months of harrowing duty and the remorseless discipline of Lees and his successor, a number of men became drunk and disorderly in Honolulu and were returned by the Shore Patrol for captain's masts and courts-martial. Others fell ill and were dispatched to the base hospital for quick naval cures. One of the latter was my good friend Ronnie Aronis, suffering a recurrence of his malaria. He had given his all to the *Pawnee* in the forward areas, another shipmate of skill

---

* In the event, it *was* a V-6 who returned with the pennant. The last member of the commissioning crew to depart the *Pawnee* was Californian Hubert I. Smith, who came on board as an apprentice seaman, qualified as a diver, served as the ship's barber and left as a shipfitter second class. Fittingly, he had been an ambulance driver in civilian life.

and valor. Now only the States, his home town of Los Angeles and his family could restore him from near collapse. He was transferred to the West Coast on 25 January 1945.

Most disturbing of all was the dispersion of the Musketeers. The first to go had been Flash Aposhian, transferred to gyro school before we left the Palaus for Ulithi Atoll in late October. At Pearl Harbor, Dale Gerber left in the draft with Aronis, destined for months of treatment in Oakland's Oak Knoll Hospital. Schleppi and I sent them off with exchanges of home addresses and plans for a great and drunken reunion as civilians.

Friends like these were irreplaceable. Sometimes, Don Aposhian had seemed oppressed by the burden of his race and its bloody history as a brilliant but persecuted minority. Sad, his mobile face reflected all the sadness of Armenia, generation upon generation. Happy, as at Sydney, he liberated my spirit. Thoughtful, as in our many long conversations, he made me think, reflect, feel. And always, as at Kossol Passage when he moved instinctively to save my life, he had been a man of rare courage. Love was a word most of us interpreted narrowly: sexual love of a woman. But I knew that a man could love also friends like Flash Aposhian.

Dale Gerber was the shipmate who had risked a possible court-martial to stand beside me at the softball game in the Russell Islands. He had stood unflinching on the fantail when the Japanese Betty passed over at low altitude in Blanche Channel. He was rude and unpolished; he talked too loud and bragged too much. Probably, his middleweight boxing career had been less successful than he claimed. Still, he was a man good and true, who valued friendship at least as much as I did. Finally, the only way he could show fear was with a bleeding ulcer.

Now only Schleppi and I were left and that for a little while. I did not claim that my judgments of character were impeccable, but I had been right about him. Considering the appearance, neither Aposhian nor Gerber would have found him acceptable as a Musketeer. I had brought him into the group, acting often as peacemaker, because he was both more and less than he seemed. A little mad he was, hostile often and dangerous on occasion. But he was loyal to his friends, a man of charm and laughing grace to balance his fierce moods. He had indeed proved fit for a bottle, a brawl or a battle, a man you could trust with your life if not your wife.

On 1 February *Pawnee* departed Pearl Harbor for Eniwetok and, scuttlebutt informed us, the Bonin Islands. As we cleared the channel and headed northwest, toward the shrinking perimeter of Japan's bootleg empire, my malaise was stronger than ever. I had heard all about the Kamikazes and seen the graphic evidence of their suicidal attacks on our ships.

The Navy seemed determined not to let me out of the Pacific Theater alive. Schleppi, Murphy and I spent hours on the fantail with the punching bag and the 12-ounce gloves.

Five-hundred miles out, the *Pawnee* broke down. In justifying his reputation as a Jonah, Lieutenant Cramer became my reluctant benefactor. I broke radio silence to send a long operational-priority dispatch to Pearl Harbor. It was the last Navy radio message I would ever send. We were ordered back to the navy yard. Crawling in at a hangdog 4 knots on one engine, there was great joy and much snickering laughter among the crew. The yardbirds had fouled up again! Or had they? The dark, unverified rumors, which I didn't believe, were that a motor mac had sabotaged the lubricating oil and fuel supplies to the main engines.

On 12 February Calvin Rempfer came into the radio shack with the good news I had long awaited. I was being transferred to the radio materiel school at Theodore Herzl City College, Chicago.

I laughed with more than elation. Now that the need was past, I was going to be instructed in radar theory and repair. I had needed that knowledge in the Solomons, the Bismarck Archipelago, the Palaus and off Formosa: I didn't need it now. But school meant thirty days' leave with travel time before reporting to Chicago. That was something I did need.

I looked around the small compartment that had been so intimately involved with my fate and the fate of my ship and shipmates. It didn't look like much here in the navy yard: an operator's position, two chairs, two receivers, a short-wave radio, an emergency transceiver, a tall TBL transmitter. The green paint was faded and smeared with greasy thumbprints; the work bench was cluttered with communications manuals, coding sheets, clipboards of logs and messages, the oscillator I had used to train my radiomen. Scotch-taped to a receiver at eye-level was the yellowing half-sheet with the words I had typed there long ago: "IF IN DOUBT, COPY THE GOD DAMN THING!"

How many hours had I spent in that radio room? Ten hours a day, at a conservative estimate, every day but five for twenty-six months. I calculated quickly: about 8,000 hours. Here I had maintained a calm, deceptive front at a hundred general quarters; firmly escorted a panicky officer to the door in the Central Solomons (as the radioman-in-charge had a right to do); spurned Lees's Sydney offer of promotion as a quid pro quo for becoming what I did not wish to be; written many a line of bad-to-mediocre poetry on many a mid-watch.

I wondered what my now-legendary chief radioman, the late Thomas J. Reeves, Medal of Honor, would think of my performance. I hoped he would say, gruffly, "Not bad, Mason," and buy me a drink. I knew he would not approve my failure on occasion to play the war game within the Navy's rules, for he had always been punctilious in his relations with officers, even the most junior Reserve ensigns.

There was one thing he would approve. My radiomen had never missed a message, never had a badly garbled one despite the always uncertain atmospheric conditions in the Southern Hemisphere, never failed to be resolute. With due allowance for the frailty, fear and folly of mortal man, each of us had done his duty to God, country and conscience as he saw it.

I left the *Pawnee* for the last time arm-in-arm with Schleppi and Murphy. Just behind us were Bowser and Bates, who had insisted on carrying my bag and hammock. At the station wagon which would take me to the receiving barracks, I looked back to the *Pawnee*. Her decks cluttered with yardbirds and their gear, she was more graceless than ever, a seagoing domestic worn and aged before her time. It didn't matter: all ships are ugly in a navy yard. I had helped to put her in commission. I knew where she had gone and what she had done, from Nomobitigue Reef through the Solomons to Peleliu and the Luzon Strait.

It didn't matter that she had broken down 500 miles out from human error or design, and it didn't matter if she never returned to action. By the grace of the nation's enormous industrial capacity, the Navy was paving a road to Tokyo Bay with new ships and men. *Pawnee* and I had been used up in war and were now supernumeraries. The rescue of the *Houston* had been the denouement of her naval career, as of mine.*

"God bless you, *Pawnee*, you lovely hunk of pig-iron," I said aloud. "You took us there, and you brought us back."

I embraced each shipmate and comrade in turn. Still, we could not say what we really felt about this transition. We spoke with laughter and studied lightness of home, girls, Kamikazes, the postwar world. As soon as I arrived at San Diego, I promised, I would toast them each and all at the U.S. Grant Hotel. In their minds, I was sure, was my unanswerable question: "Will I ever see *him* again?"

---

* *Pawnee* returned to the Western Pacific on 23 February for service around Okinawa, Leyte and Luzon but to no special accomplishments. After V-J Day, she was assigned to the Naval Occupation Forces in the Philippines. On 1 January 1947 she was decommissioned and mothballed with the Columbia River Group of the Pacific Reserve Fleet. She was struck from the Navy list on 1 September 1962 and placed in the Maritime Reserve Fleet at Puget Sound, Washington. On 9 November 1971, twenty-nine years nearly to the day after her commissioning, she was sold to Hatch & Kirks, Seattle, and broken up.

I stood on the deck of a British "Jeep" carrier as we cleared Pearl Harbor, that death-haunted place, just as I had done in the *Pawnee* two years before and the heavy cruiser *Louisville* a year before that. But now nothing remained of battleship row except the rusting hulk of the burned-out *Arizona*, minus her masts and turrets. No Japanese planes came whistling down Southeast Loch to torpedo my ship, as they had on that infamous Sunday morning. No scars remained on Ford Island to remind me of the emergency radio dugout where I had copied NPM Fox on the night of 7 December 1941. But the fluffy cumulous clouds still banked over the Koolau Range, just as they had done. And Diamond Head raised its scarred flanks, brooding over Oahu as it had when I saw it from the forecastle of the oiler *Neosho* on 12 October 1940—and for twenty-five millions of years before that. Was Pele, the goddess of the volcano, sated at last with blood sacrifice? I thought of my friends and shipmates sleeping in the military cemetery and knew that she was not. Not yet.

Well, I consoled myself from the hangar deck of the ship I had dubbed *H.M.S. Pinafore*, it will be over soon. The Nazis were in full retreat on both fronts, and surrender within weeks, months at worst, was inevitable. Then Japan, the sole remaining Axis power, would be assaulted in her home islands and overwhelmed. Almost overnight, as in our previous wars, the military would lose much of its power. All that millions of American servicemen wanted was what Aronis had wanted: to "get this shit over with so we can go home." They were poor material for any would-be American Caesars like Dugout Doug MacArthur or Georgie ("Two-Gun") Patton.

Dreaming of peace, I reviewed my plans for the future—not the expedient of radio school, but a real university and a career in teaching or journalism. With a prescience that surprised me, I realized suddenly that—no matter what my future profession and accomplishments—never again would I have the actual responsibility I had enjoyed as radioman-in-charge of a small Navy ship named *Pawnee*. There, a missed call sign could have cost a five-million-dollar ship and a hundred lives. Very possibly, other ships and lives as well. The Navy gave a young man that kind of responsibility. A certain number failed; others were destroyed by it. But most of us, in all truth, gloried in it. Nor would I enjoy those two other special virtues of Navy life: great and stirring, frightening and unforgettable action that entered the history books, and comradeship of a very high order. Civilian life could offer nothing commensurate, I was sure. Its principal offer was freedom.

I felt a curious ambivalence at this farewell. I was happy that my war was over, and that peace was on the horizon. I was sad that an unforgettable chapter of my life was now past tense. For war, despite its terrors—

perhaps because of them—was still the greatest adventure of all. I had had a chance to "share the action and passion" of my time, to put my courage and honor to the ultimate test. I could not claim that I had distinguished myself, but I had not failed. That was certainty a man could carry with him into the uncertainty of the future.

What a paradox that war, which Aposhian had once defined as "organized insanity," brings out the dark primitive, the Caliban, in some men, but the brotherhood, the Damon and Pythias, in others! From the worst of times, the worst in men—and the best. My service in the *Pawnee* had not brought the retribution for my dead *California* shipmates I once had fantasized: main batteries thundering, enemy ships burning and exploding. The *Pawnee* and her men had been mere salvagers, rescuers, litter-bearers of the seas. But that essential work had brought, finally, a quiet satisfaction.

It is better to save than to destroy.